The Role of the American Board in the World

The Role of the American Board
in the World

Bicentennial Reflections
on the Organization's Missionary Work

1810–2010

EDITED BY
CLIFFORD PUTNEY AND PAUL T. BURLIN

WIPF & STOCK · Eugene, Oregon

THE ROLE OF THE AMERICAN BOARD IN THE WORLD
Bicentennial Reflections on the Organization's Missionary Work, 1810–2010

Wipf & Stock
An Imprint of Wipf and Stock Publishers
199 W. 8th Ave., Suite 3
Eugene, OR 97401
www.wipfandstock.com

ISBN 13: 978-1-61097-640-4

Manufactured in the U.S.A.

All scripture quotations, unless otherwise indicated, are taken from the Holy Bible, New International Version®, NIV®. Copyright ©1973, 1978, 1984 by Biblica, Inc.™ Used by permission of Zondervan. All rights reserved worldwide.

Timothy Mason Roberts' essay, "Commercial Philanthropy: ABCFM Missionaries and the American Opium Trade," was originally published in the *Journal of Mediterranean Studies* 19:2 (2010) 371–388. It is republished here by permission of the journal.

Contents

Illustrations

Contributors

Stephen K. Ault (J.D.), Executive Liaison for the International Institute in Spain. He works with both the U.S-based board of the Institute and the administration at its building in Madrid, and he practices law in Boston, Massachusetts.

Paul T. Burlin (Ph.D.), Professor of History at the University of New England. His publications include *Imperial Maine and Hawai'i*.

Donald Philip Corr (Ph.D.), Pastor of the First Congregational Church of Escondido, California. He is the author of *"The Field is the World."*

Alice C. Hunsberger (Ph.D.), Assistant Professor of Religion (Adjunct), at Hunter College, City University of New York. Her publications include *Pearls of Persia* and *Nasir Khusraw, the Ruby of Badakhshan*.

Hamish Ion (Ph.D.), Professor of History at the Royal Military College of Canada. His research specialty is modern Japanese history, and his publications include *The Cross and the Rising Sun*, 2 volumes; *The Cross in the Dark Valley*, and *American Missionaries, Christian Oyatoi and Japan, 1859–1873*.

Jennifer Fish Kashay (Ph.D.), Associate Professor of History at Colorado State University. Her research on Western imperialism in Hawai'i has been published in journals such as the *New England Quarterly*, the *Pacific Historical Review*, and the *Western Historical Quarterly*.

Dorothy Birge Keller (Ph.D.), Professor Emerita of Social Work at Manchester College, Indiana, and the daughter of missionaries in Turkey. She served in Turkey as an educational missionary of the ABCFM and its successors from 1955 to 1965, and from 2000 to 2004.

Robert S. Keller (Ph.D.), Professor Emeritus of Sociology at Manchester College, Indiana. He served in Turkey as an educational missionary of the ABCFM and its successors from 1953 to 1965, and from 2000 to 2004.

Virginia Metaxas (Ph.D.), Professor of History and Women's Studies at Southern Connecticut State University. She is writing a book on war, medicine, and American medical women in the Near East from 1900 to 1950.

Char Miller (Ph.D.), W. M. Keck Professor of Environmental Analysis and Director of the Environmental Analysis Program at Pomona College. His publications include *Fathers and Sons* and *Gifford Pinchot and the Making of American Environmentalism*.

Thomas G. Oey (Ph.D.), an independent scholar based in Putney, Vermont, USA, and Shaoxing, Zhejiang, China. He is the author of several articles on the history of Christianity in Asia.

Regina Pfeiffer (D.Min.), Assistant Professor of Religious Studies at Chaminade University. She has written about important figures from her culture (Native Hawaiian), and her work will appear in *Great Lives from History*.

Ann Ellis Pullen (Ph.D.), Professor Emerita of History at Kennesaw State University. She is the co-author (with Sarah Ruffing Robbins) of *Nellie Arnott's Writings on Angola, 1905–1912*.

Clifford Putney (Ph.D.), Assistant Professor of History at Bentley University. His publications include *Muscular Christianity* and *Missionaries in Hawai'i*.

Timothy Mason Roberts (Ph.D.), Assistant Professor of History at Western Illinois University. His publications include *Distant Revolutions*.

Sarah Ruffing Robbins (Ph.D.), Lorraine Sherley Professor of Literature at Texas Christian University (TCU). Her publications include *The Cambridge Introduction to Harriet Beecher Stowe*; *Managing Literacy, Mothering America*; and (with Ann Ellis Pullen) *Nellie Arnott's Writings on Angola, 1905–1912*.

Douglas K. Showalter (D.Min.), Minister Emeritus of the First Congregational Church of Falmouth, Massachusetts (United

Church of Christ). His publications include *Chapters on the 1806 Haystack Prayer Meeting and the American Board of Commissioners for Foreign Missions* and *Chapters on the History of the First Congregational Church of Falmouth, Massachusetts of the United Church of Christ.*

Sharon A. Taylor (Ph.D.), Director and Donald G. Miller Librarian of the Clifford E. Barbour Library at Pittsburgh Theological Seminary, and a lecturer at the school on mission history.

Acknowledgments

As with all academic projects, this one would not have seen the light of day without the invaluable assistance of a number of people. In the first place, we thank Margaret "Peggy" Bendroth and her staff at the Congregational Library in Boston for hosting the conference that generated many of the essays in this book. The librarians showed themselves to be the most gracious of hosts at the conference (which was held on September 25, 2010), and we appreciate their efforts. We also appreciate the willingness of Robin Duckworth at the library to furnish us with many of our illustrations.

We were fortunate to receive funding for the publication of this book from Rodney Petersen of the Boston Theological Institute, and from Jan Aerie and Cally Rogers-Witte of Wider Church Ministries/United Church of Christ. Naturally, we thank them very much for their generosity. We also thank the Reverend John Chung of Park Street Church in Boston for his assistance on the day of the conference. The staff of Wipf & Stock have aided us greatly as well, and we are especially appreciative of Christian Amondson, our project manager, and Tina Campbell Owens, our typesetter.

Last but not least, we want to thank Cheryl Weiser of Bentley University and Holly Haywood of the University of New England for enabling us to format our illustrations correctly. For imperfections in the book, illustrative or otherwise, we as the editors are, of course, solely responsible.

Clifford Putney

Paul T. Burlin

Introduction

—Clifford Putney

In Matthew 28:19, Jesus says, "Go ye therefore, and teach all nations, baptizing them in the name of the Father, and of the Son, and of the Holy Ghost." This is the "Great Commission," which has inspired millions of Christians. It has also led to the creation of numerous missionary organizations, not the least of which was the American Board of Commissioners for Foreign Missions (ABCFM). Founded in 1810 at the outset of the Second Great Awakening, the ABCFM (whose cumbersome name belied its efficiency) was America's first sponsor of overseas Christian missions. It transported its first missionaries to India in 1812, and by 1961 it had sent nearly 5,000 missionaries to 34 different fields around the world.[1] Emissaries from the ABCFM established the first American mission in Sri Lanka (1816), the first American mission in the Middle East (1820), the first American mission in China (1830), the first American mission in Singapore (1831), the first American mission in Indonesia (1831), the first American mission in Thailand (1831), the first American mission in Africa (1833), and the first missions of any kind among the Hawaiians and other Pacific islanders. The Board's missionaries also exerted a tremendous amount of influence, chiefly through making conversions, operating schools and hospitals, spreading Western ideas and technology, and doing groundbreaking linguistic work to increase biblical literacy.

Missionaries from the ABCFM displayed a great deal of courage in pursuing their line of work. It was not easy being a missionary from the Board, particularly in the early nineteenth century, when American citizenship meant little to foreign leaders, much was unknown about the world, medical skills were limited, long distances were not easily traversed, mail and supplies traveled slowly and unreliably, and there were

1. Global Ministries, "ABCFM's 200th Anniversary," n.p.

few Protestant foreign missionaries (other than those from the London Missionary Society) who could be emulated. All of these obstacles were so daunting that many churchgoers viewed the ABCFM as a foolhardy enterprise, and they refused to support it with donations. Others admired the ABCFM for its daring, however, and a few even stepped forward to serve the Board as missionaries. This was no small step, in part because it often involved getting married (the ABCFM's primary method of keeping its missionaries chaste). Another challenge the missionaries faced was the likelihood of never seeing their families and friends again. This likelihood receded over time, but it was very strong in the early 1800s, when many missionaries from the Board remained overseas at their stations until they died.

What enabled pioneering missionaries from the ABCFM to persevere? That is a question that cannot easily be answered, but certainly one of their most valuable assets was "Yankee ingenuity." Many of the missionaries had grown up on farms in New England, New York, and other parts of the north, and they were proficient in manual arts such as farming, animal husbandry, carpentry, masonry, and the operation of machinery. Their wives (who were classified as "associate missionaries") likewise possessed practical skills, and they were particularly good at sewing, cooking, gardening, and caring for the sick. All of these abilities, the men's skills and the women's, were useful in missionary fields, and they helped the missionaries to survive on islands and in other remote places. The missionaries' skills also attracted potential converts, especially in pre-modern places such as Hawai'i, where the islanders expressed interest in learning from the missionaries how to raise cattle, make wheeled vehicles, and master other basic techniques.[2]

Missionaries from the ABCFM definitely benefited from their practical know-how, but it was their religious faith that did the most to keep them going. That faith was quite stern at first, because early missionaries from the Board belonged to staunchly Calvinist denominations, namely the Congregational Church, the Presbyterian Church, the Dutch Reformed Church, and the German Reformed Church. All of these churches supported the ABCFM in an early display of ecumenism, but it was the Congregationalists who created the organization and placed its headquarters in Boston, Massachusetts. They also stood by the ABCFM while the other denominations fell away (the Old School Presbyterians

2. Putney, 6–7, 42, 60.

in 1837, the Dutch Reformed Church in 1857, the German Reformed Church in 1866, and the New School Presbyterians in 1870).[3] As a result of these groups leaving to form their own mission boards, the ABCFM officially became an arm of the Congregational Church in 1913. It also reflected theological shifts within the church, which grew increasingly disaffected with the grim Calvinist doctrines of predestinationism and total depravity. When the church began to replace those doctrines with the perfectionist ideas of post-millennialists such as Charles Grandison Finney in the 1820s, missionaries from the ABCFM followed suit. They did not reject Calvinism outright (at least not in the antebellum period), but many of them came to see the world as perfectible rather than ir-redeemable, and they aimed with God's help to improve themselves and others.

Improving people around the world struck missionaries from the ABCFM as a task that urgently needed doing. Everywhere they looked they saw human activities to which they objected. Some of these activities were religious, others were cultural. But missionaries from the Board tended not to view the two categories as separate. This was especially true in the nineteenth century, when the missionaries often conflated Christianity and Western culture. Because of this conflation, they described their own habits as Christian, and they condemned the habits of non-Westerners as "heathenish." They also expected their converts to do more than simply accept the Gospel. That was a good first step, but the missionaries doubted whether it made one fully Christian. To achieve that status, converts needed in the eyes of the missionaries to use cutlery, wear full-length clothing, and adopt other Western ways.[4]

3. The ABCFM became associated with the Presbyterian Church in 1812, the Dutch Reformed Church in 1826, and the German Reformed Church in 1829.

4. Dunch, "Beyond Cultural Imperialism," 301–25.

Figure 1. Female missionary reading to a group of potential converts, watched over by an angel. Engraving by Samuel Worcester Rowse (artist) and Oliver Pelton (lithographer). From Daniel C. Eddy, *Daughters of the Cross* (New York: Dayton and Wentworth, 1855), front. Image courtesy of the Congregational Library, Boston.

Missionaries from the ABCFM set high standards for their converts, and they usually set even higher standards for themselves and their children. From the missionaries' perspective, time was far too precious to waste on frivolous pursuits. Rather than playing sports, reading novels, and celebrating holidays such as Christmas (which was viewed as too Catholic), the missionaries spent their leisure time praying, reading the Bible, and engaging in other activities of obvious moral worth. Their asceticism did diminish over time (even to the point where they enjoyed observing Christmas), but they retained their puritanical assessments of drinking, smoking, gambling, and other risky pastimes well into the twentieth century. They also kept focusing on self-improvement, which produced mixed results. On the positive side, the quest for personal excellence led ABCFM families such as the Humes, Binghams, Gulicks, Blisses, Riggses, and Scudders to reach remarkable heights of achievement. At the same time, however, members of those families sometimes broke down mentally and physically on account of their endeavors.

When that happened, they often went on furlough to recuperate from pushing themselves too hard.

The overall number of missionaries from the ABCFM who broke down overseas was sizeable, largely because the Board was America's biggest foreign missionary organization in the nineteenth century. As such it attracted the attention of the public, some of which read the Board's journal, the *Missionary Herald*, with avidity. Another source of information about the ABCFM was the mainstream secular press, which described missionaries from the Board as self-sacrificing heroes. That the missionaries were engaged in a noble cause was seldom disputed in the press or in public, because most Americans in the nineteenth century agreed that converting the world to Christianity was a good idea. They also shared the missionaries' tendency to view foreign cultures as cruel, decadent, primitive, or deeply flawed in some other way.

Many Americans still denigrate foreign cultures. But the American public as a whole is clearly more accepting of cultural diversity than it used to be. This increased acceptance is particularly noticeable among American academics, some of whom have moved to the point where they routinely praise foreign cultures while condemning their own. What really upsets these censors is the spread of American culture, something for which missionaries were largely responsible. For that reason among others, critics of Americanization tend to dislike missionaries. They also often disparage the evangelists, describing them as a chauvinistic bunch of busy-bodies who moved through the world in a haze of ignorance and incuriosity.[5]

The critics' negative portrayal of American missionaries does have some validity, since a number of the missionaries were in fact ignorant and incurious. Those adjectives do not fit all missionaries, however, and they are especially inaccurate when it comes to describing missionaries from the ABCFM. Rather than being untutored bumpkins, missionaries from the Board held college and seminary degrees (rare things in the nineteenth century), because they belonged to faith traditions (Congregationalism et alia) that required a learned ministry. Missionaries from the Board also prized scholarship of various kinds (scientific as well as religious), and they read voraciously, subscribed to multiple journals, and ordered boxes of books from Boston's Congregational Library

5. Anti-missionary sentiment can be found in many contemporary works, including Silva, *Aloha Betrayed*, and Trask, *From a Native Daughter*.

(which was founded in large part to serve missionaries). From their absorption of knowledge, ABCFM missionaries ascended into the ranks of America's intelligentsia. But they were not content simply to absorb knowledge; they also wanted to disseminate it through preaching and writing. Another tool that missionaries from the Board used for the dissemination of knowledge was the printing press, which they introduced to Hawai'i, Micronesia, the Pacific Northwest, and many other parts of the world.

From their printing presses, ABCFM missionaries issued great quantities of religious literature, including Bibles and parts of the Bible. Most if not all of this biblical material was in the vernacular, because missionaries from the Board believed in true Protestant fashion that people, women as well as men, ought to be able to read the Bible in their own languages. This was not a readily attainable goal, especially in places where people had no written language. But missionaries from the Board moved to address the linguistic challenges they found in preliterate cultures, and they managed with help from indigenous speakers to transform Cherokee, Hawaiian, Zulu, Umbundu, and other oral languages into written ones. Another colossal project that missionaries from the Board undertook was translating the Bible into preexisting written languages. They were not the only missionaries to engage in this enterprise, but they did play a leading role in translating the Bible into Japanese, Chinese, Tamil, Arabic, Persian, Turkish, Bulgarian, and other tongues.

The linguistic work of the ABCFM was meant to spread Christianity, and it did that. It also rather ironically played a role in cultural preservation, which was not a prime missionary objective. Missionaries from the Board were initially far more interested in reforming foreign cultures than they were in safeguarding them. But their writing down of languages preserved patterns of speech and thought that might otherwise have been lost. Another act of cultural preservation occurred when missionaries from the ABCFM recorded foundational stories from foreign cultures. At first they did this largely to demonstrate how shockingly unchristian the stories were, but as time went on they became more appreciative of the tales they collected. They even went so far as to stress the importance of cross-cultural respect and understanding, although those concepts did not really take hold within American Board circles until the late nineteenth century.

Whatever missionaries from the ABCFM thought about foreign cultures, they did assist in saving the history of some of those cultures from oblivion. They also assisted in saving people's souls, or at least they thought that they did. A skeptic might question the missionaries' claims of spiritual salvation, but he or she would have to acknowledge that they saved people physically, mainly through medical work. Indeed the missionaries' employer, the ABCFM, pioneered in such work, sending John Scudder, the first American medical missionary, to Ceylon (Sri Lanka) in 1819. Other medical missionaries from the Board followed in Scudder's wake, establishing hospitals, vaccinating people against diseases, and taking additional measures to alleviate human suffering.

The ABCFM was renowned for its medical work, but it was even more renowned for its schools, which ranged from primary schools to colleges. Among the most famous of these institutions was the Foreign Mission School, which was founded in 1817 in Cornwall, Connecticut. The school was the first in America to focus on international students, but it was only in existence for nine years. Other early ABCFM schools were also short-lived, because Rufus Anderson, who ran the Board from 1832 to 1866, did not support them. He believed that his missionaries should concentrate on preaching the Gospel rather than on teaching English language proficiency and other secular skills (which were in high demand overseas for their commercial utility), and he looked askance at the ABCFM's schools and hospitals, because he did not like the idea of having to fund and staff them in perpetuity.

Figure 2. Rev. Rufus Anderson, long-time administrator of the ABCFM.
Engraving by Joseph Andrews from a painting by Henry Peters Gray.
From Anderson, *History of the Missions of the American Board of Commissioners
for Foreign Missions—The Oriental Churches* (Boston: Congregational Publishing
Society, 1872), front. Image courtesy of the Congregational Library, Boston.

Institutional dependence conflicted with the traditional emphasis within Congregationalism on autonomy, and it undermined Anderson's goal of transforming the ABCFM's schools and hospitals into self-supporting institutions with indigenous leaders. After he retired, however, his policy of self-support lost force within the Board, which started channeling much of its wealth into its schools. Many of these institutions are still operational, and they include Robert College in Istanbul (the oldest American college in existence abroad), the American College in Madurai (one of the oldest colleges in India), the American Farm School in Greece (once a haven for Armenians and other refugees), the American University of Beirut (the first coeducational college in the Middle East), Doshisha University (the first coeducational college in Japan), Inanda Seminary (the first school for native women in South Africa), Punahou School in Hawai'i (the alma mater of U.S. President Barack Obama), and the International Institute (the first school in Spain to prepare women to obtain degrees in higher education).

Wherever they taught, missionaries from the ABCFM came out strongly in favor of education for women. This was a progressive step in nineteenth century America, and it was downright revolutionary in other parts of the world. Nevertheless, missionaries from the Board, many of whom had gone to Mount Holyoke (America's first women's college) or Oberlin (America's first coeducational college) forged ahead, creating the first women's and coeducational schools in many countries. Maintaining those schools was not always easy, but the Board accomplished the task, often with help from the Woman's Board of Missions, a powerful affiliate. Active from its founding in 1868 to its absorption by the ABCFM in 1927, the Woman's Board was run by women, and it wholeheartedly endorsed women's education. It also published a journal, *Life and Light for Woman*, and it provided financial support for female missionaries. Many of those missionaries were daring single women such as Kate Woodhull, the first Western female doctor in China. In the U.S. Woodhull had encountered opposition to her practice of medicine, but on the mission field she and other enterprising women were comparatively free to exercise their skills.[6]

Figure 3. Mary Bowker, founder of the Woman's Board of Missions.
From Frances J. Dyer, *Looking Backward over Fifty Years* (Boston: Woman's Board of Missions, 1917), 4. Photo courtesy of the Congregational Library, Boston.

6. Bendroth, et alia, "Of Faith and Courage," n.p.

That missionaries from the ABCFM and the Woman's Board supported women's rights is not surprising, because they often took progressive stands on social issues. What made them do so was a combination of their Christian principles and their adherence to the ideals of the Euro-American Enlightenment. Citing Enlightenment ideals such as liberty, brotherhood, and equality, missionaries from the ABCFM firmly opposed slavery in the antebellum period, and they chastised their employer for taking donations from slave-owners. Missionaries from the Board also defended the rights of Native Americans, whom the missionaries were charged with converting until that task passed into the hands of an affiliate, the American Home Missionary Society (AHMS), which was created in 1826.

After the AHMS took over work among Native Americans in the U.S., missionaries from the ABCFM turned their attention to other groups. But they still kept an eye on their Native American converts, and they were appalled when they heard about President Andrew Jackson's brutal plan to remove eastern Indians from their ancestral lands. For protesting against that plan, two ABCFM missionaries went to jail, generating a case, Worcester vs. Georgia, that ended up before the U.S. Supreme Court in 1832. The court ruled against Jackson's removal plan, but the president just shrugged, infamously declaring, "John Marshall [the chief justice] has made his decision: now let him enforce it!"[7]

Figure 4. The Brainerd Mission, an ABCFM mission to the Cherokees in Chattanooga, Tennessee (1817–1838). From Joseph Tracy, *History of the American Board of Commissioners for Foreign Missions* (New York: M. W. Dodd, 1842), 237. Engraving courtesy of the Congregational Library, Boston.

7. Greeley, *The American Conflict*, 1:106.

Following its involvement in the Worcester case, the ABCFM went on to appear in other notable episodes of American history. These included the Whitman Massacre in Oregon Territory (where Native Americans killed a family of ABCFM missionaries in 1847), the annexation of Hawai'i (which was largely engineered by the children of ABCFM missionaries in the 1890s), and the "Tainted Money" scandal of 1905 (when political progressives tried unsuccessfully to persuade the ABCFM to return a large gift from the monopolist John D. Rockefeller, Sr.). Other historic events in which the American Board was involved occurred in foreign lands such as Hong Kong (where Charles R. Hager, a missionary from the Board, baptized Sun Yat-sen, a future leader of China, in 1883), China (where missionaries from the Board were killed in the Boxer Uprising of 1900),[8] the Ottoman Empire (where missionaries from the Board played a leading role in helping survivors of the Armenian Genocide), and South Africa (where missionaries from the Board ran Adams College, the alma mater of John Dube, the first president-general of the African National Congress).

Listing all the activities of the ABCFM cannot easily be done. Nor is it the aim of this introductory essay. Nevertheless, certain aspects of the Board's work ought to be mentioned at least briefly before the essay ends. One of those aspects was the ABCFM's vast American support network, which included people who gave the Board money, cared for its sick missionaries, and looked after the children of missionaries on assignment. Another facet of the ABCFM was its connection to leading non-Western Christians such as Henry Opukaha'ia in Hawai'i, Liang Fa in China, and Joseph Hardy Neesima in Japan. All of these men greatly assisted the Board, but their assistance did not eclipse that of American merchants, a group with whom the Board had a complicated relationship. Sometimes merchants worked hand in glove with the ABCFM to spread Christianity and capitalism. At other times, however, missionaries from the Board clashed with merchants, especially those whom the missionaries accused of exploiting vulnerable people.

---

8. Mark Twain, an anti-imperialist, was sympathetic to the Boxers, and he was highly critical of the American Board's presence in China. In a *North American Review* article in 1901, he attacked William Scott Ament, one of the Board's best known missionaries in China, for his behavior in the aftermath of the Boxer Uprising. The attack instigated a war of words between Twain and the Board that was front page news for much of 1901. Thompson, *William Scott Ament and the Boxer Rebellion.*

By now it should be clear to readers that the ABCFM played a highly important role in U.S. and world affairs. Yet that role is not often mentioned in standard history survey textbooks. Nor do the activities of the ABCFM attract a great deal of attention from America's historians, many of whom care little about missionaries in general, let alone missionaries from a particular organization. This tendency among historians to ignore missionaries has been evident for a long time, and it troubled John King Fairbank, a president of the American Historical Association. In his 1968 presidential address to the organization, Fairbank described the missionary as "the invisible man of American history," and he called upon historians to write more about missionaries.[9] Some historians have done as Fairbank asked, producing quality scholarship on missionaries in the years after his presidential address. But historical work on the American missionary movement still does not appear to be very extensive, especially when it is compared to the vast amount of historical work that has been done on American reform movements such as abolitionism, women's suffrage, and Prohibition. These reform movements were of course tremendously important, but they ended a long time ago, whereas the missionary movement, which is no less reformatory than the others, remains active. The missionary movement also almost certainly has the distinction of absorbing more wealth and human capital than any other specific reform movement in American history (unless wars are allowed to count as reform movements).

Aware of how consequential the missionary movement has been, a group of around forty scholars gathered in the Congregational Library in Boston on September 25, 2010, to commemorate the bicentennial of the ABCFM, the oldest and most historically significant foreign missionary organization in America. The scholars at the commemoration (or conference, as it was called) were an international crowd, and they approached the ABCFM from different angles. Some presented papers that were complimentary of the Board, while others of a more secular mindset presented papers that were highly critical of the organization. After the conferees finished speaking and answering questions, they were invited to go on a customized trolley tour of ABCFM-related sites in the Boston area. Not everyone went on the tour, but those who did enjoyed seeing sites that included Boston's Park Street Church (the embarkation point for many ABCFM expeditions), Andover Newton Theological

---

9. Fairbank, "Assignment for the '70's," 877.

School (which many ABCFM missionaries attended), and the Walker Center (formerly a home for the children of absent ABCFM missionaries). Another stopping point on the tour was a burial plot for ABCFM missionaries in the Walnut Street Cemetery in Newton, Massachusetts. The plot is most notable for containing the grave of James L. Barton, a leader of the ABCFM who worked tirelessly to aid survivors of the Armenian Genocide in Turkey.

After the trolley tour and conference were over, Rodney Petersen, one of the conference organizers and the director of the Boston Theological Institute, suggested that the conferees publish their papers collectively in a book. His suggestion met with approval from many of the conferees, and it led directly to the publication of this volume, half of which consists of essays that were presented at the conference. All of the essays herein (conference pieces and non-conference pieces alike) focus on the work of the ABCFM, though the authors of the essays emphasize different aspects of that work. Douglas K. Showalter writes about the formation of the ABCFM; Sharon A. Taylor writes about the doctrinal controversy within the Board over "future probation"; Stephen K. Ault writes about a Board missionary in Spain; and Ann Ellis Pullen and Sarah Ruffing Robbins write about a Board missionary in Africa.

The remaining authors, who constitute a large majority, concentrate on two additional fields in which the ABCFM did work: Asia (which includes India and the Middle East) and Hawai'i (where in the words of one ABCFM missionary the Board was responsible for "the greatest triumph of gospel achievement of our age"[10]). Hawai'i is the basis in this book for essays by Paul T. Burlin, Donald Philip Corr, Regina Pfeiffer, Jennifer Fish Kashay, and Char Miller, while parts of Asia are the basis for essays by Timothy M. Roberts, Virginia A. Metaxas, Alice C. Hunsberger, Thomas G. Oey, Hamish Ion, and the Kellers (Robert and Dorothy [Dee] Birge).[11]

Many of the contributors to this book avoid traditional ways of writing about missionary history. Those ways often lacked nuance, especially when they were taken by scholars with strongly religious or secular points of view. Religious scholars tended to be hagiographic in their coverage of missionaries, while secular scholars often treated the

10. Gulick, "Rev. Peter J. Gulick," n.p.

11. Taylor, Ault, Burlin, Metaxas, Hunsberger, Ion, Roberts, the Kellers, and Pullen and Robbins attended the ABCFM conference, presenting papers that became essays in this book.

evangelists in a dismissive manner. Neither way, however, strikes revisionist missiologists as sufficiently revelatory. Rather than constantly praising or belittling missionaries, the revisionists "complicate" their subject, demonstrating that missionaries were a diverse group of individuals with different methods and aspirations.

Whether or not they identify themselves as revisionist, the contributors to this volume are conscientious scholars. They are also committed to illuminating the work of the ABCFM, and they show how important the organization was as a player on the world stage. The contributors' essays ought not, however, to be viewed as the last word on the ABCFM, whose work extended far beyond the places that the contributors discuss in this book. The contributors also focus mainly on the ABCFM's first century of existence, leaving much unsaid about the changes that the organization experienced in the twentieth century.

One of the changes that affected the ABCFM in modern times was a growing disinclination among well-educated young Congregationalists in America after World War I to become missionaries. Rather than proselytizing overseas for the Board as they might have done had they come of age in the nineteenth century, many young Congregationalists who wanted to see the world in the twentieth century went into secular fields such as anthropology, diplomacy, and international business. All of these fields incidentally often attracted ABCFM missionaries' children, who tended to have language skills and cultural knowledge that were useful outside of the U.S.

Seeing young Congregationalists turn away from missionary work must have upset the leaders of the ABCFM. Nevertheless, they went on with their business, hiring new missionaries to carry the Gospel overseas in the twentieth century. Many of these new missionaries were influenced by the ideas of William Ernest Hocking, a Congregational layman and Harvard philosophy professor who produced a book titled *Re-Thinking Missions* in 1932. In the book, Hocking argued that missionaries should change their behavior. Rather than preaching to people and trying to convert them, missionaries needed in Hocking's view to initiate interreligious dialogue and model the Christian life unobtrusively. These ideas obviously clashed with traditional missionary methods, but they nonetheless became guiding principles for the ABCFM and its missionaries.

In addition to experiencing ideological changes, the ABCFM underwent organizational shifts in the twentieth century. Many of those shifts reflected developments within the ABCFM's parent body, the ecumenically-minded Congregational Church, which merged with the Christian Church in 1931.[12] Twenty-six years later, most of the Congregational Christian Churches merged with the Evangelical and Reformed Church to form the United Church of Christ (UCC). Its headquarters were at 475 Riverside Drive in New York City, and at some point between 1957 and 1961 the ABCFM moved to that address, vacating its old offices in the historic Congregational House at 14 Beacon Street, Boston. The ABCFM also gave up its name when it became a part of the United Church Board for World Ministries (UCBWM) on June 29, 1961.

The UCBWM remained in New York City for nearly thirty years. But after the Board's parent body, the UCC, decided to relocate its headquarters to Cleveland, Ohio, the Board moved there in 1989. Seven years later, the UCBWM joined with the overseas ministries division of the Christian Church (Disciples of Christ) to form Global Ministries. This joint venture is still in operation, coordinating the overseas work of the UCC and the Disciples. But it is now co-directed by Wider Church Ministries (WCM) rather than by the UCBWM, because WCM was chosen as the new name for the UCBWM in 2000. WCM is a direct institutional descendent of the ABCFM, and in the tradition of its famous predecessor it seeks to help people throughout the world.

BIBLIOGRAPHY

Anderson, Rufus. *Memorial Volume of the First Fifty Years of the American Board of Commissioners for Foreign Missions.* Boston: The Board, 1861.

Bendroth, Margaret, et alia. "Of Faith and Courage: The American Board of Commissioners for Foreign Missions," 2010. Archives, Congregational Library, Boston.

Burlin, Paul T. *Imperial Maine and Hawai'i: Interpretive Essays in the History of Nineteenth-Century American Expansion.* Lanham, MD: Lexington Books, 2006.

Corr, Donald Philip. *The Field is the World: Proclaiming, Translating, and Serving by the American Board of Commissioners for Foreign Missions, 1810–1840.* Pasadena, CA: William Carey Library, 2009.

Dunch, Ryan. "Beyond Cultural Imperialism: Cultural Theory, Christian Missions, and Global Modernity. *History and Theory* 41 (October 2002) 301–25.

Fairbank, John King. "Assignment for the '70's," *American Historical Review* 74 (February 1969) 861–69.

Global Ministries. "ABCFM's 200th Anniversary." No pages. Online: http://global ministries.org/resources/mission-study/abcfm/abcfm-american-board-200.html.

12. The ABCFM incorporated the Foreign Department of the Christian Church in 1931. Thirteen years later, the Board made another important move, giving most of its records to the Houghton Library at Harvard University.

Goodsell, Fred Field. *You Shall Be My Witness*. Boston: American Board of Commissioners for Foreign Missions, 1959.

Greeley, Horace. *The American Conflict: A History of the Great Rebellion in the United States of America, 1860-'65*. Hartford: O.D. Case & Co., 1877–1879.

Gulick, Orramel. "Rev. Peter J. Gulick: Fifty Years a Missionary," December 17, 1877. ABCFM Papers on microfilm, ABC 16.4.3, Reel 383, Lamont Library, Harvard University.

Harris, Paul William. *Nothing but Christ: Rufus Anderson and the Ideology of Protestant Foreign Missions*. New York: Oxford University Press, 1999.

Hutchison, William R. *Errand to the World: American Protestant Thought and Foreign Missions*. Chicago: University of Chicago Press, 1987.

Ion, Hamish. *American Missionaries, Christian Oyatoi, and Japan, 1859–1873*. Vancouver, Canada: UBC Press, 2009.

Laymen's Foreign Missions Inquiry, Commission of Appraisal. *Re-Thinking Missions: A Laymen's Inquiry after One Hundred Years, by the Commission of Appraisal, William Ernest Hocking, Chairman*. New York: Harper & Brothers, 1932.

Miller, Char. *Fathers and Sons: The Bingham Family and the American Mission*. Philadelphia: Temple University Press, 1982.

Phillips, Clifton Jackson. *Protestant America and the Pagan World: The First Half Century of the American Board of Commissioners for Foreign Missions, 1810–1860*. Cambridge, MA: East Asian Research Center, Harvard University, 1969.

Pullen, Ann Ellis and Sarah Ruffing Robbins. *Nellie Arnott's Writings on Angola, 1905–1913: Missionary Narratives Linking Africa and America*. Anderson, SC: Parlor Press, 2010.

Putney, Clifford. *Missionaries in Hawai'i: The Lives of Peter and Fanny Gulick, 1797–1883*. Boston: University of Massachusetts Press, 2010.

Robert, Dana. *American Women in Mission: The Modern Mission Era, 1792–1992*. Macon, GA: Mercer University Press, 1997.

Silva, Noenoe K. *Aloha Betrayed: Native Hawaiian Resistance to American Colonialism*. Durham, NC: Duke University Press, 2004.

Stowe, David M. *Year 175: A Brief History of the United Church Board for World Ministries*. New York: United Church Board for World Ministries, 1984.

Strong, William E. *The Story of the American Board: An Account of the First Hundred Years of the American Board of Commissioners for Foreign Missions*. Boston: Pilgrim Press, 1910.

Thompson, Larry Clinton. *William Scott Ament and the Boxer Rebellion: Heroism, Hubris, and the 'Ideal Missionary.'* Jefferson, NC: McFarland & Co., 2009.

Tracy, Joseph. "History of the American Board of Commissioners for Foreign Missions." In *History of American Missions to the Heathen, from Their Commencement to the Present Time*. Worcester, MA: Spooner & Howland, 1840.

Trask, Haunani-Kay. *From a Native Daughter: Colonialism and Sovereignty in Hawai'i*. Monroe, ME: Common Courage Press, 1993.

Winslow, Miron. *A Sketch of Missions, or, History of the Principal Attempts to Propagate Christianity among the Heathen*. Andover, MA: Flagg & Gould, 1819.

1

The 1810 Formation of the American Board of Commissioners for Foreign Missions

Douglas K. Showalter

IN 2006 A NUMBER of us traveled to Williamstown, Massachusetts to celebrate the Bicentennial of the 1806 Haystack Prayer Meeting, which marked the birth of American foreign missions. There we remembered Samuel Mills and his fellow Williams College students who decided, at a prayer meeting in the shelter of a haystack during a sudden thunderstorm, to send the saving gospel of Jesus Christ to non-Christians in a foreign land.[1] That was a startling decision, for at that time American Protestants were only engaged in home missions. Generally, they assumed then that foreign mission work was impractical or even fanatical.

In 1808 at Williams College, Mills and four fellow students went on to organize a secret society, called the "Brethren," to promote the cause of foreign missions. Members of that society took the further step of committing themselves to take the gospel overseas themselves, not just send it with others.

---

1. See Showalter, "The Story of the Haystack Prayer Meeting"; and Showalter, *Chapters on the 1806 Haystack Prayer Meeting and the American Board of Commissioners for Foreign Missions.*

Figure 5. Haystack Monument in Williamstown, Massachusetts. The monument, which commemorates the Haystack Prayer Meeting, was dedicated in 1867. From H. C. Haydn, ed., *American Heroes on Mission Fields* (New York: American Tract Society, 1890), front. Engraving courtesy of the Congregational Library, Boston.

In 1810 Mills entered Andover Theological Seminary for ministerial training. The Brethren society was then transferred there. At the seminary Mills met fellow student Adoniram Judson Jr., who shared Mills' passion for foreign mission work. That same year their vision began to become a reality, which opened up a brand new chapter in American Protestantism. Here's what happened.

On Tuesday, June 26, 1810, Mills, Judson, and some fellow Andover students met with some Congregational leaders at the home of Andover Theological Seminary professor Moses Stuart. The students spoke of their strong desire to serve as foreign missionaries, but they did not receive a very encouraging response. Those assembled raised questions about their goals and the difficulty of raising funds to support them. A minister from Reading, Massachusetts, stated quite frankly that "while the proposal was generous and had back of it a worthy motive . . . it was premature and seemed to savor of infatuation."[2]

2. Strong, "The Founding of the American Board," 247.

The students returned to their seminary rooms with little hope of receiving support for their idea.[3] Yet, those at Stuart's home ultimately decided that the students' desire should be brought before the General Association of Massachusetts Proper (GAMP), whose annual meeting was beginning the very next day at the Church of Christ in Bradford, Massachusetts. The General Association was Trinitarian in orientation and made up of clergy delegates primarily from Congregational ministers' groups around Massachusetts. It was a predecessor to today's Massachusetts Conference of the United Church of Christ.

The next morning, Wednesday, June 27, Rev. Samuel Worcester of Salem and Rev. Dr. Samuel Spring of Newburyport shared a two hour carriage ride together, as they traveled to the General Association meeting in Bradford. Inspired by the students' comments the day before, those ministers used their time together to formulate how a foreign missionary society could be structured. They even chose a name for it, the "Board of Commissioners for Foreign Missions."[4]

Apparently, other General Association members found this idea of interest, for that very afternoon Mills, Judson, and the other Andover students received an invitation to attend the meeting the next day. The students willingly undertook that journey on foot, a distance of about ten miles from their seminary to Bradford. On Thursday, June 28, they appeared before the assembly with a prepared statement. The presenters and signers of that statement were Adoniram Judson Jr.; Samuel Mills; Samuel Nott, Jr.; and Samuel Newell.[5]

That statement originally contained the names of six students, but the students decided to omit two of them, James Richards and Luther Rice. They did this out of concern that the prospect of finding support for as many as six missionaries would discourage the General Association from trying to support any.[6] That likely was a wise move, for the organization was relatively new, having been founded in 1802/1803. It did not have representation from all the Congregational ministers' groups in

---

3. Worcester, *Discourse at the Semi-Centennial Anniversary of the Institution of the American Board of Commissioners for Foreign Missions*, 21.

4. See Tracy, *History of the American Board of Commissioners for Foreign Missions*, 25; and Strong, *The Story of the American Board*, 4.

5. The statement was drafted by Adoniram Judson Jr. It was published in *The Panoplist and Missionary Magazine United*, 3:2 (July 1810), 88–90.

6. Tracy, *History of the American Board*, 26.

Massachusetts, and it's likely that many delegates did not know before-hand that such a momentous subject would be on the agenda of their meeting.[7]

In their prepared statement, the students expressed their desire to devote their lives to missionary work with non-Christians in foreign lands "whenever God, in his providence shall open the way." But the students still asked the General Association delegates to judge if they "ought to renounce the object of missions, as either visionary or impracticable." If the answer to that question was no, the students also wanted to know if the delegates thought it best to "direct their attention to the eastern, or the western world." In their statement the students also asked if they could expect support from a missionary society in America, or if they "must commit themselves to the direction of a European Society."[8] After their statement was read the students answered questions, then returned to their seminary on foot.

The response was immediate. One delegate at that meeting said he was moved to tears and made to "feel small . . . to see those young men offering themselves to go and preach to the heathen."[9] As another delegate noted, the students' statement "was heard with profound attention. It was a sound in the tops of the mulberry trees, and some of us held our breath.[10]

(Second Samuel 5:24 says that God would stir the tops of the mulberry trees as a sign for the ancient Hebrews to prepare themselves, for God would soon be leading them into a battle in which they would conquer the Philistines.) That delegate and others were very aware that God might be working through those students to create this brand new missionary effort for Christ. Speaking of the students themselves, another delegate declared that "One thing was prominent and universal,

7. Strong, *The Story of the American Board*, 5.

8. At that point in time, Congregationalists knew of two Protestant foreign missionary societies in England. One was the Baptist Missionary Society, formed in 1792 in response to Rev. William Carey's urging. Carey, who has been called the "Father of the Modern Missionary Movement," subsequently became noted for his missionary work in India under that society's sponsorship. The other organization was the Missionary Society of London, which was formed in 1795 by Independents, Anglicans, Presbyterians, and others. In 1818, it was renamed the London Missionary Society.

9. Worcester, *Discourse at the Semi-Centennial Anniversary*, 25.

10. *Memorial Volume of the First Fifty Years of the American Board of Commissioners for Foreign Missions*, 50.

viz., a deep sense of the sublime position and devout spiritual conse-
cration of this missionary band. They were unpretending, modest, of a
tender, child-like spirit, well understanding their aim, consecrated, a felt
power."[11]

The General Association referred the students' requests to a subcommittee of its members to study the matter and report back the next
day. That subcommittee was made up of Rev. Worcester, Rev. Dr. Spring,
and Rev. Enoch Hale, a brother of the Revolutionary War hero Nathan
Hale. The next day, on Friday, June 29, that subcommittee brought
back a report which was basically favorable to the students' requests.
Guided by that report, the twenty-one voting members of the General
Association decided unanimously to create the "Board of Commissioners
for Foreign Missions."[12] They also appointed nine highly respected
Congregationalists, both clergy and lay persons, to serve on that new
board. Mills and the other students were also advised to put themselves
"under the patronage and direction" of that new board and to wait for
the "openings and guidance of Providence in respect to their great and
excellent design." In describing that historic meeting, one delegate noted
that there was "no direct opposition," "weak faith" or "genial hope," but
"a waiting posture." As he said, "It obviously was a relief to a portion of
the body that the subject was put into the hands of such men as those

11. *Memorial Volume*, 51.

12. The names and church affiliations of those voting at this meeting were as follows:
Rev. Levi White (Sandisfield), Rev. Nathaniel Turner (Second in New Marboro), Rev.
Benjamin Ruggles Woodbridge (Norwich), Rev. John Emerson (Conway), Rev. Rufus
Wells (Whately), Rev. Vinson Gould (Southampton), Rev. John Keep (Blandford),
Rev. Thomas Snell (Brookfield), Rev. Titus Theodore Barton (Fitchburg), Rev. Joseph
Goffe (Second in Sutton), Rev. Humphrey Clark Perley (Methuen), Rev. Samuel Mead
(Second West in Amesbury), Rev. Ebenezer Dutch (Second East in Bradford), Rev.
Thomas Holt (Second in Ipswich [Chebacco]), Rev. Manasseh Cutler (Hamilton), Rev.
Samuel Worcester (Third Church in Salem), Rev. Enoch Hale (Westhampton), Rev.
Jonathan Allen (Bradford), Rev. Salmon Cone (Colchester), Rev. Evan Jones (Berlin),
Rev. Samuel Wood (East in Boscawen). The average age of the twenty-one clergy voting
was about 47.

The seven honorary, non-voting members at that meeting were: Rev. Samuel
Spring (North Congregational in Newburyport), Rev. Eliphalet Pearson (retired
Andover Theological Seminary professor), Rev. William Morrison (Londonderry, del-
egate from the Presbyterian Communion), Rev. Daniel Dana (Presbyterian Church in
Newburyport, delegate from the Presbyterian Communion), and three other Andover
Theological Seminary professors who have not yet been identified. Finally, a large num-
ber of other ministers from the Bradford vicinity and some laity were present at this
meeting.

who composed the Board. In the right sense they were marked men, well suited to the emergency . . . The feeling was, Try it; if the project fail, it would have, from such men, an honorable burial.[13]

Those appointed to the Board of Commissioners were:

His Excellency John Treadwell, Esq. (Governor of Connecticut)

Rev. Dr. Timothy Dwight (President of Yale College)

General Jedediah Huntington (noted Revolutionary War officer, now serving as Customs Inspector in New London)

Rev. Calvin Chapin (Rocky Hill Congregational Church)

Rev. Joseph Lyman (Hatfield Congregational Church)

Rev. Dr. Samuel Spring (North Congregational in Newburyport)

William Bartlett, Esq. (merchant, philanthropist and major contributor to Andover Theological Seminary)

Rev. Samuel Worcester (Third Church in Salem)

Deacon Samuel Hall Walley (Federal Street Church in Boston and Trustee of Andover Theological Seminary)

On September 5, 1810, the new Board of Commissioners for Foreign Missions held its first meeting in the parlor of the home of Rev. and Mrs. Noah Porter in Farmington, Connecticut. Sitting around a small mahogany table, the five Board members who could attend adopted a new constitution for their society and changed its name to the American Board of Commissioners for Foreign Missions (ABCFM).[14] That change likely reflected their growing sense of the importance of their new mission and of God's spirit stirring within it. And so, what started as a decision made by college students under a haystack during a thunderstorm in 1806 was now an organization and a growing movement of which the world would soon take note.

In 1812 the American Board of Commissioners for Foreign Missions was incorporated by the Massachusetts Legislature. Although created by Congregational clergy, at that point the ABCFM became an independent society, which worked with different denominational groups, including Congregationalists. The ABCFM's work soon led

13. *Memorial Volume*, 51.

14. See "Minutes of the First Annual Meeting," 11; "Recollections of the Rev. Noah Porter, D.D.," *Memorial Volume*, 60–61; and Strong, *The Story of the American Board*, 4.

many American Protestants to value foreign missions and feel it was their duty to support them. Over the course of the nineteenth century, a number of other Protestant foreign mission societies also sprang up in the United States, following the lead of the ABCFM.

The ABCFM sent out its earliest missionaries to India (1812), Ceylon (1815), the Cherokee nation (1817), the Choctaw nation (1818), the Sandwich Islands (1819), and Palestine (1819). Those missionaries were expected to spend their entire lives in those mission fields.

In Mark 16:15 Christ gave his followers this charge: "Go ye into all the world, and preach the gospel to every creature." The early ABCFM took that charge as its mandate and placed those words on its seal. Accordingly, the primary work of early ABCFM missionaries was to preach the Christian message. The "great design of the Board" in sending out missionaries was to bring knowledge of Christ to non-Christians.

Figure 6. The seal of the ABCFM. From *The Day Breaking; or, Light in Dark Lands* (Boston: ABCFM, 1870), title page. Image in the collection of the author.

Many who supported the early ABCFM did so out of compassion. They believed that ABCFM missionaries could play a significant role in preventing the precious souls of those who had been living in spiritual darkness from being lost eternally. In those early years, people also supported the ABCFM for humanitarian reasons. Tales of dire practices, such as the sacrifice of children in the Ganges and the burning of widows on the funeral pyres of their deceased husbands, led supporters to hope that the Christian influence of ABCFM missionaries would help end such practices.

The early ABCFM missionaries were expected, at least in principle, to focus on preaching and pay less attention to fulfilling other basic needs of the people they were serving. In fact, in 1828 the ABCFM's Prudential Committee held the position, which it considered "unquestionable," that, "the Gospel affords the only adequate relief for the temporal, as well as for the spiritual wants of men."[15] That attitude changed over the years and the ABCFM sought to do more to meet people's physical and economic needs, as well as their spiritual needs. ABCFM missionaries themselves were credited with making significant contributions, particularly in the fields of education, geography, philology, and archaeology. In 1881 the ABCFM published a hefty volume detailing many of those accomplishments.[16] Also, in 1897, the ABCFM gave its physicians and nurses full missionary status, which reflected the Board's growing awareness of the importance of providing medical care in its mission fields.[17]

Some may be surprised to learn that not all nineteenth-century Congregationalists were happy with the creation of the ABCFM. Some complained that according to Congregational polity, the General Association of Massachusetts Proper, as a group of Congregational clergy only, had exceeded its authority when it created such a missionary society which Congregational churches were then expected to support. As was noted, the churches had no voice in the ABCFM's creation, but they should have.[18] Also, it has been said that this complaint was used

---

15. See Prudential Committee, *ABCFM Annual Report, 1828,* 113; and Goodsell, *They Lived Their Faith,* 34–35.

16. Laurie, *The Ely Volume.*

17. Goodsell, *You Shall Be My Witnesses,* 71.

18. Quint, *Congregational Year Book, 1859,* 49.

repeatedly to thwart efforts to form a national Congregational denomination. However, such a national body finally was formed in 1871.[19]

At the time of its 100th anniversary in 1910, the ABCFM was reported to have 595 active missionaries serving in 20 different mission fields around the world.[20] In the twentieth century, the ABCFM was brought within the denominational structure of the Congregational churches. Today its work is continued by the Wider Church Ministries department of the United Church of Christ. In fact, I'm told that the small mahogany table around which the Board held its first meeting, in 1810, is currently on display in the greeting area outside the offices of the Wider Church Ministries department in Cleveland, Ohio.[21]

Figure 7. Table used in 1810 at the first annual meeting of the ABCFM. From "The American Board, 1810—Centennial Leaflet—1910" (Boston: ABCFM, 1910), n.p. Image in the collection of the author.

19. Atkins and Fagley, History of American Congregationalism, 194–95.

20. Goodsell, *You Shall Be My Witnesses*, 288.

21. "Chronology of the Journey Toward The Common Global Ministries Board," 2.

BIBLIOGRAPHY

Atkins, Gaius Glenn and Fagley, Frederick L. *History of American Congregationalism.* Boston: The Pilgrim Press, 1942.

"Chronology of the Journey Toward The Common Global Ministries Board," n.p. In *History, Mission, and Organization of the Common Global Ministries Board: A Common Witness of the Christian Church (Disciples of Christ) and the United Church of Christ.* [Cleveland, OH: Global Ministries Board, 2000].

Goodsell, Fred Field. *You Shall Be My Witnesses: An Interpretation of the History of the American Board 1810–1960.* Boston: American Board of Commissioners for Foreign Missions, 1959.

———. *They Lived Their Faith.* Boston: American Board of Commissioners for Foreign Missions, 1961.

[Judson Jr., Adoniram]. Statement. *The Panoplist and Missionary Magazine United* 3:2 (July 1810) 88–90.

Laurie, Thomas. *The Ely Volume; The Contributions of our Foreign Missions to Science and Human Well-Being.* Boston: American Board of Commissioners for Foreign Missions, 1881.

Memorial Volume of the First Fifty Years of the American Board of Commissioners for Foreign Missions. Boston: ABCFM, 1862, 5th ed.

"Minutes of the First Annual Meeting." *First Ten Annual Reports of the American Board of Commissioners for Foreign Missions with Other Documents of the Board.* Boston, 1834.

Prudential Committee of the ABCFM. *ABCFM Annual Report, 1828.*

Quint, Dr. Alonzo H. *Congregational Year Book, 1859.*

Showalter, Douglas K. *Chapters on the 1806 Haystack Prayer Meeting and the American Board of Commissioners for Foreign Missions.* Privately printed, 2006.

———. "The Story of the Haystack Prayer Meeting." *Bulletin of the Congregational Library,* Second Series, 3:1 (Summer 2006) n.p.

Strong, E. E. "The Founding of the American Board." *The Missionary Herald* 106:6 (June 1910) [240–50].

Strong, William E. *The Story of the American Board: An Account of the First Hundred Years of the American Board of Commissioners for Foreign Missions.* Boston: The Pilgrim Press, 1910.

Tracy, Joseph. *History of the American Board of Commissioners for Foreign Missions, Compiled Chiefly from the published and Unpublished Documents of the Board.* New York: M. W. Dodd, 1842.

Worcester, Samuel M. *Discourse at the Semi-Centennial Anniversary of the Institution of the American Board of Commissioners for Foreign Missions: At Bradford, Mass., June 20, 1860.* Boston: T. R. Marvin & Son, 1860.

2

The Great Debate: The American Board and the Doctrine of Future Probation

Sharon A. Taylor

IN OCTOBER 1886, OVER a thousand delegates and visitors flocked to Des Moines, Iowa for the 77th annual meeting of the American Board of Commissioners for Foreign Missions. The *Boston Herald* declared that the assembly had gathered to witness the greatest crisis that the Board had faced since its establishment in 1810.[1] Boston's *Daily Advertiser* billed it the "The Battle of the Giants".[2] On the podium sat scores of eminent preachers, seminary professors and Board officials, many of whom were graduates of Andover Theological Seminary. Of particular importance was Egbert Smyth, a member of the Prudential Committee of the Board, a professor and president of Andover Seminary, and a leader in the movement that called itself "Progressive Orthodoxy" or the "New Theology." (Conservative churchmen, who were less enamored with the doctrines promulgated by the movement, dubbed it the "New Departure.") One notable figure was absent due to ill health: Edwards Park, professor of theology at Andover Seminary for fifty years and figurehead for the conservatives. His influence was palpable, however. A majority of the Prudential Committee members and officers had been his pupils. And, by the estimate of a later American Board Secretary, over half the or-

---

1. "Probation after Death," *Boston Herald*, October 6, 1886.

2. "Does Death End All? The Battle of the Giants" *Boston Daily Advertiser*, October 8, 1886.

dained men present that day and two-thirds of the Board's Corporation members were Park's admirers.[3]

The scent of high drama was in the air. Robert A. Hume, an Andover Seminary graduate, son of ABCFM missionaries, and himself a missionary in India for eleven years, found his return to the mission field barred. The American Board's Prudential Committee, the body charged with the oversight of the hiring and placement of missionaries, had deferred his re-appointment to India. Decisions concerning other promising applicants for the foreign mission field had also been postponed. The topic that triggered these decisions was the matter of future probation, also known as the doctrine of salvation after death, or, the Andover Theory. This speculative dogma proposed that persons who did not have an opportunity to hear the gospel in this lifetime would have an opportunity after death to receive the gospel message from the lips of Jesus himself. All those who heard the gospel would then be able to accept or reject an offer of salvation. At issue for the missionary endeavor was an obvious point: why squander human and fiscal resources by sending out missionaries if the "heathen" could have the opportunity to hear the untainted gospel in their own language after death from the Savior? As Edwards Park would famously say, future probation was a doctrine calculated to cut the nerve of missions.[4]

The future probation question had been a difficult one for Congregationalists for the previous twenty-five years. The issue became a pressing concern, however, with the rise of denominationalism and challenge of maintaining theological integrity within a denomination that relegated the judgment of such matters to the local congregation. Over the years the National Council of the Congregational Churches had recommended that every member of the clergy be a part of an association or organization of churches to provide some theological and moral oversight. Rather than depending upon local churches to vet their potential pastors, the National Council of 1879 called for local councils to examine all who were to be installed or ordained "to guard the rights of the churches and congregations from danger; and especially to protect them from those who are unfit or from unsoundness of doctrine".[5] Soon

---

3. Enoch F. Bell, "Then and Now . . .", March 11, 1943," ANTS Archives.

4. "A.B.C.F.M.," *Portland Daily Press*, October 5, 1882, 1.

5. *Minutes of the National Council of the Congregational Churches, October 17–21, 1877*, 49.

these installation councils became the setting for several fierce contests as men who espoused a belief in future probation, many of them Andover Seminary graduates, attempted to enter pulpits throughout the country.

To help the churches and councils clarify the content of core doctrine, the Commission Creed of 1883 was written and distributed to the churches for their edification and possible use. Conservatives were dismayed that the Commission Creed left open the door for the belief in the possibility of a future probation. For this reason Edmund Alden, the Home Secretary of the ABCFM refused to recommend the Creed even though he had served on the commission that created it. Several months after the creed's adoption, Alden began to distribute a substitute credo to all new missionary candidates of the ABCFM. This new statement of belief was adopted by the Pilgrim Church in Worcester, Massachusetts, and was known thereafter as the Worcester Creed. Though published anonymously, Edwards Park was the acknowledged author. The creed was unambiguous in declaring that judgment was tied to deeds done in the body and that death ended this probation. There was no future probation, no possibility of salvation after death for anyone.

1886 proved to be the year of the "perfect storm" for theological controversy among Congregationalists in America. That year five Andover Seminary professors, including the president Egbert Smyth, were charged with heresy in a highly publicized hearing before the Seminary's Board of Visitors. Four of the professors were eventually exonerated due to a technicality, but Smyth was found guilty among other things of "maintaining and inculcating belief inconsistent with and repugnant to the creed of the school," namely that "he believed that there is, and will be, probation after death for all men who do not decisively reject Christ in this life.[6] With appeals and counter-appeals the controversy at the seminary lasted until October 1891, leaving the school in dire straits financially and its reputation irreparably damaged.

By the time of the annual meeting of the ABCFM in Des Moines, it was inevitable that the theological controversies in the Congregational churches and their premier seminary would find their way there as well. While the ABCFM was founded as an "undenominational" society, by 1886 its identity with Congregationalism was firmly cemented. When Robert Hume had been blocked from the mission field, his integrity

---

6. ATS. *Minutes of the Board of Visitors*, June 3, 1887. ANTS Archives.

as a Congregational minister as well as the orthodoxy of the education he received at Andover Seminary was a subtext to the debates. Hume had been the poster boy for the Seminary and the ABCFM—the ideal missionary candidate. While home on furlough in 1886, he had been asked to speak during the June alumni day gatherings at the seminary. There he proudly confirmed that the new Andover Theology, including the idea of salvation after death, was spreading rapidly around the globe. The question of a post-mortem salvation was not a theoretical one for him or his colleagues, he declared. New converts overseas were desperately concerned about the destiny of their ancestors who never had the opportunity to hear the gospel. The idea of a future probation would bring them relief.[7] Hume's speech provoked a quick reaction. The Prudential Committee, responding to dozens of protests, immediately blocked Hume's return to India. The action made front page news in the Boston papers.[8]

Figure 8. Andover Theological Seminary, ca. 1830, featuring Phillips Hall, Bartlet Chapel, and Bartlet Hall. Image courtesy of Andover Newton Theological Seminary Archive.

7. "The Andover Anniversaries," *Congregationalist,* June 17, 1886.

8. "Missionary Hume refused permission to return to India," *Boston Daily Advertiser,* September 24, 1886.

At the annual meeting of the American Board, Egbert Smyth forced the issue by asking why the Prudential Committee was blocking qualified men and women, and then proceeded to read, case by case, personal correspondence from the candidates purporting to show that none of them held post-mortem salvation as a settled doctrine but only entertained hopes about it.[9] After days of debate a final resolution was quickly adopted. The Board recommended that Prudential Committee consider taking difficult doctrinal cases to a council of the churches to pass on the theological soundness of the candidate, and then to report on this matter at the next annual meeting.[10] The Prudential Committee's decisions were not overturned, and, overall, the meeting appeared to be a dramatic victory for the conservatives on the Board. However, some members immediately raised objections to the proposal of using church councils to adjudicate orthodoxy. Most of the missionary candidates were not ordained at the time they applied to the ABCFM. Using councils to determine their theological fitness would only occur, in the normal process of things, as they sought ordination after they were accepted as candidates. Moreover, what about the Presbyterians and other non-Congregationalists that might apply? What authority would a council of Congregational churches have over those from outside the ecclesiastical tradition?

A verbatim report of the Board's discussions concerning the future probation dispute was published in 1886 under the title *The Great Debate*. The press had a heyday with the reports. *Puck,* a popular New York humor magazine, ridiculed the proceedings in a cartoon that showed Andover professors in a pitched battle over seemingly esoteric theological matters while placid natives watched from the shore under a banner that read, "We want no heaven without our ancestors."[11] Meanwhile the sticky case of Robert Hume remained on the table. Alden revealed the news that Hume had spoken about Future Probation on one of his recent recruitment jaunts to Chicago. He had met privately with seminary students there and told them that he did believe in the possibility of a post-mortem salvation and it brought him great relief.[12] Meanwhile, Hume's

9. The American Board at Des Moines," *Independent,* October 14, 1886. "Address of Professor Smyth," *Independent,* October 14, 1886.

10. ABCFM. *The Great Debate: a verbatim report . . . Des Moines, Iowa, Thursday, October 7, 1886,* 80.

11. *Puck,* October 27, 1886.

12. S. M. Freeland to Mark Hopkins, November 5, 1886. ABCFM Papers, Special

colleagues on the mission field testified to his good work and pleaded for his return.[13] The Prudential Committee relented and finally voted to send Hume back to India—but the vote was not unanimous.

The resolution of Hume's case was not the only problem for the Prudential Committee. The same month that Hume was making his remarks on Andover hill, the Committee was faced with decisions concerning the candidacies of two Andover seniors, William H. Noyes and Daniel Temple Torrey. Both had applied for the mission station in Japan, and both had expressed ambivalence about the belief that those who die without making a decision for Christ were destined to eternal punishment. The Committee voted to defer both men. In the next two months two more candidates also applied and were also deferred: Robert Morse, a senior at Yale Divinity School, and Cornelia Judson, a student at Wellesley College.

The case of William Noyes proved to be as controversial as that of Robert Hume. Noyes, like Hume, was born in India, the son of ABCFM missionaries who served a lifetime on the Madura station. After college Noyes had attended Union Seminary in New York where he had experienced a crisis of faith. He transferred to Andover Seminary after one year, and after rapid spiritual renewal, he became convinced that he had a calling to missions. He applied to the Prudential Committee in May 1886, bringing with him the recommendations of two seminary presidents, two of Andover professors, as well as the association where he had been licensed to preach. Noyes answered the requisite questions from the *Manual for Missionary Candidates*, affirming his assent to the Apostle's and Nicene creeds and well as the Commission creed of 1883. In his interview before the three Board Secretaries he confirmed his belief in the traditional doctrines of the faith. Noyes seemed like the ideal missionary candidate except for one glaring irregularity: he admitted unambiguously to a belief in the dogma of Future Probation. Noyes was questioned several times and, to some members of the Prudential Committee, it seemed that he had moved beyond the point of private musings and had entered the realm of constructing or adopting a theological system in which future probation played an integral part. This set him apart from previous candidates who expressed doubts about the established doctrine but had not yet come to firm convictions about adopt-

Topics, Box Pe-Prob, HLHU.

13. "That Letter from India," *Congregationalist*, February 10, 1887.

ing future probation as an alternative. The transcript of the Committee's interview with Noyes was leaked to the *Christian Union* magazine. In a rebuttal, published in the same magazine, Noyes objected saying he had been misunderstood, that perhaps he had been enticed to use phrases that were imprecise or ambiguous, and, he denied that future probation was the centerpiece of his belief system.

About this time the public learned that Edmund Alden in his role as Home Secretary had been mailing copies of the Worcester Creed to persons applying for missionary positions. This creed had been interpreted as the official doctrinal position of the Board, which was not the case. Alden insisted that this new creed was sent out to serve as a guide for candidates as they wrote out their own statements of belief. Critics, however, were outraged. What right did the Prudential Committee have to expect a higher standard of belief from its candidates than churches expected from their pastors? Who had the authority to determine what these theological boundaries were to be, particularly in a close corporation that was related to the churches but not overseen by them?

The damage was done. The perception that Alden and handful of others on the Prudential Committee had a lock-hold on the theological policies of the Board raised the hackles of the progressive element in the Corporation. The indignation focused on Alden despite the fact that as a secretary he was merely *ex-officio* and had no vote on the Prudential Committee.[14] Augustus C. Thompson, long time member of the Committee and pastor of the Roxbury Congregational Church, rose to Alden's defense. Thompson reminded the public that the Prudential Committee had decided long before these controversies that its role was not to decide whether or not a man was fit to be a minister of the gospel, but it was its prerogative and duty to decide on the fitness of the candidate as a missionary to the heathen.[15] As Thompson pointed out, the American Board was not an ecclesiastical organization; it did not ordain clergy or operate as a congregation according to Congregational polity. It was a *close* association with a self-perpetuating membership. Nevertheless, the Board had a clear understanding that its missionaries would hold substantially the same doctrinal views as those of its patrons. Moreover, it was within the authority of the Board secretaries and the Prudential Committee to search out any discrepancies with evangelical

14. "In Brief," *Congregationalist*, August 26, 1886.

15. Thompson, *Future Probation and Foreign Missions*, 9.

orthodox theology.[16] That made scrutiny on the subject of the belief in salvation after death a matter of supreme importance to the Board. The dogma of future probation contradicted the historic belief of the lost state of the heathen, and a host of missionaries had testified that permitting it on the mission field would be detrimental to the work and moral influence of missions. It was "incipient theological dry rot."[17]

Letters and cables arrived at the offices of the ABCFM demanding that that Egbert Smyth be dropped from the Prudential Committee.[18] One pastor threatening to cut off the ABCFM financially if the view of future probation was adopted.[19] And another wrote, "I am resolved never to utter a syllable or to contribute a farthing to help build, at home or abroad, a Doubting Castle or a half-way House to Heresy."[20] Meanwhile, more cases of candidates rejected by the Prudential Committee came to light. The *Christian Union* claimed to know of seven men who had been delayed, discouraged or rejected for their belief in the Andover Theory. The *Andover Review* reported that the number was actually between twelve and twenty, men and women who had been kept back by August 1886.[21] The Prudential Committee vehemently denied these numbers and questioned how the magazine had gotten what was supposed to be confidential information. It was clear that someone was leaking reports to the press. By October 1886 the whole country was caught up in the fight, a conflict that was being waged on three fronts: within associations and churches as they wrestled over creed making and theological integrity in an attempt to assign theological boundaries to a denomination that looked at such boundaries with suspicion; within Andover Seminary, long the bastion of orthodoxy for Congregationalists and now the home of the "New Departure" and a progressive theology that many considered was better suited to a modern age; and, finally, among the officers and Corporate members of the American Board who brought

16. Ibid., 12–13.

17. Ibid., 49.

18. D. Furber to Augustus C. Thompson, September 10, 1886. ACT Papers, HSA.

19. Herbert W. Lathe to Augustus C. Thompson, September 9, 1886. ACT Papers, HSA.

20. Rev. D. Thompson (Boston, Mass.) to Augustus C. Thompson, September 10, 1886. ACT Papers, HSA.

21. "Not an Andover Question," *Christian Union*, September 2, 1886; "Secretary Alden's Difficulty: the Way Out," *Andover Review* 7 (August 1886) 198.

with them the all the apprehensions of the churches and the Seminary as well as the very real fear that the decisions that would be made over future probation would impact the very mission of the organization and the salvation of souls around the world.

Figure 9. Professors at Andover Theological Seminary, ca. 1884.
Photo courtesy of Andover Newton Theological Seminary Archive.

Meanwhile, the rejection of William Noyes by the Prudential Committee, a decision supported by the corporate members of the ABCFM at the annual meeting in 1887, infuriated his supporters. Taking matters in to their own hands, they—and Berkeley Street Church in Boston—called for a hastily assembled ordination council. The leaders of the New Theology turned out in force while the few conservative churches that were invited failed to attend. It gave all the appearances of a stacked council of supporters. Then, duly ordained and his theological stance deemed sufficiently orthodox by an official ecclesiastical council, Noyes again applied to the Prudential Committee for a place in Japan. Once again he was rejected, news that made the *New York Times*. The paper attributed Noyes rejection to "his theological agreement with the heretical Andover Seminary." While the hubbub continued at home, Noyes and his wife sailed to Japan as independent missionaries with the financial and moral support of the Berkeley Street Church.[22]

In 1889 a committee appointed by the ABCFM president, Richard Storrs, recommended that the President and Vice-president serve as *ex*

22. "Mr. Noyes Again Rejected," *New York Times*, November 12, 1888.

officio members on the Prudential Committee along with ten elected members. Even this move to broaden the constituency of the Committee did not allay fears that the whole procedure was too controlled as long as Edmund Alden remained as Home Secretary. A new Committee of Nine was appointed to look into the administration of the office. At the annual meeting the next year, the Committee of Nine made some minor recommendations about auditing and financial reporting. The main recommendation, however, dealt with how missionary candidates were examined for their theological beliefs. The Corporate members of the Board voted to amend the question in the *Manual for Missionary Candidates* so that they now read:

> *Question 1.* What are you views respecting each of the leading doctrines of Scripture commonly held by the churches sustaining this Board? In answering this question you may use your own language, or refer to any creeds of acknowledged weight as to the doctrines contained in such creeds.

> *Question 2.* Have you any views at variance with these doctrines, or any views of church government which would prevent your cordial cooperation with the missionaries of this Board?

Candidates would no longer have to use specific creedal language to explain their beliefs. The second question was refocused from the candidates' doubts to their settled convictions. Hiring procedures were also amended. Now the Secretary would receive applications and turn them over to the Prudential Committee with no further correspondence. The Home Secretary could not reject candidates out of hand as Alden had been accused of doing in previous years. Only the revised questions in the manual could be used in questioning candidates. And, finally, any Secretary could bring matters to the Committee without having consent or approval of the other secretaries. These new polices provided, in modern parlance, a means of executive limitations and served as a method of checks and balances within the administration. The decision-making power of the Home Secretary was now curtailed and his influence with potential candidates circumscribed.

With new policies in place the Committee now faced three more problematic applications all from Andover students. The first two men were turned down for health reasons, though the fact that they held views favoring future probation was well known.[23] The third man, Edward Fairbank, was an extraordinary candidate. Like Hume and Noyes he had been born in India. His father, his brother Henry, and his brother-in-law, the renowned Robert Hume, were all serving with the ABCFM in India. During his interview before the Prudential Committee, Fairbank was asked to clarify his statement at three points: future probation, the inspiration of the Bible and the Holy Spirit.[24] When he was advised that a "little verbal change in the statement" would clear the way for his appointment, he refused the suggestion and decided to stand by his own unedited words.[25] Backed by President Storrs, Fairbank's appointment was approved and he was assigned to the Marathi Mission in India. The next day the headlines of one Boston paper read "An Andover Heretic Appointed as Missionary."[26]

In 1892 another application was received from William Noyes. His application came with letters of recommendation from several large donors and fifty-one missionaries of the Japan Mission who formally requested that Noyes be allowed to join them. In light of Noyes' proven record of service, and the fact that he had caused no theological disturbances on the field, a resolution was offered at the annual meeting in October 1892 to receive the couple as regular missionaries of the Board. Alternate resolutions and counter resolutions were made. Noyes was questioned again about his views about future probation. He replied that he did not believe in a future probation if to believe meant to have certainly. He went on to say that he did not find the theory explicitly revealed in the Bible but that the Bible did leave room for it. And, concerning those who do not hear the gospel in this life, he opined, "I entertain in their behalf what I consider to be reasonable hope that somehow, before their destinies are fixed, there shall be revealed to them the love of Christ in Christ Jesus. In this, as in every question to which God has given no distinct answer, I merely claim the liberty of the gospel."[27] In April, the Committee assured by the restraint of his remarks voted to appoint Noyes and his wife to Japan. Noyes responded by saying that,

23. Edward Fairbank to Enoch F. Bell, January 20, 1943. ABCFM Papers, HLHU.

24. ABCFM. *Records of the Prudential Committee*, 22 (15 March 1892) 494. CL.

25. Edward Fairbank to Enoch F. Bell, January 20, 1943.

26. Ibid., cited by Fairbank.

27. William H. Noyes to Mr. Ellison, December 4, 1892, in "The Prudential Committee and Mr. Noyes," *Congregationalist*, July 27, 1893.

once again, he had been misunderstood. He had not meant to sound as if he was reneging on his stated beliefs but had merely responded to the Secretary's inquiry in the language that had been prescribed. While it was true that his views on future probation had not progressed dangerously or limited his missionary zeal, Noyes reiterated that he still stood by his original statements made at his ordination.[28] The Committee promptly recalled his appointment, setting off yet another round of criticism and public derision."[29]

For the third time the Prudential Committee, following the Board's guidelines refused to appoint Noyes on theological grounds. Following this latest rejection, the case was remanded to the full Board for adjudication. Noyes's supporters obtained the confidential reports of the Prudential Committee and had some 2000 copies printed and mailed to pastors and corporate members of the Board. The gauntlet was thrown down and satisfaction was demanded. This time overwhelming support was on Noyes's side. Even the *Congregationalist* backed his appointment, saying it was grieved at the Committee's action and editorialized that the Board should stop operating alike a closed corporation.[30]

In October, 1893, 148 corporate members including 96 from New England and a large crowd of visitors assembled in Worcester, Massachusetts. Once again future probation was the presenting issue. The long, drawn out fight had taken its toll. Now even those who considered themselves to be conservative in the theological realm were ready to call a halt to the wars. The pressures to require church councils to examine candidates had proved to be equally ineffective. One final maneuver remained for those who wanted a more open theological stance within the ABCFM and that was to demand a complete overhaul of the administration that would bring the Board more directly under denominational control, and subject its policies to the oversight of a broader constituency.

Under the leadership of President Storrs, a Committee of Fifteen was formed to deal with the "revolutionary" resolutions that were being heard. They proposed, and the Board voted without debate, to increase its corporate membership from 250 to 350. Two thirds of these positions

28. American Board of Commissioners for Foreign Missions. *Records of the Prudential Committee*, 23 (18 July 1893) 195.

29. "The Prudential Committee's Final Action, July 18, 1893," in "The Prudential Committee and Mr. Noyes," *Congregationalist*, 27 July 1893.

30. "Mr. Noyes' Appointment recalled," *Congregationalist*, July 27, 1893.

were to be filled by nominations from the various state associations as a way to yoke the Board more closely to the churches. The Prudential Committee was also to be expanded to fifteen persons, with the addition of some members living outside the environs of Boston but within easy reach of it. Three-year terms were initiated with a limit of three consecutive terms. No longer would it be possible for men like Augustus Thompson to serve forty-four years on the Committee. And, in a final dramatic gesture to demonstrate that the Board would not continue with business as usual, the Committee of Fifteen recommended that William Noyes be offered an appointment to the Board with the understanding that "this action is not to be understood in any way modifying its former utterances on the subject of future probation."[31]

This final proposal raised up the last gust of a dying storm. For those who supported Noyes it was a matter of justice. The Board had no right to refuse men who were now being ordained and installed by Congregational churches. This argument was only possible because of the change in perception of the moral and fiscal ownership of the Board. Many now believed that Board was *not* a close corporation, but was to be representative of every Congregational church in the country.[32] By a vote of 106 to 24, the resolution to appoint Noyes was affirmed. Edmund Alden promptly resigned as Home Secretary and Augustus Thompson and Elbridge Torrey resigned from the Prudential Committee. Seven new members were elected. The ABCFM had now constructed the Committee in such a way that there was little chance that doctrinal issues would cause the same kind of difficulties that they had in the past. The monumental decisions made at the annual meeting were published in the *Independent*, the longest article ever to appear in it pages.[33]

With the appointment of Noyes, the fight over future probation was over. As one speaker declared, the dogma was as dead as last year's oyster shells."[34] And how did the protagonists of this debate fare? Robert Hume returned to India and carried out a fruitful and celebrated ministry. For fifty-five years he ran a theological school in India, wrote articles and tracts, headed up relief work for which he received the Victoria Cross, and closed his career by becoming the first moderator of the newly

31. Minutes of the Annual Meeting," *Missionary Herald* 89 (November 1893).
32. "Remarks of Mr. Holcombe," *Independent,* October 19, 1893.
33. "The American Board at Worcester," *Independent,* October 19, 1893.
34. "The Results at Worcester," *Independent,* October 19, 1893.

formed Church of North India. Hume apparently never spoke of the events surrounding the controversy and his return to India, even when pressed.[35] If he harbored a private belief in future probation, there was no apparent detrimental effect on his ministry.

The story of William Noyes took another turn. Less than four years after William and his wife Inez, had received their appointment to Japan under the ABCFM, they withdrew from missionary service and returned to the United States. It seemed that Noyes had lost his faith. There were speculations that he had become a Buddhist but the head of the mission recalled that when he asked Noyes if he had lost faith in God, he had said yes.[36] What part future probation or the controversies surrounding the debates had on his loss of faith, we can only speculate.

With the resolution of the Noyes case and the realignment and reorganization of the ABCFM, the future probation controversy ended somewhat abruptly. There were now more urgent crises to face. The damage to the reputation of the American Board caused by the debates was catastrophic. One officer later estimated that it took twenty years for the Board to recoup. By September of 1893 the donations and bequests were down over $160,000 for the previous year. In 1894 the Board was more than $116,000 in debt. Several significant legacies were depleted and annual gifts were far below what was necessary to sustain the mission work.[37] The number of candidates for mission work had also dwindled. Fewer and fewer men from Andover Seminary, once the primary pool for candidates, presented themselves for foreign mission work, though this may have been due as much to perceptual changes in the value and nature of missions as it was to any stigma of the doctrinal controversies. The traditional pattern of sending out preachers, evangelists and church planters was curtailed and a new emphasis on cultural redemption took its place. Medical work, industrial training, and higher education now took precedence over more explicit evangelistic endeavors. Those changes, and a shifting religious climate, made the acceptance of candidates with broader theological positions feasible.

---

35. Cornelius H. Patton in "The Late Robert A. Hume, D.D. 1847–1929: Tributes of Friends and Associates," *Congregationalist*, July 11, 1929.

36. Dr. Dwight W. Learned to Enoch Bell, undated handwritten response to Bell's letter of 18 January 1943. ABCFM Papers, HLHU.

37. Fred Field Goodsell, *You Shall be My Witnesses*, 219, 220.

The impact of the future probation debates was momentous. The furor had led to a permanent reorganization of ABCFM structures as well as a considerable change in procedures dealing with missionary candidates. Never again would the Board face a theological controversy that threatened to undo what for decades had been the strongest mission sending agency in the world. Though charges of blatant heterodoxy heightened the temper of the debates, in retrospect the controversy was framed as much by competing ecclesiological issues as it was by theological ones. The symbiotic relationship between the Congregational Churches and the ABCFM meant that disagreements over future probation in local churches, ordination councils and in the seminaries became the grounds for energetic attempts to preserve theological integrity on mission stations around the world. As one mission educator would later note, in effect the American Board had become the guinea pig for the denomination.[38]

The rapidly rising tide of progressive theological opinion was lapping at the doors of churches and seminaries, and both proponents of the New Theology and defenders of traditional beliefs found it impossible to measure or predict the impact the controversy might have. Ultimately the long struggle to corral the spread of the dogma proved futile, and its proponents were heartened by speeches before the World Parliament of Religion in 1893 that future probation was now widely known and appreciated among native Christians in Japan.[39] Eventually those who doggedly fought the spread of the dogma became battle-weary, sensing the debilitating effect that the fight was having within the ABCFM and the denomination. Even Edmund Alden, years later, said that he had misjudged the theological trends of the times and that trying to ban believers in Future Probation had been a mistake.[40] He gave no sign, however, that he had modified his views about the dangers of future probation for the cause of missions. The theological controversy that reached around the world faded to a whimper—even among the giants of the American missionary movement.

38. Edward Warren Capen to Enoch F. Bell, January 24, 1943. ABCFM Papers, HLHU.

39. Quoted in George F. Magoun, "Conservatives and Compromisers in the American Board," *Our Day* 12 (November 1893).

40. Ibid., 114.

BIBLIOGRAPHY

Abbreviations

ABCFM   American Board of Commissioners for Foreign Missions

ACT   Augustus C. Thompson Papers

ANTS   Andover Newton Theological School, Newton Centre, Massachusetts

ATS   Andover Theological Seminary

CL   Congregational Library, Boston, Massachusetts

HLHU   Houghton Library, Harvard University

Texts

American Board of Commissioners for Foreign Missions. *The Great Debate: a verbatim report of the discussion of the meeting of the American Board of Commissioners for Foreign Missions: held at Des Moines, Iowa, Thursday, October 7, 1886.* Boston: Houghton Mifflin, 1886.

American Board of Commissioners for Foreign Missions. *Papers.* Houghton Library, Harvard University.

American Board of Commissioners for Foreign Missions. *Records of the Prudential Committee.* Congregational Library, Boston, Massachusetts.

Andover Theological Seminary. *Minutes of the Board of Visitors.* Archives, Andover Newton Theological School, Newton, Massachusetts.

Augustus C. Thompson Papers. Archives, Hartford Seminary, Hartford Connecticut.

Bell, Enoch F. "Then and Now, or, The American Board and Andover Candidates: a Hyde Lecture delivered at Andover Newton, March 11, 1943," Archives, Andover Newton Theological School, Newton Centre, Massachusetts.

Goodsell, Fred Field. *You Shall be My Witnesses.* Boston: American Board of Commissioners for Foreign Missions, 1959.

Taylor, Sharon A. *That Obnoxious Dogma: Future Probation and the Struggle to Construct an American Congregational Identity.* Ph.D. thesis. Chestnut Hill, Mass.: Boston College, 2004.
Some of the material found in this article was based on chapters 6 and 7 of the dissertation.

Thompson, Augustus C. *Future Probation and Foreign Missions: certain duties and usages at the rooms of the American Board.* Boston: Beacon Press, 1886, 9.

3

Commercial Philanthropy: ABCFM Missionaries and the American Opium Trade

Timothy Mason Roberts

T HIS ARTICLE EXPLORES THE interactions between American
Protestant missionaries and opium traders in and around Izmir,
Turkey (then called Smyrna), in the first part of the nineteenth century.
It argues that American missionaries placed confidence in the humani-
tarianism of American international commerce, even commerce involving opium. Opium was the main commodity that first drew American
traders to Izmir, where they bought opium and shipped it for sale in
China, making great profits, despite the emerging controversy of the
opium trade. The missionaries' faith in "free trade" helped them to ratio-
nalize the traders' efforts. It also helped them to establish a rapport with
peoples of Western Asia, especially Armenians, who, in addition to possessing a portion of "the true religion," were engaged in American-style
commercial activity in the Ottoman Empire. In the missionaries' opinion, such activity was preparatory to returning evangelical Christianity
to the Middle East.[1]

---

1. Parsons, *Dereliction*, 30. The author wishes to thank Dr. Clifford Putney for
organizing the 2010 conference, "Commemorating the Bicentennial of the ABCFM:
America's First Sponsor of Overseas Christian Missions," where this research was pre-
sented, and Michael Lowe for his assistance to revise the article to its present form.
In this article Turkish words have been italicized and Turkish characters transliter-
ated into English letters. Studies of the first American citizens in the Levant include
Finnie, *Pioneers East*; Field, *America and the Mediterranean World*; Daniel, *American
Philanthropy*; Oren, *Power, Faith, and Fantasy*; and Kieser, *Nearest East*.

In his novel, *White Jacket*, published in 1850, Herman Melville wrote that Americans "bear the ark of the liberties of the world . . . and let us always remember that with ourselves, almost for the first time in the history of earth, national selfishness is unbounded philanthropy; for we cannot do good to America, but we give alms to the world."[2] Melville, a complex American who advocated international trade as a source for democracy but condemned missionaries, actually would have found some common ground with Rufus Anderson, secretary of the American Board of Commissioners for Foreign Missions, the largest American missionary organization in the nineteenth century. Anderson gave a charge to a missionary on his way to the Ottoman Empire in 1848, declaring, "Never was it so evident that Christians cannot innocently live to themselves . . . [nor] so evident that this great and free nation of ours exists not for itself alone but more perhaps than any other nation for the benefit of the entire world."[3] Melville and Anderson conflated the impulses of self-interest and Christian philanthropy that brought the first Americans to Turkish shores, in Izmir in the first part of the nineteenth century. Long before any substantial American diplomatic or military presence developed in the Eastern Mediterranean, the area contained what have been called the key social figures in early American history, merchants and Protestant ministers.[4]

Izmir is perhaps not well known outside the Mediterranean world today, but in the early nineteenth century it was widely recognized in the West as a destination for tourism, a critical port city for trade, and a potential gateway into the Middle East. The city commonly referred to then as the "Paris of the Levant" dazzled Americans who came there. With its population of nearly 150,000 in the mid-nineteenth century it would have been the third largest city in the United States at the time.[5] Its diverse population of Western Europeans, Greeks, Armenians and Jews, as well as Turks, made it unique, "an essentially extraterritorial port city." It was Turkish but, as foreign visitors remarked, it was really a cosmopolitan republic; like other international trading ports of the

2. See Lyons, "The Global Melville." The quotation is from Perkins, *Creation of a Republican Empire*, 9.

3. Anderson, "Charge to the Reverend Thomas Laurie, South Hadley, Mass, June 7, 1848," Anderson Papers, Congregational Library.

4. Parrington, *Romantic Revolution*, 272.

5. MacFarlane, *Turkey and Its Destiny*, 1: 25.

day such as Bombay, Honolulu, and, after the 1842 Treaty of Nanjing, the treaty ports of China, Izmir was largely under the jurisdiction of European laws invoked by Western consuls and merchants. Positioned "at the intersection between two vast civilizations, one Islamic and the second Christian," it was the "rendezvous of merchants from almost all parts of the world."[6]

One of the first American missionaries in Izmir, Levi Parsons, wrote, "I cannot describe Smyrna . . . The people are of all ranks and complexions . . . What would you think of a man approaching you, of gigantic stature, long beard, fierce eyes, a turban on his head . . . long flowing robes, a large belt, in which were four or five pistols and a sword?"[7] When they arrived in the city, most foreigners, called "Franks," were taken normally by donkey ride along "Frank Street" to the city's casino, which had rooms for billiards and card playing, a library complete with European newspapers, a ballroom, and a gambling hall. The city was both exotic and genteel.[8]

Izmir, though one-third smaller than Istanbul, dominated the trade of the Ottoman Empire through the nineteenth century, including trade with regions further east in Anatolia and international trade with the West. The city developed as a major international port in the mid-sixteenth century by drawing export trade in Iranian silk, which until the early eighteenth century constituted over half of the city's exports.[9] In the eighteenth century cotton became the city's major export commodity, remaining so until the American cotton empire, enabled by the cotton gin, attracted European buyers away from the Izmir cotton market (although the city's cotton trade recovered somewhat during and after the Civil War). In the late eighteenth century American traders began arriving in Izmir, a destination more prominent and accessible than other Ottoman port cities, such as Aleppo and Istanbul.[10]

Americans first came apparently to purchase raisins, but by the early nineteenth century a small American colony developed in the city for a different commodity, which was opium. At this time the world opium

6. Malham, *Naval Gazetteer*, 2: 426; Goffman, "Izmir," 133.

7. Parsons, *Memoir*, 297.

8. Finnie, *Pioneers East*, 20–23.

9. Matthee, *Politics of Trade*, 225.

10. Frangakis-Syrett, *Commerce of Smyrna*, 24–25, 34; Frangakis-Syrett, "Trade in Cotton and Cloth in Izmir"; Beckert, "Emancipation and Empire."

trade was dominated by the British East India Company, which exported opium from its colony of India to China. The British Levant Company had supplied Americans, as subjects of the British Empire, with opium from Izmir throughout the eighteenth century, although, owing to the British Acts of Trade, that trade was indirect, through England, until American independence.[11] After independence Americans recognized the opium trade's potential and joined it, opening direct commerce with the Levant. American traders could hardly seek to gain access to Indian opium without British permission, thus they focused on the Ottoman Empire, a leading opium producer and not a British colony.[12] Ironically, however, at least until 1811 Americans traded at Izmir under protection of the British Levant Company, paying the same duties as did British traders.[13] The American-Turkish opium trade would amount to about a tenth of the Anglo-Indian opium import into China.[14]

Izmir was the destination of opium grown in the Anatolian hinterland, where state-licensed brokers, mostly Jews and Armenians, negotiated and bought, on behalf of the exporting Izmir firms, from Turkish merchants. Camels then brought the opium, typically around the beginning of June, to Izmir, where, again on behalf of American and European exporters, Jewish and Armenian brokers judged the opium for color, weight, and scent. Only rarely do records show Muslims active on the Izmir market sending opium abroad: A Dutch trader opined in 1847 that opium trading by a "rich Turk" was "very strange." Turkish merchants did not assume Western protection and as a result often could not compete with their non-Muslim peers.[15]

The first American opium trader in Izmir was probably a British loyalist named George Perkins, who fled America during the American Revolution, heading eventually to Izmir.[16] Coincidentally, he was the relative of Thomas Handasyd Perkins, of Boston, the founder of one of the

---

11. Zentner, "Opiate Use in America"; Morison, "Forcing the Dardanelles."

12. The American opium trade with Turkey is the subject of Turgay, "The Nineteenth Century Golden Triangle."

13. Schmidt, *From Anatolia to Indonesia*, 34–35, 41. American traders also paid the Levant Company a fee for its helping maintain their privileged status.

14. Fairbank, "Introduction," 4.

15. Cizakca and Kenanoglu, "Ottoman Merchants."

16. Morison, "Forcing the Dardanelles," at 209, identifies this individual as William Lee Perkins.

largest international trading firms of the early American republic. With the gaining of independence in 1783 American maritime trade naturally lost the protection of the British Navy. American ships thus became exposed through the 1820s to depredations by British and French warships seeking to prevent American trade from benefiting the other side. Barbary corsairs, erroneously called "pirates" in American documents, also seized American ships, holding their men for ransom. Nevertheless, the firm of James and T. H. Perkins wrote to George Perkins in Izmir in 1796, remarking that European wars "opened some new channels for the American commerce in the Mediterranean."[17]

In 1803 Perkins and Company established a branch in Canton, China, the city that was the main *entrepot* for the importation of opium into China. Although the Chinese emperor had banned the import of opium in 1800 because he realized it was causing the Chinese people to become addicted and draining China of hard currency, the Perkins headquarters in Boston wrote to its China branch "respecting the article of Turkish Opium; its value."[18] Ships from Philadelphia, Baltimore, and Boston began carrying Turkish opium in 1804. In 1805 Thomas Perkins wrote John Cushing, the representative of the Perkins firm in Canton, averring that since opium could be bought in Turkey at $2 per pound ($8 less than in China), "great profits may be made on it."[19] In 1811 David Offley, of the Philadelphia shipping firm of Woodmas and Offley, established the first American commercial house in the Levant.[20] The Izmir trade of J. & T. H. Perkins required the firm to open its own office in the city in 1816. From these origins, trade in opium out of Izmir, bound for China, would become the main American export from the Middle East in the nineteenth century.[21]

Not long after the first arrival of American opium merchants, another central figure in American society at the time, the Protestant missionary, came to Izmir. Two American missionaries, Levi Parsons and

17. James and T. H. Perkins to George Perkins, 27 December 1796, in Perkins, *Memoir,* 282.

18. Seaburg and Paterson, *Merchant Prince,* 265.

19. J & T. H. Perkins to John Cushing, Perkins Papers, vol. 37, 23 September 1805; Seaburg and Paterson, *Merchant Prince,* 298; Schmidt, *From Anatolia to Indonesia,* 20.

20. Goldstein, *Philadelphia and the China Trade,* 54.

21. Turgay, "Nineteenth-Century Golden Triangle," 1:117–8, 2:75–76, 86–90; Stelle, *Americans and the China Opium Trade,* 14–19, 45–57; Finnie, *Pioneers East,* 30.

Pliny Fisk, arrived on behalf of the American Board of Commissioners for Foreign Missions (ABCFM). The ABCFM, America's "first large-scale transnational corporation," was, like J. & T. H. Perkins, headquartered in Boston.[22] Seeking the moral redemption of the world, the ABCFM sent out its first missionaries in 1812 to India. The Eastern Mediterranean, however, was in some ways more attractive. Dominated by Muslims since the Middle Ages, it was nonetheless the setting for biblical narratives and the home of Jews and Orthodox Christians. For that reason, missionaries felt that the Eastern Mediterranean had been degraded by people who were ignorant of or did not follow biblical teaching.[23] Moreover, the region lay outside formal European colonial possession, a point illuminated when Samuel Newell initially was obstructed from establishing a mission in India by the East India Company. Newell wrote to the Board headquarters in Boston encouraging establishment of a mission in Turkey, because "A mission to Western Asia would be all our own, free from the objections . . . to establishing our mission in British India."[24]

Thus, the commercial port of Izmir became crucial for American missionaries, as it was for American traders. ABCFM headquarters noted in 1821, "The active commerce [that] is carried on from the many islands and ports in the Levant . . . furnish the means of conveying books and tracts to distant and populous regions . . . [H]ow essentially will this commercial intercourse promote every plan, adopted for the permanent improvement and spiritual benefit of the people."[25] In particular, one missionary wrote, "Smyrna is by far the best situation in the Levant for a permanent missionary establishment . . . having a frequent communication with all parts of the Ottoman empire . . . the best place in those regions for learning [languages] . . . for security and liberty," and for "an extensive printing establishment" to serve the region. Another confirmed that Izmir "is the largest and most commercial city. It would be the best port of entry for Western Asia." American missionaries' tracking

22. Fairbank, ed. *Missionary Enterprise,* 8.

23. Grabill, *Protestant Diplomacy,* 4–10.

24. *Report of the American Board* (1812), 39. Upon an appeal by William Wilberforce, at the request of Jedidiah Morse and Jeremiah Evarts of the ABCFM, the East India Company authorized Americans to remain in India in 1814. Wilberforce had led Parliament to pass the Charter Act of 1813, forcing the EIC to allow missionaries in the country. Phillips, *Protestant America,* 39–40.

25. *Report of the American Board* (1821), 90.

of American merchants' trade routes unshielded by U.S. military protection in fact differed from European imperial patterns.[26]

It was in short merchants and missionaries who first represented America in the Ottoman Empire, and both groups first settled in Izmir. They came in pursuit of ostensibly contradictory objectives. American traders came for financial profit. Imports of Turkish opium into China in exchange for tea and silk helped Stephen Girard, John Jacob Astor, and Thomas H. Perkins, all purchasers of Turkish opium at Izmir, to become America's first millionaires.[27]

Meanwhile American missionaries came to Izmir to spread the Gospel and reform Eastern Christians; ABCFM literature rejected the wholly self-enriching goal of commerce. In a charge to missionaries destined for China the ABCFM Prudential Committee asked, "Who would choose to be a wealthy merchant, a powerful statesman, a crowned hero, could he but be called of God to preach Christ among the millions?"[28] On the eve of his departure for Izmir Levi Parsons preached, "Every devoted Christian will enquire, not where he can . . . obtain the most wealth, but where he can most successfully . . . promote the salvation of men . . . Better, my brethren wear out and die in three years, than live forty years in slothfulness."[29] A missionary report urged "Christians [to] learn what is meant by not living to themselves . . . not limiting their beneficence to the narrow circles of their immediate . . . communities, [so they] may do good unto all men . . . Their merchandise and their hire . . . shall not be treasured, nor laid up."[30]

Yet missionaries embraced what the Congregationalist theologian Samuel Hopkins called "disinterested benevolence" to refer to Protestant Christians' calling to improve the lives of non-Christians through good work and religious reform. ABCFM missionaries in the Middle East practiced this doctrine, manifesting most famously in institutions of

26. Salibi and Khoury, eds., *Missionary Herald: Syria*, 1:29; Pliny Fisk to ?, Smyrna, 1 February 1820, in American Board Papers, Houghton Library [microfilm], reel 502.

27. Pessen, *Riches, Class, and Power*, 22; Belohlavek, "Economic Interest Groups"; Tchen, *New York Before Chinatown*, 46.

28. Prudential Committee Instructions to Caleb Baldwin, Seneca Cummings, and wives, and William Richards, 2 November 1847, American Board Papers, Houghton Library, Series 8.

29. Kling, "New Divinity," 25.

30. *First Ten Reports of the American Board of Commissioners for Foreign Missions* [report for 1818], 202.

moral and practical education.[31] Trans-cultural commerce, like education, could potentially bring Christian reformers into contact with native
peoples. When Rufus Anderson, the ABCFM secretary, visited Istanbul
in 1843, a missionary there told him that "Armenians were the traders
of the empire," particularly well placed, and therefore people with whom
missionaries should build relationships.[32] Thus missionaries focused
increasingly on Armenians in the Ottoman Empire as a means to reach
the "whole mingled population" of peoples of the Near East. According
to ABCFM headquarters, "It [was] to be hoped . . . that no small part of
those who bear the Christian name, would willingly and gladly receive
the Bible into their houses, and . . . become active in doing good . . .
towards . . . the Jews, Mahommedans, and Pagans."[33] Missionaries antici-
pated that well connected Armenians, once reformed and gathered into
viable Protestant communities, might themselves evangelize Muslims
and Jews in the Middle East.

Still, these two groups of Americans in Izmir—opium merchants
and missionaries—appear to have had opposite purposes. We might
reasonably expect historical sources to show tension or conflict in their
interactions, but there is little evidence of this. Instead, missionaries
sought out merchants for counsel, encouragement, and companionship.
In 1820, soon after the missionaries Pliny Fisk and Levi Parsons arrived
in Izmir, they informed the *Missionary Herald* newspaper, "The Messrs.
Perkins received us very politely and assured us of their friendship and
assistance."[34] The *Missionary Herald* reiterated the fraternity of their
letter, reporting, "the missionaries were received with cordiality by all
gentlemen . . . particularly, the Messrs. Perkins, eminent merchants in
that city."[35] A year later Fisk left Izmir and journeyed to Ephesus, accompanied by a Turkish janissary, an Armenian, and two Greeks, along with
"Mr. George Perkins of Smyrna and Thomas and Joseph Langdon of
Boston."[36] Perkins and Langdon were both representatives of American

31. Kling, "New Divinity," 24; Daniel, *American Philanthropy*, ix–x, 18–22, 41–70.

32. "Memoranda on discussion of meetings of missionaries during visit to Levant
1843–1844," Anderson Papers, Houghton Library, vol. 10, entry for 27 December 1843.

33. Khalaf, "Leavening the Levant," 276; Field, *America and the Mediterranean
World*, 130, 176–8.

34. Salibi and Khoury, eds., *Missionary Herald: Iraq*, 1:13.

35. *Ibid.*, I: 27.

36. *Ibid.*, I: 82.

opium-trading companies, by then long established in Izmir.[37] In Ephesus Fisk noted that he "found a few Greeks at work on the ruins . . . I gave them some [religious] tracts, which they promised to give to their priests."[38] It does not appear that Fisk gave Perkins and Langdon the same didactic literature.

Missionaries also had an active relationship with David Offley, a commercial agent who later became an American diplomatic consul. Offley was a Quaker, but in Izmir married an Armenian woman. He had initially come to Izmir representing the trading firm of Woodmas and Offley of Philadelphia, which traded extensively in opium bound for China.[39] Offley's major political achievement was to convince the Ottoman government not to charge American traders higher customs duties than they charged European traders. Thanks to Offley's initiative, the Ottoman government recognized American traders as a distinct foreign nationality in the Empire, although this would not be made permanent or official until a Treaty of Navigation and Commerce of 1830.[40]

Offley also assisted American missionaries in Izmir. On one occasion he tipped off missionaries in Izmir that Ottoman authorities were looking for a certain "Armenian priest," whom the provincial Ottoman governor wished to deport. Offley advised the missionary Daniel Temple "by all means to place [the man] in concealment." Temple also wrote approvingly of Offley's intercession with the governor, who had complained that the missionary press was printing works that "make violent attacks upon [Islam]." "Mr. Offley on my authority assured [the governor] . . . that our real and declared intention was to print elementary works for the purpose of . . . education of the young among Christian and Turk of the country."[41] Missionaries occasionally held religious services on Offley's property, and Pliny Fisk for a time served as chaplain to the British Levant Company.[42] Upon Offley's death after a serious illness

37. Downs, "American Merchants," 423.

38. Pliny Fisk to "dear Brother," 14 April 1821, American Board Papers, Houghton Library [microfilm], reel 502.

39. Finnie, *Pioneers East*, 26–27.

40. Field, *America and the Mediterranean World*, 117–18; Oren, *Power, Faith, and Fantasy*, 106.

41. Daniel Temple to Rufus Anderson, 16 January 1834, American Board Papers, Houghton Library [microfilm], reel 563.

42. Tracy, *History of the American Board*, 101–2.

Temple wrote that he had "had many . . . conversations with him . . . to lead his thoughts to the Lamb of God that takes away the sin of the world." While "the labor was apparently all lost," Temple saluted Offley for enjoying "the reputation, as I believe most justly, of being an honest man."[43] While we cannot tell if Offley expressed regret to Temple about his opium trading, or if Temple meant to allude to such commerce as a sin, it is noteworthy that Temple praised Offley as reputable and honest. In a pattern that would be repeated elsewhere in the Ottoman Empire, missionaries esteemed and relied on the influence of traders to practice what became known as "Christian philanthropy," blurring the line between commerce and humanitarian benevolence in the process.

Despite residing in Izmir for many years, American missionaries and merchants were always a small minority of the city's population, and perhaps that encouraged their banding together. "Merchants from all countries reside in Smyrna," Pliny Fisk wrote in 1820, "enjoy[ing] their political and religious opinions and practices. There are at least six or eight foreign consuls in the city who afford protection to the people of their respective countries and decide all differences among them and between them and the Smyrneans according to the laws of civilized nations."[44] Even after a quarter-century of missionaries' immersion in the peoples and cultures of Izmir, the missionary Mary Van Lennep wrote in 1844, "We Protestants are a feeble band in the midst of Greeks, Catholics, Jews, Turks, and Armenians."[45] The "feeble band" of Americans in Izmir mainly hailed from New England (although Offley was from Philadelphia). Their common ethnic and regional background served to draw them together.

Thus it seems inconceivable that missionaries were unaware that the American traders with whom they were interacting were trafficking in opium, headed for distribution in China. The first American missionary to China, E. C. Bridgman, began to condemn opium in the *Missionary Herald* in 1832. From the port city of Canton, he observed that opium was one of the "greatest evils afflicting Chinese society," and he described how "the practice of smoking the 'black commodity' is widely prevalent, from the royal palaces to the meanest hovels, exert-

43. Daniel Temple to Rufus Anderson, 5 October 1838, American Board Papers, Houghton Library [microfilm], reel 520.

44. Salibi and Khoury, eds., *Missionary Herald: Iraq,* 1: 13.

45. Van Lennep, *Memoir,* 265.

ing, from one end of the empire to the other, and through all the ranks of society, a most deadly influence."[46] In the same issues in which it printed Bridgman's condemnation of opium consumption in China, the *Missionary Herald* published numerous accounts by ABCFM missionaries in Turkey, though none included any similar criticism of the drug. An American newspaper in 1829 printed an indirect condemnation of opium in a letter from the missionary Josiah Brewer, who extolled the character of Turkish people as "mild, honest, hospitable and temperate." Among them "the practice of eating opium does not exist to any considerable extent; Mr. Brewer says he has seen tens of thousands of Turks, and never observed one making use of the drug."[47] In 1833 the journal of ABCFM missionaries in Bombay, India, the *Oriental Christian Spectator*, reported the establishment of a temperance society "upon the principle of entire abstinence from ardent spirits, opium, and other intoxicating drugs."[48] Yet it is intriguing that no missionary publicly commented on or criticized the opium trade of Izmir, conducted by American traders and their Orthodox Christian counterparts. What was the perspective of ABCFM missionaries in Izmir concerning their compatriots' involvement in the city's opium trade?

Americans' opinion of the Turkish opium trade at the time was divided. On the one hand, opium was recognized as an important painkiller and sedative. In 1782 Hector St. John De Crevecoeur remarked in *Letters of an American Farmer* how women of Nantucket, Rhode Island "adopted the Asiatic custom of taking a dose of opium every morning" to endure the absence of their whaling husbands.[49] David Ramsay, the American historian and physician, recommended opium to the educator and signer of the Declaration of Independence, Benjamin Rush, as a cure for venereal disease in 1784. The ailing Benjamin Franklin used opium extensively late in his life.[50] In his scientific instructions to the explorers Meriwether Lewis and William Clark, President Thomas Jefferson encouraged administration of opium as a cure for "watchful-

46. Lazich, "American Missionaries," 200.

47. *Farmer's Cabinet*. In 1836 the missionary Justin Perkins wrote of his effort to direct a Persian man in the city of Urmia, the site of the first American Christian mission in Iran, to stop chewing the drug. Salibi and Khoury, eds., *Missionary Herald: Iraq*, 1: 60.

48. "American Mission in the Bombay Presidency," 119.

49. Philbrick, "Nantucket Sequence," 420.

50. Brunhouse, ed., *David Ramsay*, 78; Madison, *Writings*, 747; Booth, *Opium*, 30.

ness," or insomnia, and Lewis bought a half-pound of "Opii Turk" in Philadelphia in preparation for the pioneering western expedition.[51]

Figure 10. Constantinople (Istanbul), Turkey, ca. 1843. Created by Thomas Allom (artist) and E. B. & E. C. Kellogg (lithographers). From Joel Hawes, *The Religion of the East with Impressions of Foreign Travel* (Hartford, CT: Belknap & Hamersley, 1854), front. Lithograph courtesy of the Congregational Library, Boston.

On the other hand, opium was known as a potentially addictive and destructive commodity of Asian (and therefore morally questionable) origin well before the association of opium-smoking with Chinese people began during the Opium Wars.[52] From the early modern era Muslim religious leaders and even sultans had attempted to curb or, periodically, to outlaw the popular diversions of public smoking and coffee drinking.[53] These efforts were largely unsuccessful, however, and the apparent ennui of coffeehouse patrons, coupled with the observations of travelers in the Ottoman Empire of the phenomena of eating opium paste or drinking opium in liquid form, provoked Anglo-Americans to associate opium with Turkish moral corruption throughout the modern era (notwithstanding similar habits taking hold in the West).[54] A British physician's 1700 treatise *Mysteries of Opium Reveal'd* described opium not only as a panacea but also as a sacrilegious aphrodisiac, popular among "Infidels of Turkey and the eastern nations (where polygamy is allowed)

51. Loge, "Two Dozes of Bark and Opium," 71, 73.
52. Tchen, *New York before Chinatown*, 65–68; Ahmad, *The Opium Debate*.
53. Marcus, *Middle East on the Eve of Modernity*, 232–33.
54. Matthee, *Pursuit of Pleasure*, 100; Faroqhi, *Subjects of the Sultan*, 216–7.

[who] use opium so much."[55] Popular American literature of the early nineteenth century associated the Turkish custom of smoking tobacco through a water pipe with both opium-smoking and Asian indolence. A children's schoolbook declared, "The Turks are a grave people, and also kind to those who think as they do, but they are cruel to [C]hristians. They smoke opium."[56]

American opium traders themselves did not often reveal their perspective on the morality of their trade. In 1819 Perkins & Company in Canton noted the opium trade "is considered a very disreputable business and viewed by the Chinese in the same light as smuggling." Nevertheless, "If to be got at three dollars we can afford to make the Mandarins view it in a more favorable light."[57] Normally, however, businessmen such as David Offley and Thomas Perkins mainly filled their papers with dry calculations and meticulous directions to traders working global markets in London, Boston, New York, Canton, Hong Kong, Singapore, and Izmir.[58] Their assumption was perhaps that trading partners in all ports of call entered into transactions voluntarily. Following this possible logic, Offley and Perkins merely sold opium; they did not force people to buy it. Therefore they bore no particular responsibility for any harm a commodity such Turkish opium (or New England rum) might cause.[59]

The opium trade, of course, was completely legal in the United States and the Ottoman Empire, and was maintained by Chinese traders despite its outlawing by the Chinese government. Meanwhile, many successful merchants lavished wealth from the opium trade on philanthropic institutions and relief efforts in Boston and Philadelphia, including the Perkins School for the Blind, a famed naval voyage bearing humanitarian supplies for victims of the Irish Famine, and the Wagner Scientific Institute. Opium traders thus became remembered for their funding for the arts and generosity towards the poor and underprivileged of these

55. Davenport-Hines, *Pursuit of Oblivion*, 44.

56. Marr, *Cultural Roots*, 169.

57. Perkins & Company to Thomas Handasyd Perkins, Perkins Papers [microfilm], roll 334, 7 August 1819.

58. Schmidt, *From Anatolia to Indonesia*, 40.

59. This interpretation is based on the description and justification of the opium trade published by a major American trader in Canton, China, Robert Bennett Forbes, in *Remarks on China*.

cities.[60] American Board organizers had been hastened to action originally in 1810 by the provision of a $30,000 legacy left to the ABCFM by the widow of the merchant John Norris of Salem, Massachusetts.[61]

Since discussion of the eventual immoral consequences of the opium trade might have embarrassed the well-to-do merchants of Izmir, and thus jeopardized the missionaries' social relations with them, the missionaries avoided the topic. Perhaps they would have missed the irony that strikes us today in the description by an American tourist of Izmir's foreign community living "over warehouses of opium in a state of cordial republican equality that is not found even in America."[62]

There is another reason the missionaries were tolerant of Eastern Mediterranean peoples' involvement in the opium trade: they tended to view those peoples as less "heathenish" than the peoples of India, China, Hawaii, and elsewhere. An ABCFM member and president of Yale University Timothy Dwight stated in 1813 that "the Romish cathedral, the mosque, and the pagoda, shall not have one stone left upon another, which shall not be thrown down."[63] But missionaries abroad were less likely to view the non-Protestant world so monolithically. When the missionary Samuel Newell wrote to the Board's headquarters in Boston to encourage the establishment of a mission in the Ottoman Empire, he emphasized that while their religions were vain and void, Muslims, Jews, and Orthodox Christians were monotheistic peoples "as high on the scale of intellect as any people in the world."[64]

Meanwhile, many Americans perceived that the Ottoman Empire, unlike the Empire of China, abided by the international "law of nations," which governed "civilized" nations. Americans who supported British prosecution of the Opium War of 1839–1842, perhaps most famously John Quincy Adams, cited the fact that China's refusal to trade with Western nations arose from its refusal to embrace the law of nations.[65]

---

60. Downs, "Fair Game"; Goldstein, *Philadelphia and the China Trade*; Forbes, *Personal Reminiscences*, 188–99; Gray, "Trade-Off."

61. Phillips, *Protestant America*, 33.

62. Willis, *Summer Cruise*, 391.

63. Kieser, *Nearest East*, 40.

64. *Report of the American Board of Commissioners for Foreign Missions* (1812), 39; Khalaf, "Leavening the Levant," 271. Other examples of missionaries' appreciation of Muslims' spirituality are noted in Hubers, "Making Friends with Locusts."

65. Adams, "Lecture on the War."

In contrast, the Ottoman Empire's gestures of support for free trade pleased Americans. During the War of 1812 an American newspaper observed that "Among the civilized nations of the world, the principles of maritime law . . . give equal privileges and protection to all . . . They are even acknowledged by the Turks, as little as that people are supposed to regard the established maxims of law and justice."[66] American commentators praised the end of the Ottoman Empire's monopoly on opium exports in 1839 (though the result of British pressure exerted in exchange for protection of the sultan against invasion by the Egyptian viceroy Muhammed Ali) as a turn towards "free trade" and thus a sign of Ottoman enlightened reform: "The grand commercial principle of Turkey is free trade; monopolies are prohibited, and commerce only limited and restricted by the extent of supply and demand . . . The national character and aspect of the Turk is thoroughly Oriental . . . [but] compared with other Orientals, the Turk is honest, and his word may be trusted."[67]

The capacity of American missionaries in the Ottoman Empire for humanitarian empathy with "others," as suggested by their reticence about the opium trade despite its harm in China, was thus limited by several factors. They may simply never have considered the destructive aspects of opium beyond the Mediterranean. Missionaries were confronted with local circumstances that took priority or required choices of behavior, even if that behavior conflicted with the perspective of ABCFM headquarters, to reach the world for Christ and reform it. Alternatively, missionaries perhaps carried assumptions that they shared with secular Americans about peoples within and outside "civilization"; they had a moral responsibility to act on behalf of peoples only within civilizational boundaries. Historians have explained the rise of humanitarian reform, specifically abolitionism, in the century after 1750 as an expansion "of the conventional limits of moral responsibility . . . to encompass evils that previously had fallen outside anyone's operative sphere of responsibility." The American antislavery movement, in other words, stemmed from awareness among a growing number of reformers of their capacity, and therefore their obligation, to intervene on behalf of slaves. Such a sense of capacity and moral obligation has also been conjectured to explain

66. *Washington* [Kentucky] *Union.*

67. Blake, *Volume of the World*, 675–76. For background to this treaty see Poroy, "Expansion of Opium," and Kieser, *Nearest East*, 36–37.

the timing of missionaries' interest in "deal[ing] with primitive peoples." But the reticence of missionaries in Western Asia about the effects of the opium trade in China may suggest the limits at the time of the growth of such humanitarian sensibility about long range obligation.[68]

While missionaries did not seek to end the Ottoman trade in opium, they did seek to reduce Orthodox Christians' consumption of alcohol. This attitude was shaped by the religious revival of the Second Great Awakening of the early nineteenth century, whose core belief was that an individual committing sin could repent, and through his own moral effort could obtain salvation rather than depending only on God's will for his eternal destiny. This emphasis on individual agency to achieve salvation led to the "postmillennial" contention that Christ would return to Earth upon the perfection of human society, not only in America but around the world. Thus the early American republic saw an explosion of reform movements, seeking to root out moral and social imperfections. The formation of the American Board itself was one product of the Second Great Awakening. Another reform movement—perhaps the largest one—was the temperance movement, which sought to cure Americans of their habit of drinking alcohol to excess.

ABCFM missionaries embraced temperance wholeheartedly, and sought to cultivate abstinence from alcohol in Western Asia. To their surprise, they discovered that many Muslims of the Middle East already practiced such abstinence, a phenomenon that, ironically, became a popular rhetorical weapon in American temperance literature. Such literature embarrassed American consumers of alcohol into reform by pointing out the sobriety of Middle Eastern peoples, although the conversion of them to Protestant Christianity was made more difficult by exports to the Near East of New England distilleries. One American reverend lamented, "I have been in the port of Smyrna, where barrels of New England rum . . . distilled damnation . . . may be seen lying on the wharf, with the Boston stamp." Another praised the Turkish porters of Izmir for their physical strength, attributing their prowess to the fact that "they are all water-drinkers." The culture of alcohol consumption among Greeks and Armenians, on whom the missionaries relied to reach Muslims, doubled the missionaries' quandary.[69]

68. See Haskell, "Capitalism," 359, 339; and Hutchison, *Errand to the World*, 46–47.

69. Quotations from American temperance documents taken from Marr, *Cultural Roots*, 174, 181, 182.

One missionary's reaction to alcohol production in Izmir, in fact, may help us understand his perspective on the country's opium trade. In 1838 the *Missionary Herald* carried the account of a missionary who observed the "manufacture and use of intoxicating liquors in Smyrna." "My attention," recalled the missionary, "was strongly attracted to . . . droves of camels, which almost blocked up the road, on their way to the city. They seemed to amount to thousands . . . They were carrying grapes to the Smyrna market . . . Considering these fruits of the fertile Ionia, as destined for some foreign and less genial clime, I often said to myself, here one may feel and realize something of the grandeur, the sublimity of commerce." This missionary examined the buildings where the camels were discharging their cargo. "My musings about the sublimity of commerce were soon at an end. What I had been admiring was the sublimity of the wine manufactory and the [*raki*] distillery, and the fruits of Ionia, instead of going to bless some distant clime, I found converted into poison for the ruin, temporal and eternal, of her own citizens." The missionary conducted further investigation to calculate the volume of alcohol produced and consumed by denizens of Izmir, then concluded, "My heart sickens with the subject . . . I have said enough to give you some idea of one of the great obstacles which a missionary in Smyrna has to encounter."[70] The missionary did not allude to the opium trade, but even if he had it would probably have disturbed him less than distillation of grapes, because he wrote at a time when the temperance movement was far stronger than opposition to the consumption of opium.

This missionary's anecdote suggests that for him and his colleagues in Izmir, commerce was virtuous if it was conducted honestly and without government interference, and involved commodities produced for distant destinations, not local consumption. Different from the trade in opium bound for distant China, the manufacture and consumption of alcohol in Izmir, like its importation from New England, allowed the missionary to see or imagine its effects.

By the mid-nineteenth century, the singular role of Izmir as the dual focus of ABCFM missionaries and American merchants began to decline. The 1856 decree of Sultan Abdulmecid I known as the "Hatt-i Humayun," proclaimed under pressure of European powers after the Crimean War, promised religious equality and suggested a new tolerance for Armenian and Greek Protestants especially in Istanbul, draw-

70. Salibi and Khoury, eds., *Missionary Herald: Syria*, 3: 135–37.

ing American Board missionaries up the coast. With greater religious freedom and thus more opportunities for sharing Protestant Christian teaching, the American Board of Commissioners for Foreign Missions elected to shift missionaries towards Istanbul and Anatolia, reducing the centrality of Izmir for their evangelizing efforts.

American missionaries, however, would return to Izmir in the 1870s, primarily as teachers. One such teacher, Maria West, wrote that when she arrived in Izmir in 1878 it was a "burned over district," thanks to intensive evangelistic activity there in the first part of the century. But the city also struck her as an "abandoned field," on account of earlier missionaries' dispersal. West taught "moral instruction and English" at an Armenian school operating in the city, of whose licentiousness she disapproved. Izmir, she wrote, "worships the goddess of pleasure and fashion," because, she averred, "French infidelity is poisoning the very foundations of family life under the guise of liberal learning." Apparently the city's cosmopolitan culture did not dazzle this American missionary, who was perhaps even more morally conservative, or more nationalistic, than the first generation of American Board emissaries.[71]

While American missionaries' presence in Izmir fluctuated, Americans' trade in opium there continued. During the first half of the nineteenth century the Americans were completely identified with Turkish opium in both Izmir and China, to the point that a Chinese official in Canton asked an American sailor in the city in 1839 if Turkey "did not belong to America, or form a part of it."[72] In the 1830s the British government removed the East India Company's monopoly on trade in Indian opium, allowing British merchants and ships to come to Izmir to compete with Americans. This development cut into the American monopoly on Turkish opium. Likewise, American merchants expanded their East Asian trade. Yet Izmir opium, increasingly bound for the United States to meet demand of the American pharmaceutical industry (an 1880 Sino-American treaty prohibited the China opium trade), remained the basis for an American trade deficit with the Ottoman Empire, exceptional for both countries' international trade at the time.

New England merchants and missionaries had the seemingly different motivations of commerce and religion to establish an early

---

71. West, "Statement of Work in Smyrna," American Board Papers, American Board Library, Box 19, File 1507, 25 May 1878.

72. Turgay, "Nineteenth Century Golden Triangle," 1: 123–24.

American expatriate community in the Ottoman Empire. Yet because of their background and circumstances American Board missionaries embraced the international commerce of Western Asia because it could "do good" in America and in the world. For them even opium, the main American export from the Middle East until the twentieth century, functioned as a facilitator of global commerce, an instrument of both rational selfishness and sentimental philanthropy, and thus an element of God's providence for the world's redemption. Needless to say, few today view the opium trade as redemptive, either religiously or commercially. For many (perhaps most) Americans, the prospect of extending their influence abroad would not justify making addicts of others. Such a change of perspective suggests the distance that has developed between beliefs about religion and beliefs about "free market" capitalism in the West over the last two centuries.

BIBLIOGRAPHY

Adams, John Quincy. "Lecture on the War With China Delivered before the Massachusetts Historical Society." *Chinese Repository* 11 (1842) 274–89.

Ahmad, Diana. *Opium Debate And Chinese Exclusion Laws In The Nineteenth-Century American West*. Reno: University of Nevada Press, 2007.

American Board of Commissioners for Foreign Missions. *First Ten Reports of the American Board of Commissioners for Foreign Missions with Other Documents of the Board*. Boston: Crocker and Brewster, 1834.

————. Papers. American Board Library, Istanbul.

————. Papers. Houghton Library, Harvard University.

————. *Report*. Boston: Samuel T. Armstrong, 1812.

————. *Report*. Boston: Crocker and Brewster, 1821.

"American Mission in the Bombay Presidency." *Oriental Christian Spectator* 4 (1833) 116–19.

Anderson, Rufus. Papers, Congregational Library, Boston.

————. Papers. Houghton Library, Harvard University.

Beckert, Sven. "Emancipation and Empire: Reconstructing the Worldwide Web of Cotton Production in the Age of the American Civil War." *American Historical Review* 109 (2004) 1405–38.

Belohlavek, John. "Economic Interest Groups and the Formation of Foreign Policy in the Early Republic." *Journal of the Early Republic* 14 (1994) 476–84.

Blake, William. *Volume of the World*. Columbus, Ohio: J. & H. Miller, 1855.

Booth, Martin. *Opium: A History*. New York: St. Martin's, 1996.

Brunhouse, Robert, editor. *David Ramsay, 1749–1815: Selections from His Writings*. Philadelphia: American Philosophical Society, 1965.

Cizakca, Murat and Macit Kenanoglu. "Ottoman Merchants and the Jurisprudential Shift Hypothesis." In *Merchants in the Ottoman Empire*, edited by Suraiya Faroqhi and Gilles Veinstein, 195–214. Paris: Louvain, 2008.

"Confessions of an Opium-Eater." *North American Review* 18 (1824) 90–99.

"Creole Case." *Southern Quarterly Review* 2 (1842) 55–72.

Daniel, Robert. *American Philanthropy in the Near East 1820–1960.* Athens, Ohio: Ohio University Press, 1970.

Davenport-Hines, Richard. *Pursuit of Oblivion: A Global History of Narcotics.* New York: Norton, 2004.

Downs, Jacques. "American Merchants and the China Opium Trade, 1800–1840." *Business History Review* 42 (1968) 418–42.

———. "Fair Game: Exploitive Role-Myths and the American Opium Trade." *Pacific Historical Review* 41 (1972) 133–49.

Fairbank, John. "Introduction: Patterns and Problems." In *America's China Trade in Historical Perspective*, edited by Ernest May and John Fairbank, 1–7. Cambridge, Mass.: Harvard University Asia Center, 1986.

———. *Missionary Enterprise in China and America.* Cambridge, Mass.: Harvard University Press, 1974.

Farmer's Cabinet [Amherst, New Hampshire], 18 April 1829.

Faroqhi, Suraiya. *Subjects of the Sultan: Culture and Daily Life in the Ottoman Empire.* London: I. B. Tauris, 2005.

Field, James. *America and the Mediterranean World 1776–1882.* Princeton: Princeton University Press, 1969.

Finnie, David. *Pioneers East: The Early American Experience in the Middle East.* Cambridge, Mass.: Harvard University Press, 1967.

Forbes, Robert Bennett. *Personal Reminiscences.* Boston: Little, Brown, 1878.

———. *Remarks on China and the China Trade.* Boston: Samuel N. Dickinson, 1844.

Frangakis-Syrett, Elena. *Commerce of Smyrna in the Eighteenth Century, (1700–1820).* Athens, Greece: Center for Asia Minor Studies, 1992.

———. "Trade in Cotton and Cloth in Izmir: From the Second Half of the Eighteenth Century to the Early Nineteenth Century." In *Landholding and Commercial Agriculture in the Middle East,* edited by Caglar Keyder and Faruk Tabak, 97–111. Albany: State University of New York Press, 1991.

Goffman, Daniel. "Izmir: From Village to Colonial Port City." In *Ottoman City between East and West: Aleppo, Izmir, and Istanbul.* Edited by Edhem Eldem, et al., 79–134. New York: Cambridge University Press, 1999.

Goldstein, Jonathan. *Philadelphia and the China Trade 1682–1846.* University Park: Pennsylvania State University Press, 1978.

Grabill, Joseph. *Protestant Diplomacy in the Near East: Missionary Influence on American Policy, 1810–1827.* Minneapolis: University of Minnesota Press, 1971.

Gray, Elizabeth Kelly. "Trade-Off: Chinese Opium Traders and Antebellum Reform in the United States, 1815–1860." In *Drugs and Empires: Essays in Modern Imperialism and Intoxication 1500–1930.* Edited by James Mills and Patricia Barton, 220–42. London: Palgrave Macmillan, 2007.

Haskell, Thomas. "Capitalism and the Origins of the Humanitarian Sensibility, Part 1." *American Historical Review* 90 (1985) 339–61.

Hubers, John. "Making Friends with Locusts: Early ABCFM Missionary Perceptions of Muslims and Islam, 1818–1850." *International Bulletin of Missionary Research* 33 (2009) 151–4.

Hutchison, William. *Errand to the World: American Protestant Thought and Foreign Missions.* Chicago: University of Chicago Press, 1993.

Khalaf, Samir. "Leavening the Levant: New England Puritanism as a Cultural Transplant." *Journal of Mediterranean Studies* 7 (1997) 268–92.

Kieser, Hans-Lukas. *Nearest East: American Millennialism and Mission in the Middle East*. Philadelphia: Temple University Press, 2010.

Kling, David. "New Divinity and the Origins of the American Board of Commissioners for Foreign Missions." In *North American Foreign Missions, 1810–1914: Theology, Theory, and Policy*. Edited by Wilbert Shenk, 11–38. Grand Rapids: William B. Eerdmans, 2004.

Lazich, Michael. "American Missionaries and the Opium Trade in Nineteenth-Century China." *Journal of World History* 17 (2006) 197–223.

Loge, Ronald. "Two Dozes of Bark and Opium: Lewis & Clark as Physicians." In *Lewis & Clark: Legacies, Memories, and New Perspectives*. Edited by Kris Fresonke and Mark Spence, 70–82. Berkeley: University of California Press, 2004.

Lyons, Paul. "The Global Melville," in *Companion to Herman Melville*. Edited by Wyn Kelley, 52–67. Malden, Mass.: Blackwell, 2006.

Madison, James. *Writings*. Edited by Jack Rakove. New York: Library of America, 1999.

MacFarlane, Charles. *Turkey and Its Destiny*, two vols. Philadelphia: Lea and Blanchard, 1850.

Malham, John. *Naval Gazetteer*, two vols. Baltimore: Edward J. Coale, 1812.

Marcus, Abraham. *Middle East on the Eve of Modernity: Aleppo in the Eighteenth Century*. New York: Columbia University Press, 1992.

Marr, Timothy. *Cultural Roots of American Islamicism*. New York: Cambridge University Press, 2006.

Matthee, Rudolph. *Politics of Trade in Safavid Iran: Silk for Silver, 1600–1730*. New York: Cambridge University Press, 2000.

———. *Pursuit of Pleasure: Drugs and Stimulants in Iranian History, 1500–1900*. Princeton: Princeton University Press, 2009.

Morison, Samuel Eliot. "Forcing the Dardanelles in 1810: With Some Account of the Early Levant Trade of Massachusetts." *New England Quarterly* 1 (1928) 208–25.

Oren, Michael. *Power, Faith, and Fantasy: America in the Middle East 1776 to the Present*. New York: Norton, 2008.

Parrington, Vernon. *Romantic Revolution in America, 1800–1860*. New York: Harcourt, Brace, 1927.

Parsons, Levi. *Dereliction and Restoration of the Jews. A Sermon, Preached in Park-Street Church, Boston, Oct. 31, 1819, Just Before the Departure of the Palestine Mission*. Boston: S. T. Armstrong, 1819.

———. *Memoir*. Edited by Daniel Morton. Hartford: Cooke & Co., 1830.

Perkins, Bradford. *Creation of a Republican Empire, 1776–1865*. New York: Cambridge University Press, 1993.

Perkins, Thomas Handasyd. *Memoir*. Edited by Thomas Cary. Boston: Little, Brown, 1856.

———. Papers. Massachusetts Historical Society.

Pessen, Edward. *Riches, Class, and Power: The United States before the Civil War*. New Brunswick: Transaction Publishers, 1990.

Philbrick, Nathaniel. "Nantucket Sequence in Crevecoeur's *Letters from an American Farmer*." *New England Quarterly* 64 (1991) 414–32.

Phillips, Clifton Jackson. *Protestant America and the Pagan World: The First Half Century of the American Board of Commissioners for Foreign Missions, 1810–1860.* Cambridge, Mass.: East Asian Research Center of Harvard University, 1969.

Poroy, Ibrahim Ihsan."Expansion of Opium Production in Turkey and the State Monopoly of 1828–1839." *International Journal of Middle East Studies* 13 (1981) 191–211.

Salibi, Kamal, and Yusuf Khoury, editors. *Missionary Herald: Reports from Northern Iraq (1833–1870),* three vols. Beirut: Royal Institute for Inter-Faith Studies, 1997.

———. *Missionary Herald: Reports from Ottoman Syria,* five vols. Amman; Royal Institute for Inter-Faith Studies, 1995.

Schmidt, Jan. *From Anatolia to Indonesia: Opium Trade and the Dutch Community of Izmir, 1820–1940.* Istanbul: Nederlands Historisch-Archaeologisch Instituut Te Istanbul, 1998.

Seaburg, Carl, and Stanley Paterson. *Merchant Prince of Boston: Colonel Thomas Perkins, 1764–1854.* Cambridge, Mass.: Harvard University Press, 1971.

Stelle, Charles Clarkson. *Americans and the China Opium Trade in the Nineteenth Century.* New York: Arno Press, 1981.

Tchen, John Kuo Wei. *New York Before Chinatown: Orientalism and the Shaping of American Culture 1776–1882.* Baltimore: Johns Hopkins University Press, 2001.

Tracy, Joseph. *History of the American Board of Commissioners for Foreign Missions.* New York: M. W. Dodd, 1842.

Turgay, A. Uner. "Nineteenth Century Golden Triangle: Chinese Consumption, Ottoman Production and American Connection, I: Opium Trade in International Perspective." *International Journal of Turkish Studies* 2 (1983) 105–25.

———. "Nineteenth Century Golden Triangle: Chinese Consumption, Ottoman Production and American Connection, II: Ottoman Opium Production and Government Policies." *International Journal of Turkish Studies* 3 (1984–1985) 65–91.

———. "Ottoman-American Trade During the Nineteenth Century." *Osmanli Aragtirmalari* 3 (1982), 189–234.

Van Lennep, Mary. *Memoir.* Hartford: Belknap and Hamersley, 1848.

Washington [Kentucky] *Union,* 13 August 1814.

Willis, Nathaniel Parker. *Summer Cruise in the Mediterranean, on board an American Frigate.* Auburn, N.Y.: Alden, Beardsley, 1853.

Zentner, Joseph. "Opiate Use in America during the Eighteenth and Nineteenth Centuries: The Origins of a Modern Scourge." *Studies in History and Society* 5 (1974) 40–54.

4

American Board Schools in Turkey

Dorothy Birge Keller and Robert S. Keller

OF THE MANY LANDS in which the American Board of Commissioners for Foreign Missions (ABCFM) did work, none was more important to it than the Ottoman Empire, the core of which was Turkey. ABCFM missionaries preached in Turkey, provided medical services, and operated a printing press, but this essay will focus on their schools, which greatly influenced Turkish society. The history of the ABCFM schools in Turkey can be divided into two general periods, each about a century in length. The first period began in the 1820s when the first missionaries started schools, enrolling primarily Christian students (mostly Armenian and some Greek) and teaching them in their vernacular languages. The second period began at the end of World War I with the end of the Ottoman Empire and the establishment of the new Republic of Turkey. At that point the mission schools began enrolling mostly Turkish Muslim students, and emphasizing the use of the English language as the medium of instruction. Midway through this period, in 1969, a secular, non-profit private foundation began to assume the ownership and administration of the schools as the American Board reduced its support.[1]

1. The "American Board" refers to the American Board of Commissioners for Foreign Missions, ABCFM, established in 1810. After the United Church of Christ formed in 1957, the mission board became in 1960 the United Church Board for World Ministries. In the late 1990s when the United Church of Christ mission efforts were joined with the Christian Church (Disciples of Christ), under the name Common Global Ministries Board, the United Church of Christ board was named the Wider Church Ministries. The name of its agency in Turkey has been the *Amerikan Bord Heyeti* (ABH) for the entire time. In this chapter we will use ABCFM until the 1960s

BEGINNINGS

The ABCFM missionaries who were first sent to the Ottoman Empire sought to determine not only how to bring the Gospel of Jesus Christ to the diverse peoples of the empire, but also how to carry out the ABCFM Prudential Committee's instructions: "The two grand inquiries ever present in your mind will be 'What good can be done?' and 'By what means?' What can be done for Jews? What for pagans? What for Mohammedans? What for Christians?"[2] At the time of the missionaries' arrival, the Ottoman Empire was vast and although it receded over time in territory, power, and influence, it continued its oversight of religious and ethnic "national" groups, or "*millets*," which included the Greek, Armenian, Nestorian, Assyrian, Jewish, and similar communities. In the early years of the empire, the Ottoman rulers were benevolent administrators of the *millet* system, which accorded minority groups considerable protection, rights and autonomy, so that they could run the civic and educational affairs of their own religious communities with minimal interference. These advantages of the *millet* system proved to be a boon for the missionaries. They also benefited from the Ottoman Empire "capitulations," which granted privileged status to Americans and Europeans in the 1800s. Thanks to the *millet* system and "capitulations," the missionaries were able to start and run their own schools with relative freedom.

EARLY MISSIONARIES AND EARLY WORK

Pliny Fisk and Levi Parsons, sent in 1819 to the Ottoman Empire, first stopped in Malta, where they visited colleagues who were establishing a publication office for the ABCFM. They gathered some of the religious materials in Armenian and Greek for their next stop, Izmir (Smyrna).[3] There they soon started a monthly "Concert of Prayer" and surveyed the area for its suitability as a site for mission work. Fisk concluded that

---

and then use the "American Board" or "Board" to refer to the successors of the ABCFM. In this chapter Turkey refers to the area that is currently the Republic of Turkey. It is the area that was the heart of the Ottoman Empire. At times this area is also referred to as Anatolia.

  2. Putney, *Brief History*, 1.

  3. Since the founding of the Republic of Turkey, some city names have been changed. In this chapter we will use the current names. If the city had a different name at the time under discussion, we will give the earlier name in parenthesis when the city is first introduced.

Izmir, a bustling port city hub of commerce and communication, was indeed an excellent center for future mission work. His assessment of area Greek and Armenian *millets* showed him that dissemination of the religious materials would not be fully successful until more of the population learned to read, thus necessitating that the mission establish schools.[4] Unfortunately, Fisk died prematurely in 1825 while visiting in Beirut. Parsons had died in 1822 while going to Jerusalem for work with the Arab peoples of the Empire.[5]

In 1831, the Rev. William Goodell was sent to Istanbul (Constantinople). With mission colleagues, he began four Lancasterian model (a monitorial method) schools among Greek *millet* communities, using advanced students, under guidance of a qualified teacher, to teach larger numbers of younger students. Within a year twenty such schools were operating for the Greeks in Istanbul.[6]

Called on to investigate and condemn these schools, the Ottoman administration ended up admiring them. They even wanted the Lancasterian model in schools for their military. With the help of Goodell and his friend and mentor, Commodore David Porter, the American Consul, the Ottomans established eight schools in military barracks using the Lancasterian model to educate over 2,000 common soldiers. It is possible that these schools could have influenced future Turkish military support for basic level education for the ordinary soldier.[7]

From the beginning, ABCFM missionaries were strongly committed to education for girls. In 1832, William Goodell and his wife opened a school for girls in their home. This was closed within months by Orthodox Christian leaders who felt that education for girls undermined the authority of the church and was humiliating for the church and its families. The Orthodox community had long traditions of arranged marriages and other practices that stood in the way of independence for women. Undeterred by the closure of his first girl's school, Goodell opened a boarding school for girls in 1845 which continued in Istanbul before it was eventually moved by the Mission to the Anatolian interior.[8]

4. Religious leaders in Izmir (Smyrna) resisted ABCFM educational work until 1878, when Maria West was able to open her school for girls and boys.

5. See Shelton, "Faith, Freedom, and Flag," 75–76; and Stone, *Academies for Anatolia*, 37–38.

6. Stone, *Academies for Anatolia*, 46.

7. Ibid., 47.

8. Ibid., 76–77.

Missionary wives and the single women appointed for Mission work were often graduates of New England female seminaries. Many came from Mt. Holyoke College and its daughter institution, Wellesley, both of which had the goal to develop women's full potential. Inspired by Mt. Holyoke, the Ely sisters in eastern Turkey founded the "Mt. Holyoke Girls Seminary for Kurdistan," which taught on the Mt. Holyoke model. Every student paid at least some tuition; financial aid was then granted on the basis of need. The seminary strongly emphasized Bible and religious study, domestic work for economizing and developing humility, traditional subject learning, and homemaking and child care skills.[9]

Women's mission efforts in Turkey received support from the Woman's Board of Missions (WBM), which was started in 1868 by Mrs. Albert Bowker.[10] It was run by American church women, usually working closely with the ABCFM. The WBM funded, staffed, and administered institutions throughout the world. One of these institutions was the "Home School" in Istanbul which was founded in 1871. Five years later it was moved for more space to Uskudar on the Asiatic side of the Bosphorus and in 1914 it was moved again to the European side (Arnavutkoy). After being granted a higher education charter by Massachusetts in 1890, and receiving full recognition by the Ottoman Empire in 1895, it became the prestigious American Girls College, a sister school to Robert College, which the former ABCFM missionary Cyrus Hamlin had founded.[11]

Figure 11. Graduates of the Home School in Constantinople (Istanbul), ca. 1872. From Frances J. Dyer, *Looking Backward over Fifty Years* (Boston: Woman's Board of Missions, 1917), 16. Photo courtesy of the Congregational Library, Boston.

9. Ibid., 124–25.

10. Johnson, *Enduring Transitions*, 3.

11. Stone, *Academies for Anatolia*, 77–78.

The schools for girls which became successful often had boarding departments and day programs. They offered full-scale academic training including courses on mathematics, the natural sciences, philosophy, and literature. They always had a strong emphasis on religious education and provided training for practical life skills such as teaching and child care. Sometimes they included community and health services. Although not wanting to be "finishing schools" for girls, they often offered such "ornamentals" as stitchery and music.[12]

Graduates of these schools gained recognition as cultured, resourceful women who could provide community leadership. Many married the pastors of the emerging Protestant churches or became teachers in the numerous church-related elementary schools in the Armenian Protestant *millets.*

EARLY ABCFM ACADEMY MODEL SCHOOLS

Most of the missionary men were graduates of New England academies that combined academic studies and practical skills into the "learning and labor" approach. These dual emphases strongly influenced the way the missionaries developed their school programs. An exponent of the academy model was Cyrus Hamlin, who was sent to Turkey in 1839 with these instructions: "The object of our mission to the Oriental Churches is, first, to revive the knowledge and spirit of the gospel among them; and secondly, by this means to operate among the Mohammedans. These churches must be reformed . . . The Oriental Churches need assistance from . . . their brethren abroad."[13]

When Hamlin arrived in Istanbul with his new bride, he started the Bebek Boys Seminary in his large home. This school, though moved twice, thrived for seventeen years in Istanbul until the ABCFM voted to move it to Merzifon (Marsovan). Hamlin's diplomatic and non-confrontational skills allowed him unobtrusively to develop highly successful "learning and labor" programs which involved entrepreneurial efforts and strong academic curricula. Hamlin used English, among other languages, for instruction and emphasized mathematics, the natural sciences, moral philosophy, history and geography. For all students, particularly the poverty-level ones, he opened industrial units with

12. Ibid., 83.

13. Blemker, *150 Years,* 2.

workshops for many crafts and products. Creatively designed by Hamlin himself, the crafts and products included special sheet-metal work for stoves and stove pipes, barrels designed for industrial washing machines, baking of the much sought after "bira bread" (using hops and fine flour in recipes formulated by Hamlin), and even the famous "Boston rat trap" that sold throughout Istanbul. These diverse products were functional and marketable, and they earned students and churches good income. Hamlin's model influenced the approaches used in ABCFM schools in Anatolia into the years of the Turkish Republic.[14]

Cyrus Hamlin wanted to start a college in Constantinople using the English language for a liberal education. Because the Prudential Committee did not approve this request, Hamlin resigned from the ABCFM and, with philanthropist Christopher R. Robert, founded Robert College in 1856. It now continues as the prestigious Turkish "Bosphorus University." The continuing academy-level school, now in Arnavutkoy, maintains the name, Robert College.[15]

GROWTH OF THE ARMENIAN PROTESTANT UNION

Protestant church development was strongly resisted by the Orthodox Church authorities, and in 1846 Protestants were excommunicated by the Church, thus thrusting them outside the protection of the official *millet*. With British diplomatic help, the Ottomans, in 1850, designated the Armenian Evangelical Protestant community to be an official *millet*, separate from the Orthodox, thus opening the way for rapid and dynamic expansion of communities, churches, and schools within the Armenian Protestant Union.[16]

The growth of members of the Protestant faith after 1850 led to the development of an extensive system of graded common schools throughout Anatolia. Support for the local schools was left to the churches, but the ABCFM took responsibility for establishing and running high schools for boys and girls. These secondary-level institutions served as bridges, filling the gap between basic literacy training and the colleges and theological seminaries that the ABCFM educators were opening. Their practical programs included employable skills such as wood crafts,

14. See Stone, *Academies for Anatolia*, 57–68; and Shelton, "Faith, Freedom, and Flag," 76–79.

15. Stone, *Academies for Anatolia*, 68–69.

16. Ibid., 73–74.

shoe making, baking, metal work, bookbinding, milling, and printing. Agricultural work was sometimes included with the "labor and learning" approach, which was very similar to the rationale of the Turkish "Village Institutes" that were developed by the Kemalist government in the 1930s.[17] Stone writes, "It was always the stated policy that the high schools and female seminaries would eventually become the property of the indigenous communities."[18]

After 1850, the ABCFM worked in cooperation with the Armenian Evangelical Union. The following statistics illustrate how effective the two organizations were at creating mission schools throughout Anatolia. By 1855, they had started 44 schools (boarding and other schools served 270 girls, nine small seminaries enrolled 153 men). By 1872 it was claimed that 85% of Protestants were literate. By 1909 there were 337 schools in the three mission areas (Western, Central, and Eastern Turkey) enrolling 20,014 students.[19] These schools included many common schools, 44 high schools, eight colleges, four normal schools, and five divinity schools.[20] There was also special education for blind and deaf children.[21] Frank Stone claimed "This was a virtual educational explosion in Anatolia."[22]

INSTITUTIONS OF HIGHER EDUCATION

A number of colleges of higher education were formed by the ABCFM, some in response to requests from the Armenian Evangelical Union. Perceiving that Harvard, Amherst, Yale, Williams, and Dartmouth were providing leadership and cultural uplift in the United States, the Union wanted a system of higher education that would do the same in Turkey. They drew closer to their goal with the foundation of the Girls' College in Marash and the Central Turkey College in Gaziantep (Aintab), pioneers as medical and pharmaceutical educational institutions. After years of service these two schools were moved to Aleppo, Syria, where they are still run by Jacobite and Armenian church groups. The Marash

17. Ibid., 65.

18. Ibid., 75.

19. Ibid., 76.

20. Blemker, *150 Years*, 3.

21. Stone, *Academies for Anatolia*, 345.

22. Ibid., 76.

Theological Seminary was moved to Beirut, Lebanon, where it is now the Near East School of Theology.[23]

Other colleges were not so successful. The Euphrates College of Harput and the Apostolic Institute of Konia, both run entirely by Armenians, did not survive the struggles of the Armenians in the rapidly devolving empire during the 1895–1918 period of turmoil.[24] Anatolia College of Merzifon, which educated Greek as well as Armenian students, survived with difficulty until 1921. At that point, conflict with Greece over control of western Anatolia led to the school being moved and restarted as a new institution in Thessaloniki, Greece, where it continues.[25]

The International College was another institution which primarily taught Greeks and Armenians, along with a few Jews and Turks. The college was an outgrowth of the Boys' School in Izmir, which had been founded by Maria West in 1878 and continued by Marcellus Bowen in 1880. Beginning in 1891, the school's dynamic principal, Alexander MacLachlan, greatly strengthened its program and expanded the student body. By 1902 the school had grown to 250 students and soon provided four years of college along with the four year high school curriculum. In 1903, the school was incorporated in Massachusetts as the International College of Smyrna, Turkey, with the ABCFM Prudential Committee as the Board of Trustees.[26]

In 1913, the Rev. John Kingsley Birge was commissioned by the ABCFM to work at International College, not only in the academic arena but also with the expanding extracurricular offerings, which included community outreach and YMCA activities for Christian youth (Greek and Armenian). He was especially invited to develop courses, clubs, settlement house programs, and youth camps with the Turkish youth of the area and with their families and communities. Birge helped to form a Turkish Literary Society in which he encouraged students to write and translate materials with themes on hope and tolerance.[27] During the September 1922 capture of Izmir from the Greeks by Turkish forces, Birge served as a facilitator, helping evacuate Americans, British,

23. Ibid., 141–59.

24. Ibid., 171.

25. Ibid., 183–98.

26. See Ibid., 235–47; and Johnson, *Paths to Learning*, 6–7, 9–12.

27. See Ibid., 241; and John Birge, "College and YMCA," 312–13.

Greeks, and Armenians from the burning city onto Greek, British, and American war ships waiting outside the harbor limits.[28]

Under the leadership of Cass Arthur Reed, who succeeded Alexander MacLachlan, International College survived the disruption of WWI and the Turkish War for Independence. However, in 1934 internal conflicts and a drastic shortfall in funding led to the separation of the college from the ABCFM. The college was then moved to Beirut where it continues now under the same name, International College, as a significant institution of higher learning.[29]

ORIGINS OF THE ABCFM SCHOOLS
THAT CONTINUED IN TURKEY

Uskudar American Academy

The Uskudar American Academy is the oldest of the continuing ABCFM schools. In 1876, with the support of the Prudential Committee and the official permit of the Ottoman Government, Laura Farnham opened a girls' day and boarding school in an old silkworm cocoonery in the town of Bahcecik.[30] It was so successful that in 1885 she moved her school to the nearby larger and more thriving city of Adapazari, at the request of the leaders of the Protestant community in that city. The student body became so diversified that in 1912–13, of the 311 students, 230 were Armenian Orthodox, seventy-seven Protestant, two Greek and two Jewish. The school included a kindergarten, a primary school, a preparatory school, a high school, and a teachers' training program. Students were instructed in math, science, history, geography, music, and religion, and they were taught in the English, Turkish, and Armenian languages. Special emphasis was given to English, and pupils were required to communicate solely in this tongue five days a week.[31]

Between 1892 and 1910, the school graduated and sent out approximately thirty teachers to work in different parts of Anatolia. Besides training professionals, the school sought to nurture knowledgeable young women who would have an enlightening influence in their homes

28. Birge, Robert, "Personsal Interviews."

29. See Johnson, *Paths of Learning*, 12; and Stone, *Academies for Anatolia*, 235–47.

30. Linder, *History of Uskudar*, 4.

31. Johnson, *Enduring Transitions*, 5–11.

and communities. As one American teacher stated succinctly, "Nothing is more needed in Turkey than educated mothers, and our school and others are working toward that end."[32] The school was closed in 1915 to be occupied by the Turkish military, but it reopened in 1918 after the Armistice. However, the Greek invasion of the area in 1919 forced the school to move to safer areas, first to Kocaeli (Izmit) and then to Uskudar, where it opened in September, 1921 in the former Girls' College buildings, now its current campus. A resourceful and perseverant principal, Mary Kinney, guided the school through each move during the turbulent times from 1910 to 1930.[33]

The American Collegiate Institute

The American Collegiate Institute was the second of the current schools to begin in the Ottoman era. It started in Izmir in 1878 when Maria West opened a day school in a rented house in the city's Armenian quarter. The ABCFM printing press had been moved to Izmir from Malta in 1833 to continue Greek, Armenian, and Turkish translations. But local Greek and Armenian populations resisted having ABCFM schools in Izmir until 1878. West's day school enrolled fifty girls and boys in its first year. It was separated in 1880 by then Director Marcellus Bowen into two schools: a boys' school with twenty-five students (which became International College referred to above) and a girls' school with forty students.

In 1882, the Woman's Board of Missions, in cooperation with the ABCFM, appointed Mary Lyon Page of Mt. Holyoke College to be principal of the girl's school, which was named the American Collegiate Institute for Girls in 1898. The school grew to have over one hundred students in three main departments—primary, preparatory, and collegiate. By 1910, the school's 302 girls needed more space, especially since a fire had destroyed part of its main building in Basmane. A search for another property took several years, but in 1912 the present school property in Goztepe was purchased. World War I and financial limitations prevented developing that new campus until 1921, when Olive Greene, almost single-handedly, planted trees, adapted buildings, and moved the

32. Ibid., 10.
33. Ibid., 7–14.

school to the Goztepe campus. In 1924, the school had eighty-one students and was officially recognized by the Turkish authorities.[34]

In the meantime, Nellie Bartlett, the daughter of Turkey Mission parents, returned from her special training in the new Froebel kindergarten methods at the Minnesota Normal School and started her own kindergarten in Izmir in 1885, the first such school in Turkey. It had two tracks. The first, which was for preschool children, used creative play, social participation, games, stories, and crafts for the development of imagination, learning, and social skills. The other track was a training school for future kindergarten teachers. Within a few months Bartlett's school went from seven to seventy students, and by 1900 she had graduated forty-two kindergarten teachers who started their own schools in many parts of Anatolia. In 1902 Bartlett's school was officially folded into the American Collegiate Institute, strengthening the latter school's appeal and program.[35]

Tarsus American College

Tarsus American College was the third of the current schools to begin in the Ottoman era. It was founded as St. Paul's Institute in 1888 by Thomas Christie, an ABCFM missionary in the Tarsus area, who arranged for its funding by Elliot Shepard, a prosperous New York lawyer. The school was first chartered in the state of New York, independently of the ABCFM. But in 1903 the Board assumed administrative and financial responsibility for the school.

Christie was president of the school until 1920, when he retired because of failing health. He placed his distinctive stamp on the school, having it train Christian young men to do work in their homeland as evangelists, pastors, teachers, physicians, and business men. To cultivate a work ethic, and to provide those in need with a means to pay their tuition and boarding fees, pupils were given jobs on campus, or in St. Paul's industrial department. Christie also developed a fine physical campus, adding three new buildings onto the three acres that he had purchased. This is the current campus.

By 1915, when enrollment totaled 260, the college could boast of having graduated 163 students since its founding. More than one-third

---

34. Johnson, *Paths of Learning*, 6–8, 16–17.

35. See Ibid., 13–15; and Stone, *Academies for Anatolia*, 90–91.

of them were ministers or teachers. By the 1923–24 school year, much of the Christian population had left the area and Turks became the majority of the student body. That year the first Turk graduated and began teaching at the school.[36]

Talas School for Boys

The Talas School for Boys was the last of the post World War II schools begun in the Ottoman era. It was opened in 1889 in the area of Kayseri (Caesarea) in central Anatolia. Thirty five years earlier, an Armenian Protestant Church had been formed in Kayseri and the first ABCFM resident missionaries arrived there. From this center a network of little churches and elementary schools was developed. This ambitious school system soon needed secondary schools and in 1889 boarding schools for girls and boys were begun in Talas, eight miles from Kayseri. In 1898 the Talas School for Boys had sixty Armenian and Greek students. The head of the school wrote then that many applicants for admission could not be accepted because there was no room for them. Funds were raised and a fine new building was finally completed. But the school, along with the school for girls, was closed in 1917 when their campuses were requisitioned by the Turkish military. The Talas School for Boys was reopened in 1927, but the school for girls was never reopened.[37]

ABCFM SCHOOLS IN THE NEW REPUBLIC OF TURKEY

The Republic of Turkey, which began in 1923 under the leadership of its founder, Mustafa Kemal Ataturk, made great social and cultural changes. These included developing a secular government and civil society, adopting a Latinized phonetic alphabet in place of the Arabic script, "purifying" the Turkish language to partially replace Persian and Arabic words with original Turkic vocabulary, forbidding the use of the veil for women and the fez for men, focusing on quality science based westernized education for youth, stressing equality of education and employment opportunities for women, adopting a form of the Swiss legal code, and committing to a future for democracy. Ataturk taught the goal, "Peace in Our Country and Peace in the World." He exhorted youth to be proud of their Turkish citizenship, whatever their religious

36. Johnson, *A Legacy*, 5–15.
37. Stone, *Academies for Anatolia*, 91–92.

or ethnic origins, and to be responsible leaders in Turkey and contributing members of the world society.

Following the upheavals and tragedies of World War I and the war for Turkey's independence, many schools that had served Armenian and Greek populations could not be reopened, while others had moved with their teachers and students to nearby countries. The Lausanne Treaty, signed on July 24, 1923, permitted previously established foreign schools in Turkey to be granted a "Founder Status" authorization, which allowed them to continue to operate under the laws of the new Republic of Turkey. These laws, however, prohibited teaching religion and proselytizing in any way. There was disagreement in the USA and among the missionaries in Turkey about whether the Turkey Mission should continue to exist under these conditions. Those who wanted to stay in Turkey felt they could provide service to the new nation with its modern democratic goals. They successfully persuaded the ABCFM to stay in Turkey, and to work with all groups, not just Christians.[38]

Paul Nilson was a primary exponent of the ABCFM's new approach in Turkey. He advocated "character building," a term with great cachet among missionaries in the early twentieth century. In 1926 he wrote:

> "Despite the strange changes which have taken place during the past twelve months, our missionaries in Turkey have settled down to their tasks with calm confidence and joy. They feel that the way of missionary progress is more clearly marked. It is the original way, the way of Jesus. Not institutions as much as personal relationships are the means, not classroom instruction but personal friendliness is the sure method; not converts to Christianity, but those who will follow Jesus' way of life are the fruitage of the missionary way."[39]

Receptivity to missionaries on the part of the Turkish authorities and population was mixed, but was favorable enough to allow nine ABCFM schools to continue to help with the government's intent to have education modernize the new nation. In 1928 the nine schools, six of them located in coastal cities, had nearly 1,300 students, three-fourths of them Muslim Turks.[40] Not only was the composition of their student bodies fundamentally different, but new educational programs

38. See Ibid., 252; and Johnson, *Legacy of Education*, 17–18.

39. Stone, *Academies for Anatolia*, 256.

40. Ibid., 260.

were also introduced in the ABCFM's work in Turkey, often in response to the Turkish educational authorities' new desire for practical education. In the Tarsus American College, pupils had a choice of two learning tracks: one to prepare for university entrance, the other to develop vocational skills for a career in business or trades.[41] In the Talas School for Boys, a trade program for village boys was developed in cooperation with the Turkish Ministry of Education, which paid the tuition for fifty, later eighty, village boys for two years of training. The program stressed practical production skills and tried to develop rural leaders who would be prepared to work toward village revitalization.[42]

The Uskudar American Academy (known in the 1920s as the American Academy for Girls) also stressed practicality. For its students in the tenth and eleventh grades it offered a choice among three special tracks of study—home economics, commercial, and collegiate—which were based on the students' plans to become homemakers, pursue a professional career, or enter university. The school was regarded so highly that its graduates were permitted to enroll at Turkish universities without an examination.[43]

In addition to this official recognition of the academic qualification of the schools' graduates, there was recognition of the social service ideals of its teachers by no less than the president of Turkey, Mustafa Kemal Ataturk. In 1926 he called Sidika Avar, a Turkish teacher in the Izmir American Collegiate Institute, to his office to question her about her teaching evening classes for women prisoners in the local jail. "Is it true that you are a missionary teacher?" he asked her. Confused, she slowly answered, "Sir, I am just teacher Avar." Ataturk pointed his finger at her and firmly declared, "No. You are missionary Avar! Missionaries like you are just what I need." He then commissioned her to go to eastern Turkey, where she headed a Girls' Institute for many years and became a living legend in hundreds of ballads and epic poems. Her career became an ideal for Board school teachers and students over the years.[44]

By 1930 ABCFM Schools in Turkey were in good favor with government authorities. That same year all foreign schools were required to

41. Johnson, *A Legacy*, 20.

42. Stone, *Academies for Anatolia*, 268.

43. Johnson, *Enduring Transitions*, 13.

44. Stone, *Academies for Anatolia*, 281. In the early years of the Republic, the Turkish word for missionary, *misyoner*, often meant "one who serves for the good of others."

employ a Turkish associate principal. This led to increased cross-cultural understanding and to a mutual influence between American and Turkish educational programs. The Turkish associate principals made significant contributions to the development of their schools' educational programs. In later years, some of the principals were graduates of the schools, and that enhanced the schools' relationships with faculty members, students, and alumni.[45]

Unfortunately, the financial restrictions imposed by the Great Depression resulted in the closing or merging of five schools. As World War II began only four schools were operating, three with middle and high school programs: American Collegiate Institute (girls) in Izmir; Tarsus American College (boys); and Uskudar American Academy (girls). The Talas School for Boys had only a middle school program.[46]

A SECOND TIME OF GROWTH AND INFLUENCE

After World War II, the Turkish Mission developed "The Plan for Advance" in 1948, basing it on a study of their schools by Dr. Harry Meyering and others. The experts' recommendations included: 1) improving the quality of students by using an entrance examination for admission and developing a systematic evaluation of student learning; 2) improving the teaching of English as a second language by using modern linguistic methods; and 3) developing effective libraries and media centers. Meyering advised that it was time for experimentation and cautious innovation rather than the previous emphasis on cutting costs and simplifying operations. Looking to the future, he said that the job of the American Board Schools would be "to pioneer, to demonstrate, and to try to work ourselves out of a job as new leaders are developed."[47]

Frank Stone notes that in the years between 1950 and 1970 the ABCFM schools did develop in several notable ways. First, the schools modernized and improved their curricula and instructional methods. Second, they expanded their physical plants with extensive renovation and new construction. Third, they created parent-teacher organizations and alumni associations in an effort to achieve more inclusive and participatory governance. As a result of all these innovations, the ABCFM

45. Ibid., 261.
46. Ibid., 271.
47. Ibid., 274.

schools in Turkey were revitalized. Rather than being dispirited, as they were in the immediate aftermath of World War II, they entered the last quarter of the twentieth century with confidence and optimism.[48]

ADMINISTRATORS WHO BROUGHT "VIGOR AND RIGOR" TO THE SCHOOLS IN MODERN TIMES

In 2002 Frank Stone wrote, "The American Board Schools in Turkey have been blessed with many capable leaders during the last half century. These individuals, in cooperation with those around them, brought vigor and rigor to the schools. The twenty-first century schools are, in large measure, products of their efforts."[49]

Uskudar American Academy (UAA)

Brought up in a Turkey Mission family, Jessie Martin, principal from 1936 to 1956, led the school with impeccable Turkish language skills and with deep sensitivity to the Turkish culture. She was admired for her great dignity and strong vision as she made changes in educational programs, in buildings, and in the student body, which grew considerably under her leadership.[50]

Following Miss Martin, Helen Morgan, principal from 1956 to 1977, continued on the way to dynamic modernization with her relaxed and fully collegial approach to working with American and Turkish faculty. School directors who followed Miss Morgan included Martha Millett, a long time teacher at UAA, and, still later, Whitman Shepard, great-grandson of the famous mission doctor, "Shepard of Aintab." Whitman Shepard currently serves as the liaison for the three schools with the Turkish Ministry of Education.[51]

Alice Lindsley was another important UAA educational program leader. She developed and ran one of the most effective, innovative, and much loved home economics programs in Turkey. This program included a "Practice House," which offered small groups of girls a week long experience in running a home, complete with housekeeping, shopping, cooking, and entertaining.[52]

48. Ibid., 301–2.
49. Ibid., 305.
50. Johnson, *Enduring Transitions*, 14–19.
51. See Ibid., 14; and Stone, *Academies for Anatolia*, 265, 305–11.
52. Linder, *History of Uskudar*, 45, 68.

Dorothy Blatter, art teacher for UAA and writer of children's books for the Turkey Mission Publication Department, which later became the Redhouse Press, was another mission luminary.[53] Also of note is Alison Stendahl, Academic Dean of UAA, who will be the last American Board missionary in Turkey as of 2012, following the retirement of Kenneth and Elizabeth Frank.[54]

Semiha Malatlioglu, Esin Hoyi, and Tulin Buyukalkan (who later served as Coordinator of Education for all of the schools) were three UAA graduates whose long and effective administration as Turkish associate principals contributed greatly to the development and stability of the school. Among the persons who served as American vice-principals were Alice Reed, a former missionary in China, and Ruby P. Birge, a leader at the Istanbul YWCA.[55] In addition, several Armenian professionals contributed immeasurably to the school's programs and culture into the 1950s. Dr. Zarouhi Kavaljian, the first Armenian woman to study medicine in the Ottoman Empire, helped with student services.[56] Mr. and Mrs. Alexanian, Miss Nodarian, and Miss Verkin were effective in many areas. And Miriam Hagopian brought zest and strong leadership to the school and to the wider community.[57]

American Collegiate Institute, Izmir (ACI)

Following Olive Greene, Lynda Goodsell Blake was principal from 1948 to 1971. She, along with her husband Everett (Jack), served ACI with vision, commitment, and stamina. She brought Turkish faculty and perspectives into the school, modernized the buildings and program, and was a role model for her many students, who admired her professionalism, kindness, and skillful diplomacy.[58]

53. See Johnson, *Changing Fonts*, 8–12; and Linder, *History of Uskudar*, 66.

54. Makari, "Address," 2.

55. See Johnson, *Enduring Transitions*, 19, 23; and Linder, *History of Uskudar*, 199, 229–30.

56. Stone, *Academies for Anatolia*, 78.

57. Linder, *History of Uskudar*, 84.

58. See Stone, *Academies for Anatolia*, 316–17, 342; and Johnson, *Paths of Learning*, 21. Other important long time missionaries were Harriet Yarrow, Fernie Scovel, Naomi Foster, Douglas Hill, Frederick and Mary Alice Shepard, and Kenneth and Elizabeth Frank.

Ibrahim Taner, who helped to found the Salhane Turkish division of ACI in 1919, was a Turkish leader of great importance to the college. He was its first Turkish vice-principal, serving from 1919 to 1960. His name is given to a central classroom building, Taner Hall, on the Goztepe campus.[59]

Tarsus American College (TAC)

After being guided by the Principals Thomas Christie, Paul Nilson, and William Nute, Tarsus American College came under the leardership of William Sage Woolworth (married to Pauline). He was principal of the school from 1928 to 1949, and he effectively guided it through the Depression and World War II. With his tall rangy frame and wide smile, he encouraged many to become good students and service-minded graduates. Richard Maynard (married to Georgianna) led the institution from 1949 to 1964. He was an exacting leader, but creative and warm. Wallace Robeson (married to Ruth), was principal from 1967 to 1988, during which time he guided the school through another period of turmoil and adjustment in the Turkish Mission and in Turkish society.[60]

Among the "short termers" who have made significant contributions are Donald and Roxanne Scott Barry.[61] Although long employed (and currently teaching) at Phillips Andover Academy, Donald Barry continues to develop international mathematics competition materials for the three schools profiled here as well as for schools all over the world.

Haydar Gofer, a full-time Turkish literature teacher who served TAC from 1949 to 1980, was a highly influential faculty member there. He is so respected and loved by the graduates that tears come to the eyes

---

59. Johnson, *Paths of Learning*, 18.

60. See Stone, *Academies for Anatolia*, 312–16; Johnson, *Legacy of Education*, 20–29; and Bartholomew, *History of Tarsus*, 73. Other principals to note include Robert Avery (Elizabeth), Frank Stone (Barbara), Johannes Meyer (Sylvia Nilson), Don Kesselheim (Chelsea), and Alan McCain (Sally). McCain was general secretary of the Near East Mission from 1991 to 2001.

61. As the school enrollments grew, an increasing number of teachers were "short termers." These were usually young three-year appointees who brought energy, inventiveness, and a new idealism to the schools. A significant number of short termers extended their service, and some became career missionaries who served in administrative positions. Some others, such as William Griswold and Thomas Goodrich, became academicians specializing in Turkey area studies.

of some alumni when they speak of his warmth, good teaching, and wise guidance.[62]

Talas School for Boys

The Talas School for Boys was led by the highly energetic and innovative Paul Nilson (married to Harriet), from its reopening in 1927 until 1952. Following Nilson were Principal John Scott and his wife Gwendolyn, both of whom were known for their loving demeanor and resourceful patience. The Scotts helped their students immeasurably, enabling them to experience well and then to remember with joy their little community of learning in that remote school set in the rugged mountain terrain of central Turkey. Robert Keller (married to Dorothy Birge) was principal from 1961 to 1964, during which time he conducted research among graduates of the American Board schools in Turkey for a major conference on the future of those schools.[63]

Turkish teachers, who commuted from Kayseri, were faculty members committed to the ideals of the school. The Turks included Remzi Dincol, an affable teacher, and the Turkish associate principals: the much loved and long remembered Giyasettin Tokyay, Durmus Esen, and Mustafa Dulgeroglu.

MORE EFFORTS TO TEACH IDEALS

Frank Stone notes that in the modern period the ABCFM schools increased their efforts to teach ideals. With an emphasis on community service and development, the schools operated a number of "pioneer" service programs, including: 1) the development of work camps in villages (the first of which was a week-end work camp by Tarsus students and faculty in 1954); 2) the development of village bookmobiles, a service that was taken up by Turkish public schools and eventually by the Ministries of National Education and Village Affairs; 3) the offering of adult English courses for members of the community; 4) the distribution of a basic literacy booklet designed by the Izmir Social Service Club to teach village women; and 5) the use of student assistants to develop

---

62. See Johnson, *Legacy of Education*, 27; and Stone, *Academies for Anatolia*, 313.

63. Stone, *Academies for Anatolia*, 256, 294–96, 343.

school libraries, a program which helped a generation of Turkish young people to learn about operating a modern library system.[64]

For some of the students, community service experiences inspired life-long passions and careers. One such student was Altan Unver, who after graduating from Tarsus American College in 1957 and earning university degrees, returned to his alma mater in 1965. He taught math and economics and initiated numerous community outreach activities, including Fellowship House, a dormitory in Tarsus for village boys attending local public schools. For nearly a decade he worked as the director of the International Voluntary Work Camps Association/Turkey Country Program and as field director, project officer, and advisor for Social Service Community Development and Family Planning programs in Turkey.

In 1969, Unver became the principal founder and the secretary general of the Development Foundation of Turkey (*Turkiye Kalkinma Vakfi*-TKV). He was responsible for policy formation, fund raising, supervision of program, and project preparation and implementation until his death in 2005. He pioneered breakthroughs in rural Turkey in several areas: extending family planning to rural households, starting quality queen-bee breeding, designing the campaign against varroa mites in beekeeping, extending the production of vaccination for cattle, developing indigenous rural credit programs, and introducing an integrated poultry production model based on small holders. According to one historian, "Altan Unver's achievements have epitomized the spirit of altruism and concern for others that American Board Schools have imparted in their students."[65]

Another American Board school graduate with extraordinary energy, vision, and commitment is Gulgun Tezgider, a 1974 graduate of UAA. She had just retired from a career in advertising when the devastating earthquakes of August and November, 1999, occurred. When called to help, she hesitated not an instant, packed some goods to take to survivors, and went to the earthquake zones in northwestern Turkey to offer whatever services she could as translator, program designer, or community developer.

Tezgider still works in the disaster-hit region where earthquakes destroyed buildings, took many lives, and severely disrupted all infra-

64. Ibid., 284–87. Elizabeth Frank pioneered in this work at the ACI library.

65. See Johnson, *Legacy of Education*, 30; and Tezgider, "e-mail to author."

structure networks. Through her expertise in project management, she has contributed effectively to physical, social, and economic recovery projects. She has related positively with the local authorities to draw their focus to healthy community work, and she has contributed to the establishment of centers for women's work, family life, children's services, and medical care. She has also designed and implemented local disaster mitigation programs which have been shared with national and international institutions. When asked about her motivation for this hard work, she credited not only her social service minded family, but also the bookmobile and other social service projects in which she had participated at Uskudar American Academy.[66]

FORMATION OF SEV, THE HEALTH AND EDUCATION FOUNDATION

In 1968, when the Turkish law governing foreign schools changed to require transfer of property from foreign to local ownership, a Turkish non-profit foundation was formed by American Board personnel and graduates of the Board schools. Its English name is the Health and Education Foundation; its Turkish name, *Saglik ve Egitim Vakfi*, is often referred to by its acronym, "SEV," which means "love" in Turkish. The Foundation progressively assumed ownership of the school properties in the 1970s and 1980s, and by the late 1990s SEV had assumed full management and financial responsibility for the schools.[67]

On November 2, 2010, the Turkish Government began the process of transferring full, legal "Founder Status" from Wider Church Ministries (a successor to the ABCFM) to SEV. This transfer was completed in April, 2011, ending Wider Church Ministries' formal mission connection to the American Board schools in Turkey.[68]

FRIENDS OF THE AMERICAN BOARD SCHOOLS IN TURKEY, FABSIT

Parallel to the development of SEV in Turkey, the United Church Board for World Ministries (predecessor to Wider Church Ministries) began to reduce its support of the schools in Turkey because of economic

---

66. Tezgider, "e-mail to author."

67. Stone, *Academies for Anatolia*, 327.

68. Trajuillo, "Dear Friends letter."

constraints and a changed focus of mission. To have an organization in the USA to assume certain important American-based linkages to the schools, the Friends of the American Board Schools in Turkey, FABSIT, was formed in 1986. It is the secular heir to the ABCFM, and as a 501(c)3 organization it can collect and provide donations for tuition aid to students, building funds, and other expenses. Working with SEV, FABSIT has been able to channel over four million dollars in recent years from USAID's ASHA grants for the American Board schools' infrastructure projects and educational programs. It also supports the recruitment of professional educational personnel for the schools.[69]

NEW CHALLENGES AND CHANGES

A major change in the nature of the schools in Turkey began in 1978 when the Tarsus American College started phasing out its boarding program due to financial and staffing problems. The Uskudar American Academy and the American Collegiate Institute soon followed, and by the early 1990s boarding was no longer available in the schools, ending a tradition which had existed from their founding. However, with the new management and financial resources provided by SEV in recent years, the schools have been able to develop boarding programs again. This enables them to enroll high quality students from any part of Turkey.[70]

Another major change has been the schools' shift to become co-educational. Again Tarsus American College led the way, enrolling thirty-five girls in 1979. By its one hundredth anniversary in 1988, girls comprised over one third of its enrollment. The American Collegiate Institute in Izmir first admitted boys in 1986 and in 1990 the Uskudar American Academy began admitting boys.[71]

Beginning in the 1960s the American Board had increasing difficulty in finding qualified American educators who would commit themselves to career service in the Turkey schools. Along with causing financial problems, this led to the closing of the Talas School in 1967 and the transfer of its middle school students to the Tarsus American College, where most of the Talas graduates had been going for their high

69. Stone, *Academies for Anatolia*, 319–20.

70. See Ibid., 334; Johnson, *Enduring Transitions*, 23; and Johnson, *Legacy of Education*, 33.

71. See Johnson, *Enduring Transitions*, 23; Johnson, *Legacy of Education*, 34; and Johnson, *Paths of Learning*, 22–23.

school education.[72] Remarkably, the Talas graduates maintain a strong loyalty to each other and to their school through posting on a Talas 1889 Yahoo E-Group, holding monthly gatherings, and nurturing their connections in other ways.[73]

By 1990 the last of the American Board missionary principals had left Turkey. For more than a century, they had served as the dedicated and effective principals of the Board's schools in Turkey. After their departure, the schools recruited administrators from a variety of international sources for short-term service. They increasingly did this with teachers also.[74]

In 1997 the American Board schools underwent further evolution when Turkey changed from a five year to an eight year primary education system. The Board schools gradually phased out their middle schools, and SEV established K-8 primary schools at each site.[75]

Today, the three former American Board schools in Turkey, now SEV schools, are private secondary schools whose acceptance of students is based on a highly selective, nationally administered, entrance examination. The students, when admitted to the schools, study English for a year, followed by a four year college preparatory program. Mathematics, science, and language arts are taught in the English language. Social studies and the Turkish language subjects are taught in Turkish. A second foreign language, usually French or German, is also required. Supplementing the required offerings is a wide variety of electives designed to meet the students' interests and needs. Co-curricular activities span a multitude of interests, including a strong commitment to social service programs. The schools participate in national and international activities, including science fairs, mathematics competitions, music and theatre performances, sporting events, the European Youth Parliament, and Model United Nations events. The Uskudar American Academy hosts the annual Turkish International United Nations conference, which is attended by over 300 students from Turkey, Europe, Asia, and the Americas.

72. Bartholomew, *History of Tarsus*, 58.

73. Talas alumnus, Cem Baysal, started and still coordinates this vibrant e-mail group, which connects through regular exchanges hundreds of Talas alumni from all over the world.

74. Stone, *Academies for Anatolia*, 329.

75. Johnson, *Enduring Transitions*, 23.

The objective of the schools is to develop good Turkish citizens who are "Global Citizens" as well. This ideal unites faculty members from around the world, drawing in teachers from Canada, Great Britain, South Africa, Australia, New Zealand, and France, as well as from the United States and Turkey. Many of the Turkish faculty are bilingual and some are graduates of the Board schools. The three schools are accredited by the Turkish Ministry of Education and the Council of International Schools (CIS). In addition, the American Collegiate Institute and Tarsus American College participate in the International Baccalaureate Diploma Program. The graduates of the three schools have a very high level of success on university admission examinations and are admitted to prestigious universities in Turkey, Europe, and North America.[76]

In December 2010, nearly two centuries after the first ABCFM missionaries went into the area that is now Turkey, a "Commemoration Event for the Transfer of the 'Founder Status' of the Board Schools from Wider Church Ministries (WCM) to SEV" was held in Istanbul. Representing Global Ministries at this event were the three remaining missionaries in Turkey, Alison Stendahl and Kenneth and Elizabeth Frank, each of whom has lived and served in Turkey for almost 30 years. The Franks have served since 2003 with outstanding effectiveness as liaison administrators. They were joint general secretaries for *Amerikan Bord Heyeti/ American Board*, relating WCM and Global Ministries to SEV, and overseeing the final years of Board involvement with its schools and medical work in Turkey.

Representing the former ABCFM at the commemoration event was Peter Makari, WCM and Global Ministries area executive for the Middle East and Europe. Makari expressed his admiration of SEV: "Today, we feel much appreciation for the dedication that you give to the schools. We know that the schools are in the professional and extremely capable hands of people who care deeply for them, and we appreciate how you honor the Board's legacy. You indeed carry on the legacy, and our Board is proud of and grateful for your service and mission, and your love— *sev*—of the schools. Thank you."[77]

Looking to the future, Erhan Dumanli, head of the SEV Board of Directors, has affirmed that "the goal of SEV is to continue these vener-

76. Current information about each of the three schools is available on their websites, which are provided in the bibliography.

77. Makari, "Address," 2.

able institutions, and to guarantee that they will live for centuries more without the slightest loss of quality. And this is the most important philosophy behind SEV: to protect the past and be open to what is new, and to build for the future, taking strength from tradition."[78]

WHAT GOOD CAN BE DONE IN THE FUTURE

The motto of the Tarsus American College is "Leaders for Turkey, Leadership for the World." The American Collegiate Institute has a similarly inspirational motto: "Enter to Learn, Depart to Serve." Both mottos are descriptive of the goals and accomplishments of the graduates of the three SEV schools. With their American Board school training, and subsequent university education, the graduates from the schools have become leaders in many professions, both in Turkey and abroad. The educational programs of the American Board schools in Turkey have proven to be an excellent "means for doing good." Moreover, the schools' new identity as SEV high schools has enabled them to keep the American Board's educational mission alive.[79] The schools' graduating students today might well be told what the original ABCFM missionaries to Turkey once heard: "Now, as you graduate and go out into the world, see what good can be done and by what means."[80]

BIBLIOGRAPHY

Bartholomew, Alan A. *A History of Tarsus American School, 1888–1988*. Istanbul: Redhouse Press, 1988.

Birge, John Kingsley. "College and Y.M.C.A. in Smyrna." *The Missionary Herald* 116 (July 1920) 312–313.

78. Dumanli, *Bulusma*, 1.

79. "The mission of SEV/ABH Schools is to contribute to the growth of individuals who combine self-confidence with a firm sense of personal, social, and environmental responsibility. We aim to enable our students to be strong bilinguals in English and Turkish, well-educated adults, lifelong learners, and efficient communicators, who have developed skills, accountability, and attitudes for leading a fulfilling life and for serving their country and humanity." Online: www.uaa.k12.tr; click on General Information, Mission.

80. For the readers who wish to learn more about the American Board Schools in Turkey we recommend Frank Stone's *Academies for Anatolia*. His 2006 edition brings into this century the fruits of the depth and breadth of his life long research. His writing has vigor, yet compassion, and he has been completely accurate and faithful to the values which guided all of the ABCFM work in Turkey. He has equal appreciation and respect for Turkey as it emerged from empire into a successful democracy. His book can be ordered on line from FABSIT: www.fasit.org/program.books.php.

Birge, Robert B. Personal interviews regarding the life and work in Smyrna (Izmir), Turkey, of his father, John Kingsley Birge, 2001–2010.

Blemker, Margaret R. *150 Years in the Near East, United Church Board for World Ministries*. New York: Near East Office, UCBWM, 1969.

Dumanli, Erhan. "Hello Dear Alumni." *Bulusma* (September 2009). Online: http://www.sev.org.tr/dergi/eylul/index.html.

Johnson, Brian, *A Legacy of Education: The Growth and Transformation of Tarsus American College*, 1888-1988, Istanbul: Ofset Yapimevi, 2006.

———. *Changing Fonts: The Evolution of a Press*. Istanbul: Ofset Yapimevi, 2002.

———. *Enduring Transitions: A Brief History of Uskudar American Academy, Founded 1873*. Istanbul: Ofset Yapimevi, 2010.

———. *Paths of Learning: A Chronicle of the American Collegiate Institute and Associated Schools in Izmir*. Izmir: Ofset Yapimevi, 2004.

Lindar, Fay. *The History of Uskudar American Academy, 1876–1996*. Istanbul: SEV Printing, 2000.

Makari, Peter. "Address at Commemoration Event for the Transfer of School Ownership" (December 3, 2010). Unpublished text obtained from author.

Putney, Ethel. *A Brief History of American Board Schools in Turkey*. Istanbul: Nesriyat Dairesi, 1964.

Shelton, Elizabeth. "Faith, Freedom, and Flag: The Influence of American Missionaries in Turkey on Foreign Affairs, 1830–1880." PhD diss., Georgetown University, 2011.

Stone, Frank Andrews. *Academies for Anatolia: A Study of the Rationale, Program and Impact of the Educational Institutions Sponsored by the American Board in Turkey, 1830–2005*. San Francisco: Caddo Gap, 2006.

Trajuillo, Eric. "Dear Friends Letter" (December 2010). Online: http://www.uaa.k12.tr; click on "Announcement about transference of founderhip."

Websites of Schools: www.aci.k12.tr; www.tac.k12.tr; www.uaa.k12.tr.

5

Dr. Ruth A. Parmelee and the Changing Role of Near East Missionaries in Early Twentieth Century Turkey

Virginia A. Metaxas

I N EARLY 1919, DR. Ruth Parmelee, an ABCFM medical missionary who had served in Turkey from 1914 until 1917, returned to the field with two hundred and fifty men and women relief workers, the first to enter the country after World War I. She went to provide medical relief under the auspices of two newly formed organizations, Near East Relief and the American Women's Hospitals.[1] As her colleague Dr. Mark Ward would say, relief work in Turkey was in a state of transition. From the middle of the nineteenth century until the First World War, missionaries had "won the respect of the people" along "evangelistic, educational and medical" lines. Between 1915 and 1919, he said, "funds sent from America for relief were handled by the American missionaries." But Ward observed that after 1919, when the work was "greatly enlarged and many new workers were added to the force already on the ground . . . a new era . . . [was inaugurated] . . . in [Turkey] under the Near East Relief."[2]

1. Ruth A. Parmelee, *A Pioneer in the Euphrates Valley*, 34–35. According to James L. Barton, relief units were stationed in twenty one locations: Adana, Aintab, Angora, Brusa, Caesarea, Constantinople, Derindje, Diarbekr, Izmit, Kharput, Konia, Malatya, Marash, Mardin, Marsovan, Samsun, Sivas, Smyrna, Tarsus, Trebizond, and Urfa. See Barton, *The Story of Near East Relief, 141.* For a recent treatment of Barton's work in Near East Relief, see Carpenter, "A Worldly Errand: James L. Barton's American Mission to the Near East."

2. Ward, "The Americans in Harpoot." Dr. Ward was a missionary physician and

This chapter describes the history of American missionaries in Turkey from the mid-nineteenth century until the early 1920s, paying particular attention to the life and work of Dr. Ruth Parmelee, an American physician born in Turkey to missionary parents in the mid-1880s. After describing the general history of missionary work in the Near East, the chapter details the years 1914–1919, a time in which missionaries shifted their focus, providing not only charity and education, but also what Joseph M. Grabill called "Protestant Diplomacy."[3] During this time, Parmelee embodied the dual missionary goals. In addition to dispensing medical care, education, and other forms of relief in the field, she also took on the role of reporter of vital information to the American public—especially the plight of Christian Armenians and Greeks in the area. The reporting of conditions in the field accomplished two things: the raising of funds so that relief work could continue; and the influencing of American attitudes that might underlay the country's political relations with Turkey.

American missionaries first appeared in Turkey when the ABCFM established a mission in Constantinople in 1831.[4] In the 1850s, there were only a few hundred students in the missionary schools, but by 1914, nearly 25,000 Greek and Armenian Christian students attended the several hundred missionary schools scattered all around Turkey.[5] According to an official census of the ABCFM, American staff of the Protestant missions in Turkey consisted in 1919 of 50 ordained ministers, 71 un-ordained men, 61 wives, 104 unmarried American women, and over 1,300 "native" personnel, most of whom staffed the schools, hospitals, and presses run by the ABCFM.[6] American and "native" women notably outnumbered men in the educational, social, religious, and medical functions conducted under the auspices of the ABCFM.

Studying the life of physician Ruth Azniv Parmelee (1885–1973) helps us to understand the drive and motivation of many of the American missionaries in the Near East. It is difficult not to see her as a heroic figure. She spent her entire life working to better the living conditions and

---

Acting Director of Near East Relief, January 10-April 1, 1921.

3. Grabill, *Protestant Diplomacy in the Near East: Missionary Influence on American Policy, 1810–1927.*

4. Daniel, *American Philanthropy in the Near East, 1820–1960,* 42.

5. Grabill, "Missionary Influence on American Relations with the Near East."

6. Bierstadt, *The Great Betrayal: A Survey of the Near East Problem,* 266.

health of the Armenians and Greeks who were caught up in the violence and war that occurred in the region between the late nineteenth century and the mid-twentieth century.[7] Her devotion to humanitarian work was something she internalized in childhood; it was almost unavoidable given her family background, in which work and sacrifice was the norm. Both of her parents served as role models for the adult woman whom Dr. Parmelee would become.

Ruth Parmelee's father, Moses Payson Parmelee, M.D., graduated from Union Seminary in 1861. Two years later, in April 1863, Parmelee married Nellie A. Frost, and shortly thereafter the young couple set off as missionaries to Erzrum (Ezurum) Turkey.[8] The births of two daughters, Addie (born in 1864) and Jennie (born in 1866), delighted the Parmelees, but this happiness was short-lived. In February 1870, Jennie, "considered to be more vivacious than the shy and reserved Addie," died of diphtheria at four years of age.[9] Her mother Nellie, after a long struggle with tuberculosis, died less than two weeks afterward, leaving Addie and the Reverend Doctor Parmelee in deep mourning. Surrounded by a small group of American missionaries, and a collection of "sympathizing Armenian friends," the Reverend Doctor Parmelee buried his dear wife and daughter within sight of the missionary house sitting room. Shortly after that, and probably adding to six-year-old Addie's traumatic loss, Parmelee left for a journey into the interior, during which time he found solace for himself in relieving "the distresses of others."[10] Addie, the "motherless girl," was left with one of the missionary women, Mrs.

7. Dr. Parmelee left a very thorough record of her work, much of which is in a collection at the Hoover Institution Archives' holdings on International Relief at Stanford University. This collection includes diaries, notes, correspondence, reports, clippings, printed matter, and photographs relating to Parmelee's refugee relief work and medical service in the Near East and Greece from 1914–1945. The Records of the American Women's Hospitals, located at Drexel University College of Medicine Archives and Special Collections on Women in Medicine (Philadelphia, Pennsylvania) hold a great deal of material about Parmelee's work in Greece as well.

8. Vinton, *Vinton Book, Volume III, Near East American Board Missions to 1886 in the Near East; ABCFM in Turkey*, 80–81. Moses Payson Parmelee was born on May 4, 1834, in Westford, Vermont. Julia Farr Parmelee was born on November1, 1840, in Williamstown, Massachusetts.

9. Moses P. Parmelee, *Home and Work by the Rivers of Eden*, 42. According to an online family geneology database, Adeline Parmelee grew to adulthood, married Frederick S. Johnson, and died in 1912. (Parmelee Family website: http://www.geocities.com/mrjimwalters/index.html.)

10. Moses P. Parmelee, *Home and Work*, 41–53.

Pierce, as her father traveled 100 miles away to Kars, an Armenian city that the missionaries saw as "an important strategic point in our religious work." There, and in neighboring towns, Parmelee and his missionary companions taught the Protestant Bible to native Armenians, using modern Armenian, which apparently attracted much attention, since most were not used to hearing the Gospel in anything but the ancient form of their native tongue.[11]

In 1871, during a trip back in the United States with Addie, the Reverend Doctor Parmelee married Julia Farr Parmelee, another woman who was enthusiastic about serving as a missionary wife. In 1872 they went to Turkey, he to continue his medical and religious work, and she to be his helpmate and model Christian wife.[12] Over the next ten years, the missionary couple moved from Erzrum to Trebizond (Trabzon), Turkey, and they produced several children. The first to arrive was Isabella, born in 1872. Another daughter, Charlotte, born in 1876, and a son, Edward Lewis, born in 1878, both died in early childhood in 1880. The Parmelees returned to the United States for a few years after the deaths of their children because Julia had fallen into ill health. The American Board hesitated to send the Parmelees back into the field until "medical authority" determined Julia's well-being.[13] This the couple finally obtained in 1882, when physicians from the Clifton Springs Sanitarium in upstate New York wrote a certificate stating that Julia was physically able to return "to her much loved field of labor."[14] After convalescing at the sanitorium, and getting back on her feet, Julia returned to Turkey with her husband, to be placed in a new and more isolated station, which somewhat alarmed Dr. Parmelee, who worried that his wife might not fare well there.[15] His worries were unfounded; they adjusted well and

---

11. Ibid., 49–51.

12. Vinton, *Vinton Book*, Volume III, Near East, 41, 80–81.

13. Moses Parmelee to Nathaniel Clark, February 23, 1882, ABCFM Papers, Reel 623. Several libraries own copies of the ABCFM papers on microfilm. I used the microfilms at the Divinity School Library at Yale University.

14. Certificate signed by two physicians (illegible signatures) dated March 24, 1882 in ABCFM Papers, Reel 623.

15. Moses Parmelee to Nathaniel Clark, February 23, 1882, ABCFM Papers, Reel 623; Moses Parmelee to Nathaniel Clark, November 20, 1880, ABCFM Papers, Reel 623. Dr. Parmelee wrote several times of his concerns about going to Trebizond, on the Black Sea and far from any seaport in the Mediterranean. Eventually he gave in and agreed to go there with his family.

produced three more children, all of whom survived to adulthood. Their son Maurice was born in 1882, their son Julius in 1883. Ruth, the only child who would closely follow her parents into missionary work in her adult life, was born on the third of April, 1885.[16]

The role of women in missionary work changed during the two generations of time in which Julia and Ruth lived and worked in Turkey. In the early years of missionary presence in the Near East, wives were expected to serve as "helpmates" to their husbands, but by the end of the nineteenth century, missionary wives and single women who traveled to foreign lands played a more public role by involving themselves in schools, orphanages, and other missionary institutions.[17] As a result of educational reforms that were designed to educate girls and boys in secular schools in Central Turkey, Eastern Turkey, and the European Ottoman territories, many new schools were established, ranging from kindergartens to high schools and even including colleges and seminaries. These schools needed teachers, and hundreds of educated women were recruited from America to serve. Christian Greek and Armenian girls and women attended these secular schools while most Turkish women attended Islamic Ottoman schools, where reforms were also underway. By the end of the nineteenth century, the American missionary schools were widening educational opportunities for young people throughout the Ottoman Empire, even making higher education accessible for women as well as men.[18]

The education of missionary children differed from that of most of their Near Eastern counterparts. Most American children were returned to the United States after receiving a primary education in the territory in which their parents served. In a speech given several decades after leaving Turkey, Julius, the son of Julia and Moses Parmelee, gave an account of the childhood he shared with his siblings at the mission in Trebizond.[19] He described the mission house as a large three story

16. Ruth Parmelee's birth date comes from "Outline of the Work of Dr. Ruth Parmelee," Ruth Parmelee Papers, Stanford University. Birth and death dates of Parmelee family children taken from a Parmelee Family website(http://www.geocities .com/mrjimwalters/index.html) and a family group record received via email in April 2006 from Jim Walters of Long Beach, California, who keeps the online database.

17. Giannuli, "'Errand of mercy': American women missionaries and philanthropists in the Near East, 1820–1930," 221–62.

18. Ibid., 234–34.

19. Julius H. Parmelee, "Turkey: the Crescent Republic," (1937), 11. A copy of this

building in which they lived and worked. Part of the building was their living quarters; another section was where his mother Julia and other missionary wives taught school. On the first floor was the consulting office where his physician father "held clinics, gave medical treatment, administered vaccinations, and prepared his medicines." The family had three full-time and several part-time Greek and Armenian servants to help run the household, including a cook, a maid, a gardener and repairman, a "sewing girl," a "laundress," and "an occasional cleaning woman." Although the children's "official" education was obtained from their parents, Julius said that their "unofficial" education was derived from their nursemaids, from whom they learned to speak Armenian and Greek "as rapidly as [they] did English." [20] Ruth's education followed the typical pattern of many missionary children, who were usually sent to the United States for a formal schooling. Ruth stated that she had "[s]tudied with [her] parents and did not go to school until coming to the United States at eleven years of age when she entered sixth grade." She "[p]repared for college in Oberlin High School," graduating in 1901 at sixteen years of age.[21] Ruth returned to Turkey to be with her parents after graduation.[22]

Ruth's going to the United States during her adolescence resembled her elder sister Isabella's educational experience. Rev. Dr. Parmelee sent Isabella to live with his brother's family in the United States at the age of fourteen, saying that she "needed the advantages of a good school. She had pursued her studies alone, with such help as we could give her," but the time finally came for her to receive an American education. Her father later wrote about the difficulty the family had in separating from Isabella, explaining that "she had grown to be companion to us all," and

---

speech is in Ruth Parmelee Papers, Box 3, folder marked "miscellaneous." Julius does not mention his half-sister Addie in this account of his childhood. Addie, Reverend Parmelee's daughter from his first marriage, had probably already been sent to the United States for her education.

20. *Ibid.*

21. "Outline of the work of Dr. Ruth Parmelee" Ruth Parmelee Papers, Box 1, Stanford University.

22. In *A Pioneer in the Euprhates Valley*, Dr. Parmelee mentions meeting Dr. and Mrs. H. H. Atkinson in her party when she crossed the ocean in 1901, (5). The Atkinsons helped to ensure her appointment to the Harpoot mission station after her completion of medical school. In *A Pioneer in the Euprhates Valley*, she mentions a "teenage visit" to her home in Trebizond (7).

that "the separation . . . caused indescribable bitterness."[23] In later years, Julia Parmelee recalled a period of estrangement from her eldest daughter, "who had always been the apple of [her] eye." In the summer of 1895, word came that Isabella was suffering a "long illness," which prompted her mother to return to the United States to oversee her recovery. Isabella refused to see her mother at first upon Mrs. Parmelee's arrival in the States, even though the two had been separated for seven years. When Julia insisted on seeing Isabella, she promised to "make a little home for us," to which her daughter replied "I have a home!" (underlining in original) This exchange took place in August; not until November did Isabella finally sort out her feelings enough to make a reunion possible. Julia also noticed that her husband's relatives, with whom Isabella lived, were "cool" towards Julia and the younger children. She worried that they might think she was ungrateful, which was far from the truth. On the contrary, she was very appreciative of all they had done for her daughter and she was filled with shame and anguish because of the tensions she sensed. [24]

Once reunited, Mrs. Parmelee, Isabella, and her brother Maurice, who had traveled to the states with his mother from Turkey, spent some time at a sanatorium in Clifford Springs, New York. By winter, Mrs. Parmelee and Maurice traveled to visit family in the Midwest. Maurice stayed with his oldest sister, Addie, who by then was married to a businessman. They lived in a small town near Lincoln, Nebraska, and Maurice later wrote in his autobiography of the delightful time he spent fishing, boating, and swimming with his "ardent sportsman brother-in-law."[25] In the meantime, violent events in Turkey occurred which would spur the Parmelees to remove all of their children from the field.

While Mrs. Parmelee was still in New York, a local Rochester newspaper reported massacres of Armenians by Turks taking place in the area where her husband and youngest children, Julius and Ruth, resided.[26] It took days before she received a cable stating that the Americans were unharmed. Ruth witnessed the atrocities, in which at least six

23. Moses P. Parmelee, *Home and Work By the Rivers of Eden*, 192.

24. Julia F. Parmelee to Dr. Judson Smith, August 6, 1901, ABCFM Papers, Reel 623.

25. Maurice Parmelee, "Autobiography, Later Draft," 34–35, Maurice Parmelee Papers, Box 3.

26. Dr. Judson Smith to Julia F. Parmelee, August 6, 1901, ABCFM Papers, Reel 623.

hundred people were killed.[27] More massacres in other nearby cities followed, lasting until 1896. The violence undoubtedly led the Parmelees to send the remaining children to school in America, where they would be out of harm's way. Moses P. Parmelee accompanied Ruth and Julius to the States in 1896, rejoining his wife there.[28] The Parmelees, along with Maurice, Julius, and Ruth, met in Oberlin, Ohio, and the children were quickly settled into the newly founded Tank Home for Missionary Children.[29] Mrs. Parmelee stayed at Oberlin for a year, studying French, before she rejoined her husband in the field. All three children enrolled in the high school in Oberlin, and later in Oberlin College. Ruth graduated from Oberlin College in 1901, but her brothers transferred to Yale to finish their baccalaureate degrees.[30]

By 1897, the Parmelees "gladly" returned to Turkey to continue their work.[31] When their daughter Ruth graduated from Oberlin High School in 1901, they persuaded the ABCFM to allow her to return to Turkey to be with them. By this time, her father Moses was chronically ill with bladder and prostate problems, and Julia longed to have Ruth with her for emotional support. In a letter to the Board, Julia reminded them that she had "no female companions [in Trebizond at that time] speaking [her] mother tongue."[32] In 1902, Ruth's father died in Beirut, where he had gone for a surgical operation.[33] Julia later said that when her husband brought "his baby girl to come and spend a year with us [it] was . . . a blessed year" indeed. Ruth had only been twelve years old when she left for Oberlin; her return at the age of sixteen allowed her, in her mother's mind, to "appreciate her father" as an older child would, and to see her father "endure" his sufferings, which were "great, as a hero."[34] Perhaps this experience inspired Ruth to pursue a career in medicine; certainly it brought her closer to her mother. According to

27. Ruth Parmelee, *A Pioneer in the Euprhates Valley*, 15.

28. Julia Parmelee, "Excerpt from Talk by Julia Parmelee (Mrs. M.P.)," April 22, 1903, in Ruth A. Parmelee Papers, Box 2, Stanford University.

29. "Tank Home," 311.

30. Julia F. Parmelee, "Excerpt from a talk by Julia Parmelee (Mrs. M.P.)," April 22, 1903, in Ruth A. Parmelee Papers, Box 2, Stanford University.

31. Julia F. Parmelee to Dr. Judson Smith, August 6, 1901, ABCFM Papers, Reel 623.

32. *Ibid.*

33. Vinton, *Vinton Book*, Volume III, Near East, 80–81.

34. Julia F. Parmelee to Dr. Judson Smith, November 15, 1902, ABCFM Papers, Reel 623.

ABCFM records, Julia and Ruth left Turkey and returned to the United States around 1903.[35] Yet it would only be a matter of time before they would go back to their beloved missionary work in Turkey.

෧ ෧ ෧

The ABCFM appointed Dr. Ruth Parmelee as a medical missionary in January 1914, just two years after she finished her medical education at the University of Illinois, and immediately following her internship at the Philadelphia Women's Hospital in 1913. Having gained much practical experience in laboratory work and in obstetrical and gynecological practice during her internship, Dr. Parmelee was more than eager to get to work as soon as she could.[36] A few days after her appointment had been announced, she wrote in her diary, "I am glad to be of service—that is what I need."[37]

After a few months of preparation, Dr. Parmelee and her mother left together for the Harpoot (Harput) Turkey missionary station, which was described in an ABCFM brochure as "a center of influence in Eastern Turkey." Harpoot was located "near the headwaters of the Tigris and Euprhates Rivers, [and] on the hills and plains surrounded by the lofty ranges of the Taurus and Anti-Taurus Mountains . . . in the very heart of Armenia." To reach the town, one had to travel 380 miles by sea from Constantinople to Samsoon (Samsun) on the Black Sea, and then journey by horseback another 320 miles south.[38]

35. Vinton, *Vinton Book*, Volume III, Near East, 41.

36. See "Outline of the Work of Dr. Ruth Parmelee"; and Ruth A. Parmelee, "A Line a Day" diary, 1913–1916. I have not been able to find any information about Ruth Parmelee from the time she departed from Turkey in 1902 to her graduation from medical school in 1912.

37. Ruth A. Parmelee, "A Line a Day" diary,1913–1916. This quote was taken from an entry written on January 7, 1914, less than a week after the ABCFM had appointed Parmelee as a full-fledged medical missionary.

38. "Harpoot Station." brochure, ABCFM Papers, reel 714.

Figure 12. Harpoot Staff Unit, August 1919: Front left, little girl seated on the carpet is Beatrice Arshalouys Dingilian, affectionately called "Bessie" by Miss Maria P. Jacobsen, who is seated next to her (Bessie was adopted by Miss Jacobsen); Dr. Ruth A. Parmelee; Anna R. Ward, wife of Dr. Mark H. Ward. Second row seated, Karen M. Petersen; (?); (?); Henry H. Riggs; Henry H. Riggs' sister, Mary W. Riggs; Dr. Mark H. Ward. Third row standing, Frances C. MacDaniels; unidentified nurse, possibly Pearl G. Larson; Cornelius Janney; Margaret H. Niles; Lee Vrooman; Laurence H. MacDaniels; Florence M. Stively, nurse; Gardiner C. Means. Photo courtesy of the Oberlin College Archives.

Dr. Parmelee's mother Julia had already done over three decades of missionary work, but in spite of her experience it is surprising that she was given permission to go to Harpoot. At the time of the journey, Julia was seventy-four years of age, and in poor health. She had suffered a stroke in 1906 and was in a semi-invalid state, being partially paralyzed on her left side.[39] Nevertheless, her presence in Turkey was important to Ruth, who might not have gone there without her mother. Dr. Parmelee was close to her mother, and even though she was among the first generation of American women to get a university education and a medical degree, her family responsibilities still strongly influenced her decisions[40] Simply put, her professional endeavors did not negate her duties to take care of her ailing mother. During her internship, for example, Dr. Parmelee lived very close to her mother's home in

39. Ruth A. Parmelee *A Pioneer in the Euprhates Valley*, 5.

40. For discussions of the "family claim" see Antler, "'After College, What?' New Graduates and the Family Claim,"409–34; and Antler, "Was She a Good Mother?," 57.

Philadelphia so that she could visit her often and supervise her live-in nurse. In February 1913, when Mrs. Parmelee's nurse "left town," Dr. Parmelee took over her mother's care, even making a visit to "combe" [sic] her mother's hair. Mrs. Parmelee spoke of finding a replacement nurse, which relieved Dr. Parmelee of her worries. Writing in her diary, she noted that her mother would no longer have to "depend on me in my uncertain life."[41] Uncertainty in life would become second-hand to Dr. Parmelee in Turkey, for she got there at the outset of the First World War and the infamous "Armenian deportations."

In 1914, Reverend James L. Barton, who would later head Near East Relief, said that "Turkey stood . . . at the focal center of . . . conflicting international political forces."[42] As the Ottoman Empire underwent its final death throes in the first decades of the twentieth century, several of the European powers circled the Empire like vultures, hoping to gain economic and territorial pieces of it. Germany had already "strength-ened her hold on Turkey" by building a Berlin-Baghdad railroad that guaranteed access to Near East resources. Even though Barton saw this was a "peaceful [and] economic penetration," he believed the Germans clearly had a "military advantage" in mind. Russia had territorial ambi-tion in its "envious intentions toward the Bosphorus and the Dardanelles as an ice-free outlet into the Mediterranean." The British had an interest in maintaining clear access to the Suez Canal, on the western boundary of Turkey, which would provide them with continuous access to their colonial interests in India and Australia. The French, "always eager to expand" according to Barton, had an eye on Syria. The Italians wanted financial and trade access to Rhodes and Adalia, in Southwestern Anatolia.[43] These various parties handled the "vexing Turkish question" sometimes in concert but more often in conflict, and the Turkish gov-ernment in turn "placed no confidence in the pretensions of friendship of the European nations."[44]

The Empire's suspicions were well grounded, given the territorial losses it had already sustained in nearly a century of conflicts and wars.

41. Ruth A. Parmelee, "A Line A Day" diary, February 25, 1913.

42. Barton, *Story of Near East Relief*, 21.

43. Ibid., 30.

44. Ibid., 31. Relevent secondary works include: Lewis, *The Emergence of Modern Turkey*; Quataert, *The Ottoman Empire 1700–192*; Shaw and Shaw, *History of the Ottoman Empire and Modern Turkey*, 2 vols.; Zurcher, *Turkey, A Modern History*.

Greece, Bulgaria, Serbia, Romania, Bosnia, Herzegovina, Albania and Macedonia had "one by one . . . revolted and won their independence," as Barton put it. By the time the Balkan Wars ended in the 1910s, Turkey's only "foothold" in Europe was "Constantinople and East Thrace." It still held Asia Minor, Mesopotamia, Kurdistan, Syria, Palestine and Arabia, and it was in these territories and in this context of shifting and contested national boundaries that the new Young Turk Party, established in 1909, struggled to achieve its goal of developing a modern nation state.[45]

Along with pressures and conflicts coming from the outside, Turkey struggled with internal strife. Building a modern nation-state is inherently a violent project, often including what we call today 'ethnic cleansing.' Within Turkey's many territories lived non-Turkish ethnic groups such as Arabs, Armenians, Greeks, Kurds, and Syrians, populations who had lived side by side with the majority ethnic Turks well before the establishment of the Empire. Violent conflicts between Christian and Muslim populations had a long history in the Empire. In particular, clashes between the majority population of Turks and the Armenian minority group flared up with frequency. After the Ottoman Empire began seriously to decline in the nineteenth century, Armenians suffered severe legal, political, and economic discrimination together with several armed attacks. As Christians in the Empire, they had little legal recourse to defend themselves, even after some minor reforms were instituted in the latter part of the nineteenth century. Numerous massacres of Armenians took place between the years 1894–1896; others occurred in 1909, even as Turkey began to modernize under the Young Turk Party.[46] Its new constitution promised democratization and fair treatment of minorities, and for a short time Armenians were hopeful that their oppression would end and that they would be considered full citizens, with representation in Parliament and opportunities to serve in government posts. But that hope was cruelly dashed. In 1915, the "Ottoman government inaugurated severe repressive measures against minority groups whose loyalty to the Empire was suspect." The Armenians in particular were singled out for extermination.[47]

---

45. Barton, *Story of Near East Relief*, 21.

46. Ruth Parmelee mentioned witnessing a massacre of Armenians in Trebizond in 1895 in *A Pioneer in the Euphrates Valley*, 15.

47. Daniel, "The Armenian Question and American-Turkish Relations, 1914–1917," 252–76.

During the First World War, Turkey aligned with Germany against the Allied powers, fighting the French and the British on the west, the Russians on the east, and a perceived enemy within: Armenians with ambitions for an independent Armenia. The vast majority of the Armenian population in Turkey lived in the area adjacent to Russia; indeed many ethnic Armenians lived within Russia itself. During the war the Turkish military and government, suspicious of Armenian loyalty, took the opportunity to solve "the Armenian problem" once and for all. In 1915, the military was given orders to eliminate Armenian community leaders. Armenian soldiers serving in the Turkish army were separated and executed. Also in 1915, the Turkish government gave a general order for Armenians all over the country to prepare for "deportation." Soon thousands were marched into the deserts of Syria, Mesopotamia, and Arabia. Many were executed or died of starvation and exhaustion along the way. Thousands of women were raped or abducted and taken into what Americans called "Turkish harems." Thousands of children were left orphaned. At least a million and a half Armenians died in this horrendous genocide of 1915–1916.[48]

People in the U.S. first learned about the genocide from the American missionaries who were located in stations all around Turkey. As the Turkish military began rounding up Armenian men and boys and ordering the Armenians to disarm, the missionaries sounded an alarm. They also encouraged their supporters in America to organize relief efforts. The American ambassador to Turkey, Henry Morgenthau, Sr., supported such efforts. The State Department worked with the ABCFM, encouraging the latter to raise funds for emergency relief. James L. Barton and Cleveland H. Dodge organized the American Committee for Armenian and Syrian Relief in 1915, and through public rallies and church collections the Committee raised millions to save "the starving Armenians." Funds and supplies were funneled through the American embassy in Constantinople, and distributed by missionaries in Turkey. In 1918, the organization was renamed the American Committee for Relief in the Near East. A year later it was incorporated by an act of Congress and came to be known as Near East Relief.[49] This big and very

48. See Barton, *Story of Near East Relief*, 3–69; and Daniel, "The Armenian Question and American-Turkish Relations, 1914–1917," 252–276. See also Ruth Parmelee, *A Pioneer in the Euphrates Valley*, 14–16; and Rockwell, *The Deportation of the Armenians*.

49. See Barton, *Story of Near East Relief, passim*; Morgenthau, *An International*

important organization, which stayed in operation until 1930, can be credited with largely saving ethnic Armenians from extinction.

Figure 13. Cover of Dr. Ruth A. Parmelee's Book.

Dr. Parmelee made a thorough record of her work in Turkey during the years 1914–1917, when she served as a missionary physician. She also kept records in 1919–1922, during which time she worked under the auspices of Near East Relief and the American Women's Hospitals. Some of her accounts were in her diaries; others were in the correspondence she had with U.S. authorities in the missionary organizations and relief agencies. In materials sent during the First World War, she was

Drama; and Morgenthau, *I Was Sent to Athens*. By 1930, when Near East Relief ended operations, it had distributed over one hundred million dollars in aid. It delivered food, clothing and materials for shelter from America, and had set up refugee camps, clinics, hospitals, and orphanages for over 132,000 orphans.

prudent in her descriptions of how the Turkish authorities interacted with the missionaries and the Armenian people, because she feared that her mail or personal papers would be seized and read. She censored herself, yet she made it clear to the reader that she was doing so. In one letter to a friend she managed to get information through about the Turkish atrocities against the Armenians by using code language that signaled the reader to lift the stamp and see her secret message. "I am glad you are so good a fisherman," Dr. Parmelee wrote at the end of the letter, alerting the reader to "fish" under the "pool" (i.e., stamp), where she found the following words: "[W]hen the people were hauled to the government buildings, most let off, some exiled. That probably means death. Our summer camping region is now filled with bodies. Cruel Manner."[50]

This communication may have been sent before the Turkish authorities uncovered a secret code that had been devised by the missionaries. Dr. Parmelee spoke of having knowledge of that code, and making "haste to destroy it and other papers such as carbon copies of letters . . . . Sure enough, [she said] we had our turn at being searched . . . [and] it did discourage us from keeping any sort of a record, not even a diary, from that time on."[51] Later, after the war ended, the papers and speeches that she wrote were more passionately outspoken with regard to the violence she had seen the Turks do to the Armenians. Clearly she wanted to ensure continued American support for the Armenian cause. In these materials there is also a very good recounting of the ways whereby the missionary medical facilities were taken over by the Turkish military or government for their own uses during and after the war, and how she and others coped with these incidents.

Almost immediately after Turkey mobilized for the war, American missionaries felt the effects. Two of the ABCFM's Euphrates College buildings were requisitioned by the Turkish government to be used as barracks for the army. Then a third building that had been used as a boys' dormitory was taken, causing severe problems for the school authorities. In April 1915, Dr. Parmelee estimated that about two thousand soldiers were living in the missionary buildings.[52] A telephone system which

50. Ellen W. Catlin to Miss Daniels, January 16, 1916, ABCFM Papers, Reel 714. In this letter, Caitlin quotes from a postcard she received from Ruth Parmelee, dated November 9, 1915.

51. Ruth Parmelee, *A Pioneer in the Euphrates Valley*, 25–26.

52. Ruth Parmelee, "A Line a Day" diary, April 6, 1915.

had allowed the missionary group in Harpoot to stay in touch with the ABCFM's Annie Tracy Riggs Hospital and the American Consulate on the plain some miles away was later confiscated. Parmelee and the others felt isolated, not being able to get either local or outside news. Supplies became scarce, and finally the Harpoot hospital in which Dr. Parmelee worked was taken by the Turkish army and filled with soldiers.

As wartime conditions worsened, Dr. Parmelee threw herself directly into her medical work. Not allowed to admit women patients into the hospital any longer, she took some rooms in the city of Harpoot and opened a clinic there with her Armenian student nursing assistant, Sarra Saprichian. Since many Turkish and Armenian physicians had been drafted into the army, she and Sarra filled an emergency need to take care of Turkish and Armenian patients in their homes—especially but not exclusively women and children. They made their own sterile supplies, using a coal-heated iron and boiling water made with a kitchen tea kettle, and set up packages for home visits that held clean towels and bandages. Realizing a need for trained midwives, Dr. Parmelee started a class in which she taught five Euphrates College graduates basic anatomy, physiology, nursing, and obstetrics. The students accompanied her to help patients deliver in their poverty-stricken homes. As the war wore on and more refugees began to enter the city from the countryside to escape the deportations, Dr. Parmelee's clinic grew busier and busier. [53]

53. Ruth Parmelee, *A Pioneer in the Euphrates Valley,* 8–18. Sarra, an Armenian graduate from Euphrates College, had been accepted to the Bellevue Hospital School of Nursing in New York City, but the war prevented her from going. She survived the Armenian genocide and eventually ended up in New York City, serving as a graduate staff nurse in New York Hospital for 25 years before retiring.

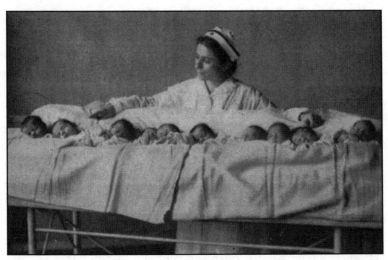

Figure 14. Sister Sarra. This woman, refugee from Turkey, served with the American Women's Hospitals at Salonica and Kokinia, Greece, 1922–27. She was graduated from the Bellevue School of Nursing, New York City, in 1933. [Source: Esther Pohl Lovejoy, *Certain Samaritans,* 1927.]

In her diary, Dr. Parmelee chronicled the atrocities she heard of and witnessed. One entry reads: "In Harpoot the first shocking action by the local government in carrying out this deportation order was the arrest and imprisonment on May 1st, 1915, of some eight hundred leading Armenian men." These tradesmen, merchants, and professional men were tortured in prison, "with the use of medieval methods [in order] to elicit confession of plots against the government, the preparation of bombs, or of where they had hidden fire-arms." Sarra's father was among a group of leaders who had been tied together and massacred late one night in a deserted spot away from town. While most of the male leaders were still in prison, the directive came for the rest of the Armenian community to be deported. This meant certain death for most of those forced to leave their homes. Dr. Parmelee managed to save Sarra's life by insisting that she needed her help with medical work. Sarra's sister Altoon was likewise saved by a cousin who taught in a nearby German Mission. [54]

54. Ruth Parmelee, *A Pioneer in the Euphrates Valley,* 16–19. Altoon Saprichian survived and worked as a kindergarten teacher in Turkey and in Greece (with Armenian refugees) for 34 years.

In the next few months, Dr. Parmelee's worst fears about the fate of her Armenian friends came true. In late May, all arms were collected from the Armenians. Rumors abounded about the destiny of Armenian soldiers, who had been "sent off—where, and for what?" By late June, they heard that all the Armenians would be exiled by the following week. Some tried to bribe officials or hide; others promised to become what Dr. Parmelee called "Mohammedan." The missionaries saw fires on the horizon, theorizing that they probably signaled the burning of nearby villages. By July, Dr. Parmelee concluded that the "attempt to extirminate [sic] a nation is diabolic, to the extreme," because she had heard that both men and women were being massacred *en masse*. By late September, word came that no more Armenians would be exiled; she hoped it was true.[55] But in November 1915, the Armenians of Harpoot were dragged before the Turkish governor and told that they would be deported. For some unknown reason, the orders were cancelled, and although the Armenians were grievously mistreated, the threat of death ended, at least temporarily.

During the summer of 1915, Dr. Parmelee and some of the missionary women visited an exile camp in Mezereh (Meszre), the town below theirs.[56] She would later write a report about what she saw there for the missionary authorities in Boston. They found the people "in wretched condition," wearing filthy and ragged clothing. Hunger, illness and emotional suffering among the Armenian refugees overwhelmed the camp, and as the American women entered, the inmates surrounded them, begging for food. Most of the camp refugees were women, children, and a few old men from towns north of Mezereh. The younger men had been killed along the way. In the center of the camp a "square trench" had been built to hold dead bodies as the refugees died; each layer was covered with a small amount of earth until "further bodies" furnished the next layer. Bread, supplied by the Turkish guards, was scarce, and those who had a little bit of money left would send out to try to buy some from outside. Dr. Parmelee was careful to recount stories about the women in the camp, saying that a few had told her that they

55. Ruth Parmelee, "A Line A Day" diary, May 23-September 25, 1915.

56. Dr. Parmelee made the visit to the camp in Mezereh, which was situated in an Armenian Apostilic cemetery, with another missionary, Mrs. Tacy Atkinson. During the visit the women took notes. Mrs. Atkinson described the grave, which had been dug by the Turkish soldiers, as "a big room [some] six feet deep." Moranian, "Bearing Witness: the Missionary Archives as Evidence of the Armenian Genocide," 119.

used various ways to hide their money. They placed gold pieces in the bottom of their water jugs, or swallowed coins. Sometimes, the doctor said, the women inserted money in "the vaginal orifice." Unfortunately, the guards "would suspect these tricks and would pour out the drinking water onto the ground, and in some cases [go] so far as to examine the women internally or to search all their clothes." One woman told how she tricked the guards by hiding some money in her "monthly napkin." The "Mohammedan" guards followed their religious law and did not touch this "unclean woman."[57]

Figure 15. Compound at Mezreh. View from within the compound in Mezreh, the lower town, 1919. Annie Tracy Riggs Hospital, commonly referred to as the American Hospital by the relief workers, was formally dedicated in October 1910 and can be located on the left side of the picture; the home of Dr. Herbert Henry Atkinson and Mrs. Tacy Adelia Wilkinson Atkinson is on the right within the walled compound. The Harpoot Mission buildings are visible on the horizon. Photo courtesy of the Oberlin College Archives.

Death visited the missionary compound as well as the refugee camp. As in all wars, the movement of troops and refugees caused infectious disease and epidemics to flourish. Anticipating that the summer of 1915 would bring disease, Dr. Parmelee wrote in her diary in April that

57. Ruth A. Parmelee, "A Visit to the Exiles in Mezereh" (n.d.), ABCFM Papers, Reel 714. This was probably written in 1917, shortly after Dr. Parmelee left Turkey. In a letter to Reverend J.L. Barton, who would soon become the head of Near East Relief, she promised to "try to remember data which will be helpful" to him "in the work you plan to undertake." Ruth Parmelee to Rev. J.L. Barton, September 14, 1917, ABCFM Papers, Reel 714.

"hot days will be unsafe for the children, with soldiers here." In another entry she said that "the soldiers have made this neighborhood filthy and unhealthy."[58] Countless refugees crowded into Harpoot and moved into the houses vacated by the deported. Caring for these unfortunates led a number of missionary relief workers to contract the dreaded disease typhus. One of the teachers, Miss Jacobsen, and a missionary physician's wife, Mrs. Atkinson, became ill but survived the disease. Dr. Atkinson, however, contracted typhus and died. Annie, the daughter of Pastor Riggs, died of a throat infection. Dr. Parmelee herself became infected while visiting patients who were sick and lying on beds of filthy rags. She theorized that she had encountered an "infected louse," even though she tried to gather up her long coat as she crouched to examine patients.[59]

Dr. Parmelee started exhibiting symptoms of typhus on the first day of 1916 when she noticed having fever and numb hands and feet. Bedridden for weeks, she sent her students to take care of patients. They also nursed her as she continued to "give directions about a number of things" in spite of her high fever. On the 6th of January, one of the "girls," Maria, shaved Ruth's head, a necessity in the treatment of typhus. By January 7th, she felt better but worried about neglecting her work "when there [was] so much to do." Unfortunately [she declared] we M.D.'s are human, too!" When Maria became infected as well, Ruth worried even more. She declared that "the poor people [are] without [any] medical help, but God is helping them." Luckily her mother Julia did not contract the disease and was able to visit Ruth, sometimes reading to her. [60]

In March 1916, however, Julia became ill, and went into a rapid decline. She suffered another stroke, which left her right arm weak and both legs useless. As Dr. Parmelee recovered from her attack of typhus and began caring for her mother in her final illness, the diary entries dropped off. Her medical work must have suffered neglect as well, because in mid-May she noted that she held her "first clinic in Mezereh since my illness. As mother's illness may go on indefinitely, I must not neglect my outside work too much."[61] Ruth blamed herself for her mother's final illness, saying that her own bout with typhus caused the anxiety that brought on Julia's "severe stroke of apoplexy." Ruth's assistant nurses

58. Ruth Parmelee, "A Line a Day" diary, April 8 and 13, 1915.

59. Ruth Parmelee, *A Pioneer in the Euprhates Valley*, 26.

60. Ruth Parmelee, "A Line a Day" diary, January 1–17, 1916.

61. *Ibid*, May 17, 1916.

helped turn, bathe, feed, and generally care for her mother until her death on June 27th, 1916. In the funeral services, missionary Reverend Henry Riggs and the local Armenian pastor praised Julia's "life of Christian service," and noted that she had spent thirty four years doing missionary service. She was buried on the Harpoot mission's grounds.[62]

After her mother's death, Dr. Parmelee fully resumed her medical duties, fulfilling them until Turkey severed relations with the United States in 1917 and expelled American missionaries. She and her missionary colleagues found themselves overwhelmed with general relief and medical work. The Reverend Riggs and his wife fed at least two thousand refugees daily. Dr. Parmelee trained a class of midwives and cared for patients with her assistants day and night.[63] Frustrated that she did not have enough supplies or staff, she nonetheless carried on, taking care of people "on the hill" in town as well as those "on the plain."[64] Some of the missionaries in her group served as volunteer nurses in a Turkish military hospital. Others supervised their American-trained Armenian nurses, who worked as nurses in the Turkish army.

Physical plant adjustments accompanied changing personnel assignments. The Turkish army continued to be quartered in the mission's school facilities. The infirmary building, once their first hospital, housed fifty poor and ill women and children. Their other building, the so-called "Garden" just outside of the city, served as a home for several Armenian mothers and their infants. On Christmas Eve, 1916, the infirmary building caught fire, and the missionaries and their orphan schoolgirls put the fire out, in full view of the Turkish soldiers who stood by and did nothing. Incensed by their behavior, Dr. Parmelee noted it in her report on the fire incident. She complained that it should have been "natural" for the soldiers to carry water to put out the fire. But instead of behaving in a gentlemanly and civilized manner, "the Turkish men . . . either stood around and watched, or . . . shouted themselves hoarse." The girls, who had "adopted the motto 'saved to serve,'" carried two buckets of water at a time from a block away, while the older women guarded them from the jeering crowd of men.[65]

62. Parmelee, *A Pioneer in the Euprhates Valley*, 27–28.

63. Ruth Parmelee to Miss Lemson, December 3, 1916, ABCFM Papers, Reel 714.

64. Ruth Parmelee to Rev. James L. Barton, September 10, 1916, ABCFM Papers, Reel 714.

65. Ruth Parmelee, *A Pioneer in the Euprhates Valley,* 28–29; and Ruth Parmelee,

Dr. Parmelee and the rest of the American missionary community were forced to leave Turkey in the middle of May, 1917, following U.S. entry into World War I on the Allied side. Filled with anxiety about what would happen to their Armenian charges, the thousands of men, women, and children who were ill and hungry in the wartime environment, the missionaries set up an arrangement with the Danish missionary Maria Jacobsen, a subject of a neutral country, to receive relief funds through a mediary in Switzerland.[66] Nurse Sarra Sapprichian and some of the other Armenian nurses remained in Harpoot to assist Jacobsen. Even before they left, the missionaries had run out of food to support the widows and children, forcing many of the women to seek work in surrounding towns. Soon many children were abandoned in the streets, prompting Jacobsen to gather over four hundred of them into eleven houses, where she cared for them with the American-trained assistants. Even so, Dr. Parmelee was not sure the children would survive, given the fact that they were "nothing but skin and bones, too weak to want to play, and it was a question whether they could keep alive on the small amount of bread they were getting." Many of the children were succumbing to sickness and hunger. Dr. Parmelee regretted leaving Turkey, believing that the missionaries would have been left alone to do their work if they had stayed.[67]

Dr. Parmelee was determined to go back to Turkey as soon as it was officially possible. She saw her brief repatriation to the United States as an opportunity to get more training, so that when she went back she would be better equipped for "future work, both mentally and materially."[68] She also realized that her return would depend upon continued American support for the relief efforts, so she endeavored to communicate the terrible conditions she had witnessed. She spent her first months in the U.S. writing descriptions of what she had seen, and she sent some of these accounts to James L. Barton at the ABCFM's headquarters in Boston. He, in turn, used the information to raise money for what would eventually become Near East Relief.

"Two Christmas Incidents at Harpoot, Turkey," ABCFM Papers, Reel 714.

66. Ruth Parmelee, *A Pioneer in the Euphrates Valley*, 29–30.

67. Ruth Parmelee to Rev. James L. Barton, July 29, 1917. ABCFM Papers, Reel 714. The letter was written after Parmelee returned to the U.S.

68. Ruth Parmelee to Rev. James L. Barton, September 7, 1917, ABCFM Papers, Reel 714.

While in the States, Dr. Parmelee gave several talks, broadcasting to the American people what she had witnessed during the days of the Armenian deportation.[69] In one of her addresses, she quoted extensively from the official Turkish government orders that set out the rules for Armenian removal. The orders stated that the Armenians had to be sent away because they were disturbing public order and allying themselves with Turkey's enemies. Parmelee countered these charges, averring that "of all the races dwelling in the Ottoman Empire there could be none more peace-loving and industrious than the Armenian race." Lastly, she condemned the "terrible things endured by all those hundreds and thousands . . . [of] poor creatures" (the Armenians). Lastly she condemned "the outrages of the human beasts who set upon [the Armenians] to do their worst," and she made it clear that it was mainly the Turks who had committed those outrages.[70]

Dr. Parmelee placed a special emphasis in her talks on the plight of the Armenian women, and she sought sympathy for them. She spoke about how Armenian mothers "saw their girls kidnapped by Kurds or Turks" and taken into the dreaded harem, where they would be sexually violated. The women also saw their "husbands and sons taken away to be killed, or even shot down before their own eyes." Often women were forced to abandon "their dear ones left sick by the roadside," and sometimes "in desperation, women would throw their little babies into the river." Parmelee wondered how Armenian women could survive such severe psychological loss, but she reasoned that they disassociated themselves emotionally from events as a means of survival. "[I]t was a mercy, perhaps," she concluded, "that [this] capacity to suffer had become somewhat dulled, or they could not have endured it all." [71]

Dr. Parmelee wanted to be sure that her audience understood the gravity of the situation, which she had come to see as a state-sanctioned genocide. She argued that there was "a definite plan to wipe out the whole nation" of Armenians, and she quoted a damning conversation that allegedly took place between the Turkish minister of war, Enver Pasha, and

69. Ruth Parmelee to Rev. James L. Barton, May 18, 1918, ABCFM Papers, Reel 714. In this letter Dr. Parmelee mentions staying at her sister's home in Montana. From there, she went on to give some talks Portland, Oregon and Chicago, where she took a post-graduate course.

70. Ruth Parmelee, "The Armenian Deportations," 2, Ruth Parmelee Papers, Stanford University.

71. Ibid., 2.

the American ambassador, Henry Morgenthau, Sr. In the conversation, Pasha supposedly said, "It was the plan of the Turkish government to get rid of the Armenians, then the Greeks, then the foreigners, and have Turkey for the Turks."[72] Parmelee pleaded with her audience, arguing that "because we are Americans and are in the [First World W]ar to give liberty to the oppressed peoples of the earth, we must send help to the martyr nations over in Asia Minor and the Caucasus." She equivocated slightly in her harsh characterization of Turks, distinguishing between the government's actions and those of the ordinary Turkish citizen. "We are hoping and praying that the Turkish Empire may never have the power it has had in the past." She said "Not that the Turkish people must be annihilated—they need good government just as much as their subject races. But the rulers of Asia Minor, now these many centuries, have proved themselves unfit to rule even their own people, let alone their oppressed races." Trying to get the American public to condemn the actions of the Turkish government, she sought to reach their religious conscience. "It will be a blot on Christendom," she averred, "if when peace is made, the Sick Man of Europe remains in power."[73]

Dr. Parmelee was part of a transitional generation of missionaries who served in the Near East. These missionaries worked against a backdrop of rising nationalisms which disrupted the Ottoman Empire in its final years. Observing this disruption, Americans focused in particular on the conflicts between the Turks, the Greeks, and the Armenians. They often characterized the Turks as feared, despised, and uncivilized "Mohammedans," while they tended to describe the Greeks and Armenians as "Christian martyrs" who suffered under Ottoman rule. Clearly, late nineteenth and early twentieth century reports from American missionaries and diplomats had resulted in widespread public awareness in the U.S. of the plight of Armenians and Greeks in the Ottoman Empire. Many grassroots organizations, both religious and secular, conducted massive public fundraising campaigns, ensuring that American schoolchildren knew of and contributed to saving the thousands of "starving Armenians" displaced by the conflict in Turkey.[74] These unprecedented international human rights campaigns helped

72. Ibid., 3.

73. Ibid., 4.

74. For a recent treatment of the Armenian genocide and America's response to it, see Balakian, *The Burning Tigris: The Armenian Genocide and America's Response*.

shape America's national and international identity and in some ways laid the groundwork for an emerging American Empire.[75]

Dr. Parmelee returned to Turkey in 1919. World War I had ended, but the country was still in turmoil, because conflict had broken out between Muslim Turks and Christian Greeks. Amidst the deportation of the latter group and an influx of Turks from Greece, Parmelee dispensed medical care and trained nurses. She also communicated what she saw to Americans back home. In 1922, she left Turkey and moved to Salonika, Greece, where she provided medical aid to the waves of refugees fleeing from Turkey. From 1925 to 1933, she directed the medical services of the American Women's Hospitals in Kokkinia, near Athens, which held wards for men, women, and children, serving the large refugee community of 70,000 people in that area. Parmelee, always identifying herself as a missionary, would serve the Greek people for the rest of her professional career as a physician. From 1922 until the 1950s, she cooperated in Greece with a variety of organizations, including the American Women's Hospitals, Near East Relief, local governments, and the Red Cross. By creating bridges between these organizations and the missionary community, she participated in the development of new international humanitarian and medical movements heretofore unknown.

BIBLIOGRAPHY

American Board of Commissioners for Foreign Missions. ABCFM Papers (Microfilm): Near Eastern Missions. Eastern Turkey, Harpoot. Unit 5 (ABC 16.9.7), Reel 714. Yale Divinity School, New Haven, CT.

American Women's Hospitals. Records of the American Women's Hospitals 1917–1982. Drexel University College of Medicine, Legacy Center Archives and Special Collections, Philadelphia, Pennsylvania.

Antler, Joyce. "After College, What?" New Graduates and the Family Claim," *American Quarterly* 32 (Fall 1980):409–34.

———. "Was She a Good Mother?." In *Women and Social Structure*, edited by Barbara Harris and Jo Ann McNamara, Durham, N.C.: Duke University Press, 1984.

Balakian, Peter. *The Burning Tigris: The Armenian Genocide and America's Response* New York: Harper Collins, 2003.

Barton, James L. *The Story of Near East Relief, 1915–1930,* New York: Macmillan, 1930.

Bierstadt, Edward Hale. *The Great Betrayal A Survey of the Near East Problem* New York: Robert M. McBride and Company, 1924.

---

75. For a critical study of the role of American women missionaries in shaping U.S. ambitions for empire in the Ottoman Empire during the nineteenth century, see Reeves-Ellington, "That Our Daughters May Be as Cornerstones: American Missionaries, Bulgarian Nationalists, and the Politics of Gender."

Carpenter, Kaley M. "A Worldly Errand: James L. Barton's American Mission to the Near East." Ph.D. Diss., Princeton Theological Seminary, 2011.

Daniel, Robert L. *American Philanthropy in the Near East, 1820–1960,* Athens, Ohio: Ohio University Press, 1970.

———. "The Armenian Question and American-Turkish Relations, 1914–1917," *Mississippi Valley Historical Review* 46 (September 1959): 252–75.

Giannuli, Dimitra. "American Philanthropy in the Near East Relief to the Ottoman Greek Refugees, 1922–1923," [microform] Ph.D. Thesis, Kent State University, 1992.

———. "'Errand of mercy': American Women Missionaries and Philanthropists in the Near East, 1820–1930," *Balkan Studies* 39 (1998): 221–262.

Grabill, Joseph L. "Missionary Influence On American Relations With the Near East." Paper Presented at Malone College in First Annual Seminar on Christianity and History, March 31 and April 1, 1966.

———. *Protestant Diplomacy and the Near East: Missionary Influence on American Policy 1810–1927* Minneapolis MN: U. of Minnesota Press, 1971.

Lewis, Bernard. *The Emergence of Modern Turkey,* London: Oxford University Press, 1961.

Lovejoy, Esther Pohl. *Certain Samaritans,* New York: Macmillan, 1933.

Moranian, Suzanne Elizabeth. "Bearing witness: the missionary archives as evidence of the Armenian genocide." In *The Armenian Genocide History Politics and Ethics,* edited by Richard G. Hovannisian, 103–29. New York: Palgrave, 1992.

Morgenthau, Henry. *An International Drama* London: Jarrod, 1934.

———. *I Was Sent to Athens* Garden City, New York: Doubleday, 1929.

Parmelee, Maurice. "Autobiography, Later Draft," n.d. Maurice Parmelee Papers, Box 3, Manuscripts and Archives, Yale University, New Haven, Connecticut.

Parmelee, Rev. Moses P., M.D. *Home and Work By the Rivers of Eden,* Philadelphia: The American Sunday-School Union, 1888.

Parmelee, Ruth A. "A Line a Day" diary, 1913–1916,

———. Papers, Box 1. Stanford University.

———. *A Pioneer in the Euphrates Valley,* n p.: privately printed, 1967 Papers, 1922–1945. Hoover Institution Archives Holdings on International Relief. Stanford University, Palo Alto, California.

Quataert, Donald. *The Ottoman Empire, 1700–1922,* Cambridge: Cambridge University Press, 2000.

Reeves-Ellington, Barbara. "That Our Daughters May Be as Cornerstones: American Missionaries, Bulgarian Nationalists, and the Politics of Gender," Ph.D. Dissertation, Graduate School of Binghamton University, State University of New York, 2001.

Rockwell, Walker. *The Deportation of the Armenians,* New York: American Committee for Armenian and Syrian Relief, 1916.

Shaw, Stanford J. and Ezel Kural Shaw. *History of the Ottoman Empire and Modern Turkey Volume II Reform, Revolution and Republic: The Rise of Modern Turkey, 1801–1975,* Cambridge, London, and New York: Cambridge University Press, 1977.

"Tank Home," *Oberlin Review,* (April 14, 1897), 311. Oberlin Missionary Home Association Printed Materials, 1890–1916, Folder 38, Oberlin College Archives, Oberlin College, Oberlin, Ohio.

Vinton, John Adams. *Vinton Book, Volume III: Near East American Board Missions to 1886 in the Near East; ABCFM in Turkey.* Manuscripts and Archives, Yale Divinity School, New Haven, CT.

Walters, Jim. The Family Parmelee: Jim Walters' Home Page for the Parmelee Family. Online: http://www.geocities.com/mrjimwalters/index.html.

Ward, Mark H., M.D. "The Americans in Harpoot," in the Ruth A. Parmelee Papers, Box 2, Folder Turkey, 1922.

Zurker, Erik J. *Turkey A Modern History.* London and New York: I. B. Tauris and Co, 1998.

6

From Brimstone to the World's Fair: A Century of "Modern Missions" as Seen through the American Hume Missionary Family in Bombay

Alice C. Hunsberger

INTRODUCTION

THE AMERICAN BOARD OF Commissioners for Foreign Missions (ABCFM) established its first foreign mission—its first anywhere in the world—in Bombay (now Mumbai), India, in 1813. A year before, on February 6, 1812, five young men had been hurriedly ordained as Congregational Church ministers in the Tabernacle in Salem, Massachusetts, and then rushed (with three wives) to different cities, for ships in harbor ready to sail to India. Gordon Hall, Luther Rice, and Samuel and Rosanna Nott sailed from Philadelphia, while Adoniram and Ann Judson sailed from Salem with Samuel and Harriet Newell. After delays deemed auspicious for allowing the ABCFM to raise funds for a year's expenses, both ships were en route to Calcutta by the end of February. In June 1812, the United States declared war on Great Britain. When the ships arrived in Calcutta soon after, the British East India Company refused to let the missionaries land in any British domain. It wasn't just the war; the Company did not want missionaries from any country to upset their commercial dealings with the Indians. The Newells left for the Isle of France (now Mauritius), and during the stormy voyage a daughter was born to them, but she never rallied and was buried at sea. The mother, Harriet Newell, barely nineteen years old, weakened by dysentery and tuberculosis, died within days of reaching the Isle of France. In August, Adoniram and Ann Judson went to Serampore, under Danish control; for theological reasons they joined the Baptists and he resigned his ABCFM connection. In October, Luther Rice also joined the Baptists and returned to the United States. That left four of the original eight.[1]

Still in Calcutta, on the east side of the Indian subcontinent, Gordon Hall and the Notts were under British pressure to leave immediately. They were waiting for a ship so they could join Samuel Newell on the Isle of France. But upon learning that the new English governor of western India, Sir Evan Nepean, was also a vice president of the British and Foreign Bible Society, Hall and Nott wrote a letter requesting passage there, to its capital city Bombay. The British police had placed them on the next passenger list to England, but the three young people managed to use their general passport document, evade a heavy military search for them, and sail out of the Calcutta port undetected. Forty miles downriver they successfully passed without detection another ship that had been stopped and searched for missionaries. Gordon Hall and Mr. and Mrs. Nott entered Bombay harbor on February 11, but did not land until the next day. Hall considered February 12, 1813, as the official date of the establishment of the American Board Mission in Bombay. Newell, holding scant hope for their admittance to Bombay, sailed to Ceylon (today Sri Lanka) but after a year joined them on March 7, 1814. This was the first Protestant mission in western India.[2]

1. How the ABCFM Prudential Committee, with no authority to admit missionaries and no funds to support them, decided to act on the enthusiastic wish of the young preachers and capitalize on the presence of two ships bound for Calcutta is described in "Report of the Prudential Committee," 228–31; and Tracy, *History of the American Board of Commissioners,* 32–38. For their travails with the British, see "Religious Intelligence," 561–62; "American Missionaries," 470–74; and extracts from Harriet Newell's and Rosanna Nott's letters and journals, "Extracts from Mrs. N.'s Letters," 468–70, and "Letter from Mrs. Newell," 515–20.

2. Stowe, "Gordon Hall," 275 and Stowe, "Samuel Newell and Harriet (Atwood)," 492–93.

Figure 16. Indian temple—"*The temple in whose veranda Rev. Gordon Hall slept the night he was suddenly seized with Cholera is most probably in the center of the accompanying picture.*" (Caption typed on the back of original photograph.) This photograph, taken between 1903 and 1911 by missionary Elizabeth Hume Hunsberger, indicates that Gordon Hall's memory was so vivid and moving to subsequent generations of ABCFM Bombay missionaries that they took pilgrimages to the site of his death in 1826. From the collection of the author.

By 1824, the Bombay Mission had expanded to include two additional stations, one in Mahin, the other in Tannah.[3] The mission was not an easy post; in their reports back to Boston, the missionaries frequently mentioned illnesses that slowed their work. Newell died in 1821, and in 1826 Gordon Hall, who had already buried two sons and sent his wife home with the other two, contracted cholera and died. The American Board sent out replacements and eventually new stations were opened farther inland, in the Deccan region, including one in Ahmednagar, later the site of a major seminary. On April 1, 1839, the ABCFM sent another contingent to Bombay. It comprised one single woman and three newly married couples: Miss Cynthia Farrar, Rev. and Mrs. Ebenezer Burgess, Rev. and Mrs. Ozro French—and Rev. and Mrs. Robert Wilson Hume.[4]

The missionaries and the Board saw their work as "modern missions," a new Christian practice that followed the model of Jesus's original apostles, such as Paul and Peter, who went out into the world of pagans and idolaters to preach the gospel. For the ABCFM missionaries of the

3. "Mission at Bombay," 1.

4. Peggy Bendroth (Congregational Librarian), personal communication. Robert Wilson and Hannah Hume are the great-great-grandparents of the author.

nineteenth century, the intervening centuries represented evangelical lethargy. These missionaries considered their global endeavor to be a modernized form of the original apostolic effort. As he prepared to save the souls of those he considered to be perishing in darkness, Rev. Robert Wilson Hume was so confident in the power of God's word to change human hearts that he could scarcely have imagined that a century later his great-grandsons and great-granddaughters would still be preaching in India for the ABCFM. But even less could he have imagined, as he stood beneath the sails of the ship that bore him and his wife to India, clutching his Bible close, that his own son would take the spotlight in a heresy controversy that, for a time, shook missions to their roots, challenged the authority of creeds and institutions, and ultimately changed how American Protestant Christians viewed other religions.

This article looks at three generations of the American Hume family of ABCFM missionaries to India, focusing on the lives of three important individuals. All were named Robert and will be often represented here by their initials, Robert Wilson Hume (RWH), Robert Allen Hume (RAH), and Robert Ernest Hume (REH). There are of course many other threads to the story—those of wives, sisters, brothers, cousins, and others—but here we will let these three men serve the missionary cause again, using their history to examine how the goal of missions evolved in conjunction with ideas about "the modern."

I. ROBERT WILSON HUME (RWH), 1809–1854

Born in 1809, in Delaware County, New York, Robert Wilson Hume was the son of a first-generation immigrant from Scotland, also named Robert Hume.[5] RWH graduated in 1834 from Union College in Schenectady, New York, and then from Princeton Theological College in 1837.[6] Planning to go abroad as an ABCFM missionary, he served one summer as a guest preacher in Babylon, Long Island, New York. There he met and wooed a young schoolteacher, Hannah Derby Sackett. She had been born and raised in West Springfield, Massachusetts, near where Mary Lyon established a female college, Mount Holyoke, which sent its "girls" out into the world as missionaries, following Jonathan

5. See "Online Genealogy, Hume Family"; and Stowe, "Robert Wilson Hume," 310. RWH's parents were Robert Hume (1787–1859) and Catherine Rose Hume (1791–1878). There is a discrepancy in the birthplace of Robert Wilson Hume: the website genealogy says Delaware City, New York, while the article by Stowe reports Stamford, New York.

6. Stowe, "Robert Wilson Hume," 310.

Edwards's theological principles.[7] Hannah dreamed of attending Mount Holyoke[8] and graduating with others to go around the globe as "cornerstones of world redemption."[9] But a new option presented itself. By marrying Hume, she could set out immediately.

American Board policy would not let them rush, however. Even after ordaining Hume in 1839, and accepting and approving the couple's application for missionary work, the Board would not allow them to marry until their ship was in the harbor.[10] In the middle of March 1839, they received a letter instructing them to present themselves at the port in Salem no later than March 30.[11] They hastily made wedding arrangements and were married in Hannah's own church in West Springfield on March 25.[12]

Hannah was twenty-three years old and her husband thirty when they and their five fellow missionaries to India went down to the Salem wharf.[13] American Board Secretary Rufus Anderson accompanied the large crowd that watched the two-masted, 232-ton freighter, the *Waverley*, sail away on April 1.[14] Later, Anderson reportedly admitted that he had worried about Hannah. With the deaths of Gordon Hall and others in India on his mind, Anderson had "great confidence in the physical equipment of all except poor, frail Mrs. Hume, for whom he feared there was not a very long life of service."[15] But Hannah would outlive them all.[16]

7. Porterfield, *Mary Lyon*, 44–47.

8. Lotta Carswell Hume, *Drama at the Doctor's Gate*, 12–13. Edward Hicks Hume was a grandson (through Edward Sackett Hume) of RWH and Hannah; Lotta was his wife. Though he was born and raised in the Bombay mission, Dr. Edward H. Hume and Lotta eventually devoted their lives to medical missions in China.

9. Porterfield, *Mary Lyon*, 45.

10. Lotta Carswell Hume, *Drama at the Doctor's Gate*, 13.

11. Salem is specifically named in a grandson's memoirs: Edward Hicks Hume, *Doctors East, Doctors West*, 22. It is also mentioned in Edward Hicks Hume's wife's account: Lotta Carswell Hume, *Drama at the Doctor's Gate*, 3, 13.

12. Lotta Carswell Hume, *Drama at the Doctor's Gate*, 13.

13. Ibid., 17.

14. Ibid., 3, 13–15. The *Waverley* carried ice to Bombay from Spot Pond in Arlington, Massachusetts. Arlington residents "were proud of the fact that every pound of this ice" came from the pond in their village. "Natives in India paid fabulous prices for these shining, cold cubes, but when, on the next day, they found that all the cubes had melted, they complained furiously to the shipowners."

15. "Death Notice of Mrs. Hannah D. Hume," 249.

16. Hannah Hume died at 87 years of age, on April 18, 1903. She outlived her five daughters (the eldest, Sarah J., died at 63 years of age, just days before her mother). Hannah's two sons, Robert Allen Hume and Edward Sackett Hume, went on to become celebrated missionaries in Bombay and Ahmednagar, while Sarah, and probably other

Figure 17. The two-masted brig *Waverley*, in which the Rev. Robert Wilson Hume and his wife Hannah sailed from Salem, Massachusetts, to Bombay in 1839 with two other missionary couples and one single woman. Reprinted from Lotta Carswell Hume, *Drama at the Doctor's Gate: The Story of Doctor Edward Hume of Yale-in-China* (New Haven, Connecticut: The Yale-in-China Association, Inc., 1961), 21, with kind permission of the Yale-in-China Association.

Modern Missionaries in Western India

Robert Wilson Hume and the other Bombay-headed missionaries were most likely familiar with the *Instructions* written two years earlier for a similar group leaving for southern India. This eloquent and fulsome document argues, first, that the missionary is, "perhaps more than any other man," a successor to the original apostles of Jesus. But then it asks how slavishly must the missionary of the present day follow the apostles' example, "since the circumstances both of Christian and heathen nations have so greatly changed."[17] In other words, the ABCFM saw the

daughters, too, were very active in mission work. One granddaughter, Ruth Peabody Hume, MD, managed the medical services and nurses training in Ahmednagar; another granddaughter, Elizabeth Norris Hume (Hunsberger), graduated from Hartford Seminary, chose a husband (Byron Keyser Hunsberger), and took him to Bombay in 1903 to run the mission school.

17. "Instructions," 83–93. The instructions read to the 1839 group were of a much more general nature, focusing on the aims, dangers, and nobility of their endeavor. The author thanks Congregational Librarian Peggy Bendroth for obtaining the 1839 source.

original apostles as the first missionaries and this new generation as their modern successors, but it advocated employing new methods for new circumstances.

The Board listed six ways the apostles were models for modern missionaries: (1) "in the holiness of their character," meaning modern missionaries should live in a way that would display the Gospel message; (2) in the doctrines and precepts which they taught—thus, "if the missionary does not proclaim to the heathen the doctrines which the apostles were inspired to preach and write, what shall he preach? Does he carry a new revelation?"; (3) in their relations with all classes of people, meaning that the missionary should act like the apostles when "they sympathized with the afflicted; wept with those that wept; and rejoiced with those that rejoiced; being all things to all men, *that they might by all means save some*"; (4) in their zeal and untiring laboriousness; (5) in their readiness to encounter danger and hardship; and (6) in their love for their work: "The missionary who does not delight, not only in his *office*, but also in his *work*, will certainly be dilatory and inefficient."[18]

But what about changed conditions? To what extent might modern missionaries vary their methods? By using the phrase "by all means" and italicizing it, the ABCFM emphasized its openness to new methods. As the *Instructions* noted, Christians now occupied a position of political power as well as a numerical majority in some places, and methods of communication were now different. Should the missionary adopt the same attitudes and practices as their New Testament forebears? The Board said no. "To suppose that Christ would have his servants quit the high vantage ground which they might occupy in this age, and prosecute their work as their predecessors did at the commencement of the Christian Era, is wholly improbable."[19]

In addition, the *Instructions* to the missionaries described six areas in which modern methods for propagating Christianity might legitimately differ from those of the apostles, and the document elaborated on reasons and methods for these differences. The tone of the *Instructions* was assertive, because the Board was trying to settle a debate over missions that was being conducted in churches at home. The Board made a clear case for accepting modernization in missions, and it approved a wide variety of methods other than public preaching for "proclaim-

18. "Instructions," 84–88.

19. Ibid., 88.

ing" the Gospel. The following is a highly abbreviated summary of the Board's position, retaining original italicized headings:

(1) *The auspices under which they were sent forth.* While the early apostles were galvanized by persecution into becoming missionaries, modern missionaries offer themselves as a "free-will offering" and are supported by churches at home.

(2) *Missionaries in this age need not generally itinerate as the apostles did.* Modern missionaries need to learn foreign languages and translate Scriptures, establish schools, and train reading communities.

(3) *Missionaries now need not limit themselves to the means used by the apostles.* The apostles were confined to oral proclamation, but the modern missionary has the printing press to put God's word into every house.

(4) *Modern missionaries need not present truth in the same order and connection as the apostles did.* Indeed, the apostles also varied their message to fit the audience.

(5) *The modern missionary need not aim so exclusively at the religious improvement of men as the apostles did.* Spiritual conversion remains the primary goal, but modern missions should strive "in every practicable manner to improve their [the people's] intellectual and social condition."

(6) *The modern missionary need not, in all cases, aim so exclusively at immediate results, as the apostles seem to have done.* Modern missionaries need to take on introductory work, such as establishing schools and printing books, in order gradually to prepare the way for direct and open preaching of the word.[20]

The *Instructions* thus argued that, based on changed conditions, it was legitimate, even required, to change methods. In this document, the ABCFM outlined a wide scope of legitimate activities for "preparing the way" for eventual conversions. On societal as well as individual levels, the missionary was to strive to establish fertile conditions for the reception and realization of the light of Christian truth. This would be challenged later, as the church at home sought higher conversion numbers.

20. Ibid., 88–93.

Preaching the End to Idolatry and the Caste System

ABCFM missionaries throughout India focused on what they saw as two primary sins of the Hindus and Jains who comprised the bulk of the indigenous population: the worship of idols and the caste system. As sins, idolatry and the caste system condemned the souls of their practitioners to the perdition of eternal fire and brimstone. Muslims, on the other hand, were monotheists and needed a different approach. In fact, Muslims often served as the missionaries' allies in the crowd, testifying, in line with Muslim doctrine, that there was only one true God and that Jesus was a holy prophet. Muslims were equally, if not even more adamantly, against idolatry. And because some areas of India were under Muslim rule, Muslims were often able to provide missionaries with aid.[21] The missionaries for their part developed respectful approaches to the Muslim population, but they still sought to change Islamic practices. Once, while itinerating in Unjunwel, accompanied by a Muslim cleric, Rev. Hume did not refrain from criticizing a Muslim saint's shrine. He reproached the cleric for allowing the people to degenerate "even from Mohammedanism, conforming to Hindoo practices, and worshiping dead men."[22]

The ways whereby missionaries addressed idol worship and the caste system included preaching in public places; providing education for all, including girls; running health programs; and teaching industrial skills. Missionary reports frequently mentioned caste strictures as obstructions to the understanding of God's word.[23] The lack of explicit Biblical condemnation of the caste system necessitated a more interpretive theological response to it, but idolatry was a clearer target. In light of considerable Bible verses against idol worship, missionaries viewed the souls of idol worshippers as definitely condemned to eternal hellfire.

21. "Report of Rev. Bowen," 163. Rev. Bowen reports that Moorood (Rajapur) was controlled by an Abyssinian Muslim named Hubshi. Bowen counted only two Africans in the town, however.

22. "Report of Rev. Bowen," 163–64.

23. See "Communication from Mr. Allen," 308–9; and "Madras Missionary Conference," 305–8. The articles are responding to a major law passed by the British on April 11, 1850 which made converts to Christianity no longer subject to the punitive laws of the religions they left. This provided missions with legal protection for their converts.

Establishing Schools as Part of Modern Missions

As the 1837 *Instructions* had argued, modern missions had new tools for new circumstances. One of these was the ability to print materials in local languages, another was the establishment of schools. As the *Instructions* argued (with italics), "*preaching* the gospel—*publishing* it—may as readily be done in the schoolroom, in the family visit, or by the Bible or tract distributor, as in the public Sabbath assembly."[24] But the building and operation of schools became a source of contention within ABCFM. Any success with schools had to be tempered by avowing that it was "highly subservient to the great object of a Christian mission," as a joint letter from Gordon Hall and other early missionaries in Bombay declared even in 1824. Nevertheless, these same missionaries then asserted their "ardent" wish to have "many, very many such schools."[25]

Schools figure in one of RWH's earliest letters. In February 1840, after first giving assurances of the good health that he and Mrs. Hume were enjoying, he wrote that the continuing illness of their colleague Mrs. Allen meant that all the schools were now the responsibility of the Hume family. Rev. and Mrs. Hume were also learning the local Marathi: "We have advanced so far in the language as to be able to hear the lessons without difficulty, and with a little previous attention, to explain them in some measure . . . The girls in the female boarding school are affectionate, intelligent children. They give Mrs. Hume much care and much pleasure."[26] During their years in India, RWH and Mrs. Hume together were credited with founding about forty day schools in Bombay and nearby. And for ten of those years, Mrs. Hume conducted a boarding school for girls in her own home.[27]

The years 1853 and 1854 were considered disastrous for the Bombay Mission. After his wife's death, Rev. Allen returned home in ailing health and, "without any prospect of resuming his labors, [was] released from his connection with the Board."[28] Rev. Hume also became so ill that the decision was made to return home. He was carried on a stretcher to the ship, while Mrs. Hume and their six children, all aged eight and under,

24. "Instructions," 92.

25. "Mission at Bombay, Joint Letter of the Missionaries," 146–47.

26. Robert W. Hume, "Letter from Mr. Hume," 500.

27. See [Hannah Hume.] Obituary; and Mitchell, *History of the United Church*, 86–87.

28. "Bombay," 6.

followed. Perhaps more hurtful to the heart of the Bombay Mission, however, was a series of decisions by the ABCFM. The belief in Boston had been growing that too much attention and funding was being expended on schools. Headquarters wanted more direct preaching to lead to more conversions.

A bifurcation of the purpose of missions took place. Oral preaching and mission schools were seen as antagonistic. With people advocating in Boston that the Bombay Mission be closed, local missionaries each penned a fiercely eloquent letter, energetically defending the principle that education, while secondary, was vital for conversions. Robert Wilson Hume, S. B. Fairbank, George Bowen, Henry Ballentine, and S. B. Munger each composed his own letter, while A. Hazen and L. Bissell wrote a joint letter, and Ebenezer Burgess and William Wood wrote another joint letter. One witness to the events was Rev. Royal G. Wilder, who had headed the schools in Ahmednagar. He compiled a 420-page history of mission schools, defending their achievements and arguing for their survival.

Wilder included selections from the missionaries' letters.[29] Rev. Hume's lengthy letter of May 25, 1853 comes first in Wilder's volume, and its selections alone total seven pages. In his letter, RWH wrote to Rev. Rufus Anderson, secretary of the ABCFM, saying that they had been "called to add an educational institution" to the mission. He argued that all the missionaries "came to India to be preaching missionaries; and we have sought to be a preaching mission. We have no wish to relinquish the work of preaching, nor any intention of doing so. But we are satisfied that the mission can not properly accomplish its work, and reap the fruit of its labors, without a superior educational institution."[30]

Hume's argument fell upon deaf ears. In 1854, the "Deputation" of the ABCFM—consisting of Rev. Rufus Anderson, then Senior Secretary, and Rev. A. C. Thompson—sailed for India to assess the situation. The Deputation closed the schools, including the girls' boarding school, the English high school, and all the schools taught by unconverted Indians. This decision outraged Wilder. After citing the Missionary Herald's praise of Mrs. Hume's schools in 1853, just the previous year, he declared in his history that the action of the Deputation "swept overboard

29. Wilder, Mission Schools in India, 84.
30. Ibid., 86.

nearly every thing of interest in the mission."[31] The opening of Wilder's polemic against the ABCFM's ruling is particularly interesting; with all capital letters he opens his defense of schools by stating that "MODERN MISSIONS have become a fact and a power in the world."[32]

The same year that the schools were closed, RWH weakened and died while he was on board the *Merchantman*, sailing home around Africa in 1854. Amid the tears of her children, and against the pressure of the seamen who wanted a rapid burial at sea, Mrs. Hannah Hume pleaded with the captain to keep her husband's body for burial in port in Capetown. He invited her into his cabin to discuss it. And while she was with him, the seamen took the body and delivered it to the sea.[33]

THE REV. ROBERT A. HUME

Figure 18. Portrait of Robert Allen Hume. From Mary Hewitt Mitchell, *History of the United Church of New Haven* (New Haven, Connecticut: United Church [Congregational], 1942), 88. Reprinted with kind permission of the United Church of New Haven.

31. Ibid., 83.

32. Ibid., 11.

33. Lotta Carswell Hume, *Drama at the Doctor's Gate*, 18.

II. ROBERT ALLEN HUME (RAH), 1847–1929

The Foundation of a Missionary Life in the Age of Progress

Robert Allen Hume was born in the Bombay city district of Byculla on March 18, 1847, elder son of Robert Wilson Hume and Hannah Derby Sackett Hume. He had five sisters (one of whom died in infancy) and one brother, Edward Sackett Hume. When the family left India in 1854, Robert was eight years old and Edward six. Hannah, now widowed, returned with her six children to Massachusetts, spending some time in her hometown of Springfield. But her ultimate destination was New Haven, Connecticut, so the boys could eventually attend Yale University in preparation for going back to India. She installed the family in New Haven and lived a long and vibrant life there, supporting missions throughout the world. Not only did her two sons fulfill her plan, but her eldest daughter, Sarah Jane, also returned to India as a missionary.[34]

Robert Allen Hume received his BA from Yale in 1868. For the next two years, he studied at Yale Divinity School, from which he received his AM degree and, twenty years later, his doctor of divinity.[35] He attended Andover Theological School, graduating in 1873, and was ordained a Congregational minister on May 3, 1874. The sermon preached at his ordination ceremony by Rev. Dr. T. D. Woolsey opened with the ironic observation that the apostle Paul saw more success with the Gentiles than with Jesus's own people, the Jews, in spreading the gospel message. Underscoring the need for new foreign missions, Woolsey declared, "the same effects follow modern missions which followed apostolic preaching—in short, it is proved that the gospel and only the gospel is the world religion." Encapsulated here is confidence both in the modern revivification of apostolic missions, as well as in Christianity as the only religion dynamic and flexible enough to be universally received.[36]

In the rapid calendar of the ABCFM, RAH's ordination, wedding, and departure for the mission field all occurred within a few weeks. On July 7, 1874, he married Abbie Lyon Burgess (a grandniece of Mary Lyon), who had been born in Ahmednagar and was in the United States

---

34. See Mitchell, *History of the United Church*, 86–90; and Lotta Carswell Hume, *Drama at the Doctor's Gate*, 21–24.

35. "Robert Allen Hume," 147.

36. Woolsey, "Christian Missions," 770–84.

to complete her education.[37] A month after their marriage, on August 12, they arrived in Ahmednagar, ready to begin their lives as missionaries. Ahmednagar, a town southeast of Bombay in the dry climate of the Deccan region, became the center of RAH's career. He is credited as the founder and driving force of the Ahmednagar Theological Seminary. A generation had passed since RWH's experience, and education was now an unquestionable part of missionary work. It certainly attracted RAH's brother, Edward Sackett Hume, who arrived in Bombay the following year, 1875, with his wife Charlotte Chandler (of the Chandler missionary family in southern India[38]). Edward energetically revived the boarding school that his mother had run in her home, expanding it to the point where it included six hundred students and was one of the leading high schools in western India.[39] With Edward and his family in Bombay, and Robert and his family in Ahmednagar, the hopes of Robert Wilson and Hannah Hume were grandly fulfilled. Many of the schools and churches their children built still flourish.

Robert and Abbie had four children. Their first child, daughter Ruth Peabody Hume, would later become a missionary doctor; for many decades she headed the hospital and nurse's training service of western India. The couple's second child, Robert Ernest Hume, would become a missionary scholar; his life is chronicled below. Two more children followed, but six years after Abbie arrived in India, she died in Panchganj on July 25, 1881, and was buried next to her mother in Mahabaleshwar,[40] a mission station admired for its healthy climate.[41] Her husband's sister,

37. Abbie Lyon Burgess (b. September 9, 1849) was the daughter of Ebenezer and Abigail (Moore) Burgess of Ahmednagar. Her mother Abigail, a niece of Mary Lyon, graduated from Mount Holyoke College in 1838 and died in India in 1853. See *One Hundred Year Biographical Directory*. For the influence of Mary Lyon and her women-only Mount Holyoke College and Seminary on the missionary endeavor in the Bombay Presidency, see Porterfield, "The Presence and Impact of Mary Lyon's Students in Maharashtra," in *Mary Lyon*, 87–111.

38. A descendent of this branch, Alice Chandler, became the namesake of the author.

39. Mitchell, *History of the United Church*, 87. Today the school is known as Hume High School, in honor of Edward Sackett Hume. The author visited the school and the Hume churches of Mumbai and Ahmednagar in 2005 and 2006. She is grateful to the many kindnesses shown to her by the congregations and the Hume School trustees, principal, vice principal, teachers, staff and students

40. *Report of the American Marathi Mission*, 1–2.

41. "Survey of the Missions of the Board," 8.

Sarah Jane Hume, went to India and took care of her brother's mother-less children for five years.[42] RAH did not marry again for ten years.

Celebrating Fifty Years of the Ahmednagar Mission

Abbie died a few months before the fiftieth anniversary celebration of the founding of the ABCFM Mission in Ahmednagar. To mark the occasion of the semicentennial, the entire Marathi Mission dedicated its annual meeting, October 26–31, 1881, to historical reflection. The meeting was overseen by RAH, and numerous papers were presented.[43] Rev. S. B. Fairbank, DD, outlined the history of the evangelistic work of Ahmednagar.[44] Fairbank noted that the activities of the pioneer missionaries, Gordon Hall, Samuel Nott, and Samuel Newell, reflected "three of the great divisions of missionary effort": education, preaching, and translating and printing in the local language. The fourth division, medical missions, was not made distinct until after the late 1850s, even though the earliest missionaries certainly preached to the sick and dispensed medicine. Fairbank emphasized that each division "earns the 'Well done' from the Master." Nevertheless, he continued, "Evangelism [is] our Primary and Paramount Work. Preaching the Gospel has been our *primary work* in the city of Ahmednagar, and in the villages of the region round about it" (italics in the original).[45]

Fairbank's article describes different forms of evangelism: holding services at set times; street preaching; singing hymns in the Indian *kirttan* form, "sure to draw a crowded audience"; slideshows with the "Magic Lantern" or the Sciopticon (an early form of slide projector whose novel visual projections were very popular); lectures in English; and discussion sessions. The article also describes three types of itinerancy: visiting the same site from time to time, such as once a year; long tours, "much in vogue in the first 23 years of the mission"; and occupying one place for

---

42. Mitchell, *History of the United Church*, 87–90. Sarah "was never a commissioned missionary, but for five years did the work of one. After her return to America she was for fourteen years city missionary under the Woman's Board of the City Missionary Association. Her special work was among women and children, and one result of her visits to their homes and knowledge of their ignorance and need was the organization of the Visiting Nurse Association."

43. *Memorial Papers.*

44. Fairbank, "A Historical Sketch," 42–56.

45. Ibid., 43.

several days.[46] RAH is mentioned as one of the key mission lecturers in English. Fairbank's elaboration of mission preaching methods suggests a defensiveness. Low numbers of conversions led him to defend the mission's preaching activities, and he promised that "the intellectual belief in Christianity that is like dormant seed in the minds of many" would bring forth its fruit.[47] This idea that an understanding of Christianity lies within every pagan and heathen would later surface in the writings of RAH and his son REH.

Modern Missions: The Heresy Trial

The 1880s put Robert Allen Hume into an even greater struggle for God's truth. This time, it was on the home front. While on furlough in the United States, RAH preached and advocated for more attention, more funds, and more preachers to be sent to India. In his 1886 speech at Andover Theological Seminary, he "expressed incidentally . . . that the heathen who had never heard of Christ might not be condemned to everlasting perdition."[48] Traditional Christian doctrine held that anyone who did not accept Jesus Christ as lord and savior was doomed to eternal hellfire. The later years of the nineteenth century saw widespread challenges to this absolutism in Europe and North America. At Andover Theological Seminary, the liberal new theology was championed by Professors Munger and Smyth. RAH and other missionaries who worked closely with Hindus, Jains, Buddhists, and Muslims heard their fears and reservations about converting to Christianity. One of their main concerns was that, by converting, an individual might well secure his or her own future salvation but would thereby condemn all ancestors to eternal hell.[49] At the same time, missionaries witnessed intense Hindu and Muslim religious devotion, embraced in full faith and humility.

RAH, and others beyond the missionary field, came to believe that their beloved God and savior would not, could not, be so unmerciful as to create human beings and then doom them to eternal damnation without giving them the chance to hear the message of Jesus. From this conviction arose the doctrine of "second (or future) probation." This

46. Ibid., 46–53.

47. Ibid., 56.

48. Mitchell, *History of the United Church*, 89. It was RAH's 1886 address to the Andover alumni that launched him into the Andover Controversy.

49. "Mr. Hume Returns to India."

doctrine holds that at the end of time rather than at death the final judgment of eternal reward or punishment—heaven or hell—will be delivered. From death to Judgment Day, however, souls can continue to learn
and understand the Christian message. On Judgment Day every human
soul will hear the message of Jesus from Jesus himself, and will have a
chance consciously to accept the message.[50]

For many traditionalist Christians, future probation threatened to
"cut the nerve of missions."[51] If everyone will have a chance to hear the
truth from Jesus himself, why are missions needed at all, in the here
and now? Promoting future probation seemed suicidal to many. At this
point, the phrase "modern missions" took on new meaning. Those who
accepted the logic of future probation were seen as modern and following the route of reason. Traditionalists were seen as old-fashioned,
unbending to new understanding. What could have remained an incon-
sequential point of theology turned instead into a nationally watched
controversy that questioned whether God's mercy had limits. It also
pitted the freedom of individual belief and expression against the en-
trenched institutions of power and authority.

The "Andover Controversy" is covered in more detail by another
article in this volume, so only a few points need be mentioned here. A
committee at Andover tried to remove Professors Munger and Smyth
from their posts, and the Prudential Committee of the ABCFM declared
Rev. Hume and several Andover applicants unfit for missionary service on the grounds that they supported the doctrine of future probation. RAH was forbidden to return to India as an ABCFM missionary.
Furthermore, the issue caused many to wonder whether a missionary
need adhere to one specific interpretation of the Andover Creed.[52]

Throughout his ordeal, RAH had many supporters. Among those
weighing in on his behalf was the United Church of New Haven. The
church sent a letter signed by its pastor and deacons, "setting forth Mr.
Hume's special and inherited fitness for missionary work, telling of the
results which had already come from his labors, and of the unanimous

50. One source for the history of this doctrine is Hudson, *Future Probation in
Christian Belief.*

51. For this famous phrase by the Board of Visitors of Andover Seminary, see Hutchison,
The Modernist Impulse, 259, also 134, 141, 155; and Dorrien, *Social Ethics,* 22.

52. Hamilton, "That Everlasting Andover Controversy," 477–86. For more on the
controversy of creeds at the time, see Robinson, "Assent to Creeds," 284, 292–93.

wish of the Mission that he be returned." Specifically, the church leaders "questioned the right of the Prudential Committee of the Board to decide the theological fitness of missionaries and said that this was a matter to be settled by a Church Council regularly called for that purpose."[53]

In the end, the ABCFM yielded to years of popular, lay, and theological protest, and allowed RAH to return to India. At a farewell meeting for the missionary in New Haven in late June 1887, Dr. Munger said, "I have been helped more in my difficulties by the Christian graces and love which Mr. Hume has shown under the grossest injustice and misunderstanding than by any other human cause." A few days later in Boston, Professor Smyth accompanied RAH to the dock and bade him farewell as the modern steamship *Pavonia* set out for Bombay.[54]

The New York Times, which had already written extensively about the Hume case,[55] gave its opinion about the outcome in a news article, "Mr. Hume Returns to India," whose title in its simplicity reveals how deeply American elites knew and cared about Hume's situation. The *Times* observed that "it will be remembered that around [RAH's] case the controversy has raged with even more earnestness than has marked the discussion about the young applicants," and it wondered whether Hume would conceal or repudiate his views once back in India. After quoting some who felt he ought to conceal his beliefs, the paper opined, "But we do not understand that he is under any obligation whatever not to teach his opinions concerning probation."[56]

In letting RAH return to India, the ABCFM gave witness to a significant change in American Protestant thought. The beliefs of one missionary had been dealt with, but a much larger theological debate had crystallized in the public mind. People were looking into the infinite future and taking into account all the souls of human beings around the world. They were beginning to think that the idea of progress was not simply material; it was also spiritual. Moreover, it was not simply American or European, it was also international. RAH would develop these ideas and publish them in his books decades later. He could also work assured in knowing that the effort of his employer, the Prudential Committee of the ABCFM, to make missionaries adhere to a creed had been thwarted.

53. Mitchell, *History of the United Church*, 87.

54. "Mr. Hume Returns to India."

55. See "Not Forbidden to Work"; and "They Dodged the Issue."

56. "Mr. Hume Returns to India."

Modern missions would now include freedom of conscience for the individual, even within a decidedly religious environment.

Robert Allen Hume returned to Ahmednagar to a richly productive missionary life, which included serving as dean and professor of homiletics and pastoral theology at the Ahmednagar Theological Seminary. In 1891, he married his second wife, Katie Fairbank, daughter of two Ahmednagar missionary families, the Fairbanks and the Ballentines. Katie knew missionary life well, and had graduated from Mount Holyoke in 1877. The couple had four children together, and Katie shared her husband's work for more than forty years. RAH stayed in India long after retirement age, and even after he returned to America he continued actively to promote modern missions. He died in 1929 at the age of eighty-two, regarded as "the outstanding missionary of the American Board in his day."[57] In the more than forty years between the time of his return to India and his death, RAH devoted himself to shaping a new vision for modern missions, a legacy that deserves further discussion.

57. Mitchell, *History of the United Church*, 89. RAH's obituary appeared in *The Times*, London, on Friday, June 28, 1929. A memorial article about him by Rev. Alden H. Clark, DD, principal of the Union Theological College, Ahmednagar, was published in *The Missionary Review of the World*. Clark, "Hume of Ahmednagar," 821–27. Clark's article took its title from the series of articles RAH published a bit reluctantly about his life: Robert Allen Hume, "Hume of Ahmednagar—His Story." The author is grateful to the kind and efficient librarians of the Congregational Library for copies of these articles.

अहमदनगरचे लाडके मिशनरी

रेव्ह. डॉ. रॉबर्ट ऑलन ह्यूम

Figure19. The Robert A. Hume Memorial Church (Congregational) of Ahmednagar, India. Cover of a pamphlet in the Marathi language on the history of the church, with a cameo portrait of Robert Allen Hume. Built on principles of RAH "to quicken reverence" and foster Christian activity, the church is situated in the center of town and includes a dome modeled on the Taj Mahal and lotus flower symbolism (signifying the Universe flowering from the Infinite) in windows and carvings to appeal to Indian spiritual aesthetics. "Hume of Ahmednagar—His Story," *The Congregationalist* 106 (November 3, 1921) 566. The pamphlet is from the collection of the author.

New Modern Missions: "Things are Different Now"

After his successful return to India in 1887 as an accredited missionary of the ABCFM, Robert Allen Hume embarked on a new stage of his missionary career. Through an energetic schedule of preaching, teaching, travel, writing and publishing, he helped to build up a truly Indian church with Indian leadership.[58] He also led the fundraising in America

58. "R. A. Hume." *The Times of London* stated, "His most distinctive contribution to

for the 1900 famine in India,[59] defended the rights of Indian-Americans to own land in the United States,[60] and raised a new family with a new wife and four new children.

RAH spread his new message of modern missions to many continents. Indeed, he looked not only into the hearts of Indians sitting before him, but back over his shoulder toward Americans sitting at home. Rather than focusing only on the most effective way to achieve spiritual conversions, RAH worked to convert the people back home to a new "modern" view of missions, in which ideas of progress, evolution, forward movement, scientific and social advancement, and change for the better (not to mention reactions against such change) were transformative. RAH saw material progress as only one side of God's positive manifestation in the world. The other side was the spiritual progress of mankind.

RAH published two books proclaiming his philosophy of missionary theology, *Missions from the Modern View* (1905) and *An Interpretation of India's Religious History* (1911). Each of these books warrants close study. *Missions from the Modern View* contains RAH's lectures from a speaking tour in the United States.[61] Growing up in the missionary environment of India and New Haven, RAH was familiar with the common, "though unreal," early image of the missionary who only needed a Bible to "go out and preach the Gospel." RAH criticized the early attitudes and assumptions about evangelizing and wanted to move beyond them. He was especially critical of the early image of "the missionary as wearing a tall hat and a dress coat, standing under a palm tree, with a book in his hand, and talking to a company of half-clad savages crouching around and gazing at him in wonder."[62]

RAH also criticized a favorite piece of advice to new missionaries, "beware the man of one book," which meant that a man who could eas-

---

missionary statesmanship was his strong support of the movement for the upbuilding of an Indian church."

59. "R. A. Hume."

60. Robert Allen Hume, et al., "Indian Rights in the United States," 447. This was a memorandum signed by RAH and eleven other American missionaries in India.

61. Robert Allen Hume, *Missions from the Modern View*, 7. RAH delivered lectures at Andover Theological Seminary, the University of Chicago, the Chicago Theological Seminary, and Bangor Theological Seminary (Maine). His volume contains "exact illustrations of how I have given the Christian message to Indians."

62. Ibid., 88.

ily quote from the Bible would be "mighty in saving souls." For people giving and following this advice, the Bible was not only central; it was all. "The Bible without note or comment was thought to be the very best thing to place in the hands of anyone whom it was sought to lead to Christ," RAH recalled,[63] and he faulted another missionary practice: preaching to the exclusion of everything else. That practice led him to write: "In the narrow conception that all that the missionary ought to do is to tell men that Christ died for their sins and that if they believed in Him He would forgive them and take them to heaven, there was no adequate justification for the missionary's spending strength and time in educating people in schools, in carrying on medical work except to a limited extent, and certainly no justification for efforts to improve the social and economic condition of peoples in other lands."[64]

RAH's bitter childhood experience of watching his parents' life-work dismantled by the ruling of the Deputation, and his decades of working and reflecting on the most efficacious methods of proclaiming the Gospel, had taken form in a new vision. "Things are different now," he wrote. Missionaries should know "with some degree of fullness and accuracy"[65] about the religion of the land they are going to, both its present form and the history of its development. Missionaries also needed in Hume's view to know about psychology and sociology. These were new sciences in his age, and he devoted a chapter to each one in *Missions from the Modern View*. But he still saw religion as central because it underscored the oneness of humanity. "It is as important to appreciate that human nature is essentially one in all the world," he wrote, "as to appreciate that there are differences in the minds of different races."[66] The oneness of human nature was the foundation RAH built upon in reaching out to other souls.[67] One of his chapter titles, "Missions from

63. Ibid., 88.

64. Ibid., 37.

65. Ibid., 88.

66. Ibid., 90.

67. RAH was not speaking alone at this point. For example, Hartford Theological Seminary's "Basis and Aims" for many years stated: "[The Seminary] discerns in human history the working of the Eternal Spirit, and the persistent growth of the Kingdom of God. It investigates that history in its manifoldness, in order to discover traces of the gradually unfolding divine purpose, that the problems of today may be met in the light of the lessons of the past" (*Hartford Theological Seminary, 1897–98*, 12). As for the

the Modern View of God and the World," shows that more than missions were undergoing a modernist review.

New Modern Missions: The Comparative Study
of Religions and Religious History

RAH's conception of modern missions included a careful study of other religions and a critical investigation of Christianity, both from a historical perspective. He advocated these approaches because he believed that religions continually evolve through time. In his first book, *Missions from the Modern View,* he focused on religious history in two chapters, "The Historical Development of Hinduism," and "A Comparison of Christianity and Hinduism." In his analysis of Hinduism, he was able to include not yet published selections of the Hindu *Upanishad* scriptures translated by his son, Robert Ernest Hume. Six years later, RAH expanded on these chapters in his book *An Interpretation of India's Religious History* (1911).[68] The book was introduced by Henry Churchill King, president of Oberlin College, who wrote: "[T]he distinguishing characteristic of the lectures is, that they are in earnest with Christ's conception of God as Father of all men, and strive to look at the complex religious phenomena of India in that light." King appreciated the detailed way whereby RAH showed parallels between Indian and Western religious development, a risky proposition in a missionary environment.[69]

RAH's main assumptions in *An Interpretation of India's Religious History* were that "God has been ever seeking His Indian children; that He has never left Himself without witness among them; that with many limitations and errors the people of India have diligently sought after God in eager desire that, haply they might find Him."[70] Just as God spoke to the Hebrews through prophets, he had, according to RAH, been speaking to Indians through their thinkers and saints. With its detailed description of how history reveals a path of doctrinal develop-

---

"three-fold comprehensive endeavor" that RAH calls for in *Missions from the Modern View* (38), see Hartford Theological Seminary's description of student life: "Care is taken to promote physical health and vigor as the basis for mental activity and spiritual soundness" (*Hartford Theological Seminary, 1897–98*, 59).

68. Robert Allen Hume, *An Interpretation of India's Religious History.*

69. Ibid., 6.

70. Ibid., 13.

ment, RAH's book argued that "God has been ever seeking His Indian children," a universalistic contention that was the main foundation of new modern missions. Countering the old missionary view that Indians were godless heathens, RAH wrote:

> The best illustration of the statement that man is "incurably religious" is found in the Hindu people. "Religion" influences their thought and conduct from before birth until after death. What made the Hindu such? God. Have we not all one Father? Is He the God of the Christians only? Is He not the God of the Hindus also? Yea, of the Hindus also. The Christian must more fully and more gladly accept Christ's assumption and teaching of the Heavenly Father's impartial blessing on all His children.[71]

For RAH, the progressive development of religious sentiment in India could be seen with the coming of Islam, when millions of Hindus converted to monotheism. "In the coming of Islam into contact with Hinduism the devout man should see the guiding hand of God. Indian pantheism had metaphysically prepared the way for the monotheism of the Mohammadans."[72] RAH considered a society's advancement from polytheism to monotheism to be a momentous step in its history, one that demonstrated the human aspiration for God. For RAH, this aspiration meant that Christians should be humble and recognize that non-Christians were God's children, too. Clearly God had been ministering to them even when they did not possess the message of Christ.

"The So-Called Modern Missionary"

Not everyone agreed with the new ideas of modern missions. Opponents and supporters of new missiological ideas gathered in Bombay in 1892 at the third Decennial Conference, a meeting of all the missionaries of India that was held every ten years. Among the proponents of progressive theology was Rev. T. E. Slater of Bangalore, whose paper, "Work Among the Educated Classes," presented an optimistic picture for ongoing success in converting educated Hindus and Brahmans.[73] "The *most remarkable transformation*" that has occurred in this class, he wrote, was in the "idea of God" and the "conception of a personal and Holy Being—the

71. Ibid., 14.
72. Ibid., 91–92.
73. Slater, "Work Among the Educated Classes," 272–89.

foundation truth of all real religion" (italics in the original).[74] Slater was confident these would increase for two reasons: first, because Christian ideas were "in the air everywhere;" and second, because scientific ideas ("which have already done much to purify mediaeval Christianity") were gaining more and more acceptance in India.[75]

"Following the trend of modern thought," Slater concluded that an interest in science would lead Indians to an ever truer understanding of natural theism (though he noted that even in Christian countries a tendency toward deistic thought was often observed among scientific minds). He also evoked Darwin, declaring that "the 'strongest' must eventually 'survive'" and in the future produce "in a true Eastern church, a type of Christian culture and saintliness as yet unseen." To achieve more conversions, Slater called for "a simple and broad presentation of Christianity," which would appeal to "rational intuitions," attach "less importance to dogma and far more to life," be "in touch with all true social and political aspirations," and not be "prejudicial to Native customs and habits."[76]

Slater's paper did not appeal to the Rev. Gunpatrao Navalkar of Alibag, Bombay. He did not think that the repackaging of Christianity would lead to more converts in India. In his opinion, the problem lay not in the message but in the messengers, namely "half-hearted Christian propagandists," such as Slater.[77] For Navalkar, Slater "represents the modern missionary . . . and the views of that new product of superficial Christianity which arrogates to itself the name of the *Modern Church*" (italics in the original). For these modernists, Navalkar said, "There is no such thing as absolute truth—absolute Christian truth. It is something 'simple and broad,' conditioned by rational intuitions and social and political aspirations, and tyrannized over by native customs and habits of life!"[78] Navalkar criticized Slater and others for separating Christ's teachings from his life and "contemptuously" calling the former "dogmas":

> When so much uncertainty prevails in the mind of the so-called modern missionary, who would measure Christian truth by the conventional standards of national habits and political as-

74. Ibid., 282.

75. Ibid., 282–83.

76. Ibid., 283.

77. Navalkar, "Third Speech," 293–98.

78. Ibid., 296.

pirations, it is no wonder that he is devoid of enthusiasm . . .
It is absolutely necessary to assure the educated natives of their
bounden duty to make a decision for truth and Christ without
stooping to any considerations of personal advantage or political
expediency; for Christianity is a system of religion, and not of
philosophy, and as a revelation of the mind and will of the Deity,
it has supreme claims upon the faith and obedience of men.[79]

Navalkar feared that the "so-called modern missionary's" views
would dilute the Gospel message and relativize absolute truth. Giving local customs and political aspirations too much importance in missionary
methods, he argued in 1892, would distort the message of Christ. Nearly
twenty years later, RAH reflected on this concern in his *Interpretation of
India's Religious History.* Like Slater, RAH called for an understanding of
national habits and local traditions. His aim was not to accommodate
them and achieve immediate converts, but rather to show their relation
to Christ's absolute truth. RAH wanted to learn the historical roots of
traditions in order to discern God's original purpose, even if the social
expression of this purpose had become distorted. For example, the
present "tyranny" of caste, he averred, was based on a "legitimate basis
that glad service is the natural crown of special privilege."[80] Rather than
distorting the message of Christ, the acknowledgment of local customs
(such as reverence for idols) showed respect for God's fatherly relationship with the Indians over thousands of years.[81]

Contrary to the former missionary view that God's message had
never reached India, RAH argued that local customs must be seen as
the Indian response to God's eternal call to his children. As such, the
Indians were as worthy of Christian respect as the Hebrews to whom
God spoke millennia ago.[82] As for dogmas, RAH noted that for nineteen
hundred years Christianity had been evolving, and yet still none of the
required Christian creeds functioned as an "all-sufficient creed entirely
in New Testament language." For that reason, the spiritual Indian who
converted would depend on the Holy Spirit as a guide, rather than "think

---

79. Ibid., 296–97.
80. Robert Allen Hume, *An Interpretation of India's Religious History*, 144, 213.
81. Ibid., 13.
82. Ibid.

subscription to the Western creeds of the past" was essential to his or her Christian faith.[83]

Indeed, RAH declared at the 1903 Parliament of Religions in Chicago that the Hindus could help the Christians: "The Hindu's recognition of the immanence of God in every part of his universe will quicken the present movement of western thought to recognize everywhere a present and a living God. The Hindu's longing for unity will help the western mind . . . appreciate . . . that there has been and will be one plan and one purpose."[84]

This may not have assuaged Navalkar's fears of a watered down Christianity. Yet for RAH, Christianity itself was moving toward a much larger view—an inkling of what RAH saw as God's larger view—of the Christian message. If Christianity in one part of the world was built upon God's speaking to Hebrew prophets, why could it not be built in another part of the world upon God's speaking to Indian prophets? In both cases, "now He is speaking to His children by His Son."[85] Since even Western Christians did not possess the final perfection of the message, Hume argued, different versions were not only possible, but could be accepted as authentic.

Readjusting Ideals and Methods for the New Modern Missions

In 1905, Charles Cuthbert Hall of Union Theological Seminary in New York (later the seminary's president) penned a perceptive introduction to RAH's *Missions from the Modern View*, in which he acknowledged the difficulty of readjusting "missionary ideals and methods to the modern state of knowledge."[86] Like RAH, Hall drew upon contemporary views of science, reason, and progress to argue for change in spiritual activity: "To admit the need of readjustment in the field of missions is to place that field in the same honorable category with every other field of lofty human enterprise. Readjustment means growth, progress, augmentation of power, as the effects of increased knowledge and experience." But Dr. Hall did not think that the need to modernize missions meant that missionaries were undeserving of admiration, and he chided the

83. Ibid., 185, 220.

84. "Later Theology," section 10.

85. Ibid., 13.

86. Charles Cuthbert Hall, introduction to *Missions from the Modern View*, by Robert Allen Hume, 1–5.

church at home and "armchair theorists of the West" for considering missionaries narrow. He called on the critics to note "how far beyond much of our relatively narrow and provincial thinking many of our foremost missionaries have advanced." Hall contended that even though modern missionaries subscribed to a variety of creeds, they "are quite at one" in recognizing certain essential points, which can be summarized as follows:

(1) "The heart of the East already contains the principle of religious aspiration."

(2) The heart of the East is "hungering and thirsting for God."

(3) "The policy of Christian Missions toward existing religious experience must be that of Christ, Who came not to destroy but to fulfill."

(4) Christian missions must conserve the existing reality while investing it with the "rich content of the revelation of God in Christ Jesus."

(5) "Christianization of the Asiatic consciousness does not mean its transformation into the likeness of the West."

(6) "The Mission of the Holy Ghost in the East may be to produce an Oriental Christianity different in institutional form and in temperament from the Christianity of Europe and America."[87]

Challenging one popular view of missionaries as narrow-minded, crimped, and conservative, Hall suggested missionaries were inspired visionary leaders in new and modern thinking who could guide churches at home. And RAH ranked at the top. Few modern missionaries appeared to Hall as more advanced than RAH. "Dr. Hume's lectures admirably illustrate the readjustment of ideals and methods that has taken place already in the most intelligent circles of foreign missionary workers," Hall wrote. "These lectures are a gospel for the West."[88]

87. Ibid., 4.
88. Ibid.

III. ROBERT ERNEST HUME (REH), 1877–1948

Raised in New Modern Missions

Robert Ernest Hume was the second child (first son) of RAH and Abbie Lyon Burgess. Born in Ahmednagar, Bombay Presidency, India, on March 20, 1877, Robert Ernest went on to achieve unique success on several levels. When he died in his home in New York City on January 4, 1948, the *New York Times* ran a long obituary with a headline that summed up his life: "Dr. Hume, Expert on Religions, Dies; Professor Emeritus at Union Seminary, Once Missionary, Wrote Several Books." Raised in India, educated in the missionary schools run by his parents in Ahmednagar[89] and thoroughly fluent in the local vernacular, Marathi,[90] Robert Ernest was sent to Newton High School in Massachusetts "to be fitted" for college. When he graduated high school in 1894, he earned the highest score on the Greek examination required for admission to Yale College that year.[91] REH received his BA from Yale in 1898, his MA in 1900, and his PhD in 1901.[92] He then went to seminary at Union Theological in New York City, but had to interrupt his studies to tour the world for a year as special secretary to the seminary's president, Dr. Charles Cuthbert Hall. REH was awarded his BD, summa cum laude, in 1904 from Union, and the next year was ordained a Congregationalist minister in the New Haven Association.[93]

89. REH would also have been closely familiar with the school in Bombay headed by his uncle (RAH's brother), Edward Sackett Hume, and his aunt, Charlotte Elizabeth Chandler Hume. The school that Edward and Charlotte ran in Byculla, Bombay City, is still vibrant, and is now named Hume High School.

90. Robert Ernest Hume, *The World's Living Religions*, vi.

91. "Competitive Debates at Yale."

92. *Alumni Directory of Yale University*. The MA class of 1900 is a particularly noteworthy group. It consisted of twenty-two men, including three Japanese and divines such as Rev. John W. Blythe, Rev. William Hazen, and Rev. Prof. Henry Sloan Coffin.

93. "Robert Ernest Hume."

Figure 20. "*Bombay Church*" under construction, 1903. Built through the efforts of Robert Allen Hume's ABCFM missionary brother (and REH's uncle), the Rev. Edward Sackett Hume (1848-1908), this church was renamed 'Hume Memorial Congregational Church' in a February 11, 1913, ceremony presided over by RAH. This would have been the church in which REH worshipped during his four years in Bombay. Located in the Byculla district, Mumbai. From the collection of the author.

Finally prepared for missionary service at thirty years of age, REH returned to India in 1907 under the ABCFM and worked as a teacher in Ahmednagar Theological Seminary for three years. After that, he moved to Bombay to take over from his father the position of editor of the bilingual Christian weekly magazine *Dnyanodaya (Rise of Knowledge)*. He worked at this publication for four years (1910–1914),[94] while also teaching at Wilson College, Bombay. Besides teaching and writing, REH was socially active, helping to organize the Western India Missionary Association and the Social Service League of Bombay.

94. See Ibid.; and "Dr. Hume, Expert on Religions, Dies."

Figure 21. *"Hume Hall—1910"* (caption typed on the back of the original photograph). One of the buildings of the Hume School complex in the Byculla district of
Bombay. Photo from collection of RAH's niece/REH's cousin (Edward S. Hume's
daughter), Elizabeth Norris Hume Hunsberger, who was an ABCFM missionary in
Bombay, 1903-1911; now in the collection of the author.

In 1914, REH left his missionary work in India to accept the post of
Marcellus Hartley Professor of Philosophy and History of Religions and
Missions at Union Theological Seminary. He held this post for four years,
after which Union appointed him Charles Butler Professor of History
of Religions. He was a professor of religions at Union for nearly forty
years, before retiring in 1943. Part of what set REH apart from other
Christian seminary professors was his academic expertise in Hinduism
as well as Sanskrit and other Indo-European languages, not to mention
his personal knowledge of Zoroastrianism, Buddhism, and Islam as living religions in India. In 1932, he received an honorary doctorate from
the University of Strasbourg, France in recognition of his translation of
philosophical and theological documents.

REH traveled back to India throughout his decades as a scholar,
once as a delegate to universities in India for the Carnegie Endowment
for International Peace. He lectured at Bombay University on early
Indian history, and also lectured at University of the Punjab, Hindu
University in Benares, Moslem University, the College of the Maharajah
of Baroda, and the India Institute of Oxford University. At Oxford, he

spoke at the World's Congress of Faiths in 1937; the next year he chaired a session of that congress.[95]

REH fit well into Union's "gospel-oriented and explicitly modern Protestantism."[96] Indeed, he helped shape it, along with Henry Sloane Coffin, George Albert Coe, Harry Emerson Fosdick, and Frederick J. Foakes Jackson. These and other "second-generation liberals . . . turned Union into a chief bastion of the liberal theology movement. Theologically, they advocated evangelical liberalism, biblical criticism, ecumenical cooperation, interreligious understanding, and the social gospel."[97]

Conviction in Practice and Publication

Throughout his career, first as an ABCFM missionary and then as a professor and author, REH expressed in word and deed his conviction that the study of history reveals mankind's ongoing "endeavor to grasp the fundamental truths of being."[98] This conviction he shared with his father, RAH. But REH believed more explicitly than his father that a study specifically of sacred scriptures from throughout the world and across time would reveal the essence of human culture at different stages of development. He contended that each religion's scriptures show its culture's most important beliefs, understandings, and aspirations, and he thought that a comparison of world scriptures would show the progress of the human race as a whole at different stages of development.

According to REH, different religions displayed not only the variety and richness of human conception, but also progress from initial aspiration toward more subtle and sublime thoughts. He saw all religions as attempts "to solve the problems of the origin, the nature, and the destiny of man and of the universe."[99] But he added that, while all religions share this common goal, they each respond to different "forces—climatic, economic, sociologic, nationalistic, etc.,"[100] and therefore manifest them-

---

95. See "Dr. Hume, Expert on Religions, Dies"; "Robert Ernest Hume"; and Robert Ernest Hume, *Treasure House.* "Docteur de L'université de Strasbourg" is written on the title page of *Treasure House of the Living Religions,* along with REH's Yale degrees and title at Union.

96. Dorrien, ed., *The Making of American Liberal Theology,* 21.

97. Ibid., 21.

98. Robert Ernest Hume, *The Thirteen Principal Upanishads,* vii.

99. Ibid., vii.

100. Robert Ernest Hume, *The World's Living Religions,* v.

selves differently. The main differences he saw between religions were the "ethical and religious ideals concerning man and the Divine which are continuously taught and accepted as sacred. Accordingly, the most important single systematic source of information among the historic religions is their canonical scriptures."[101]

Acting on his ideas, REH began his study of Sanskrit very early, hoping to explore the world's most ancient extant scriptures of a living religion. Tutored by leading masters in India (his "native land"[102]) and scholars in Europe and America, he developed his skills to the point where his translations of the Hindu scriptures, the *Upanishads*, became the standard for most of the twentieth century. But to complete his goal of understanding all living religions,[103] Hume also studied other ancient languages of the world, including Avestan (for Zoroastrianism) and Hebrew (for Judaism). Among his writings, three books stand out: *The Thirteen Principal Upanishads* (1921), *The World's Living Religions* (1924), and *Treasure House of The Living Religions* (1932).

The Thirteen Principal Upanishads (1921; 1931)

REH's first book, *The Thirteen Principal Upanishads*, became the standard in its field and is still suggested reading in university classes nearly a century after its publication. Hume's *Upanishads* comprise his translation from the Sanskrit of theological/philosophical treatises of Hinduism and his introductory analysis. Published twenty years after REH received his PhD from Yale, Hume's *Upanishads* benefited from his subsequent study at Union Theological Seminary and seven years of ABCFM missionary work in India (1907–1914). Demand for the book was steady, causing Hume to write in the preface to the second, revised edition (1931) that "the call for the book has been sufficient to exhaust the first edition in a fairly brief period of years."[104]

101. Ibid., v.

102. Robert Ernest Hume, *The Thirteen Principal Upanishads*, x.

103. See Robert Ernest Hume, *The World's Living Religions*, where REH writes, "The author has found very rewarding the results of learning to handle in their original languages the sacred texts of most of the religions of the Near East, the Middle East and the Far East" (v). In *Treasure House of the Living Religions,* REH writes, "This labor has involved scrutiny of the original languages in the case of Hebrew, Greek, Chinese, Sanskrit, Prakrit, Pali, Gurmukhi and Avestan" (1). Further research is ongoing into his university studies.

104. Robert Ernest Hume, *The Thirteen Principal Upanishads*, x.

Of all possible Sanskrit scriptures to translate, REH explains in his preface why he chose the Upanishads: "In the long history of man's endeavor to grasp the fundamental truths of being, the metaphysical treatises known as the Upanishads hold an honored place." To Hume, it was not only their antiquity, but their sublime content that was critical. He believed that the Upanishads reveal mankind's early efforts to pose and ponder deep philosophical and spiritual questions, and he was taken with these texts because they show "intimations of the inadequacy of nature worship and of the falsity of an empty ceremonialism," thereby demonstrating spiritual progress in a specific culture. As "the earnest efforts of the profound thinkers of early India to solve the problems of the origin, the nature, and the destiny of man and the universe," the texts seemed to REH to be proof that mankind had always been searching for ultimate truth.[105]

The World's Living Religions (1924; many editions)

In 1924, REH published what *The New York Times* later called his best-known book,[106] *The World's Living Religions*. A compact volume (only six inches by four), *The World's Living Religions* laid out a comparative study of the eleven religions that Hume identified as "organized religions of culture which have lived for more than a century." While he admitted to the existence of new cults and ongoing animism, he explained, "the scope of this volume includes only those movements in mankind's religious life which have maintained continuous social organization, art and literature, as well as worship, through a succession of centuries."[107] The fact that some important religions have faded from the world and are no longer practiced (e.g., Egyptian and Greek religions), stood as proof to REH that human beings have advanced spiritually through the millennia.

The World's Living Religions caught the American public's attention in the middle of the so-called Roaring Twenties. And, as repeated printings and even a translation into Spanish[108] reveal, the book retained its

105. Ibid., vii.

106. "Dr. Hume, Expert on Religion, Dies."

107. Robert Ernest Hume, *The World's Living Religions*, v.

108. In *The World's Living Religions*, REH does not name the language, but simply states in the preface, "The book has been translated and published in a foreign language" (vi). It is in the front pages of his later *Treasure House of the Living Religions*

appeal through the dark decade of the Great Depression in the 1930s. It then achieved a great (and highly unusual) honor in recognition of its significance for contemporary American society: it was the one book on religion (other than the Bible) selected to be included in the 1939 New York World's Fair time capsule.[109] For a World's Fair focused on progress toward the future, the time capsule was designed to preserve the best of the present until it would be opened five thousand years later, in the year 6939. Fair organizers and Westinghouse Corporation, which developed the materials and mechanisms of the time capsule, explained that they chose the capsule contents "to provide an organized record of the world as they knew it for future generations."[110]

REH's little 300-page volume, in describing the history and beliefs of the living religions of the world, neatly fit the requirements of the time capsule. The book was international. It was detailed. It offered a variety of careful and respectful ways to study religions. But more than that, it pointed to spiritual progress on a universal level, born of a universal human aspiration to higher faith that had been proceeding through all time and would continue to evolve in the future. Of course for REH, the ABCFM missionary, this aspiration culminated in Christianity and its message. As he predicted, and called for, knowledge of religions grew in subsequent years. His book remained popular, so that even in 1959, ten years after his death and thirty-five years after it had first been published, *The World's Living Religions* was again republished in what purported to be an updated and "completely revised edition."[111] Such long-lasting popularity showed that the book struck a deep chord in America that echoed for decades.

---

where Spanish is identified and the title given as *Las Religiones Vivas.*

109. *The World's Living Religions* was included in the millions of pages on microfilm, while a Bible was included as a physical artifact.

110. *America in the 1930s.*

111. Religious scholarship had advanced by the 1950s. In a scathing review of the 1959 edition of *The World's Living Religions*, William P. Woodward called the chapter on Shinto so "out-dated" and its revisions so "inadequate" that "it would have been better if the book had not been republished." He also wrote that two of the texts that REH relied on, the *Kojiki*, the *Nihon Shoki*, "are not considered 'sacred' in any sense that the word is generally used," while another text that Hume used, the *Manyoshi,* "has never been regarded as a scripture of the Shinto faith." Woodward, "Book Review: *The World's Living Religions,*" 73–74.

Treasure House of the Living Religions (1932)

Professor Hume's third book, *Treasure House of the Living Religions*, combined the aims and methods of his two previous works: the global-survey approach of *The World's Living Religions* and his careful study of sacred writings in the *Upanishads*. With his conviction that scriptures are both the key to understanding religions and the reason they "survive the devastations of time," REH compiled illustrative scriptural texts from nine living religions. He explained, "All the living religions have been able both to maintain the continuity of their dominant teachings and to adapt themselves to changing conditions, just because of their reverence for their sacred scriptures, in whose ancient formulas every succeeding generation may perceive fresh applications of eternal truths."[112] Here we see him squarely in the American mode of progress, espousing evolution and change. Thus, while he saw truth as everlasting, he also held that each generation keeps that truth alive for itself through "fresh applications" of the eternal wisdom in sacred texts in response to changes in society.

REH's main purpose in *Treasure House* becomes apparent with his last chapter, which is practical and directive. The chapter is titled "Program of Joint Worship (includes Readings which could be arranged as a Responsive Reading."[113] With this, Hume had moved beyond translating and presenting the texts, beyond teaching about other faiths, to outlining a social and public worship service that incorporates sacred scriptures and readings from other faiths. His aim was to move individuals and society forward, outside of their own scriptures. He wanted them to experience the universal connection among all mankind, and to feel themselves part of a continuous human spiritual development that extends from a distant past, beyond the present and into the future.

CONCLUSION

Three generations of Hume family missionaries in Bombay and the larger American Marathi Mission of the ABCFM demonstrate the changing understanding of the phrase "modern missions"—a transformation they helped to lead. Each one, in a way that was true to his time, sought the enlargement of Christian compassion to extend to the people of India.

112. Robert Ernest Hume, *Treasure House*, 3.
113. Ibid., 287–300.

Changes in their methods and thinking over the course of a century, from 1839 to 1939, reflect not only changes in the ABCFM but also changes that took hold in American society and its popular understanding about religions in the world.

Robert Wilson Hume went to Bombay in 1839 as one of the first modern missionaries. Like his peers, his goal was to bring the light of Christ to a people who had not had the opportunity to hear the Gospel and whose souls, according to Christian theology of the day, were considered lost to eternal hellfire. While he believed in the supremacy of preaching—to let the Gospel words simply be heard and explained—RWH soon saw the necessity of schools in providing a wider educational context for faith, and he and other missionaries built a strong school system in western India. The closing of all the schools in 1854 by the ABCFM shows that a deep fault line had emerged in the philosophy of how to conduct modern missions.

A generation later, when RWH's son, Robert Allen Hume, returned to start his missionary work in 1874, his father's view had prevailed and schools had become an unquestioned component of mission work. But RAH's experience in the field led him to new ideas about the role and responsibilities of "modern missions." This changed understanding of modern missions took hold in the second half of the nineteenth century, when progress was the leading concern in all arenas, and when Darwin's theory of evolution, geological discoveries showing the age of the earth, and advances in technology and industry pointed to natural evolution in every sphere. For RAH, modern mission work now required an understanding that faith and spirituality evolve over time. It also required a new, larger conception of God; he needed to be a father to all mankind, one who had been speaking to and caring for all people around the world through all time. Therefore, modern missions became committed to a deep understanding of other religions, and to hearing God's voice in them as well as in Christianity.

RAH's son, Robert Ernest Hume, inherited this concept of modern missions and worked to share this view of Christianity more broadly. He grew up in India and mastered many of its languages, particularly Sanskrit. After years of practical experience in the field as a missionary, he became a professor of comparative religions in one of the most important Christian theological seminaries in America. This post and the sustained popularity of his writings on world religions indicates that

American society came to accept his view that Christianity was part of a spiritual unfolding, not just in each individual but in the world, and throughout history. The selection of his book for the time capsule of the 1939 World's Fair made a public statement about American understanding of religions in the world. It encapsulates how much the ideas underlying modern missions had changed in a century, over the course of three generations of the Hume family.

BIBLIOGRAPHY

Alumni Directory of Yale University (Graduates and Non-Graduates). New Haven, Connecticut: Yale University Press, 1920. Online: http://www.archive.org/stream/ alumnidirectoryo00yalerich#page/n5/mode/2up.

"American Missionaries." *The Panoplist, and Missionary Magazine* 5, no. 10 (March 1813): 467-74.

America in the 1930s. University of Virginia. Online: http://xroads.virginia.edu/~1930s/ front.html.

Biographical Dictionary of Christian Missions. Edited by Gerald H. Anderson. Grand Rapids, Michigan: Wm. B. Eerdmans, 1999.

"Bombay." *Missionary Herald* 50, no. 1 (January 1854): 6.

Clark, Alden H. "Hume of Ahmednagar." *The Missionary Review of the World* 52, no. 11 (November 1929): 821-27.

"Communication from Mr. Allen of the Bombay Mission on Caste and How the East India Company Ruled On It." *Missionary Herald* 46 (September 1850): 308-9.

"Competitive Debates at Yale; The New Law School Building to be Ready for Use by New Year's." *The New York Times*, October 15, 1894.

"Death Notice of Mrs. Hannah D. Hume." *Missionary Herald* 99 (June 1903): 249.

Dorrien, Gary J., ed. *The Making of American Liberal Theology: Idealism, Realism, and Modernity, 1900-1950*. Westminster: John Knox Press, 2003.

Dorrien, Gary J. *Social Ethics in the Making: Interpreting an American Tradition*. West Sussex, United Kingdom: Wiley-Blackwell, 2009.

"Dr. Hume, Expert on Religions, Dies; Professor Emeritus at Union Seminary, Once Missionary, Wrote Several Books." Obituary. *The New York Times*, January 4, 1948.

"Extracts from Mrs. N.'s Letters." *The Panoplist, and Missionary Magazine* 5, no. 10 (March 1813): 468-70.

Fairbank, S. B. "A Historical Sketch of the Evangelistic Work Done by the Ahmednagar Branch of the Marathi Mission of the American Board of Commissioners for Foreign Missions, in the Half Century, Closing with This Year of 1881." In *Memorial Papers of the American Marathi Mission, 1813-1881*, 42-56. Bombay: Education Society's Press, 1882.

Hamilton, Gail. "That Everlasting Andover Controversy." *The North American Review* 144, no. 366 (May 1887): 477-86.

Hartford Theological Seminary Annual Register for 1897-98. Hartford, Connecticut: Hartford Seminary Press, 1898.

Hudson, Albert O. *Future Probation in Christian Belief*. Middlesex, England: Bible Fellowship Union, 1975. http://www.auburn.edu/~allenkc/fut-prob.html.

Hume, Edward Hicks. *Doctors East, Doctors West*. New York: Norton & Co., 1946.

[Hume, Hannah.] Obituary. *The Hartford Courant*, April 21, 1903.

Hume, Lotta Carswell. *Drama at the Doctor's Gate: The Story of Doctor Edward Hume of Yale-in-China*. New Haven, Connecticut: The Yale-in-China Association, Inc., 1961.

Hume, Robert Allen. *An Interpretation of India's Religious History*. New York: Fleming H. Revell, 1911.

———. "Hume of Ahmednagar—His Story." Pts. 1–7. *The Congregationalist* 106, no. 41 (October 13, 1921): 467–68; 106, no. 42 (October 20, 1921): 499–500; 106, no. 43 (October 27, 1921): 534–36; 106, no. 44 (November 3, 1921): 566–67; 106, no. 47 (November 24, 1921): 665; 106, no. 48 (December 1, 1921): 705–6; 106, no. 51 (December 22, 1921): 817–18.

———. *Missions from the Modern View*. New York: Fleming H. Revell, 1905.

———, et al. "Indian Rights in the United States." *The Nation*, October 17, 1923, 447.

Hume, Robert Ernest. *The Thirteen Principal Upanishads*. 2nd ed. Oxford: Oxford University Press, 1931.

———. *Treasure House of the Living Religions: Selections from Their Sacred Scriptures*. New York: Charles Scribner's Sons, 1932.

———. *The World's Living Religions: An Historical Sketch*. New York: Charles Scribner's Sons, 1942.

Hume, Robert W. "Letter from Mr. Hume, Dated Bombay, February 7, 1840." *Missionary Herald* 36, no. 12 (December 1840): 500.

Hutchinson, William R. *The Modernist Impulse in American Protestantism*. Durham, North Carolina and London: Duke University Press, 1992.

"Instructions Delivered to the Members of the late Reinforcement of the Mission in Southern India." *Missionary Herald* 32, no. 2 (February 1837): 83–93.

"Later Theology." In *Later National Literature, Part II*, vol. XVII of *The Cambridge History of English and American Literature in 18 Volumes* (1907–21). Online: http://bartleby.com/227/0910.html, accessed January 17, 2006.

"Letter from Mrs. Newell." *The Panoplist, and Missionary Magazine* 5, no. 11 (April 1813): 515–20.

"Madras Missionary Conference on Caste." *Missionary Herald* 46 (September 1850): 305–8.

Memorial Papers of the American Marathi Mission, 1813–1881: Presented at the Semi-Centennial Anniversary of the Commencement of the Ahmednagar Mission, October 26–30, 1881. Bombay: Education Society's Press, 1882.

"Mission at Bombay." *Missionary Herald* 20, no. 1 (January 1824): 1.

"Mission at Bombay, Joint Letter of the Missionaries: The State of the Schools." *Missionary Herald* 20, no. 1 (May 1824): 146–47.

Mitchell, Mary Hewitt. *History of the United Church of New Haven*. New Haven, Connecticut: United Church (Congregational), 1942.

"Mr. Hume Returns to India." *The New York Times*, July 3, 1887.

Navalkar, Gunpatrao. "Third Speech." In *Report of the Third Decennial Missionary Conference Held at Bombay, 1892–1893*, 293–98. Bombay: Education Society's Press, 1893.

"Not Forbidden to Work." *The New York Times*, February 12, 1887.

One Hundred Year Biographical Directory of Mount Holyoke College, 1837–1937. South Hadley, Massachusetts: Alumnae Association of Mount Holyoke College, 1937.

"Online Genealogy, Hume Family." Accessed July 23, 2011. Online: http://www.hunsberger.org/humegenealogy.htm.

Porterfield, Amanda. *Mary Lyon and the Mount Holyoke Missionaries*. New York and Oxford: Oxford University Press, 1997.

"R. A. Hume." Obituary. *The Times*, London, June 28, 1929, p. 18, column D.

"Religious Intelligence: American Missionaries." *The Panoplist, and Missionary Magazine* 5, no. 12 (May 1813): 561–62.

Report of the American Marathi Mission for the Year 1881. Poona: Orphanage Press, 1882.

"Report of the Prudential Committee." *The Panoplist, and Missionary Magazine* 5 (October 1812): 228–31.

"Report of Rev. Bowen," *Missionary Herald* 45 (May 1849): 163–64.

Report of the Third Decennial Missionary Conference Held at Bombay, 1892–1893. Bombay: Education Society's Press, 1893.

"Robert Allen Hume." In *Catalogue of the Officers and Graduates of Yale University in New Haven, Connecticut, 1701–1910*, 147. New Haven, Connecticut, 1910.

"Robert Ernest Hume." In *Alumni Catalogue of the Union Theological Seminary—City of New York, 1836–1936*. Quoted in "Robert Ernest Hume, Biographical Notes," *Internet Archive*, September 13, 2007. Online: http://www.archive.org/details/RobertErnestHumeShortBiographyAndOrbituary.

Robinson, Henry C. "Assent to Creeds." *New Englander and Yale Review* 47, no. 211 (October 1887): 284–93.

Slater, T. E. "Work Among the Educated Classes." In *Report of the Third Decennial Missionary Conference Held at Bombay, 1892–1893*, vol. 1, 272–89. Bombay: Education Society's Press, 1893.

Stowe, David M. "Gordon Hall (1784–1826)." In *Biographical Dictionary of Christian Missions*, edited by Gerald H. Anderson, 275. Grand Rapids, Michigan: Wm. B. Eerdmans, 1999.

Stowe, David M. "Robert Wilson Hume (1809–1854)." In *Biographical Dictionary of Christian Missions*, edited by Gerald H. Anderson, 310. Grand Rapids, Michigan: Wm. B. Eerdmans, 1999.

Stowe, David M. "Samuel Newell (1784–1821) and Harriet (Atwood) (1793–1812)." In *Biographical Dictionary of Christian Missions*, edited by Gerald H. Anderson, 492–93. Grand Rapids, Michigan: Wm. B. Eerdmans, 1999.

"Survey of the Missions of the Board: South Asia, Bombay." *The Missionary Herald* 46 (January 1850), 8.

"They Dodged the Issue." *The New York Times*, February 13, 1887.

Tracy, Joseph. *History of the American Board of Commissioners for Foreign Missions*. New York: M. W. Dodd, 1842.

Wilder, R. G. *Mission Schools in India of the American Board of Commissioners for Foreign Missions, with Sketches of the Missions among the North American Indians, the Sandwich Islands, the Armenians of Turkey, and the Nestorians of Persia*. New York: A. D. F. Randolph, 1861.

Woodward, William P. "Book Review: *The World's Living Religions*." *Contemporary Religions in Japan (CRJ)* 33 (September 1960): 73–74.

Woolsey, T. D. "Christian Missions and Some of Their Obstacles." *New Englander and Yale Review* 33, no. 129 (October 1874): 770–84.

7

David Abeel, Missionary Wanderer in China and Southeast Asia; with Special Emphasis on His Visit with Walter Henry Medhurst in Batavia, January–June 1831

Thomas G. Oey

D AVID ABEEL WAS UNIQUE in several respects.[1] He was one of the first two American missionaries to China, and later he became the first American missionary to Southeast Asia outside of Burma.[2] He

1. A satisfactory scholarly monograph on Abeel has yet to be written. See Williamson, *Memoir*; Wylie, "Abeel," 72–75; Poppen, "Life"; Staufer, "David Abeel"; Rubinstein, *Origins*, 238–340; Stowe, "Abeel," 1–2. For Abeel's contribution to German sinology, see Walravens, *Deutschland-Kenntnisse der Chinesen*, 147. A collection of David Abeel's personal papers and journals is at Houghton Library, Harvard University, Cambridge, Massachusetts, USA and is available on microfilm. Additional letters of David Abeel are at New Brunswick Theological Seminary, New Brunswick, New Jersey. Nineteenth-century works quoted in this article were accessed from Google Books.

2. The first American missionaries to enter Asia were Adoniram Judson (1788–1850), Ann Hasseltine Judson (1789–1826) and Luther Rice (1783–1836). All three entered Serampore, India in 1812 under the auspices of the American Board of Commissioners for Foreign Missions (ABCFM), and in fact Judson was one of the founders of the ABCFM. However, under the influence of British Baptist missionary William Carey, the three decided to become Baptists and underwent believer's baptism by immersion. Adoniram and Ann Judson entered Burma in 1813, and Luther Rice returned to America to establish the General Missionary Convention of the Baptist Denomination in the United States of America for Foreign Missions (GMCBDUSAFM) in 1814. The ABCFM and the GMCBDUSAFM, also known as the Baptist "Triennial Convention" were in effect almost twin missionary organizations with the same roots. During the period 1831–42, they were both rivals and partners in various mission fields of East Asia such as Singapore, Bangkok and Macau. See Oey, "Baptist Missionaries." Rev. Dr.

arrived in 1830 in Guangzhou, China, with his missionary colleague, Elijah Coleman Bridgman. But as Murray Rubenstein has stated, they differed from one another. Bridgman was from a rural, middle class New England background, whereas Abeel was from the upper middle class of Dutch America.[3]

Among the nine Americans who arrived in the China mission field between 1830 and 1834, Abeel stood out as having a non-New England, non-Congregationalist background.[4] His father was a descendent of the Dutch immigrant Christopher Janson Abeel, who arrived in New Netherlands with his family in 1651, only a generation after the founding of New Amsterdam in 1609. His mother was apparently of more recent immigrant ancestry. She could still speak the language from the Netherlands old country, which might explain Abeel's linguistic talents. His family's spiritual beliefs can be traced back to Theodore Jacob Frelinghuysen, whereas the spiritual beliefs of his colleague Bridgman can be traced back to Jonathan Edwards.

Another difference between Abeel and Bridgman was the type of missionary work they chose to pursue. There were two types of missionaries in the nineteenth century: 1.) stationary missionaries such as the Britons Robert Morrison and Walter Henry Medhurst (both of the London Missionary Society) and the Americans E. C. Bridgman and Peter Parker; and 2.) itinerant missionaries such as the Prussian Karl Gützlaff, and the Americans David Abeel and Edwin Stevens. Stationary missionaries engaged in literary, educational, and medical mission work in one mission station for many years, while itinerant missionaries were primarily interested in "sowing" gospel seeds and traveling from place to place.[5]

John Scudder, Sr. (1793–1855), an American Dutch Reformed missionary affiliated with the AFCFM, in 1819 entered Ceylon (Sri Lanka) where he established a medical hospital, and established a mission in Madras (Chennai), India in 1836. David Oliver Allen (1799–1863), a native of Barre, Vermont and graduate of Amherst College, served under the ABCFM in Bombay, Ahmednuggar and other parts of Western India from 1827 to 1844. See Montague, *Alumni of Amherst College*, 10.

3. Rubenstein, *Origins,* 239.

4. These missionaries included E. C. Bridgman (arrived 1830); Edwin Stevens (arrived 1832), Samuel Wells Williams (arrived 1833), Ira Tracy (arrived 1833) Henry Lyman (arrived 1833), Samuel Munson (arrived 1833), Stephen Johnson (arrived 1833), Peter Parker, MD (arrived 1834). With the exception of Williams, who was born in Utica, New York, all of these men were from New England.

5. See Lutz, *Opening China*; Klein and Zöllner, *Karl Gützlaff.*

Among the early itinerant missionaries, Abeel was the only one who traveled around both sides of the Atlantic, preaching up and down the American Atlantic Coast and on the shores of the European North Sea.[6] He was active in Northeast and Southeast Asia. Simply put, Abeel was a wandering missionary phenomenon, who was at home preaching anywhere, whether it was in Boston, Georgia, Guangzhou, Batavia, Bangkok, Singapore, London, Paris, Amsterdam, Basel, or Xiamen. From his background and missionary wanderings through three continents, he developed the ability to communicate in four European languages (English, Dutch, German, and French), three Asian languages (Chinese, Malay, and Thai) and two Chinese dialects (Hokkien and Shantounese).

While Abeel was in China and Southeast Asia during the years 1830–33, his letters and other reports of his work were being published in America and Europe, thereby forming the basis of a missionary sensation. After completing four years of mission work in East Asia and visiting Europe, Abeel returned to the United States on September 4, 1834, for four years of furlough. He was the first China missionary to return to America to promote mission work, and he used the occasion to produce his magnum opus: *Journal of a Residence in China, and the Neighboring Countries, from 1829–1833* (New York and Boston, 1834). This influential work, and his earlier published letters, attracted new missionaries from various denominations to enter China and Southeast Asia. The materials appealed specifically to the group that initiated American missionary work in China in 1830 (namely the ABCFM and its Congregationalist, New School Presbyterian, and Dutch Reformed supporters), and they appealed to the groups that entered the new fields in East Asia subsequently, namely the Baptists (1835), the Episcopalians (1835), the Old School Presbyterians (1838) and others. The first group came mostly from the north (especially New England), while the other groups included a number of Southerners.

Because of the widespread appeal of Abeel and his book, Abeel can be seen as a cross-denominational missionary leader. He is also notable because he extended the influence of American missions in East Asia beyond "Zion's Corner" of Guangzhou,[7] and promoted the development

6. On the phenomenon of cooperation between British and continental European Protestant missionaries, see Railton, *No North Sea*.

7. See Rubenstein, *Zion's Corner*, and Rubenstein, "The Protestant Missionary enterprise," 133–74.

of new mission work in the Netherlands East Indies, Siam, Singapore and Macau prior to the Opium War, and in the coastal cities of China thereafter.

EARLY LIFE AND MISSIONARY CALLING

David Abeel III was born June 12, 1804, in the family home in New Brunswick, New Jersey, a largely rural area. Wylie states his family background very succinctly: "His family was originally from Amsterdam in Holland; and his father was an officer in the United States navy during the revolution. His mother Jane Hassert was distinguished for her piety." At the age of fifteen, he applied to West Point Military Academy, but discouraged by the large number of prior applicants, he decided to study medicine for a year instead. He studied medicine for one year at the medical school of Queen's College (now Rutgers University), but apparently did not have any other college training.[8] At age seventeen, he underwent a religious conversion. He developed a deep conviction of sin, and a strong religious piety which would thereafter permeate his writings.

Deciding to become a preacher, Abeel entered the Reformed Theological Seminary at his home town of New Brunswick in 1823, graduating in April 1826. He was licensed to preach on April 20, 1826, and in the following month was commissioned as pastor in Athens, New York, where he served for two and a half years.

Abeel was influenced by reading the journal of David Brainerd and the life of Henry Martyn to consider missionary work. In December 1827, he resolved to submit an application to the ABCFM in the spring. In 1828 Abeel suffered from chronic dyspepsia, which caused depression, and his medical condition forced him to resign from his pastorate.[9] He embarked on his first missionary adventure in November 1828, when he sailed for St. John's in the Danish West Indies, both to "recruit his energies" and "with the expectation of proclaiming the Gospel as he found opportunity." Already Abeel found himself unable to distinguish between taking a vacation and conducting missionary work. For the next

8. Alicia Graham, email to author, June 9, 2011, citing Poppen, "The Life of David Abeel."

9. Williamson, *Memoir*, 44. I do not see any evidence that Abeel's medical condition influenced his decision to become a missionary.

18 years until his death, the ailing Abeel was a worldwide whirlwind of activity, continuously traveling and preaching.

Abeel began regular preaching at St. John's in the late spring of 1829. He was so successful that after only two months the local government forced him to stop. Abeel returned to New York in August 1829, and soon received a proposal to go to Guangzhou, China, as a chaplain for the Seamen's Friend Society. "This he accepted," a biographer wrote, "with the understanding that, after one year, he was to enter the service of the American Board of Foreign Missions, for the purpose of exploring the islands and countries in eastern Asia, to ascertain the best position for mission stations."[10] Accompanied by E. C. Bridgman, Abeel sailed from New York on October 14 aboard the *Roman,* and traveled through the islands of the East Indies. On February 18, the ship passed the latitude of Formosa (Taiwan), and Abeel commented in his *Journal* about Dutch mission work among the Taiwan aborigines in the 17th century. After stopping at Macau, they reached Guangzhou on February 25, 1830.

IMPRESSIONS OF CHINA (1830)

As a chaplain for the American Seamen's Friend Society during his period of service in Guangzhou, Abeel had what he described as "a conditional appointment from the American Board of Commissioners for Foreign Missions, in case he should consider it his duty to devote himself exclusively to the heathen."[11] His companion E. C. Bridgman has been described by Michael C. Lazich as "America's first missionary to China,"[12] but in fact Abeel was as much a missionary as Bridgman, who worked directly for the ABCFM from the beginning, and shared also in the chaplaincy work. Comments in Abeel's *Journal* demonstrate his missionary intentions even prior to his arrival in Guangzhou.

While in Guangzhou, Abeel served as a chaplain to the foreign English-speaking community and studied the Chinese language. He and Bridgman encountered the British missionary Robert Morrison, who had established a Protestant mission to China in 1807, and Liang

---

10. Wylie, "David Abeel," 72–73.

11. Abeel, *Journal* preface, 7.

12. Lazich, *E. C. Bridgman.*

Fa, a Chinese preacher who had been converted by British missionary William Milne in Malacca.

Abeel spent several chapters in his *Journal* describing China. In one chapter he addressed things he saw as needful of reform, such as the practices of female infanticide, female foot binding, the lack of education, and grotesque criminal punishments. His descriptions are rather picturesque, but often condescending and deprecatory. For example he makes the following comment in a footnote concerning the literature of the Chinese:

> Their philosophy, history, poetry, are so mixed up with the marvelous and absurd, that with the exception of the maxims of their sages, some of which are excellent, there is nothing worth exploring in the whole field of their sciences.[13]

Like other early American Protestant missionaries, Abeel combined his piety with condescension that bordered on anti-intellectualism. Pioneers such as Abeel were more interested in mission itineracy than in studying Chinese literature and culture. They saw themselves as representatives of western Christian civilization and sought to remake the "heathen" after their own image. They had no intention of indigenizing the Christian message for Asia.

ABEEL AND WALTER HENRY MEDHURST IN BATAVIA (JANUARY–JUNE 1831)

Only ten months after arriving in Guangzhou with E. C. Bridgman, Abeel had acquired enough proficiency in the Chinese language to make him anxious to get on the move. At the end of 1830, he had finished his contract to serve "one year as chaplain" to American seamen in Guangzhou, and on December 20 he transferred to the care of the ABCFM. He accepted an offer of free passage aboard the *N.C.S. Castle Huntley*, which departed Guangzhou on December 29. Passing by the coast of Cochin China (Vietnam and Cambodia), Abeel wrote in his journal about sighting a pagoda, and the influence of French Catholic missionaries.[14] He arrived in Angier, Java, and from there he traveled on land. On January 20, 1831, he reached Batavia, where he stayed five months before proceeding to Siam. Leaders of the Reformed Dutch Church (now known

13. Abeel, *Journal*, 138.
14. Ibid., 149–50.

as the Reformed Church in America), when they learned that Abeel had embarked on this mission activity, formed a Board of Foreign Missions in 1832 to support the work of Abeel in China and Southeast Asia "in concert" with the ABCFM, and also to support existing mission work in South Asia. [15]

As a Dutch American bound for mission work in Asia, Abeel naturally wished to visit that part of Asia which was colonized by the "Old" Netherlands, namely the Netherlands East Indies (now known as Indonesia). A collection of islands in Southeast Asia which included the Moluccas (the Spice Islands), Celebes (Sulawesi), Borneo (Kalimantan), West Timor, Bali, Java, Sumatra, and Riau, the Netherlands East Indies began to be colonized in the early seventeenth century. Two centuries later in 1829, the year before Abeel arrived in Guangzhou with Bridgman, an announcement was made in a Dutch American religious journal of Abeel's intention to visit the British Protestant missionary Walter Henry Medhurst in Batavia (now Jakarta), the administrative capital of the Netherlands East Indies.[16] Batavia was located on the northwest coast of Java, a fertile volcanic island which was the most populous in the East Indies. Medhurst was a missionary of the London Missionary Society who had arrived in Malacca in 1817 and transferred to Batavia in January 1822.

Abeel had passed through the Netherlands East Indies as he voyaged to China at the beginning of 1830. On that voyage he reflected in his journal about the history of the area. The Portuguese had entered the East Indies in the sixteenth century and they were largely supplanted by the Dutch in the early seventeenth century. Both groups brought Christianity to the islands. By the close of the seventeenth century, roughly 40,000 Indonesians were professing Christians. Abeel contended, however, that Christianity on the islands subsequently declined:

> A declension soon commenced, and continued with such rapidity, that whole districts speedily relapsed into their former abominations. The causes of this decline, or rather of the apparent conversion of such numbers, who afterwards apostatized, are various. Many of the chaplains opposed, in spirit and conduct, their worthy coadjutors; too much stress was laid upon a knowledge of the technicalities, or a compliance with the formalities

15. Ibid., preface.
16. Brownlee, "Religious Intelligence," 382.

of Christianity, too little upon the renovation of the heart; professing Christians were preferred to their heathen neighbors in the distribution of petty offices under governments and even a monthly allowance of rice was served out to those, and those only, who had received the rite of baptism.[17]

By 1814, new missionaries had arrived in Java, and the Dutch missionary Joseph Kam arrived in the Moluccas in 1815 in an attempt to revitalize Christianity in that region of the Netherlands East Indies. But there still remained much to be done in this regard when Abeel arrived in Batavia. On the Sunday after his arrival, he visited Medhurst's mission chapel, where two English services and a Malay service were held, and met Medhurst's two assistants, William Young and a native Amboynese convert, Lucas Monton. Speaking with an unnamed longtime English-speaking foreign resident, Abeel learned that Java had a population of six million, including four million who spoke Javanese, one and a half million who spoke Sundanese, and half a million who spoke Malay. The three principal towns were Batavia (with 300,000 thousand inhabitants, including 30,000 Chinese), Semarang (with 200,000 thousand inhabitants, including 10,000 Chinese), and Surabaya (with 300,000 inhabitants, including 5,000 Chinese). An additional 10,000 Chinese were scattered throughout the island. The foreign resident observed that the Dutch colonizers were reluctant to support mission work:

> The Dutch systematically avoid establishing missions among Mohammetans, and endeavor to thrust their missionaries away, into bye places, as much as possible. Hence on the whole island of Java, entirely under their own dominion, they have not a single missionary. Formerly, two missionaries were stationed at Christian villages, but with the exclusive object of ministering to those who already professed Christianity. These are both dead.[18]

17. Abeel, *Journal*, 18.

18. Ibid., 158–59. In fact the foreign resident was somewhat misinformed. At least five persons were engaged in missionary or quasi-missionary activities in Java. Medhurst, who also served as chaplain of the English-speaking church in Batavia, had thereby attained the status of burgher or resident, and had the freedom to conduct mission activities. Johannes Emde, a German watchrepairer, was associated with an indigenous missionary society in Surabaya. The German Gottloeb Brückner had arrived in Semarang in 1814 and since 1817 was supported by English Baptists. At the time of Abeel's visit, Brückner was in Serampore, overseeing the printing of his Javanese New Testament translation. J. F. C. Gericke, a German linguist and agent of the Netherlands Bible Society, had arrived in 1826, and was based in Surakarta, Central Java. He was

In his *Journal*, Abeel wrote positively about the beginnings of Dutch missionary work in in the East Indies:

> The Dutch church in these islands was planted nearly the time, when our forefathers colonized New Amsterdam. That zeal for the Saviour's glory, and attachment to the doctrines of her standards characterized the eastern branch of the mother church equally with the western, is proved by historic testimony. We have one of the least ambiguous evidences of this fact in the ardor and enterprise with which her ministers engaged in the duty of evangelizing the heathen around them. The bible was translated—works of much utility and merit were written—preaching was commenced—schools opened—in fact, every thing which was attempted for the heathen, was done by these men; missionary societies were unknown at the time.[19]

Abeel clearly admired the early Dutch missionaries in Indonesia. He was less enthusiastic, however, in his assessment of their successors who served prior to 1814. In fact, he blamed them for undermining Christianity on the islands:

> The deterioration of the churches at home—the neglect to appoint chaplains, when the [Dutch East India] company was disorganized—the subordination of the ministry to the secular power,—the dissipated habits of Eastern society, added to the worldly spirit and unsound faith of many of the chaplains—are quite sufficient to account for the sad change which came over this once flourishing part of the Saviour's vineyard.[20]

Abeel spent five months in the company of Medhurst, preaching, distributing tracts, and observing the customs and practices of the indigenous Malay speakers and ethnic Chinese in Batavia and its environs. On April 7, Abeel and Medhurst visited a Chinese temple, and Medhurst described how he witnessed the practice of divine possession:

> Mr. M. has witnessed some of the incantations which they practice, to obtain the inspiration of such deified men. Upon the performance of some ridiculous ceremony, the subject becomes

---

engaged in producing a grammar and word book of the Javanese language and in producing another translation of the Bible into Javanese. Dirk Lenting, a Dutch minister in Batavia, engaged in missionary activities, and with Medhurst edited a Malay New Testament produced by the Surabaya missionary society.

19. Ibid., 178.

20. Ibid., 178–79.

convulsed, exerts himself with violence, frequently cuts his body with a sword, and when necessarily composed from the exhaustion of effort and pain, is thought to be tranquilized by the influence of the deity, and prepared to answer such questions as are proposed. As the subject of inquiry is generally one of deep interest, his replies are noted down with all possible dispatch, and his advice carefully and confidentally followed. The evidence of true inspiration, is the rapidity with which his wounds heal, and the success which attends his prescription.[21]

On April 14, Abeel and Medhurst witnessed a Chinese fire-walking ceremony. It became an opportunity for them to distribute a tract Medhurst had written for precisely such an occasion:

This afternoon, we rode about six miles in the country, and attended a Chinese ceremony, which reminded us of the "bloody rites of Moloch." It occurs on the birth-day of one of the Taou gods, and is performed by running barefoot through a large heap of ignited charcoal. The pile was about ten or twelve feet square, and nearly two feet in height. It threw out a sweltering heat. The crowd was large, and the crash of gongs almost deafening. When we arrived, we found two priests standing near the fire, earnestly reading a book, though the noise drowned their voices, and performing a variety of strange acts, which they appeared to derive from its pages. One of them held a cow's horn in his hand, with which he occasionally assisted the noise, while the other, after burning paper, and making his obeisance, advanced to the fire— sprinked water upon the heap, struck it violently with a sword, threw in more of the paper, bowed his head, and frequently gazed upwards with an expression of most intense earnestness, while his whole body, as might be supposed, was bathed in perspiration. After this, they both approached the fire, went through a number of antics, and finally dashed through the coals. A passage was kept clear from an adjacent temple to the spot, and as soon as the priests had set the example, a number of persons, old and young, came running from the temple with idols in their hands, and carried them through the fire. Others followed the example, and among them, an old man, who rather halted and staggered in the midst of the heap . . . It is thought to be a test of the moral character of those who attempt it . . . One of the votaries last year fell down in the midst of the pile, and was severely burned.

21. Ibid., 182–83.

Our budget of Chinese tracts was disposed of, as speedily as they could be handed out.[22]

Abeel emphasized how few missionaries were in the islands of the Netherlands East Indies. He was aware of only two missionaries in Java including Medhurst, and one in the Moluccas. Abeel's appeal to revitalize the Christian message in the Netherlands East Indies did have certain consequences. Other events further stimulated interest in the East Indies. Notable among them, in 1833, American Congregationalists Henry Lyman and Samuel Munson arrived in Batavia, and in the following year they were killed when they attempted to conduct mission work among the Bataks in Sumatra. Their work, however, was later taken up by the German missionary Ludwig Nommenson (1834–1918). During his visit to Europe in 1833–34, Abeel might have been influential in recruiting new missionaries to enter the East Indies. American Episcopalians entered Batavia to conduct missions among the Chinese in 1835, and around a dozen American Dutch Reformed missionaries serving under the auspices of the ABCFM labored in difficult conditions in Borneo up until the time of the Opium War in China.[23] In 1843, Medhurst transferred to Shanghai, and by 1851 the American missionaries also withdrew from the Netherlands East Indies, leaving the field to German and Dutch missionaries.

VISITS TO SINGAPORE, SIAM, MALACCA, AND RIAU (1831–1833)

After departing from Batavia, Abeel arrived in Singapore June 14, 1831, where he met Jacob Tomlin of the London Missionary Society, a colleague of Medhurst. Along with Karl Gützlaff, Tomlin had engaged in pioneering Protestant mission work in Bangkok for nine months in 1828 and 1829, and was anxious to return there.[24] Abeel and Tomlin departed Singapore on June 17, 1831, and arrived in Bangkok on July 2, 1831. Gützlaff was no longer there, having departed for China after the death of his wife and child. While in Siam (now known as Thailand), Gützlaff, Tomlin and Abeel—who undoubtedly made use of his prior medical

---

22. Ibid., 183–84.

23. A description of the work of ABCFM missionaries in Southeast Asia during the 1830s is found in Latourette, *History*, 104–9.

24. See Tomlin, *Early Missionaries in Bangkok*.

training—treated patients as a method of evangelistic work; thus they became models for Peter Parker of the ABCFM, the first full-time medical missionary to China.[25]

Abeel labored in Bangkok until January 7, 1832, and returned to Singapore January 13, 1832. On March 6, Abeel departed from Singapore and arrived in Malacca on March 12. He observed the work of the London Missionary Society in Malacca until his departure on March 27. He then returned to Singapore on April 2, but left on April 18, arriving in Bangkok on May 19 for a second missionary visit there. He worked in Bangkok for the next five and a half months. He departed Bangkok on November 5, and returned to Singapore. On the 28th of the same month, he accompanied Claudius H. Thomsen, a missionary of the London Missionary Society in Singapore, on a visit to Rhio (Riau), an island near Singapore which was controlled by the Dutch.

After returning to Singapore in December 1832, Abeel accepted an invitation to serve as the preacher to the colony's English language congregation of western foreign residents, taking the place of the ailing Rev. Robert Burn, who died on January 17, 1833. Although his previous visits to Singapore had been brief, Abeel stayed there almost six months this time, becoming acquainted with the English-speaking residents of Singapore, conducting mission work among the Chinese inhabitants, and studying Chinese and Malay. He also noted the effective educational mission work with girls being done by Miss Sophia Martin, the sister-in-law of Walter Henry Medhurst, who along with Mrs. Elizabeth Medhurst had been born in the regency of Madras (Chennai), a southern port city of British-colonized India. Ill health forced Abeel to leave Singapore on May 25, 1833, but before he departed he published an anonymous tract, *To the Bachelors of India by a Bachelor,* to discourage western foreign residents from taking native concubines.[26]

Abeel blazed a trail for other American missionaries who wanted to work in Singapore and Siam. Inspired by his example, American Baptist, ABCFM, and American Presbyterian missionaries entered Siam. The Baptists developed a permanent mission among the Shantounese-

25. Jones, "letters." John T. Jones, originally a Congregationalist trained at Amherst College, was the first American Baptist and the second American missionary to enter Singapore in 1832 and Bangkok in 1833.

26. Wylie, "David Abeel," 73–75. The information about Miss Martin and Mrs. Medhurst comes from R. G. Tiedemann, conversation with author, July 5, 2010, and subsequent correspondence.

speaking Chinese, while the Presbyterians developed a permanent relationship with the ethnic Thai. In Singapore, Ira Tracy of the ABCFM entered in 1834 and established a printing press with the help of several colleagues. American Baptist missionaries also frequented Singapore from 1832 to 1844, and American Presbyterian missionaries entered Singapore in 1838. However, the ABCFM and American Presbyterian Singapore missions were closed after the Opium War. Benjamin Keasbury was a British printer who was significantly influenced during Abeel's visit. Keasbury, who travelled with Abeel from America during his return to East Asia in 1839, went back to Singapore and made a significant contribution to its Christian history.

VISIT TO EUROPE (1833–4)

Abeel arrived in England on October 21, 1833. His heath had recovered, and he began to promote mission work. He remained in Europe for ten months. At the end of December 1833, he left England, and by January 1, 1834, he was in Paris, where he spoke to members of the Protestant community. In the span of just two weeks, he visited the Netherlands, Prussia, and the German Rhineland. Then he arrived in Basel, Switzerland, where he was based for six months. Details of Abeel's visit to the European Continent are scanty in his *Memorial,* but it appears Abeel may have visited the Protestant French portion of Switzerland. He may also have revisited the German Rhineland and the Netherlands to meet religious leaders and promote mission work.

A series of experiences in the East Indies stimulated Abeel's interest in promoting missions in the German-speaking portions of Europe. Abeel had been appointed as a chaplain to foreign sailors in Guangzhou in 1830. There in the early summer Abeel met two German sailors: a man who was undergoing medical treatment for a factured limb, and his companion, a Lutheran, whose Bible had been stolen by a monkey.[27] As Dutch was Abeel's mother tongue, it was probably not difficult for him to learn from the sailors how to communicate in German. When Abeel visited Batavia in 1831, he probably learned about the work of the German missionary Karl Gützlaff, who had stayed with Medhurst a few years earlier.

27. Richardson, *Memoir,* 69–70.

Abeel made a significant visit to the Basel Mission Society in the German-speaking portion of Switzerland. The Society, which wielded enormous influence in the German-speaking portions of Europe, had taken notice of Medhurst's work in the inaugural issue of its mission's magazine in 1821. Abeel for his part was interested in the Society. Back in January, 1832, he had written them regarding his recent mission work in Siam.[28] A German translation of an excerpt from Abeel's *Journal* about his visit with Medhurst in Batavia appeared in the Basel mission's magazine.[29] Abeel's *Journal* was published in two editions in the German language.[30]

On July 25, 1834, Abeel returned to England, and preached in London, Birmingham, and Edinburgh. He also issued the pamphlet "Appeal to Christian Ladies in behalf of Female Education in China." Together with Rev. Baptist Noel and a few ladies, Abeel established the Society for Promoting Female Education in China and the East. Profits from the sale of his *Journal,* for which Rev. Noel arranged a London edition in 1835, were devoted to its support. By the time Abeel returned to Asia in 1839, the society had sent out five British and Swiss single female missionaries to Batavia, Singapore and Macau, and by 1849 it had sponsored nearly 40 lady missionaries of different denominations.[31]

Abeel also noted the presence of Catholic missionaries in Korea. He concluded his *Journal* with descriptions of Borneo, the Philippines, and Japan, which he knew from the writings of others rather than from personal visits. These chapters completed his desired portrait of East Asia. He made an appeal for new missionaries to the fields described. As he had related to the expatriate communities of East Asia, he supported the laicization of mission work and appealed for not only the best theological graduates but also for women, teachers, physicians, merchants, and even mechanics to enter the field.[32]

28. Abeel, "German-language letter."

29. Abeel, "Ueberfahrt," 186–212.

30. Abeel, *Reise in den Ländern Hinterindiens; Reise des nordamerikanischen missionars.*

31. See Williamson, *Memoir,* 141–42; 145 and Tiedemann, *Reference Guide,* 213.

32. Abeel, *Journal,* 388, 391.

FURLOUGH IN AMERICA (1834–38)

Abeel returned to New York on September 6, 1834. One week later, the mission board of the Reformed Church in America met to approve the publication of his *Journal*, which appeared in October 1834. It also appeared in British (1835) and German (1836) editions, and a second American edition was issued in 1836. Although a rather superficial work, the *Journal* became a milestone of American sinology and the American understanding of East Asia. Infused with the religious social reform sentiment of antebellum America, it presented a humble, American, homegrown analysis of the spiritual, societal, educational, and developmental needs of East Asia. Religious audiences throughout the country could have direct access to its author through his manifold speaking engagements, and even participate in the challenge of mission work.

Space does not allow for a detailed description of Abeel's activities in America. Suffice it to note that he traveled extensively throughout the country, promoting mission work on an interdenominational basis. Visits to the the South were good for his health, which benefited from the region's warmer climate. Nevertheless, recurring attacks of illness kept him from returning to the mission field for four years. While recruiting his heath he received many speaking invitations from churches, colleges, and theological seminaries. The fall 1836 election of Martin Van Buren, the first Dutch American and mid-Atlantic state resident to become president of the U.S., served to enhance Abeel's stature as a missionary statesman. He planned to sail for China in October 1836, but he suffered from a health relapse, and did not go. Instead, he traveled to the West Indies to recuperate the following winter. There he learned that he suffered from an organic disease of the heart.

During Abeel's four years in America, about two dozen American missionaries and their spouses were inspired to enter Batavia, Borneo, Singapore, Siam, and Macau with support from the ABCFM, Baptist, Presbyterian, and Episcopalian mission societies. In 1838, Abeel's second influential missionary work, *The Missionary Convention at Jerusalem; or an Exhibition of the Claims of the World to the Gospel* was published in New York by John S. Taylor.

RETURN TO ASIA: MISSION WORK IN GUANGZHOU, MACAU, SINGAPORE, BORNEO, AND XIAMEN (1839–45)

Abeel was finally well enough to sail from America on October 17, 1838, with the Rev. Samuel R. Brown, of the Morrison Education Society and Benjamin P. Keasbury and their wives. On February 20, 1839, the group reached Guangzhou, where Abeel was reunited with his former colleague, E. C. Bridgman. The Rev. Morrison had died since Abeel's departure over eight years earlier, but Peter Parker, who had arrived in 1834, was doing effective mission work through the practice of medicine.

Within a month of Abeel's arrival in Guangzhou, trouble arose from the interdiction of opium by Chinese commissioner Lin Zexu. The dispute eventually broke out into open hostilities between China and Britain, whose subjects were the chief suppliers of opium to the Chinese. There were also Americans who sold opium to the Chinese, although their quantities were not as large as the British. Whereas the British held a monopoly over opium produced in their colony in India, the Americans bought opium in Izmir, Turkey. Both British and Americans shipped opium to China via Singapore.[33] Both Bridgman in Guangzhou in 1832 and Medhurst in London in 1838 wrote against the opium trade. In his 1835 visit to the coast of China, Medhurst even refused to travel on any vessel that engaged in the opium trade, whereas Gützlaff often traveled on ships that carried opium. Abeel criticized the trade and the consumption of opium in several passages in his 1834 *Journal*. At one point while on a voyage to Siam, Abeel took transportation in a vessel which had opium in its hold, and he commented on the degrading effect of the trade on the crew members.[34]

Abeel watched as Britain defeated China in the Opium War of 1839–41. According to his nephew G. R. Williamson, Abeel was opposed to the opium trade but saw the British retaliation as a justifiable measure:

> While he considered the opium trade as fraught with ruinous consequences to the bodies and souls of the inhabitants of China, on the other hand he deemed the war necessary to overcome the prejudices, and destroy the exclusive policy of the self-styled subjects of the "Son of Heaven." He looked beyond political questions; and saw in these difficulties, the providence of God

33. Roberts, "Commercial Philanthropy," 371–88.

34. Abeel, *Journal*, 284–85.

working great results for good out of seeming evil, and causing the wrath of man to praise him. Nor were his anticipations in regard to those things disappointed.[35]

By August 1839, Abeel had transferred to Macau. Established as a Portuguese trading enclave in the mid sixteenth century, Macau became a base for Catholic missionaries. The British Protestant missionaries Robert Morrison and William Milne visited Macau in connection with their mission work. Abeel and E. C. Bridgman were the first two American missionaries to visit Macau, which they saw in the beginning of 1830.[36] In 1831, Karl Gützlaff chose Macau to be his base for missionary trips to the coasts of China, Korea, and Okinawa. In 1836, American Baptist missionaries J.L. and Henrietta Shuck established themselves in Macau, followed by Samuel Wells Williams of the ABCFM and the American Baptist I.J. Roberts in 1837.

After Abeel entered Macau for the second time in 1839, he studied the Chinese language and wrote articles in the *Chinese Repository*, which was published by his ABCFM colleagues E. C. Bridgman and Samuel Wells Williams. Abeel focused his missionary efforts on the Chinese speaking the Hokkien (Xiamen) dialect, which he had encountered previously among overseas Chinese in Batavia and Singapore.

Accompanied by Rev. and Mrs. Samuel Brown, Abeel left Macau and arrived in Singapore in April 1841. While in Singapore, he stayed at the home of Benjamin Keasbury. After a brief visit to Malacca, Abeel spent over a month (September 18 to October 30) visiting Borneo with Rev. Thomas L. MacBryde, a Presbyterian missionary from South Carolina.[37] About a dozen American Reformed missionaries, personally recruited by Abeel and working under the auspices of the ABCFM, had been serving in the Netherlands East Indies, focusing mainly on Borneo. Laboring under difficult circumstances, several had died, and others had been forced to leave the field on account of illness. Abeel, however, received positive impressions from his Borneo visit.

Abeel returned to Macau on December 21, 1841. Citing an obscure reference from Isaiah which many Protestant missionaries believed referred to China, he opined that British military intervention in the

---

35. Williamson, *Memoir,* 180.

36. See Sena, "Macau," 23–90.

37. Wylie, "Abeel," 128.

Opium War was providential, because it enabled missionaries to enter China:

> Hence we have drawn the cheering conclusion, that the accept-able year of the Lord—the set time to favor the land of Sinim—is at hand. In either case, whether the Emperor yield or resist, tol-eration must be obtained. God has often made use of the strong arm of civil power to prepare the way for his own kingdom, that kingdom which is righteousness and peace, which cometh not with observation, and is not of this world.[38]

The treaty gained by the British at the end of the Opium War in 1842 ratified the presence of traders and missionaries in Guangzhou, ceded the island of Hong Kong, and designated the port cities Xiamen, Fuzhou, Ningbo and Shanghai as open to trade and missionaries. Even though the American treaty with China was not signed until 1844, the Macau-based American missionaries seized the opportunity to enter the new coastal cities beginning in early 1842. The American Baptist mis-sionaries I.J. Roberts and J. Lewis Shuck, together with their colleague William Dean from Bangkok, preferred to enter Hong Kong, whereas other Protestant China missionaries, including Abeel, chose to focus on Xiamen in southern Fujian.

Figure 22. The center of the "Bund" in Shanghai. The Bund is an embankment along the Huangpu River in Shanghai that was settled and developed by Westerners in the nineteenth century. Lithograph by Thomas Picken. From William Lockhart, *The Medical Missionary in China: A Narrative of Twenty Years' Experience* (London: Hurst and Blackett, 1861), front. Image courtesy of the Congregational Library, Boston.

38. Ibid., 215. Rather than creating a receptive atmosphere for Christianity in China, British and French military intervention led to a deep-seated hatred of Western missionaries among the Chinese literati. See Cohen, *Chinese Hostility to Christianity*.

Abeel led the vanguard of Protestant missionaries who entered the Chinese coastal cities early in 1842.[39] Moreover, Abeel had the appointment as American consul for Xiamen, the first American to have such a political appointment for a port north of Guangzhou.[40] As he held two hats as both missionary and American consul in Xiamen, Abeel was in the ambiguous position of supporting both the political and the cultural agenda of the United States in China. It was not entirely unusual at the time for Western Protestant missionaries to serve as official translators and to engage in political as well as missionary activities and roles at different times in China and East Asia, as the cases of Gützlaff, John Robert Morrison (the son of Robert Morrison), Bridgman, Parker, and Williams show. However, the dual function of the missionaries brought confusion as to what belonged to Christ, and what belonged to Caesar.

On February 2, 1842, Abeel left Macau in the company of the Episcopalian missionary William Jones Boone (who had transferred from Batavia), and established a mission at Gulang Island, Xiamen. Missionaries from the the American deep South became prominent in Xiamen and subsequently other port cities such as Ningbo and Shanghai. Most of those joining Abeel in Xiamen in June 1842 were Episcopalian or Presbyterian missionaries from South Carolina and Georgia.[41] They included Sally DeSaussure Boone, Rev. Boone's wife, who by virtue of her ancestors' Huguenot origins was, like Abeel, of seventeenth century continental European Reformed scionage. Abeel quite possibly had met the Boones when he visited their native South Carolina in the spring of 1835. Sally Boone died on Gulang Island on August 30, 1842, becoming the first American woman missionary to die and be buried in China.[42]

In 1843, Abeel left Gulang Island to reside in Xiamen proper. In the summer of 1844, he received an honorary D.D. degree from Rutgers College in his native state of New Jersey, but out of humility he declined the honor. In November 1844, he visited Jinmen, a small island opposite

39. I recall visiting the historical museum on Gulang Island in 1999. It depicted Abeel as the "vanguard of Western imperialism."

40. Sena, "Macau," 73.

41. These included William Jones Boone and Sally DeSausure Boone from South Carolina; Rev. and Mrs. Thomas MacBryde from South Carolina, and William Henry Cumming, MD, an independent missionary from Georgia.

42. The story of the early missionary career of William Jones Boone and his first wife, Sally DeSausure Boone, in Batavia and Gulangyu, Xiamen, is found in Boone, *China*, 9–103. In 1845, Boone established the first American mission in Shanghai.

Xiamen. By December 19, 1844, his health had so deteriorated that he had to leave Xiamen and make his way back to America.[43]

Before Abeel left China, he passed through Hong Kong and Macau. He had already written a Chinese tract, 論世間獨有一真神 (Discourse on the Unity of God).[44] Two other Chinese tracts were published posthumously: 真神耶穌之論 (Discourse on the True God, Jesus) was published in 1846, and 耶穌之要道 (The Important Way of Jesus), co-authored by Elihu Doty was published in 1854. The term that Abeel used for God, 真神 (*Zhenshen*), was derived from the generic term for spiritual beings, 神 (*Shen*) which was preferred by his American colleagues E. C. Bridgman and William Jones Boone.[45] Although Abeel had visited Medhurst in Batavia in 1831, he had rejected the indigenous term 上帝 (*Shangdi*), which Medhurst, based on an in-depth study of classical Chinese religious texts, used for God in Chinese Bible translation.

FINAL TOUR IN AMERICA (1845–1846)

Abeel arrived in New York aboard the *Natchez* on April 3, 1845. He was so weak he had to be carried from the ship. However, he recovered sufficiently to begin touring, going as far south as Georgia, and also visiting Rhode Island. After seeing his relative Rev. Gustavus Abeel in Geneva, New York, he died at Albany, New York, on September 4, 1846. He was buried at Greenwood cemetery outside New York City, and a monument was erected in his honor.[46] His nephew, G. R. Williamson, prepared a memoir from his diary, journal, and correspondence: *Memoir of the Rev. David Abeel, D.D.: late missionary to China*. The book included two appendices: "Religious Vade Mecum," which Abeel had composed in Guangzhou in 1830, and "Sermon on Heaven." His Dutch language tract, *Wenken omtrent den arbeid van Christelijke vrouwen onder de heidenen* (*Hints about the Work of Christian Women among the Heathen*), was published posthumously in 1851.

---

43. Wylie, "Abeel," 74. Other missionaries from the American Reformed Dutch Church continued the work of Abeel in Xiamen and southern Fujian province. In 1857 their work became independent from the ABCFM. See De Jong, *The Reformed Church in China*.

44. Ibid., 75.

45. Oey, "Essay," 1–13.

46. Wylie, "Abeel," 74–75.

CONCLUDING REFLECTIONS

David Abeel was an important figure in the establishment of American cultural influence in East Asia. He was clearly a person of enormous vision and piety; however, he possessed breadth without depth or critical interpretation of knowledge. His enormous Christian piety was commendable, as were his attempts at holistic expression of Christianity in developing health, education, economic capital, and moral and religious values in East Asia. His ecumenical approach to Christian relations was also laudable. He saw a need for social reform in East Asia, and he wanted to provide it with economic capital, education, western medicine, religious and political freedom, and civil rights for women. He was a talented linguist, but he had an insufficient knowledge of East Asian literature, history, and culture. He also had an anti-intellectual tendency to deprecate attempts at acquiring such knowledge.

In 1837, while Abeel was on furlough in America, American Congregationalists and Old School Presbyterians went their separate ways, unable to agree on the desirability of the new style of revivalism employed by Charles Grandison Finney and other Congregationalists as well as on theological issues. The majority of Congregationalists as well as New School Presbyterians supported Finney, but the Old School Presbyterians did not. Even more divisive was the issue of slavery. Religious leaders were beginning to wrestle with what became the the dominant social issue that divided antebellum America, slavery. Abolitionism was beginning to affect the New England religious mind in the antebellum period, and Congregationalist missionaries, even those in far away Siam, were to adopt it, serving in a different society from the ABCFM, which took a neutral stance on the issue. As a native of a mid-Atlantic state whose Dutch forebears had introduced slavery to Virginia in 1619, Abeel was less than outraged about the "peculiar institution," feeling it to be less a less important matter than interdenominational and interregional cooperation. His cooperation with church leaders from the South, though laudable for its ecumenism, was critically unreflective on the need to combine the Christian message with social reform in his home country.

Abeel lacked a full comprehension of the Christian message and its social and cultural applicability to non-Western societies. I do not see him reflecting either on the devastating psychic effects of African-American slavery in America in the 1830s, or on the negative influences of Western colonialism in East Asia. Perhaps because of the highly collegial relations he had with British and American traders in East Asia, Abeel failed to see the injustice of Britain in its conduct during the Opium War. He had a religiously naïve view of America, Holland and Britain, seeing them as new Israels or lights upon a hill, providentially ordained to bring Christianity to the non-Western world. Like other first-generation America China missionaries, he tried to remake East Asia into the Western image rather than to bring Christianity to East Asia. He did not understand that the message of Christianity should ensure rather than annihilate non-Western culture, and affirm equality and justice for non-Westerners. The fact that he did succeed in bringing Protestant Christianity to East Asia may be attributed to the inherent nature of Christianity, that its message exceeds its messengers.

SELECTED BIBLIOGRAPHY

Abeel, David. German-language letter, Singapore, January 15, 1832. In Evangelische Missions-Gesellschaft in Basel, *Magazin für die neueste Geschichte der protestantischen Missions- und Bibelgesellschaften*, 13 (1833), 29–30.

——. *Journal of a Residence in China, and the Neighboring Countries, from 1829 to 1833*. New York: Leavit, Lord & Co, 1834.

——. *Reise in den Ländern Hinterindiens in den Jahren 1830–1833*. 1836.

——. *Reise des nordamerikanischen missionars herrn David Abeel, in den ländern hinterindiens in den Jahren 1830–1833*. Germany, 183?.

——. "Ueberfahrt nach der Insel Java, etc." *Evangelisches Missions Magazin* (Basel), 16 (1836): 186–212.

Boone, Muriel. *The Seed of the Church in China*. Philadelphia: Pilgrim Press, 1973.

Brownlee, William Craig. "Religious Intelligence," *The Magazine of the Reformed Dutch Church*, 4 (1829), 382.

Cohen, Paul A. *Chinese Hostility to Christianity: A Study in Intercultural Conflict, 1860–1870*. Cambridge, Massachusetts: Harvard University Press, 1960.

De Jong, Gerald Francis. *The Reformed Church in China, 1842–1951*. Grand Rapids, Mich.: Eerdmans, 1992.

Jones, John T. Singapore, November 14, 1832 and February 19, 1833 letters to Rev. L. Bolles. *The Baptist Missionary Magazine*, vol. 13 (1833), 246–8, 403.

Klein, Thoralf and Reinhard Zöllner, eds. *Karl Gützlaff (1803–1851) und das Christentum in Ostasian: Ein Missionar zwischen den Kulturen*. Sankt Augustin, Germany: Institut Monumenta Serica, 2005.

Latourette, Kenneth Scott. *The History of Early Relations Between the United States and China 1784–1844*. New Haven, CT: Yale University Press, 1917.

Lazich, Michael C. *E. C. Bridgman (1801–1861), America's First Missionary to China*. Lewiston, New York: Edwin Mellen Press, 2000.

Lutz, Jessie. *Opening China: Karl F.A. Gützlaff and Sino-Western Relations 1827–1852*. Grand Rapids, Mich.: Eerdmans, 2008.

Montague, W. L., ed. *Biographical Record of the Alumni of Amherst College*. J.E. Williams: Amherst, MA, 1883.

Oey, Thomas G. " 'Essay on the Term for Deity,' a Key Text of William Jones Boone in His Nineteenth-Century Debate with Walter Medhurst on the Protestant Chinese Term for God." *Sino-Western Cultural Relations Journal*, 31 (2009), 1–13.

———. "Prolegomena to the American Northern Baptist Mission in Shantou: An Analysis of Selected Baptist Missionaries in Southeast Asia and China from 1814 to 1842." In *Chaoshan Christianity: Past and Present*. Shantou, China: Shantou University Press, forthcoming.

Poppen, Alvin John, "The Life of David Abeel." S.T.M. thesis, Union Theological Seminary, 1959. [Translated and published in Chinese, 1963.]

Railton, Nicholas M. *No North Sea: The Anglo-German Evangelical Network in the Middle of the Nineteenth Century*. Leiden: Brill, 2000.

Roberts, Timothy M. "Commercial Philanthropy: American Missionaries and the American Opium Trade in Izmir during the First Part of the Nineteenth Century," *Journal of Mediterranean Studies* 19.2 (2010), 371–88.

Rubinstein, Murray A. *The Origins of the Anglo-American Missionary Enterprise in China, 1807–1840*. Lanham, Maryland: Scarecrow Press, 1996.

———. "The Protestant Missionary enterprise, 1807–1860." In *Handbook of Christianity in China*, Vol. 2, edited by R.G. Tiedemann, 133–74. Leiden: Brill, 2009.

———. *Zion's Corner: Origins of the American Protestant Missionary Movement in China, 1827–1839*. New York: New York University Press, 1976.

Sena, Teresa. "Historical Background of Macau with Particular Focus on the First Americans in China." In *Macau: Cultural Dialogue Towards a New Millenium*, edited by Iêda Siqueira Wiarda and Lucy M. Cohen, 23–90. [Washington, DC]: Xlibris, 2004.

Stauffer, Milton. "Our Beloved Brother, David Abeel." Typescript, New Brunswick Theological Seminary, 1941.

Stowe, David M. "Abeel, David." In *Biographical Dictionary of Christian Missions*, edited by Gerald Anderson, 1–2. Grand Rapids, Mich.: Eerdmans, 1999.

Tiedemann, R. G. *Reference Guide to Christian Missionary Societies in China; From the Sixteenth to the Twentieth Century*. Armonk, New York : M.E. Sharpe, 2009.

Tomlin, Jacob. *Early Missionaries in Bangkok: the Journals of Tomlin, Gutzlaff, and Abeel, 1828–1832*. Bangkok: White Lotus Press, 2001.

Walravens, Hartmut. *Die Deutschland-Kenntnisse der Chinesen (bis 1870), nebst einem Exkurs über die Darstellung fremder Tiere im K'un-yü t'u-shuo des P. Verbiest*. Köln: W. Kleikamp, 1972.

Williamson, G. R. *Memoir of the Rev. David Abeel, D.D.: Late Missionary to China*. New York: Robert Carter & Brothers, 1849.

Wylie, Alexander. "David Abeel." In his *Memorials of Protestant Missionaries to the Chinese. Giving a List of Their Publications and Obituaries. Notices of the Deceased with Copious Indices*, 72–75. Shanghae: American Presbyterian Mission Press, 1867.

8

Japanese Evangelists, American Board Missionaries, and Protestant Growth in Early Meiji Japan: A Case Study of the Annaka Kyôkai

Hamish Ion

PART OF THE MARKING of the bicentenary of the American Board should include acknowledging the propagation of the Christian Gospel that American missionaries associated with the ABCFM insti-gated in Japan. One of the great successes of the Japan Mission of the American Board was that within ten years of the arrival of its first mis-sionary in Japan in 1869 it had been able to attract and train Japanese evangelists, who became the most effective spreaders of the Christian message in the interior of Japan.[1] Unless they obtained special permission, missionaries were prohibited by treaty regulations from living outside a few coastal treaty port settlements. Thus, the expansion of Christianity into rural provincial Japan and its rapid growth there, which character-ized the decade from 1879 to 1889, was largely the work of Japanese evangelists rather than missionaries. This paper is a case study of the formation of one of the most important early churches in provincial Japan, the Annaka Kyôkai (安中教会, Annaka Church) in West Gunma prefecture. In looking at the development of a Congregationalist Church at the local level, the paper is conforming to the recent trend of research into Japanese Protestantism. In adopting a microhistorical approach, the

---

1. For a useful Japanese study of early American Board missionaries in Japan, see Dôshisha Daigaku Jinbun Kagaku Kenkyûjo hen, *Rainichi Amerikan senkyôshi*.

aim here is to provide fresh insights into the way Japanese came to form Christian groups in rural early Meiji Japan, and that will be done by focusing on the personal, familial, and economic connections through which Japanese were influenced toward Christianity.

It is fitting in marking the bicentenary of the American Board to acknowledge the Annaka Kyôkai, because the church would not have been formed without the ABCFM's Japan Mission and the Japanese Christians associated with it. But before looking in detail at Annaka, it is important to provide context by investigating some of the themes within the broader Protestant movement in Meiji Japan. A look at the role that American Board missionaries played in inspiring Japanese toward becoming Christian is also in order.

I

For political and economic reasons, the Tokugawa bakufu that ruled Japan from 1603 to 1868 decided in the mid seventeenth century to proscribe Christianity, which had been propagated in the country by Portuguese and Spanish Roman Catholic missionaries since the middle of the sixteenth century. The bakufu simultaneously adopted maritime exclusion laws that severely limited foreign contact with Japan.[2] In 1853 the American commodore Matthew Perry and his squadron of black ships engaged in a display of gunboat diplomacy, supposedly ended Japan's isolation, and opened the country to Western intercourse. The American-Japanese Treaty of Kanagawa of 1858, which came into effect in the summer of 1859, allowed for the residence of Christian missionaries in the three treaty ports of Kanagawa, Nagasaki and Hakodate, and later Kobe, Osaka and Tsukiji on the Tokyo waterfont.[3] In 1859 and 1860 the first American Protestant missionaries (specifically Protestant Episcopal, Presbyterian, Dutch Reformed and Baptist missionaries) established themselves in Nagasaki and Kanagawa.[4] They were not allowed to propagate the Christian message to the Japanese. Christianity would, in fact, remain a prohibited religion until the promulgation of the Meiji Constitution in 1889, although Western protest about Japan's policy toward Christianity led to the removal of the publicly displayed

2. See Hellyer, *Defining Engagement.*

3. See Auslin, *Negotiating With Imperialism.* For a recent Japanese view, see Mitani, *Peri raikô.*

4. See Ion, *American Missionaries.*

proscription edicts against it, in 1873. Missionaries in Japan interpreted this action as meaning that they now could openly preach the gospel to the Japanese. What they did not appreciate, however, was that there was a deeply ingrained Japanese bias against Christianity as a result of the two centuries of edicts proscribing it as a potential danger to the state. This bias would make the Christianizing of Japan an extremely difficult task.

The first interest in a Japan mission for the American Board was shown by a donor in Brookline, Massachusetts. His (or her) donation of $27.87 for such a mission was noted in the *Missionary Herald* in March 1828. By the time some forty years later that the American Board decided to start its Japan mission, interest on the donation contributions to it amounted to over four thousand dollars. The first American Board missionary, Daniel Crosby Greene (1843–1913),[5] arrived in Japan in late November 1869. A year later, after living briefly in the Tsukiji treaty settlement on the edge of Tokyo, he established himself in Kobe, which together with Osaka had been recently opened as a treaty port. With the arrival of Orramel H. Gulick (1830–1923) in early 1871,[6] missionary work was extended to neighbouring Osaka. But it did not expand outside the treaty ports until 1875 when Niijima Jo (新島襄, 1843–1890)[7] returned to Japan from his studies in America. The most famous of the Japanese evangelists who were associated with the American Board (and arguably the most famous Japanese Christian of all), Niijima took advantage of his ethnicity to move to Kyoto, a city which was out of bounds for foreigners except with special permission.

---

5. There is a dated but still valuable biography of Greene, see Greene, *A New-Englander in Japan*. Of very considerable use for Greene's work in Kobe, see Shigeru *Meiji shoki Kobe dendô*. For a brief biographical note about Greene, see Nihon Kirisutokyô Rekishi Dai Jiten Henshû Iinkai, *Nihon Kirisutokyô rekishi dai jiten*, hereafter cited as *NKRDJ*, 466.

6. For the Gulick family and its early connection with Japan, see Clifford Putney, *Missionaries in Hawai'i*, 137, 145–52. For brief biographical notes of Gulicks who were important in Japan, see *NKRDJ*, 375–76.

7. For a brief biographical note on Niijima, see *NKRDJ*, pp. 1017–1018. A massive canon of literature has been written about Niijima by Dôshisha graduates and Japanese Christian historians. Different from the usual run of hagiographical studies is a critical study that is to be recommended, Ôta, Yûzô, *Niijima Jô:Ryôshin no zenshin ni jûman shitaru masurao*. For a short article on Niijima and the American Board, see Motoi Yasuhiro, "Amerikan Bodô no dendô hoshin to Niijima Jô." in *Kirisutokyô Shakai Mondai Kenkyû*, hereafter cited as *KSMK*, 54 (December, 2005), 99–122.

Over the years, Greene and many other American Board missionaries helped to form the Kumiai Kyôkai (組合教会, Congregational Church) which became the second largest Protestant denomination after the Nippon (Nihon) Kirisutokyôkai (日本基督教会, Japanese Presbyterian Church). Both joined with other Protestant denominations in 1941 to form the Japan United Church (日本キリスト教団, Nihon Kirisutokyôdan).[8] But to return to the early years of Protestantism in Japan, it is important to note that the American Board missionaries made many significant contributions to the cause, including their medical and evangelistic work, their translation of the Bible into Japanese, a task associated particularly with Greene, and their establishment of influential schools such as Dôshisha University (同志社大学) in Kyoto and Kobe Jo Gakuin (神戸女学院) in Kobe.[9] Many of these activities were made possible because direct evangelistic work was largely undertaken by Japanese. This allowed missionaries to become relatively detached. Rather than preaching in the streets, they could focus on educational, medical, and administrative tasks within the controlled environment of the mission compound, which served to cocoon them from the confrontational challenges posed to their spiritual and cultural values by the alien outer culture of Japan.

The standard interpretation of American missionary attitudes about Asian culture can be seen in the work of Koshiro Yukiko, who argued that American missionaries in 19th century Asia were "motivated by a sense of *noblesse oblige*, that made them dismiss the importance of understanding Asia as equal to the West."[10] Both John Howes and Cyril Powles reached similar conclusions about American Protestant missionaries in the Bakumatsu and early Meiji Japan mission field. [11] Helen

8. For a useful history of Christianity in Japan during the Meiji period, see: Morioka Kiyomi.*Meiji Kirisutokô keisei no shakaishi*; see also Takahashi, Masao *Meiji no Kirisutokyô*. See also Ôhama Tetsuya, *Meiji Kirisutokyô kaishi no kenkyû*, For its penetrating insights into the nature of early Japanese Protestantism, the following is essential reading, Yamaji Aizan, *Essays on the Modern Japanese Church*. The best general English-language study of Christianity in Japan is Mark R. Mullins, ed., *Handbook of Christianity in Japan*, of special interest in it is the short general survey, Helen J. Ballhatchet, "The Modern Missionary Movement in Japan," 35–68.

9. See, for instance, Nihon Seisho Kyôkai, *Nihon Seisho Kyôkai hyakunenshi*, 10, 45–50.

10. Koshiro, "Introduction—Bridging an Ocean: American Missionaries and Asian Converts Reexamined," 218.

11. Howes, "Japanese Christians and American Missionaries," 342; and Powles,

Ballhatchet has pointed out that the majority of early Meiji Protestant missionaries saw Christianity as the religion of Western civilization and believed the simple preaching of the Gospel message, combined with the introduction of Western ideas and technology, would naturally lead both to the collapse of Japan's indigenous religious systems and to the toleration of Christianity.[12] Although there is much truth in this, it is perhaps a little too harsh. Powles has shown that there was a wide range of missionary responses to Japanese culture and has persuasively maintained that the four main Christian traditions represented by missionaries in Japan (namely American Protestantism, French Roman Catholicism, Russian Orthodoxy and British Anglicanism) had different approaches to Japanese culture. He described these approaches respectively as dialectical, dualistic, absorption into culture, and affirmation of variety.[13] American Protestantism, by which Powles meant Calvinism, modified by Pietism and Manifest Destiny, "challenged the Japanese tradition. Theologically, it regarded the latter as pagan and corrupt. Culturally, it believed it to be archaic and outmoded." Powles argued that the American missionary "looked for the conversion of Japan to Christianity, which implied the destruction of the old cults." Secondarily the American missionary "hoped for the modernization of Japanese society, which meant for him democracy and a general progress toward similarity to America."[14] However, it is important to stress that there was a broad range of missionary responses to Japanese culture, together with differing Japanese responses to the Christian message. In any case, the purpose here is not to challenge the above interpretations but rather to suggest that they need to be nuanced.

American Board missionaries arrived in Japan when revolutionary changes were occurring. The political movement that gave rise to the Meiji Restoration had combined with a cultural movement aimed at transforming society to create an intellectual milieu that was open to Christian ideas in the decade after 1868. During this so-called age of

---

Victorian Missionaries, 3.

12. See, for instance, Ballhatchet, "The Religion of the West versus the Science of the West: The Evolution Controversy in Late Nineteenth Century Japan," in Breen and Williams, eds., *Japan and Christianity*, 107–21.

13. Powles, *Victorian Missionaries*, 1–18.

14. Ibid., 3.

English masters,[15] the question of the role of Christianity in Western civilization and the practical benefits that might accrue from its acceptance by the Japanese was raised. This was part of a broader intellectual debate about whether or not the development of Japan's military strength on Western lines could take place without the need to adopt other aspects of Western civilization, including religion. Fukuzawa Yukichi (福沢諭吉, 1835–1901) was one key intellectual figure who felt that until the power of the arts, thought, and temperament of the West was recognised, the concentration of effort on increasing military power might be wasted.[16] The proponents of freedom of religion and Christianity belonged to the first generation of Japanese students who had gone overseas, conducting their studies in the 1860s.[17] Other Japanese had gone overseas as diplomats in the 1860s and their view of Japanese problems often differed from that of the students. But the students and diplomats agreed that Japan was in a crisis because they had seen with their own eyes the overwhelming difference in military strength between the Western powers and Japan.[18] Christianity was seen by some Japanese as the essence of Western civilization (and missionaries certainly did not dissuade them of this idea). Consequently, some concluded that in order for Japan to gain equality with the West, it therefore seemed necessary and patriotic for Japanese to become Christian.

The majority of those few Japanese whom missionaries helped to convert to Christianity were *shizoku* (士族, descendants of samurai). Upper class individuals whose outlook was conditioned by Confucianism, they mainly looked down on Buddhism and Shinto as the religions of the masses. Some *shizoku* converts accepted Christianity because they thought it possessed a superior moral code that could be grafted onto the Confucian root. The political and religious events of the early Meiji period (1868–1912) saw the loss of Confucian influence in the intellectual and religious life of Japan, especially after the disestablishment of the feudal samurai class in 1874 and the rise of importance of Buddhism

15. The importance of Japanese English language experts during these ten years in the intellectual milieu of Japan is stressed by Ōta Yuzō, see Ōta, *Eigo to nihonjin*, 72–75.

16. Kano, *Kindai Nihon shisō annai*, 24–25.

17. Before the collapse of the Tokugawa bakufu, some 150 students and a further 300 people attached to Bakufu or various *han* embassies had gone overseas. See Matsuzawa Hiroaki *Kindai Nihon no keisei to seiyō keiken*, 58.

18. Kano, *Kindai Nihon shisō annai*, 24.

and Shintô. While missionaries could point, in contrast to China, that they were converting in Japan members of the social and intellectual elite, their message lacked resonance with the masses, who remained Buddhist or Shintôists.

The argument put forward by sympathetic historians is that even though the actual number of converts was small, Christianity still had a substantial influence on Meiji Japan. However, one has to be very careful about attributing too much influence to Christianity and asserting success without concretely demonstrating what that success was. In so many cases, interest in Christianity was just one interim stage in a Japanese enquirer's intellectual development and not the final stage. The apostates are often more interesting, especially those who became more important than those who remained Christian. One of the early historians of Japanese Protestantism, Yamaji Aizan (山路愛山, 1865–1917), for instance, was a defender of a liberal Christianity and demonstrated in his writings that Christianity was important in the transformation of Japan from a traditional to a modern society, yet toward the end of his life he confessed that he himself was not a Christian.[19] The transmission of Christian values and beliefs across cultures is not simply a matter of acceptance or rejection. A smorgasbord of different ideas and knowledge was offered up by missionaries, and from their veritable Viking's feast the Japanese freely picked, selecting items they considered most delectable and valuable to them. It was not all or nothing when it came to Christianity.

The missionaries struck those Japanese who sought them out in Kobe or Osaka as "walking encyclopaedias" of Western life. In the age of the English masters during the 1870s, when knowledge of the English language could lead to plum jobs, the Japanese were looking for English teachers, and Greene, Gulick, Marquis Lafayette Gordon (1843–1900), Jerome Dean Davis (1838–1910), John Cuting Berry (1847–1936)[20] and

19. Ito Yushi, "Conflicting Views of Japan's Mission in the World," 326 footnote 6. Yamaji, who was baptized in 1883, served as the editor of Christian journal *Gokyô* 護教 [Defend the Faith] from 1891 to 1897.

20. For brief biographical notes on Gordon, Davis and Berry, see NKRDJ, 530, 895 and 1267 respectively. Both Gordon and Berry were medical doctors, although Gordon quickly gave up medical work in favour of direct evangelistic work and teaching. Both Gordon and Davis were intimately associated with Dôshisha in Kyoto. A good portrait of Jerome Davis, during his Kyoto heyday can be found in John Merle Davis, *An Autobiography*. For the impact of Berry's medical work in Kobe, see Tanaka Tomoko,

other early American Board missionaries fitted the bill. As Paula Harrell has pointed out, "missionaries may have hoped to develop interest in Christian ideas as they taught the elements of English, but for most of the Japanese youth who flocked to the mission schools, English functioned more like the Internet, as a gateway to new knowledge, in this case of technical and organizational systems that fuelled the power of modern Western societies. It was a case of *dôshô imu* [同床異夢] (same bed, different dreams)."[21] Yet the Japanese were not only attracted by the missionaries' knowledge of English, they were also fascinated by the missionaries' family life and way of living, how they treated their wives and children, the clothes that they wore and the food that they ate all were fascinating to Japanese. Many Japanese had never seen a foreigner before, and for them the missionary and his family represented a microcosm of life in America, a country which very few Japanese would ever have the opportunity to visit.

The early missionaries were willing to cater to the Japanese who desired to learn more about things Western. In 1875 Gulick was instrumental in establishing the influential Christian journal *Shichi Ichi Zappô* (七一雑報, *Once in Seven Days General News*), getting two Japanese Christians, Murakami Shunkichi (村上俊吉, 1847–1916) and Imamura Kenkichi (今村謙吉, 1842–1898) to act as proprietors.[22] This journal combined a focus on Christianity with practical information about things Western, including scientific explanations. It had wide appeal because it answered a Japanese thirst for Western knowledge (of a practical sort), which was the magnet that first attracted Japanese to missionaries. In late 1878 Gordon wrote that the Annaka Kyôkai alone had taken and paid for 24 copies.[23]

But while a missionary could put forward Christian ideas, he had little control over how these ideas would be accepted or interpreted by Japanese to whom they were directed. This, of course, was intensified by problems of language and lack of common cultural background between missionary and enquirer. Still, Christianity managed to expand along

---

"Meiji shoki no Kobe to senkyô i Beri: iryô o Meguru chiiki no rikigaku."

21. Paula Harrell review, 148.

22. For the *Shichi Ichi Zappô*, see Dôshisha Daigaku Jinbun Kagaku Kenkyûjo hen, *Shichi Ichi Zappô no Kenkyû.*

23. ABCFM Japan Mission (Microfilm), reel 340, Gordon to Clark, 16 November 1878. For a brief biographical note on Gordon, see NKRDJ, 530.

skeins of friends and family. If a missionary could make an influential convert, that person could broadcast Christianity. Greene was exceptionally fortunate in having contact with Sawayama Pôro (Paul Sawayama, 沢山保羅, 1853–1887),[24] a Chôshû 長州 *han* 藩 (feudal domain) samurai, whom he met in 1870 and was instrumental in sending to Northwestern University in Evanston, Illinois, in 1872.[25] Returning to Japan in 1875, having converted to Christianity while in the United States, Sawayama had the social standing among Japanese and a knowledge of Christianity that allowed him to serve as an interpreting intermediary between missionary and Japanese concerning Christian ideas. In a practical and real sense, a missionary was only as good as his Japanese assistants and helpers. As it was usual that the missionary could only speak broken Japanese at best, a process of discussion and interpretation had to take place among the Japanese to fathom the meaning of what the missionary had said, making the role of the Japanese assistant very important. It is also to be borne in mind that Japanese were not always totally reliant on missionaries for Christian ideas; many *shizoku* could read the Chinese Bible which had been published in Shanghai in the late 1850s, long before the first Gospels were translated into Japanese. Missionary work in Japan benefitted from the earlier opening of China.

In 1900 Greene wrote "I came to Japan 31 years ago with the idea that I had undertaken a Mission in a country that differed in nothing from China where 50 years of labour, showed such poor results. But I soon found out my mistake and before I had been here long baptized my first two converts, and began to make friends among the Japanese."[26] This is an important observation because it relates missionary work in Japan to the missionary experience in China, even though Greene himself had no experience of China. The investigation of linkages between missionary work in China and the later work in Japan is a new area being explored by missionary scholars in Japan, who are especially interested in the translation of the Bible into Chinese by the end of the 1850s, and early attempts to translate parts of the Bible into Japanese by Chinese missionaries such as Elijah Coleman Bridgman, an American Board missionary. The existence of printing facilities in Shanghai, which could

24. For a brief biographical note on Sawayama, see *NKRDJ*, 586–87.

25. Tanaka Tomo, "Rev. Paul Sawayama," 16.

26. "Christianity in Japan: Views of Two Missionaries of Long Service," 134–37.

produce Japanese texts, contributed greatly to the spread of Christianity in Japan.

Much of the success that came to the American Board in Japan arose from its ability to attract a stellar constellation of Japanese converts. The American Board is associated with Niijima Jô, a samurai from Annaka who stowed away on an American merchant ship in order to go to the West to study gunnery. In 1865 he arrived in Boston, where he came into contact with Alpheus Hardy, who introduced him to Amherst College and Christianity. Niijima would return to Japan as an American Board missionary in 1875 and go on to found what is now Dôshisha University in Kyoto. He was not the only prominent Japanese Christian figure associated with the American Board. Educational and evangelistic work were the two great streams of activity within the nascent Kumiai Kyôkai. Niijima was clearly the leading Japanese Christian in educational work, and his counterpart in evangelistic work was Sawayama Pôro.[27]

Yet it was not an American Board missionary but a West Point ex-cadet, Leroy L. Janes, who was instrumental in leading a group of young students in Kumamoto to Christianity. Janes taught Christianity at the Yogakkô (洋学校) school in Kumamoto in southern Japan. While there he converted a number of his students, who gathered together in 1876 to form the so-called Kumamoto Christian Band, one of the three major groups of early Christians who came to dominate the leadership of the Japanese Protestant movement until the 1930s.[28] Members of the Kumamoto Band under the influence of Janes moved from Kumamoto to continue their studies with Niijima at Dôshisha in Kyoto. Some of them became leading pastors in the Kumiai Church, most notably Ebina Danjô (海老名弾正, 1856–1937), Kozaki Hiromichi (小崎弘道, 1856–1938), and Yokoi Tokio (横井時雄, 1857–1927). Tokutomi Sohô (徳富蘇峰, 1863–1957), the youngest of the Band and Yokoi's cousin, became an influential journalist.[29] Of the three major Protestant Christian convert groups, the Kumamoto Band (Congregationalist) represented a nationalistic (*kokkateki* 国家的) type of Christianity, while the Yokohama Band (Presbyterian/Dutch Reformed; formed in 1872) represented a church-

---

27. Tanaka, "Rev. Paul Sawayama," 15.

28. For a superlative biography of Janes, see F. G. Notehelfer, *American Samurai*.

29. For brief biographical notes on Ebina, Kozaki, Yokoi and Tokutomi, see *NKRDJ*, 195, 520, 1463, 944 respectively. For a still useful study of Tokutomi, see Sugii Mutsurô, *Tokutomi Sohô no kenkyû*.

orientated type (*kyôkaiteki* 教会的), and the Sapporo Band (Independent/ Anglican/Methodist Episcopal; formed in 1879) represented an individualistic type (*kobetsuteki* 個別的).

The question of whether the American Board should pay Japanese for preaching was a contentious one. Gordon for one was very critical of the ABCFM because it insisted on the self-support of Japanese churches at the cost of turning away those who might have wanted to become evangelists and pastors but did not enough money to support themselves while they underwent training.[30] The American Board's failure to provide for struggling theological students was contrasted by Gordon to the American Presbyterians and their aid for their prospective ministerial candidates.[31] It meant a very considerable sacrifice for most to become a Kumiai pastor.

The stress on nationalism in the thinking of the Kumamoto Band would lead to the "Dôshisha Crisis," which pitted Japanese Congregationalists against American Board missionaries over control of funds from the United States and facilities that had been built by donations from American supporters. The crisis (1895–1899) also took on the form of a power struggle between Japanese who espoused new liberal theological ideas and American Board missionaries who were more conservative in their theology. The liberals were led by Kozaki and Yokoi, while the conservatives were led by Davis.

But before the crisis drove a wedge between the American Board and Japanese in Dôshisha and the Kumamoto Band, these Japanese led the charge to gain more converts for Protestantism in the 1880s. Among the most famous of these Japanese evangelists was Ebina Danjô, who was instrumental in helping to develop the Annaka Kyôkai in western Gunma prefecture in the Kantô region of Japan.

II

Kudō Eiichi has pointed out that the ten years from 1877 to 1887 saw a tremendous growth in the Japanese Protestant movement, much of which came from the creation of new churches in rural areas.[32] The formation of the Annaka Kyôkai by Japanese evangelists influenced by

30. See ABCFM Japan Mission (Microfilm), reel 340, Gordon to Clark, 17 October 1879; 12 August 1880.

31. Ibid., Gordon to Clark, 12 August 1880.

32. See Kudō Eiichi. *Nihon Kirisutokyō shakai keizaishi kenkyū*, 112.

American Board missionaries was part of this growth. Gunma prefecture and Annaka had special meaning for Kumiai Kyōkai because Annaka was the home of the parents' of Niijima Jō.[33] Further, it represented the first excursion of the Kumiai Kyōkai into rural eastern Japan. Indeed, the development of the Annaka Kyōkai, because it was associated with such leading figures as Niijima and Yuasa Jirō 湯浅次郎[34] (and later with the influential pastor Kashiwagi Gien 柏木義円, 1860–1938)[35], tends to overshadow the emergence of other Christian churches in the region. Between 1878 and 1888 some twelve churches were established in the Prefecture with a total membership of 1,466.[36] Among them was the independent church (Nishi Gunma Kyōkai 西群馬教会, later known as the Takasaki Kyōkai 高崎教会)[37] established in May 1884 by Hoshino Mitsuta (星野光多, 1862–1932).[38] The Nippon Kirisuto Ichi Kyōkai (日本基督教一教会, Presbyterian/Dutch Reformed), the Baptists and the Methodists each established one church in Gunma Prefecture. But nine of the churches in the Prefecture belonged to the Congregational Church, indicating the dynamism of the young graduates from Dōshisha who helped to found them. The majority of these churches were on the main road leading west across Honshū toward Niigata. Such was the case with Kiryū, Maebashi, Takasaki, Annaka and Harashi. Other churches were on the route of the railway, such as Isesaki. Professor Ōhama has pointed out that Gunma Prefecture had 985 Christians in its churches in 1888, and ranked fifth in terms of numbers of Christians living in Japanese Prefectures or major cities, and fourth overall at 14.75 in terms of Christians per thousand of population.[39]

33. Morioka Kiyomi, Joshu no shodai Kirisutokyoshatachi, 188–89.

34. See Ōta Aito. *Jōshū Annaka aritaya*. For a short biographical note on Yuasa, see *NKRDJ*, 1451.

35. For Kashiwagi Gien, see *NKRDJ*, 293. Kashiwagi was baptized by Ebina Danjō in the Annaka Church in 1883, and, after attending Dōshisha where he came under the influence of Niijima, became a distinguished Congregational pastor. In 1897 he became pastor of the Annaka Church with which he is always associated

36. Sumiya Mikio. *Nihon Purotesutanto shiron*, 25.

37. For this church, see *NKRDJ*, 822. In 1888 the church joined the Kumiai Kyōkai.

38. Hoshino Mitsuta was baptized by James Ballagh in 1875, and was a student at both Nakamura's Dōjinsha and later Fukuzawa's Keiō Gijuku, see *NKRDJ*

39. Ōhama, *Meiji Kirisutokyōkai shi no kenkyū*, 111 (see table 4 between 36–37). In 1888, the leading places for Christians numerically were Tokyo (5267), Osaka (1678), Kanagawa (1423), and Hyōgo (1022). In regards to Christians per thousand of population, Tokyo (36.16), Kanagawa (15.87), and Hokkaidō (15.04) were above Gunma, with

Kumiai evangelists began actively to propagate Christianity in the Kantō region from the late 1870s. At their head was Ebina Danjō,[40] who was instrumental in helping to form the Annaka Kyōkai. He was an especially important member of the Kumamoto Christian Band, which had been formed at the Yōgakko in Kumamoto in Kyūshū through the agency of Leroy Janes in 1876 and forged by Niijima Jō and Jerome Davis at the Dōshisha in Kyoto into Christian leaders.[41] Another important member of the Kumamoto Band was Wada Masaki 和田正幾. After being baptized at Nakamura Masanao 中村正直's Dôjinsha 同人社 school by George Cochran, the Canadian Methodist missionary, in August 1876,[42] Wada became a student at the Kaisei Gakkô 開成学 in Tokyo. From there he went to join his Kumamoto Band friends at Dôshisha, and in 1879 he started helping Ebina in Annaka and undertaking the first evangelistic trips to Maebashi.[43] Sadly Wada died soon afterwards, and it was another Kumamoto Band member, Kurahara Korehiro 蔵原郭 (1861–1949),[44] who truly laid the foundations of Christian work in Maebashi in 1883.

III

Annaka was the castle town of the Annaka *han*. Situated on the road to Niigata, it was positioned to take advantage of the growth of the silk trade through Yokohama which developed rapidly in the years after the Meiji Restoration. In 1870 the Meiji Government established a model silk factory at Fukuoka, a village a few kilometres to the south of Annaka.[45] Annaka was a very prosperous town, lying in the heart of one of the finest silk districts in Japan. Large quantities of silk-worm eggs were produced there for export to Italy, and silk reeling machinery was

the overall figure for whole of Japan standing at 4.85.

40. Ebina graduated from Dōshisha in 1879 and was the pastor of the Annaka Church from 1879 to 1884.

41. Although Dôshisha was founded in 1875, it was only with the arrival of the Kumamoto Band members in July 1876 that the school really got underway. Before they came the standards had hardly been academic. See, Sugii Mutsurô. "Kumamoto Bando."

42. Ôhama, *Toriizaka Kyôkai Hyakunenshi*, 28

43. Nihon Kirisutokyôdan Maebashi Kyôkai Kyôkaishi Henshû Iinkai. *Maebashi Kyôkaishi*, 1.

44. For a brief biographical note on Kurahara, see NKRDJ, 461.

45. Ôta, *Jōshū Annaka aritaya*, 17.

introduced there to produce silk thread for the Japan and export market.[46] Annaka, therefore, was on the cusp of the rural industrial changes that were taking place in Japan in response to the need to export goods overseas to help pay for the transformation of the country. More importantly to Protestants, Annaka was the home of Niijima Jō, who came from a middle samurai family. When Samuel Robbins Brown, the Dutch Reformed missionary, and his party were on their way across country to Niigata, where Brown had accepted a teaching post, they stopped in Annaka to visit Niijima's parents in 1869.[47]

On his return to Japan from the United States in late November 1874, Niijima went home to Annaka to visit his aged parents.[48] He did not stay long there, only some three weeks, as he wanted to go on to Osaka, which was then the main mission station of the American Board. Nevertheless, he did engage in evangelistic work in his hometown.[49] It has been suggested that Niijima suffered from cultural shock when he talked about Christianity and his experiences in the United States with people in Annaka and surrounding villages whose way of life was only just beginning to be changed by the political, industrial and intellectual events of recent years.[50] Niijima's activity annoyed both the authorities in Gunma Prefecture and in Annaka itself because it upset the Buddhists there. However, such difficulties were overcome because Niijima had established, while he had been in the United States, links with officials at the highest level of government who could vouch for him. Further, on his arrival in Osaka, Niijima had conversations with Kido Takayoshi 木戸孝允, the influential government minister whom he had known and helped in the United States, and received from him support for the creation of a school,[51] which Niijima would establish in Kyoto.

Even though Niijima's energies were directed away from Annaka to Kyoto, where he established his school, interest in Christianity still persisted in his hometown. Among the former samurai and promi-

---

46. Gordon, Thirty Eventful Years, 91.

47. Ōta, Jōshū Annaka aritaya, 11–12.

48. Ōta Yūzō, Niijima Jō, 194.

49. See Gendaigo de yomu Niijima Jō henshū iinkai, Ha-de fujin e no tegami, [A Letter to Mrs. Hardy] 22 December 1874, Gendaigo de yomu Niijima Jō. See also Morioka, "Jōshū no shodai Kirisutokyōshatachi," 188.

50. Ōta, Jōshū Annaka aritaya, 17..

51. Ibid., 195–96.

nent landowners in Annaka, there had been a long-standing interest in things Western, resulting in the formation of a study group that included Chigira Shōan 千木良昌庵 (1842–1879),[52] a former Annaka *han* doctor. Some of the local samurai had been first introduced to Western studies in the 1850s and 1860s, when the Annaka *han* had decided to specialize militarily in Western artillery, and had ordered numbers of young samurai, including Niijima Jō, to learn about it.[53] Chigira's study group was able to obtain books, some of them Bibles, to study from Tokyo. From within this study group there emerged a smaller Bible study group of some thirty persons, including seven members who had not belonged to the original larger study group.[54] Yuasa Jirō 湯浅次郎 (1850–1932) was among those who belonged to the Bible study group. He was an odd man out because he came from a family that was commercially significant in Annaka rather than from a family that owed its influence to its samurai lineage. The Yuasa family owned the Yutaya, a significant soy sauce manufacturing business.[55] From 1872 onward Yuasa and some friends met every Sunday to study the Bible.[56] At Annaka, with the notable exception of the Yuasa family, almost all of the Christian enquirers were *shizoku*, that is of samurai stock, which was very different from the Presbyterian/ Dutch Reformed church at Kiryû whose members were farmers.

The Christian study group at Annaka received a tremendous boost in 1877. During the summer holidays that year, the authorities at Dōshisha decided that the theological students should engage in evangelistic work. While most were sent to places in the Kansai or to areas south of it, Ebina Danjō was chosen to go to Annaka.[57] The difficulties of internal travel were indicated by the fact that Ebina journeyed to Annaka by the circuitous route of sailing from Kobe to Yokohama and then going from there to Annaka. He was in Annaka from the middle of July to the

52. For Chigira Shōan, see NKRDJ, 862.

53. Ōhama, *Meiji Kirisutokyōkai shi*, 115.

54. Ibid., 120.

55. Ibid., 123. There were also some family connections between the Niijima family and others in this Bible study group.

56. Sumiya, *Nihon Purotesutanto shiron*, 16.

57. Kanamori Michitomo (1857–1945) was sent to Okayama, Kozaki Hiromichi to Hikone; Miyakawa Tsuneteru (1857–1936) to Osaka; Fuwata Dajirō (1857–1919) to Fukuoka. All of these, like Ebina himself, were former members of the Kumamoto Christian Band. See Sunakawa Banri. *Ebina Danjō*, 35. See also Morioka, "Jôshû no shodai Kirisutokyôshatachi," 190.

end of August, approximately two months. There he conducted lectures on the Bible which attracted from fifty to a hundred people.[58]

The results of this evangelistic foray were so heartening that Niijima decided to send Ebina back to Annaka in February 1878. There was some fear on the part of Niijima that Okuno Masatsuna (奥野昌綱, 1823–1910),[59] the Presbyterian minister of the Takanawa Kyōkai 高輪教会 in Tokyo, had contact with the Annaka group, and Niijima did not want them to fall into Presbyterian hands. Neither did Ebina.[60] When he arrived back in Annaka, he threw himself into evangelistic work. As a result Niijima, coming from Kyoto for the occasion, was able on March 30, 1878, to baptize thirty people (sixteen males and fourteen females), all of whom were *shizoku* except for three people.[61] Among those baptized was Yuasa Jirō, whose wife, Yuasa Moto 湯浅初子, was also baptized. Indeed, while the thirty members came from eighteen different families, eight families alone produced twenty of them. Of those eight families, all included husband and wife. The Asada family, made up of Nobuyoshi, his mother Yone, his wife Haru and his daughter Take, was at four the largest single family group.[62] As in the case of the Asadas, the initial husband and wife of most of the families would expand to include daughters, parents and sisters. The linkage between family and Christian growth should not be underestimated.

Although he had intended to return to Kyoto, Ebina was asked to remain in Annaka, which he did for the next four months, leaving only in July. This was important for it allowed the consolidation of the congregation. On his way back to Kyoto, Ebina took time to attend as a representative of the Annaka Kyōkai the All Japan Christian Great Gathering (*zenkoku Kirisutokyō shinto dai shimbokukai*, 全国基督新徒大親睦会) held on July 10 at the Shin Sakae Kyōkai 新栄教会 in Tokyo.[63] This meeting brought together some 500 Christians, and it gave

---

58. Ibid.,190. See also Sunakawa, *Ebina Danjô*, 35–36.

59. Okuno, a member of the Yokohama Christian Band was a Nihon Kirisuto Ichi Kyôkai (Presbyterian/Dutch Reformed) minister. See *NKRDJ*, 253. The Takanawa Kyôkai was one of the earliest churches in Tokyo, standing very close to where the present Christian private university, Meiji Gakuin Daigaku, is located. For this church, see *NKRDJ*, 825.

60. Sunakawa, *Ebina Danjô*, 36.

61. Ōhama, Meiji Kirisutokyōkaishi, 124.

62. Ibid., 266–67.

63. Sunakawa, *Ebina Danjō*, 36.

Ebina the opportunity to meet many of the leading Christian figures in the Kantô region.

By the end of 1878, the number of people who had joined the Annaka Kyōkai had risen to forty-four. Some seventy-five percent of them were *shizoku*. The percentage of *shizoku* would, however, steadily decline. Only 52.8 percent were descendants of samurai in 1881, and only 10.5 percent were *shizoku* in 1886.[64] When the church was established, Yuasa Jirô was the richest member. Most of the *shizoku* members were not rich. In fact, most of the *shizoku* members had lost wealth as a result of the Restoration.[65] Only two families, the Niijimas and the Yuasas, improved their positions after the Restoration.

From the first, Annaka Kyōkai was an independent church in that is it was self-supporting and did not look to the American Board for financial assistance. The underlying problem with the majority of its members being *shizoku* was that most of them were poor. Further, one of the setbacks that the *shizoku* group within the church received was the death of its key leader, Chigira, in 1879, which left Yuasa Jirō as the leading force in the church. Another problem for the church in 1879–1880 was that its growth stagnated, partly because there were not many evangelists visiting Annaka. Students were sent from Dōshisha in the summer, but through the long period from winter to spring there was nobody from outside to help explain and teach the church members, let alone new inquirers, about Christianity.

The situation was set right in November 1879 with the appointment of Ebina, newly graduated from Dōshisha, as the pastor of the Annaka church. However, there were still problems through 1880 in drawing new people into the church. The *shizoku*, who lived mainly in Annaka itself, only joined in very small numbers after the initial converts had been made. Attempts to attract students into the church through the introduction of a night school for girls did not bring in new Christians, partly because the young were leaving Annaka in order to find jobs. In 1880 Yuasa and others began to focus their attention on neighbouring villages and converting ordinary folk. In early October 1882, Gordon,

64. Ōhama, *Meiji Kirisutokyōkaishi* , see table 14 on 130.

65. Ibid., see table 10 between 120–121. Ōhama goes into considerable detail about the economic condition of the first *shizoku* members of the Annaka Kyōkai, comparing the hereditary rice stipend that they received prior to the Restoration to their financial position in 1878.

the American Board missionary, wrote from Dôshisha that "our young men who have been out during the summer come back much encouraged. Considerable interest is reported in the region of Annaka Mr. Neeshima's parents' home. The people paid the expenses of the young man who went to them."[66] It might well have been the last point that pleased Gordon the most. In late February 1883 he went out of his way to assure the American Board authorities at home that "we still hold intact the Board's rule that foreign money shall be administered by the missionaries."[67]

The number of members in the Annaka church did not start to climb until the Christian revivals in Yokohama (1883) and Dôshisha (1884). These figures reached a peak of 303 in 1885 before slipping back to 206 in 1887.[68] In early October 1883 Greene wrote enthusiastically that "the Annaka Church is lengthening its cords and strengthening its status. It is sustaining more or less regular services in eighteen different towns and villages . . . one of our students who has recently returned from Annaka where he spent his vacation in assisting Mr. Yebina, the pastor, informs us that the church numbers over 180 members at the close of last month."[69] Greene also pointed out another satisfactory point about the growing Annaka Kyôkai: "late important additions have been received from outside the Samurai ranks so that the church may be said to include all classes. Though class distinctions are not nearly as troublesome as in India, still they are often times a serious hindrance to the progress of Christianity in some of the old castle towns in Japan, and we are glad to congratulate the Annaka Church and its pastor upon this new evidence of progress."[70] It is interesting that Greene would recognize that there was a class problem with the growth of Christianity, even though he did not consider it as extreme as in India. He was right, of course, in seeing that other classes were now joining the Annaka Church. In late December 1883 the signs of growth were also evident to Gordon, who wrote that "in the six years since this church was organized, about one hundred persons have become members of it—the addition of the past few months have been about seventy—They are planning and doing a

66. ABCFM Japan Mission, reel 340, Gordon to Clark, 2 October 1882.

67. ABCFM Japan Mission, reel 340, Gordon to Clark, 20 February 1883.

68. Ōhama, *Meiji Kirisutokyōkaishi*, 131–33, especially table 15, 132.

69. ABCFM Japan Mission, reel 341, Greene to Clark, 1 October 1883.

70. Ibid.

broad work for the surrounding villages."[71] There was certainly evidence of a revival going on.

It was not only American Board missionaries who paid attention to what was happening in Annaka. The group that Niijima led in Dôshisha was interested, as were a variety of non-Congregationalists, Dohi Akio points out that during the early 1880s Uemura Masahisa (a Presbyterian minister) and Guido Verbeck[72] (a Dutch Reformed missionary), visited the Annaka Church three times, while Kozaki Hiromichi (a Congregationalist pastor) and Uchimura Kanzô 内村鑑三[73] (an independent Christian leader) came twice. Yokoi Tokio (a Congregationalist pastor) and Tsuda Sen 津田仙[74] (a leading lay Methodist) also came, as did Bishop Channing Moore Williams of the American Church Mission, Jerome Davis (a Congregational missionary) and Merriman C. Harris (a Methodist Episcopal missionary).[75] In looking at Uemura and Verbeck, it has to be remembered that it was not until 1886 (when the separate Kumiai Kyôkai was formed) that the idea of a union church that would include the Presbyterian, Reformed, and Congregational Churches finally foundered. The cooperation of Uemura and Verbeck with the Congregationalists in Annaka, Takasaki and Maebashi can be seen as part of the church union effort, although it was also tied to the ongoing Nippon Kirisuto Ichi Kyôkai evangelistic work in Kiryû to the north of Annaka. Likewise, the appearance of Bishop Williams was not altogether surprising given the Protestant Episcopal endeavour at Kawagoe (closer to Tokyo but connected to Annaka by rail). The Methodist Episcopalians also had evangelistic interests in Gunma prefecture, which accounts for Tsuda and Harris coming to Annaka.

In the summer of 1883, the town received a visit from Uchimura Kanzō and his friend Nitobe Inazō 新渡戸稲造,[76] two members of

71. ABCFM Japan Mission, reel 340, Gordon to Clark, 21 December 1883.

72. For Guido Herman Fridolin Verbeck (1830–1868), see NKRDJ, 1265–1266.

73. For a brief biographical note on Uchimura Kanzô (1861–1930), a member of the Sapporo Christian Band and the founder of the Non-Church Christian Movement, see *NKRDJ*, 176. See also Howes, *Japan's Modern Prophet.*

74. For a brief biographical note on Tsuda Sen (1837–1909), the great Methodist Episcopal layman, see *NKRDJ*, 886.

75. Dohi Akio, *Rekishi no shôgen*, 317. For biographical notes on Channing Moore Williams (1829–1910) and Merriman Colbert Harris (1846–1921), see *NKRDJ*, 155, 1141 respectively.

76. For a brief biographical note on Nitobe Inazô (1862–1933), see *NKRDJ*, 1030. For a more thorough treatment, see Howes, ed., *Nitobe Inazô.*

the Sapporo Christian Band who had moved south to Tokyo following their graduation from the Sapporo Nōgakkō 札幌農学校 in July 1881. Uchimura was familiar with this part of Gunma prefecture because he had spent some of his childhood fairly close by in Takasaki. Probably as a result of hearing about the active church at Annaka from Ebina at the Third All Japan Christian Conference held at Ueno in Tokyo in May, Uchimura and Nitobe were inspired to make the trip to Annaka to see for themselves. It was reported at this time that between 150 and 200 people were coming to the new church building every Sunday and that many people were coming forward for baptism.[77]

It was during this visit that Uchimura met and fell for Asada Take 浅田タケ, who had been baptized by Niijima together with her parents and grandmother in March 1878. Uchimura would marry Take in 1884 but would divorce her some seven months later.[78] Asada initially struck Uchimura as a good choice of wife, for she was a Christian and the beneficiary of a Christian education. She had entered the Dōshisha Girls' School 同志社女学校 in Kyoto in August 1878 (which indicated the close connection between her family and that of Niijima) but in 1881 had transferred to the Normal School in Yokohama from which she graduated in March 1884.[79] The failure of his marriage helped to precipitate Uchimura's decision to leave Japan and go to study in the United States.[80] His divorce was a traumatic incident in Uchimura's life and theological development, but his suffering did not compare with that of Take. Uchimura sent her back to her brother, pregnant. A daughter, Asada Nobu 浅田ノブ, was born, then brought up by the Asada family. She played little part in Uchimura's life, although he wrote to her occasionally.[81] After the divorce Take remarried, but one cannot help feeling that her prospects had been blighted by Uchimura.

What happened between Asada Take and Uchimura was unfortunate, but it did not stop the Take family from participating in the Annaka

---

77. See Howes, *Japan's Modern Prophet*, 53.

78. Matsuzawa, *Uchimura Kanzô*, 21.

79. Ōta Aito , *Jōshū Annaka aritaya*, p. 64. See also Ōta Yuzō, *Niijima Jō*, 243.

80. Ballhatchet, "Christianity and Gender Relationships in Japan," 192.

81. See Howes, *Japan's Modern Prophet*, 170. See Howes, *Japan's Modern Prophet*, 170. Miyagawa was a member of the Kumamoto Christian Band and a Dôshisha graduate. His name is associated with the Osaka Kumiai Church, of which he was the pastor for some forty-three years.

church (where Take's grandmother, Asada Yone 浅田ヨネ, was an active leader of women's Bible study classes). Nor did the divorce scandal prevent the church from spreading Christianity into nearby towns. One of the first openings outside of Annaka itself was in Minami Goka Village in North Kanra County some thirteen kilometres to the south of Fukuoka. This opportunity owed its beginnings to Motegi Ichirō 茂木一郎, who had been baptized in Annaka by Ebina. A clothier by trade, Motegi went to the village on business in 1881 and 1882 and introduced the villagers to Christianity. In this activity, he was assisted by his son-in-law, Motegi Heisaburō (茂木平三郎, 1850–1902). Baptized by Ebina in March 1881, he went on to study at Dōshisha and become a Congregational Church evangelist.[82] Ebina himself would travel to the village once a month to explain Christianity to audiences which in 1884 were reaching between 130 and 140 people. On February 21 1884, the independent Kanra Dai Ichi Kyōkai was formed with a congregation of twenty males and fifteen females.[83]

In his evangelistic work, Ebina was, like Fielding's Parson Adams, a veritable pedestrian. He introduced Christianity by first talking about Washington and Lincoln; and then he moved on to speak about Luther and the apostles Paul and John.[84] By doing this, Ebina meant to show a clear connection between Western civilization and Christianity. Interestingly, he did not dress in Western clothes and wore geta or other Japanese traditional footwear as he walked on average eighty kilometres a week to visit villages near Annaka. His evangelistic program saw him take only one day a week off, namely Monday. He gave services and Bible training classes at the Annaka church on Sunday, Wednesday and Saturday evenings. On Tuesdays, Wednesday mornings, Thursdays and Fridays, he was on the road, visiting villages and leading Bible classes.[85] Despite his evangelistic activities, Ebina still found time in October 1882 to marry Yokoi Miya 横井ミヤ,[86] the sister of Yokoi Tokoi and the daughter of Yokoi Shonan 横井小楠, the famous thinker. Like her brother and her future husband, Miya had studied English under Leroy

82. For Motegi Heisaburō, see *NKRDJ*, 1402.

83. For the Kanra Kyōkai, see *NKRDJ*, 352. See also Sumiya, *Nihon Purotesutanto shiron*, 18–19.

84. Dohi, *Rekishi no shôgen*, 316.

85. Iwai, *Ebina Danjō*, 102-103.

86. Sunakawa, *Ebina Danjô*, 43. See also *NKRDJ*, 195.

Janes at the Kumamoto Yôgakkô. In 1877 she had gone to the Dôshisha Girls' School in Kyoto. That same year Niijima Jô baptized her. While Ebina and Miya had known each other for some years, their marriage underlines the close ties that existed between the families of Kumamoto Band Christians. The marriage also reflected the fact that there was a relatively small number of Christian women of marriageable age available for Christian men to marry. Once married, Miya joined Ebina in doing evangelistic work in and around Annaka. Certainly, they cannot be slighted for any lack of energy when it came to trying to advance their evangelistic work outside of Annaka. Miya would accompany Ebina on some of his evangelistic outings, which included going by rickshaw six *ri* (23 kilometers) from Annaka to Maebashi.[87]

The next place after Kanra which was opened up was the village of Hara City. Evangelistic work in the village, an important farming center, was especially productive of new church members. Ebina began evangelistic work there in the netmaking shop of Yuasa Jirō's wife's parents' family, and he quickly came into contact with other merchant families, including that of the most influential person in Hara City, Tanaka Kyōshirō, whose family had turned from alcohol making to soya sauce manufacturing.[88] In 1881 seven people from Hara City were baptized in the Annaka church, including Hanada Heijirō and his wife Kera. These latter two were also influential people within Hara City.[89] The next year Hanada Kera's grandfather and mother were baptized, underlining the fact that converts were being made along family lines. By April 1885 a church had been built, and in October 1886 Hara City Kyōkai became independent of Annaka.[90] It was reported that during the first six years of the Annaka church about a hundred people became church members who were very active in reaching out to the surrounding towns and villages. By 1889 there were seven Kumiai churches and nine outstations in the prefecture. Furthermore, seven members of the local prefectural legislature were Christians; six of them were Kumiai members. The Christian legislators were keen reformers, as evidenced by their leadership in the attempt to ban licensed prostitution in Gunma prefecture.

---

87. Nihon Kirisutokyôdan Maebashi Kyôkaishi Henshû Iinkai, *Maebashi Kyôkaishi*, 3.

88. Ōhama, *Meiji Kirisutokyōkaishi,* 135.

89. Sumiya, *Nihon Purotesutanto shiron*, 19.

90. *Ibid.*

As early as 1880, Yuasa Jirô and thirty-five other members of the Gunma Prefectural Assembly had presented a petition for the abolition of prostitution to the governor of Gunma prefecture. In Annaka alone Christian influence led to the closure of five brothels.[91] Puritanism was very close to the heart of Annaka Christians, for it was noted that Miyagawa Tsuneteru 宮川経輝,[92] the Kumiai pastor in Osaka, had told them about the English Puritans and the Pilgrim Fathers in a visit to Annaka during the mid-1880s. One elderly gentlemen told Niijima that "since then he had been trying to imitate what the Pilgrim Fathers did when they landed on the wild shores of America, that is, they built a meeting-house, which was also used for a school; and it was his desire to do the same thing for his townspeople. Through his influence and effort a church-building, and also a schoolhouse was completed within the past year."[93] Clearly, this reveals that Annaka Christians saw that Christianity and education went hand-in-hand and were coupled with reliance on one's own financial resources. Puritanism, however, put the Annaka Christians at odds with their non-Christian neighbours. By advocating temperance and the abolition of prostitution, the Annaka Christians were deliberately challenging the permissive atmosphere of Japanese society, which condoned prostitution and did not disapprove of drink.

Yet it was not the Christians' support of social reform that seemed to pose the most difficulties for Christianity in this region. Reflecting on the challenges that faced Christianity in this part of Gunma prefecture during the 1890s, Gordon enumerated them with bitterness in 1901. His ideas need to be quoted at some length because they show how many missionaries felt about the kind of evangelistic work that was overwhelmingly conducted by Japanese evangelists. He wrote:

> The spirit of insidious and reckless nationalism which entered Japan at this time and in the name of scientific theology and higher learning denied the best established truths of Christ's revelation and the most certain facts of his career; made "atone-

91. Gordon, *Thirty Eventful Years*, 91.

92. For a brief biographical note on Miyagawa Tsuneteru (1857-1936), see *NKRDJ*, 1366. Miyagawa was a member of the Kumamoto Christian Band and Dôshisha graduate. His name is associated with the Osaka Kumiai Church of which he was the pastor for some forty-three years.

93. Gordon, *Thirty Eventful Years*, 92.

ment, salvation and the future life" the "deadest of issues;" put Christianity on a level with other faiths, turning Christmas-tide into a festival in memory of "the four sages, Socrates, Buddha, Confucius and Jesus;" called Christ a morose Jew; berated America for giving so high a place to woman; lauded "the value of species in religion," etc., and did not fail to bear fruit; and in no part of Japan was that fruit more visible than in that of which we are now writing [Annaka and district]. Here Christianity has spread most rapidly; here was the greatest attempt to carry it into practical and political life; here was the least of that careful instruction which the missionaries have always emphasized; here the blow of Mr. Neesima [Niijima Jô] was most severely felt; and here the influence of certain "wandering stars" had freest course. Under such influences the inexperienced and unindoctrinated Christians relaxed their grip.[94]

Gordon was obviously upset not only with the fickleness of Annaka Christians but also with the work of local Japanese evangelists who in his words did not ground Christians there sufficiently in "the best established truths of Christ's revelation." His reference to the influence of "wandering stars" is a criticism of Ebina, Kozaki and Yokoi, whose liberal theological views stood at variance with the conservative views of many American Board missionaries. This liberal/conservative split contributed to the Dôshisha College crisis in the 1890s, after the death of Niijima, when Japanese staff led by Kozaki challenged missionaries for control over the college. Further it is evident that the debate on the merits science versus those of Christianity—a debate that began in Tokyo in the late 1870s—had a negative impact on Christian growth in the provinces, albeit an impact that postdated that in metropolitan areas. It is clear that growth in the Kumiai Church, but not in the Anglican Church, slowed in the early 1890s in the wake of the promulgation of the Meiji Constitution of 1889, the Imperial Rescript on Education in 1891, and the jingoistic atmosphere of the Sino-Japanese War (1894–95). All of these served to promote Japanese nationalism. Nevertheless, there can be no doubt that Ebina and other Japanese Kumiai evangelists met with very considerable success in their evangelistic work in Annaka and the surrounding district. During the 1880s Christian growth in this region did much to increase the overall numbers of Christians in Japan. It

94. Ibid., 92.

also offered hope for the future by showing that Christianity spread by Japanese evangelists could take hold in provincial areas.

In Annaka Christianity was spread mainly along familial lines, although personal connections and economic ties also played an important part. The Yuasas were a wealthy merchant family who were able to exploit their position to help develop the Annaka Church and later to gain political office. It has to be borne in mind that Annaka was wealthy as a result of the export trade in silk, a business that perhaps made the town's citizens more open to new ideas. The fact that Christianity was seen by some to be the essence of Western civilization or modernity must have helped to make it attractive to those in a community where new Western machines and ideas were being introduced to help modernize the silk industry. English was seen as a gateway to new knowledge, and the linkage between Christianity and learning English was one that missionaries, certainly, were not afraid to exploit. Ebina, the pastor of the Annaka Church, was a very capable English speaker, and a model of an "English master" for the young people of the church to emulate.

After he left Annaka, Ebina became the pastor of the famous Hongo Kyôkai 本郷教会 in Tokyo, close to the campus of Tokyo Imperial University. He was able to influence many university students and faculty there, including Yoshino Sakuzo 吉野作造, one of the most famous of Christian laymen in the early 20th century and a leader in the movement for democracy in the Taisho period. By that time the first generation of American Board missionaries—Greene, Gulick, Gordon and Davis—had died. While Gordon toward the end of his life might have griped at the fickleness of Japanese Christians, American Board missionaries had served as catalysts and supporters for a generation of Japanese evangelists who not only brought Christianity into the interior of Japan but also helped to bring about societal changes in places like Annaka and West Gunma Prefectures. These changes definitely had a lasting regional impact.

BIBLIOGRAPHY

Auslin, Michael R. *Negotiating With Imperialism: The Unequal Treaties and the Culture of Japanese Diplomacy.* Cambridge, Mass.: Harvard University Press, 2004.

Ballhatchet, Helen J.. "Christianity and Gender Relationships in Japan: Case Studies of Marriage and Divorce in Early Meiji Protestant Circles," *Japanese Journal of Religious Studies*, 34:1 (2007), 177–201.

———. "The Modern Missionary Movement in Japan: Roman Catholic, Protestant, Orthodox," in Mark R. Mullins. *Handbook of Christianity*, 35–68.

———. "The Religion of the West versus the Science of the West: The Evolution Controversy in Late Nineteenth Century Japan," in Breen and Williams, eds.. *Japan and Christianity*, 107–121.

Breen, John and Mark Williams, eds.. *Japan and Christianity: Impacts and Responses.* Houndmills, Basingstoke: Macmillan Press Ltd., 1996.

"Christianity in Japan: Views of Two Missionaries of Long Service: Bishop Nicolai and D. C. Greene," *The Church in Japan*, 6:8 (August 1900), 134–137.

Davis, John Merle. *An Autobiography.* Tokyo: Kyo Bun Kwan, n.d..

Dohi, Akio. 同肥昭夫. *Rekishi no shôgen: Nihon Purotesutanto Kirisutokyôshi yori.* 歴史の証言：日本プロテスタント。キリスト教史より. [The Testimony of History: From Japanese Protestant Christian History]. Tokyo: Kyôbunkan, 2004.

Dôshisha Daigaku Jinbun Kagaku Kenkyûjo hen. 同志社大学人文科学研究所編. *Shichi ichi Zappô no Kenkyû.* 七一雑報の研究. [Research on the *Shichi Ichi Zappô*]. Kyoto: Dômeiya Shuppan, 1986.

———. *Rainichi Amerikan senkyôshi: Amerikan Bodo senkyôshi shokan no kenkyû, 1869–1890.* 来日アメリカ宣教師：アメリカンボード宣教師書簡の研究 1869–1890 [American Missionaries Resident in Japan: Research on the Correspondence of American Board Missionaries 1869–1890]. Tokyo: Gendai Shiryô Shuppan, 1999.

Gendaigo De Yomu Niijima Jō Henshû Iinkai. 現代語でよむ新島襄編集委員会. Ha-de fujin e no tegami, [A Letter to Mrs. Hardy] 22 December 1874. *Gendaigo de yomu Niijima Jō.* 現代語でよむ新島襄. [Niijima Jō's Writings in Modern Japanese]. Tokyo: Maruzen, 2000.

Gordon, Marquis L. *Thirty Eventful Years: The Story of the American Board's Mission in Japan 1869–1899.* Boston: American Board of Commissioners for Foreign Missions, 1901.

Greene, Evarts Boutell. *A New-Englander in Japan: Daniel Crosby Greene.* Boston: Houghton Mifflin, 1927.

Harrell, Paula. Review of Hamish Ion, *American Missionaries, Christian Oyatoi, and Japan, 1859–1873* in *Journal of Japanese Studies*, 37: 1 (2011), 146–149.

Hellyer, Robert I. *Defining Engagement: Japan and Global Contents, 1640–1868.* Cambridge, Mass.: Harvard University Asia Center, 2009.

Howes, John F. "Japanese Christians and American Missionaries," in Jansen, ed., *Changing Japanese Attitudes*, 337–368.

———. *Japan's Modern Prophet: Uchimura Kanzô, 1861–1930.* Vancouver: University of British Columbia Press, 2005.

———, ed., *Nitobe Inazô: Japan's Bridge Across the Pacific.* Boulder, Co.: Westview Press, 1995.

Ion, Hamish. *American Missionaries, Christian Oyatoi and Japan, 1859–1873.* Vancouver, British Columbia: University of British Columbia Press, 2009.

Ito Yushi, "Conflicting Views of Japan's Mission in the World and National Moral Education: Yamaji Aizan and his Opponent Inoue Tetsujirô," *Japan Forum*, 22: 3–4 (2010, September-December), 307–330.

Iwai, Fumio. 岩井文雄. *Ebina Danjō*. 海老名弾正. Tokyo: Nihon Kirisutokyōdan Shuppan Kyoku, 1973.

Jansen, Marius B., ed. *Changing Japanese Attitudes Toward Modernization*. Princeton, New Jersey: Princeton University Press Paperback, 1969.

Kano, Masanao, 鹿野正直. *Kindai Nihon shisô annai*,　近代日本思想案内 [An Outline of Modern Japanese Thought]. Tokyo: Iwanami Shoten, 1999.

Koshiro, Yukiko, "Introduction—Bridging an Ocean: American Missionaries and Asian Converts Reexamined," in *Journal of American-East Asian Relations*, 6:3–4 (1996), 217–226.

Kudō, Eiichi.　工藤英一. *Nihon Kirisutokyō shakai keizaishi kenkyū: Meiji zenki o chûshin toshite*. 日本キリスト教社会経済史研究：明治前期を中心として. [Research on the Economic and Social History of Japanese Christianity: With Special Emphasis on the Early Meiji Period]. Tokyo: Shinkyô Shuppansha, 1980.

Matsuzawa, Hiroaki. 松沢弘陽. *Kindai Nihon no keisei to seiyô keiken*. 近代日本の形成と西洋経験. [The Formation of Modern Japan and Western Experience]. Tokyo: Iwanami Shoten, 1993.

———. *Uchimura Kanzô*. 内村鑑三. [Uchimura Kanzô]. Tokyo: Chuôkoronsha, 1973.

Mitani, Hiroshi. 三谷博. *Peri raikô*. ペリー来航 [The Arrival of Perry]. Tokyo: Yoshikawa Kôbunkan, 2003.

Morioka, Kiyomi. 盛岡清美. "Jôshû no shodai Kirisutokyôshatachi." 上州の初代キリスト教者たち. [Jôshû's first Christians]. *Bungaku* 文学[Literature], 47: 4 (1979), 187–197.

———. *Meiji Kirisutokô keisei no shakaishi*. 明治キリスト教会形成の社会史. [The Social History of the Development of Meiji Christianity]. Tokyo: Tokyo Daigaku Shuppankai, 2005.

Motoi, Yasuhiro. 本井廉博. "Amerikan Bodô no dendô hoshin to Niijima Jô: Turuko Misshun to Nihon Misshun o taikurabe shite."アメイカン。ボードの伝道方針と新島襄：トルコ。ミッシュンと日本ミッシュンを対比して。"[The Mission Policy of the American Board and Niijima Jô: A Comparison between the Turkish and Japan Missions] in *Kirisutokyô Shakai Mondai Kenkyû*.キリスト教社会問題研究. [The Study of Christianity and Social Problems]. hereafter cited as *KSMK*, 54 (December, 2005), 99–122.

Mullins, Mark R. Ed., *Handbook of Christianity in Japan*. Leiden and Boston: Brill, 2003.

Nihon Kirisutokyôdan Maebashi Kyôkai Kyôkaishi Henshû Iinkai.日本基督教団前橋教会史編集委員会. *Maebashi Kyôkaishi: Hyaku jûnen no ayumi*. 前橋教会史編集委員会：百十年の歩み.　[A History of the Maebashi Church: The Course of a Hundred and Ten Years]. Maebashi: Nihon Kirisutokyôdan Maebashi Kyôkai, 1996.

Nihon Kirisutokyô Rekishi Dai Jiten Henshû Iinkai. 日本キリスト教歴史大事典編集委員会. *Nihon Kirisutokyô rekishi dai jiten*. 日本キリスト教歴史大事典. [A Dictionary of the History of Christianity in Japan]. Tokyo: Kyôbunkan, 1988. Cited as *NKRDJ*.

Nihon Seisho Kyôkai.日本聖書協会. *Nihon Seisho Kyôkai hyakunenshi*. 日本聖書協会百年史. [A Centennial History of the Japan Bible Society]. Tokyo: Nihon Seisho Kyôkai, 1975.

Notehelfer, F. G.. *American Samurai: Captain L. L. Janes and Japan*. Princeton: Princeton University Press, 1985.

Ôhama Tetsuya. 大濱徹也. *Meiji Kirisutokyô kaishi no kenkyû*. 明治キリスト教会史の研究. [Research on the Social History of Meiji Chistianity]. Tokyo: Yoshikawa Kôbunkan, 1979.

———. *Toriizaka Kyôkai Hyakunenshi*. 鳥居坂教会百年史. [A Centennial History of the Toriizaka Church]. Tokyo: Toriizaka Kyôkai, 1987.

Ôta, Aito. 太田愛人. *Jōshū Annaka aritaya: Yuasa Jirō to sono jidai*.上州安中有田屋：湯浅治郎とその時代 . [Jôshû Annaka Aritaya: Yuasa Jirô and His Times]. Tokyo: Ozawa Shoten, 1998.

Ôta, Yûzô. 太田雄三, *Eigo to nihonjin*, 英語と日本人[English and Japanese People]. Tokyo: Kodansha, 1995.

———. *Niijima Jô:Ryôshin no zenshin ni jûman shitaru masurao*. 新島襄：良心之全身二充満シタル丈夫. [Niijima Jô: A Man Who Completely Followed His Conscience]. Tokyo: Mineruva Shobô, 2005.

Powles, Cyril Hamilton. *Victorian Missionaries in Meiji Japan: The Shiba Sect, 1873–1900*. Toronto: University of Toronto-York University Joint Centre on Modern East Asia, 1987.

Putney, Clifford. *Missionaries in Hawai'i: The Lives of Peter and Fanny Gulick, 1797–1883*. Amherst: University of Massachusetts Press, 2010.

Shigeru, Yoshiki. 茂義樹. *Meiji shoki Kobe dendô to D. C. Gurin*. 明治初期神戸伝道とD。C。グリーン [D. C. Greene and Evangelistic Work in Kobe at the Beginning of the Meiji Period]. Tokyo: Shinkyô Shuppansha, 1986.

Sugii, Mutsurô. 杉井六郎. "Kumamoto Bando. Dôshisha to bungaku: '*Dôshisha Bungaku*'no taidô." 熊本バンド。同志社：同志社文学の胎動. [The Kumamoto Band, Dôshisha and Literature: The Quickening of Dôshisha Literature]. *Bungaku*, 47: 4 (1979), 167–186.

———. *Tokutomi Sohô no kenkyû*. 徳富蘇峰の研究. [Research on Tokutomi Sohô]. Tokyo: Hôsei Daigaku Shuppan Kyoku, 1977.

Sumiya, Mikio. 隅谷三喜男. *Nihon Purotesutanto shiron*.日本プロテスタント史論. [Historical Treatise on Japanese Protestantism]. Tokyo: Shinkyô Shuppansha, 1983.

Sunakawa Banri. 砂川萬里. *Ebina Danjō: Uemura Masahisa: Nihon no daihyōteki Kirisutokyōsha* . 海老名弾正：植村正久：日本代表的キリスト教者. [Ebina Danjô, Uemura Masahisa: Japan's Representative Christians]. Tokyo: Tôkai Daigaku Shuppankai, 1965.

Takahashi Masao. 高橋昌郎. *Meiji no Kirisutokyô*. 明治のキリスト教. [Meiji Christianity]. Tokyo: Yoshikawa Kôbunkan, 2003.

Tanaka Tomo, "Rev. Paul Sawayama," *The Japan Evangelist*, 2:1 (October, 1894), 15–20.

Tanaka Tomoko.田中智子. "Meiji shoki no Kobe to senkyô i Beri: iryô o Meguru chiiki no rikigaku." 明治初期の神戸と宣教医ベリー：医療をめぐる地域の力学. [The Missionary Medical Doctor Berry in Kobe: The Regional Dynamics of Medical Work in the Early Meiji Era], *KSMK*, 52 (December, 2003), 58–81.

Yamaji, Aizan. *Essays on the Modern Japanese Church: Christianity in Meiji Japan*, translated by Graham Squires with introductory essays by Graham Squires and A. Hamish Ion. Ann Arbor: Center for Japanese Studies, The University of Michigan, 1999.

9

Nellie J. Arnott, Angola Mission Teacher, and the Culture of the ABCFM on Its Hundredth Anniversary

Ann Ellis Pullen and Sarah Ruffing Robbins

A s the American Board of Commissioners for Foreign Missions (ABCFM) celebrates its two-hundredth anniversary, the writings of Nellie J. Arnott provide insight into how the organization's vision and culture were being disseminated by women working in one of its more remote mission areas, Portuguese West Africa (Angola), on its one-hundredth anniversary. Arnott's oeuvre provides a portrait of the fluid and complex status of ABCFM work in Angola during the early twentieth century. Diaries and letters of Arnott, who served as a mission teacher in Angola from 1905 to 1912, as well as magazine articles by and about her, actually provide differing perspectives for analysis of her experience and of the ABCFM context in Angola at that time. Arnott's personal diaries describe the ABCFM's work in the field in Angola as it was impacting one missionary woman, while her official reporting in letters and publications, as well as magazine articles in which she is a "character," illustrate what various American audiences interested in the mission learned about that work. [1]

One reason behind the complex and sometimes contradictory view of mission work in Angola as seen in the archive of Arnott's experiences there is that she came to ABCFM service at a time when the organization's goals and strategies were in flux. Though the ABCFM encom-

---

1. In some details and occasional phrasings, this essay draws on portions of our book, *Nellie Arnott's Writings on Angola*. © Parlor Press. Used by permission.

passed diverse mission stations around the world in the early twentieth century, certain elements of the institution's vision dated from the early years of the organization, according to D. Philip Corr. He argues that both ABCFM administrators and missionaries viewed "propagating the Gospel to be the highest priority, with Bible translation an important complement to preaching." Corr continued that "social concern" was "clearly subordinate" to these tasks.[2] The establishment of self-sufficient indigenous churches was a clear component of this vision, though just when such churches would be prepared for autonomy was often not clear. Instruction in vernacular languages was a key ingredient in educating eventual leaders for these churches. By the late 1800s, arguments had arisen within the ABCFM and other Protestant mission organizations as to the extent to which social issues and "civilizing functions" such as advanced schools and hospitals should be an adjunct to preaching and teaching.[3] Arnott's writings illuminate challenges and successes in meeting these sometimes ambiguous goals.

Given the expanding sense of what mission work included, professional single women missionaries (and not just mission spouses) were becoming central to the enterprise. But women missionaries working for the ABCFM at this time were in a complex social position. As agents of Western culture, they had been schooled to view white, Anglo-American Christian social practices as superior and to see intervention in the local societies being served by missionaries as a civilizing task. At the same time, due to their gender, their position as inferiors in the ABCFM's own hierarchy, coupled with their daily interactions with women in the foreign communities where they served, could lead them to resist some of the institution's agenda. Though female missionaries, both married and single, were going to ABCFM missions in ever-increasing numbers, males held authority in mission stations; women generally followed the "Woman's Work for Woman" model that Dana Robert has described. That is, they concentrated on teaching and other nurturing tasks aimed

2. Corr, "Field is the World," 3. According to Paul W. Harris in Nothing but Christ (4), Rufus Anderson, ABCFM Corresponding Secretary from 1832 to 1866, played a "decisive role" in forming the organization's mission policy of "winning individual souls to Christ" and developing indigenous churches.

3. See Corr's discussion of ABCFM Secretary Rufus Anderson's "three-self" theory for indigenous churches (self-governing, self-supporting, self-propagating) in "Field is the World," 135–36; Harris, Nothing but Christ, 4; Hutchison, Errand to the World, 91–124. Harris describes controversies within the ABCFM over higher education in Nothing but Christ, 38–58.

primarily at women and children. At home in the U.S., women's activities in the ABCFM were coordinated through the Woman's Board of Missions in Boston and the Woman's Board of Missions of the Interior (WBMI) in Chicago; the WBMI provided the main financial support for Arnott's service.[4]

The writings of Nellie J. Arnott reflect ways in which female missionaries of her era embodied aspects of the ABCFM's culture or, in some cases, modified or questioned its practices in the field. A particularly detailed record exists of Arnott's service in Angola, as she left diaries, photographs and scrapbooks related to her experiences. Late in her life, she made careful annotations on many of her photos and other memorabilia so that her grandchildren could better understand her years in Africa. Arnott's granddaughter eventually donated the collection of scrapbooks, diaries, and personal journals to the Bancroft Library at the University of California, Berkeley.[5] Besides the Bancroft-held materials and ABCFM official documents, including the written reports she sent back to headquarters, Arnott's place in the gendered ABCFM network is also partially traceable in the organization's mission magazines aimed at a female audience, especially *Mission Studies* and *Life and Light for Woman*. By the time she left Angola in 1912 for a furlough, her byline would have been recognizable to thousands of U.S. women supporters of the ABCFM's overseas stations.

Nellie Arnott, born in Iowa in 1873, spent five years teaching in American Missionary Association (AMA) schools in Savannah, Georgia, and Meridian, Mississippi, before first applying to become an ABCFM missionary in 1899. Arnott requested posting to the Portuguese West Africa mission in hopes of joining Sarah Stimpson, her colleague in Meridian, who by that time was already serving in Angola. As preparation for mission service, Arnott enrolled in Moody Bible College, an institution whose conservative teachings suited her own premillennialist views. In addition, she took courses in kindergarten teaching at Oberlin College.[6] Arnott's selection process for service was lengthy and rigorous,

4. Robert, *American Women in Mission*, 130–37. For a history of what Grace T. Davis calls "'women's work for women'" in the founding of the WBMI, see *Neighbors in Christ*, 4–9.

5. Nellie Jane Arnott Darling Papers (hereafter cited as NJADP). We thank The Bancroft Library, University of California, Berkeley, for permission to use material from this collection.

6. For a full discussion of Arnott's childhood, education and early career, see Robbins and Pullen, *Nellie Arnott's Writings on Angola*, 3–11. Premillennialists like

demonstrating the commitment of the ABCFM to hiring candidates who were both professionally and personally qualified to serve in the field. In Arnott's case, lengthy correspondence was exchanged between ABCFM officials in Boston and those in the WBMI in Chicago before she was deemed eligible. Arnott's experience teaching in schools for African Americans was deemed a plus for her, though she lacked a college education. Her initial application, however, was rejected due to perceived health issues, and she was not approved for service until 1905.[7]

The West Central Africa mission to which Arnott was going had been established in 1881 at the urging of ABCFM Secretary John O. Means, who believed that ABCFM missions could help to combat both the domestic and commercial slave trade in Angola.[8] ABCFM stations were located in the highlands, some 250 miles inland from the coast, in an area accessible only by foot or donkey. In the early twentieth century, the backbone of the economy of the area's Umbundu peoples was trade in wild ("red") rubber and other products. Subsistence farming was generally the responsibility of women. Though Portugal was the colonial power in Angola, it had only brought Umbundu kingdoms in the area under its administration after the "Bailundu War" in 1902. Arnott's ap-

---

Arnott generally saw evangelization as their key role in missions; they were less enthusiastic about the development of higher education, hospitals and other institutions that were supported by postmillennialists caught up in the Social Gospel movement. See also Hutchison, *Errand to the World*, 91–124.

7. This correspondence is in ABCFM Archives, ABC 6, Candidate Department, Vol. 75, 1900–1919: Papers of Accepted Candidates, Vol. I. "Record of Candidates for Missionary Appointment, Number 70, Miss Nellie J. Arnott," Houghton Library, Harvard University. Material from the ABCFM Archives is used by permission of the Houghton Library of Harvard University and Wider Church Ministries of the United Church of Christ.

8. Means presented his argument for establishing a new mission in the highlands of Angola at the ABCFM Annual Meeting of 1879 in a paper entitled "The Proposed Mission in Central Africa." The paper appeared in *Missionary Herald* (see especially 446 and 458–60), followed by a response to his presentation by a "Special Committee of the Board" (460–61). The Special Committee recommended acceptance of his proposal, noting eloquently that "the evangelization of Africa has peculiar claims upon American Christians. Whatever the horrors of the slave trade as it exists to-day among these African tribes, some part of the responsibility lies unquestionably at our doors . . . . We can make no reparation, it is true, for the wrongs and shames of the slave trade. But one thing we can do. For as many years as American ships tracked the seas with curses and blood, in the interest of American slavery, we can keep them re-tracking it with Bibles, and missionaries, and prayers, and songs of jubilee, in the interest of the gospel of our Lord Jesus Christ, and of the evangelization of Africa" (461).

pointed station, Kamundongo, was very much in a frontier area. The Catholic colonial government was not in fact particularly friendly towards the ABCFM at this time, for the Portuguese were suspicious that mission leaders were siding with Umbundu rulers as the government sought to pacify the highlands.[9] Over time, actually, in the years after Arnott's service, the Portuguese would come to see the Umbundu-based teaching of the ABCFM schools as particularly subversive, since such work could enable a covert, shared literacy skill to resist the colonial government in a language European officials could not fully control.

Arnott was apparently unaware of the volatile political situation in Angola as she went to ABCFM headquarters Boston in 1905 to make preparations for her voyage. During this time, she stayed in Auburndale at the home of ABCFM Secretary E. E. Strong and his family, including his sister, Jane Means, widow of John O. Means. Jane Means, like her husband, had long been a supporter of the Angola mission and remained a role model for Arnott. With Arnott on her journey to Angola were Reverend William Henry Sanders, one of the original ABCFM missionaries in Angola, and his wife Sarah Bell Sanders, who were returning to the Kamundongo station from furlough. While in the U.S., William Sanders had met with government officials in hopes that they might persuade their Portuguese counterparts to better protect the Angola mission stations.[10]

Unbeknownst to the Sanderses, Arnott was full of personal anxieties as she prepared to leave the U.S., despite her conviction that God had called her to teach in Africa. On a pre-departure visit to her parents,

9. The name of the indigenous people in the Angola highlands is Ovimbundu; the descriptive adjective and name of the language is Umbundu, according to former missionary Gladwyn Murray Childs in *Umbundu Kinship & Character*, xi. For accounts of the early history of ABCFM missions in Angola, see Strong, *Story of the American Board*, 336–40, and Henderson, *Church in Angola*, 51–59. On ABCFM relations with the Portuguese, see Soremekun, "Religion and Politics in Angola," 341–77. For a discussion of economic issues and Ovimbundu-Portuguese relations in this period, especially useful sources are Heywood, *Contested Power in Angola*, 9–11, 20–32, and Soremekun, "The Bailundu Revolt, 1902," 447–73.

10. Arnott's account of her visit with Reverend Strong and his family is in her Circular Letter (to friends at home), May 3, 1905, NJADP. In her papers, Arnott saved a letter from Reverend Strong informing the West Central Africa Mission of Jane Means's death on June 12, 1912. He indicated that Mrs. Means was in the process of writing to the mission when she became ill (E. E. Strong to Dear Friends, June 15, 1912, "Loose Letters," NJADP). On continuing problems with the Portuguese that led Sanders to go to the U.S., see Soremekun, "Religion and Politics in Africa," 355–58.

who were then living in California, Arnott had turned down a marriage proposal from long-time family friend Paul Darling. A businessman, Darling had no interest in African mission service. Arnott's private anguish is evident from a diary entry as she left Boston: "Do not feel satisfied with my own heart. The love of the last few weeks, I fear is taking from me the hearty spirit I had in going. I do want to do God's *will* & I want to love to do it, but human love draws my heart the other way."[11] Arnott's seemingly clear-cut decision between marriage and a mission career reflects the reality that married women missionaries in her day could receive an overseas posting only by virtue of their minister husbands' assignments. Whether she had made the correct decision regarding Paul Darling's proposal and whether she would be an effective missionary were frequent topics in her diaries during her initial years of service overseas. (She would write Paul Darling, midway through her African tenure, to announce her plan to remain single and fully committed to the mission endeavor.) If her diaries exposed her doubts and fears, however, her Circular Letters and magazine articles for mission supporters back home were cheerful and positive; she was quite aware that it was donations from her middle-class women readers that made her ongoing service possible.

Arnott's personal and public writings provide a window into the beliefs shared by numerous ABCFM women at the turn into the previous century. At the core, her service was religiously motivated. Arnott was convinced that her highest calling in Angola was to teach Umbundu children about Christ. Reading scriptures "brought to me a new realization of what Jesus suffered for me. Oh! That I might make known such a Saviour to His little ones is my earnest prayer," she wrote in her diary shortly after she left Boston.[12] At the same time, Arnott sought to build cross-cultural connections. She strongly supported the commitment of ABCFM missionaries in Angola to teach in Umbundu, a language she mastered only after three or so years of study. She agonized over how slowly she developed proficiency, reflecting in her diary on New Year's Eve of 1906 that "I am just holding on the ropes [it] seems to me & being no real blessing to anybody." Yet, while still struggling with her language studies, Arnott found other ways to support the work William Sanders and their colleagues were doing in translation of mate-

---

11. Arnott, Diary, April 29, 1905, NJADP. Emphasis in original via underlining.

12. Arnott, Diary, May 14, 1905, NJADP.

rials into Umbundu. In late 1906 and early 1907, for example, she wrote often about her role in a mission project to print and bind copies of an Umbundu-English hymnal, a project considered critical to mission translation goals because music was an integral part of Umbundu culture.[13] Eventually, Arnott became so proficient in Umbundu that some entries in her personal writings slip into the local language to designate concepts and practices not easily translatable into American English.[14]

Arnott was horrified by the contract labor system, whereby African men and women were sent to cocoa plantations on the islands of São Tomé and Príncipe and were "really held as slaves," as she explained in one of her early Circular Letters to friends at home. ABCFM missionaries sought the most effective means to prevent Umbundu men and women from being captured as contract laborers, as well as to inform the U.S.-based audience about abuses the enslaved workers suffered. Thus, from the perspective of Portuguese colonial authorities and traders, the missions represented a threat to the system. A series of mysterious fires at Kamundongo, Arnott reported in a subsequent letter, was thought to be the coerced work of slaves of Portuguese traders disgruntled by the activities of the ABCFM mission.[15] Arnott herself was quite frightened, as she confided in her diary: "We go to bed with fear & trembling for fear of another fire. We have no help or hope apart from God." In a Circular Letter describing one of the fires, however, she assured her readers that "[w]e hardly think our enemies will dare to set fire to any Mission prop-

13. In her diary on November 20, 1906, Arnott recorded that she and the Sanderses "folded 1500 copies of the first folio of the hymn book." A number of other entries through the first months of 1907 indicated progress on the work. Arnott took a great deal of pride in this project; a copy of the hymnal was one of the items she carried with her when she left Angola and is now in NJADP. The title page is written in Umbundu, except for the notation that it was published by the "West Central African Mission, A.B.C.F.M." In the body of the hymnal, English words and music are on the right side of the page, Umbundu words on the left.

14. Having struggled to attain fluency in Umbundu, Arnott lamented as she left for her furlough in 1912 that she had likely done her "last Umbundu teaching" until she returned. "I do hope I will not forget the language," she commented in a Circular Letter dated February 17, 1912 ("Loose Letters," NJADP).

15. Arnott, Circular Letter, June 6, 1905, and Circular Letter, June 22, 1905, NJADP. For the history of the contract labor system in Angola, the classic work is Nevinson, *Modern Slavery*, first published in 1906. Nevinson was in São Tomé just a short time before Arnott's visit there. For a current assessment of Nevinson's investigation and a history of the contract labor system in Angola, see Satre, *Chocolate on Trial*, 1–12, 41–43.

erty."[16] Such discrepancies between Arnott's public and private writings reveal an awareness that her home audience would be more likely to support a stable, thriving mission than one in a seemingly precarious position.

As Arnott grew more experienced in the Angola mission field, she became convinced that preparing Umbundu men and women for leadership in their own schools and churches was her central responsibility as a missionary. Once she developed some competence in Umbundu, she spent much of her time teaching reading, writing, and numbers to young boys and girls at Kamundongo or at its outstations.[17] "[I]t pays to give one's life to the training of native teachers," she explained in a letter to her home supporters in 1910. "They are the ones who must reach the Angola population."[18] In her emphasis on evangelization, vernacular teaching and the growth of indigenous institutions, Arnott supported ABCFM goals of that time. Evaluating Arnott's relationship with Ovimbundu with whom she worked is a more complicated task. Dana L. Robert argues that in the late 1900s, "even the best missionary efforts . . . were tainted by paternalism and assumptions about the superiority of western culture. But compared to the overt racism of ordinary westerners at that time, missionaries come across as surprisingly enlightened."[19]

Arnott in many ways fits this pattern. She certainly opposed aspects of traditional Umbundu society such as polygyny, domestic slavery, and forced marriage. She regularly communicated to her readers the horrors young girls might experience in a culture that endorsed such activities.[20] In articles such as "A Visit to an African Village (Continued)" in *Mission Studies*, Arnott drew contrasts between mothers who followed tradi-

16. Arnott, Diary, August, 19, 1905, NJADP; Circular Letter, September 11, 1905, NJADP.

17. See, for example, an account of her school in "Letter from Miss Nellie J. Arnott," one section in a larger article, "Lesson: Our New Missionary," 315–17.

18. Arnott, Circular Letter, August 5, 1910, in Ideal Scrapbook, NJADP.

19. Robert, *Christian Mission*, 89.

20. Mission leaders might privately admit that traditional practices like polygyny had advantages for Umbundu women; William Sanders reported in his "Reminiscences" (ABCFM Archives, the Houghton Library, Harvard University) that women told him that having "two or three" wives made the work easier (93). The mission also went slowly in addressing the issue of domestic slavery, for fear that forcing Umbundu Christians to free dependents would leave those freed in an even more vulnerable position. Historian Linda Heywood argues that Angola missionaries were "relatively powerless" to change practices related to domestic slavery because of its complex role in Umbundu society ("Slavery and Forced Labor," 424).

tional practices and the improved lives of their daughters who sought out the mission station and became Christianized.[21] Those who followed traditional ways she sometimes negatively characterized as "heathen." Witnessing a traditional funeral ceremony, though her description was lengthy and vivid, led her to hope: "May the Light soon be revealed to all these dark villages."[22] Arnott frequently confided to her diary her sadness at deaths of women caused, in her view, by a reliance on traditional healers or by bearing children at a young age. The neat, orderly settlements of Umbundu converts she found far preferable to traditional communities, which she judged to be chaotic and unhealthy, causing "many of the babies [to] die leaving their mothers with broken hearts and no comfort."[23] To her home readers, she communicated scenes of Umbundu women's lives designed to show mission work as worthy of donations. Overall, Arnott, like many others within the ABCFM, came to embrace a complex mix of social goals, some affirming the capacity of her students, others reasserting the "rightful" superiority of Anglo-American Protestant culture.[24]

In her writings, Arnott expressed little doubt that her students had the capability to lead their schools and churches. Her criticisms of traditional Umbundu customs certainly reflect contemporary assumptions about racial hierarchies. However, they are more closely related to her belief in the benefits of literacy, education, and improved health care, as well as the cultivation of a Christian life. Umbundu men and women were unfortunate to have been born far from "the blessings that surround our lives in America," Arnott wrote, but they were "just as dear to the Father as any one of us," she reminded her readers. "My heart often fills

21. Nellie Arnott Darling, "Visit to an African Village (Continued)," 184–86.

22. The description is in Arnott's journal (NJADP), entitled "Happenings in Africa," and is dated February 1909. Arnott "went to watch them [the Umbundu participants] play & dance" at the funeral and seems to have been fascinated, if in some ways repelled, by such ceremonies. On another occasion she and her colleague Elisabeth Ennis observed a divination ceremony, which Ennis described as "wearisome," but interesting enough that she returned for a second day of the event. Mrs. Merlin [Elisabeth] Ennis, "African Witchcraft," 317–19. A copy of the article is pasted in Arnott's Ideal Scrapbook with the notation "I was with them & saw this. N.J.A." (NJADP).

23. This quote is from remarks included in Arnott's Ideal Scrapbook (NJADP); titled "What it Means in Africa to the Mother and Child to be Without the Christ Child," the notes were evidently used for a talk she gave after returning to the U.S. on furlough.

24. John von Rohr comments upon difficulties within the ABCFM in distinguishing Christianity itself from its "cultural embodiment" in Western societies (*Shaping of American Congregationalism*, 375–76).

with joy at the privilege of being here," she declared.[25] In her journal titled "Happenings in Africa" she recorded descriptions of Umbundu life, many aspects of which she admired. In one lengthy entry, she gave an enthusiastic account of attending an *onjuluka*, a women's corn-shelling bee, in the fields of a young woman named Cipuku, about whom Arnott wrote often. Arnott had considerable respect for the agricultural skills of Cipuku and other Umbundu women, though she lamented that long hours in the fields kept young women from school. Arnott also appreciated basketry and other traditional handicrafts. She wrote admiringly about a group of masked dancers with their "garments . . . of bark string . . . made soft & pliable by oil. They are really quite wonderful." [26] Arnott lamented that few young women were learning to make clay pots and baskets that she regarded as both functional and beautiful. She imagined a future for Umbundu women in which they had specific responsibilities as "helpmates" to their husbands in teaching and in Christian education, while continuing, to some degree at least, their established role in food cultivation and storage.[27] While this model had obvious components of cultural intervention, there is also evidence that Umbundu women and men saw advantages in becoming part of Protestant communities that might offer protection and education as the highlands increasingly opened to European settlers. For example, Umbundu leaders, even those who were not Christians, might permit mission schools in their settlements or seek medical help at the missions; missions also interceded regularly on behalf of Ovimbundu who had run afoul of Portuguese authorities.

25. Arnott, "News from Kamundongo," 107. Her mission colleague Thomas Woodside wrote a more pointed argument, also published in 1908, asking his readers to consider how much of seeming "race superiority" was really "due to race and how much to environment, not only . . . of the man himself, but that of his father and grandfathers?" See "Is the African Worthwhile?" (320).

26. Arnott's journal, which she titled "Happenings in Africa, not recorded in letters or diary" (NJADP) gives detailed accounts of events she witnessed and of incidents in the lives of Umbundu Christians with whom she worked. She made occasional entries in the journal during the years 1907 to 1910. Some of these narratives are lengthy, in contrast to her daily diary entries, which are written to fit the available space in a day-by-day dated book of entries. Her account of the corn-shelling bee is in her entry of August 26, 1908; her description of the masked dancers was recorded on February 8, 1909.

27. "To the Friends of Mrs. Jane C. Means," undated [1912?], in Ideal Scrapbook (NJADP). A description of Umbundu women's pottery and baskets is in Cushman, *Missionary Doctor*, 141–45. Arnott brought a collection of baskets home with her; her granddaughter Mary D. Caris later donated them to the Lowie Museum of Anthropology (now the Phoebe A. Hearst Museum of Anthropology) at the University of California, Berkeley.

Umbundu women, in some instances, saw mission stations as havens from Portuguese settlers and traders. "Our people are in great fear these days," Arnott reported in 1908. "The price of rubber has gone way down so the traders are loseing [sic] money & have no prospects before them. So it is reported that *people* are being caught & sold . . . . Women are reported of being caught in the fields & several times our women have been frightened & ran in" to the mission station [emphasis in original via underlining].[28]

Arnott's writings about Umbundu society demonstrate that ABCFM women's mission culture was evolving, as Arnott herself represented a middle figure between the attitudes of some first-generation women serving with their spouses in Angola and younger teachers who were more in line with those historian Jane Hunter calls "New Woman" missionaries. Bertha Dodge Stover, one of Arnott's colleagues who came to Africa with her husband Wesley in 1882, for example, presented Umbundu women's lives, before Protestant intervention, as filled with "utter blankness, desolation, and hopelessness." But, Stover continued in a pamphlet entitled "Women of West Central Africa," "Christian motherhood" brought a new vision: a "neatly dressed, placid-faced woman" with "no palm oil on her hair."[29] In contrast, Elisabeth Logan Ennis, a college-educated woman who arrived in Angola in 1907 with her husband Merlin, represents a newer type of female missionary whose racial views and respect for Umbundu women were more equitable. Ennis, in an article in *Life and Light* entitled "The Umbundu Baby and Its Mother," takes a different tack from Stover, indicating that she sometimes thought of the Umbundu woman as "the original suffragette." "True," Ennis wrote, "she tills the soil and wins her daily 'mush' by the sweat of her brow, but possessing the key to the granary she possesses the key to the situation." Though Ennis was critical of certain child-rearing practices, the ar-

28. Arnott, "Happenings in Africa," May 10, 1908. Descriptions of other instances of medical assistance and of helping Ovimbundu in conflict with the Portuguese are in "Happenings in Africa" during April and May of 1908. In her entry of April 8, 1908, for example, she describes the imprisonment of a witness in the case of *Soma* (royal leader) Kanjundu, who was imprisoned himself as a result of false accusations made by a Portuguese trader. Kanjundu was eventually freed, due in part to intervention by ABCFM leaders. Missionary John Tucker wrote of Kanjundu's case in *Drums in the Darkness*, 108–10. Linda Heywood discusses advantages that might accrue to Umbundu rulers "who hitched their wagons to Protestants" in *Contested Power in Angola*, 54–57.

29. Hunter, "Women's Missions in History," 22–31; Stover, *Women of West Central Africa*, 8–9.

ticle nonetheless presents a notably more affirmative view of Umbundu women than did Stover.[30]

"New Woman" missionaries were also confident of their own ability to offer something unique and important to the mission enterprise, not merely support endeavors of husbands or male authorities. Here, again, Arnott's career is illustrative, as her writings reflect a shift in her own attitude over time and reveal some discomfort with traditional gender roles still favored by the ABCFM. Arnott, initially quite deferential and quick to note her own inadequacies, came to oppose male mission leaders upon occasion. In one telling instance, she and Sarah Stimpson questioned a male-only vote, at the 1909 Annual Meeting, opposing their plan to go and teach alone at a remote new outstation. She and Stimpson wanted "to get the native teachers better fitted to carry on these schools by themselves," a worthy goal in Arnott's view. Arnott acknowledged that "They have done very well without a resident missionary. Responsibility has seemed to develop them."[31] She and Stimpson continued their cam-

30. Ennis, "The Umbundu Baby and Its Mother," 390, 394–96. The article was also printed in pamphlet form by the Woman's Board of Missions in Boston. Jeremy Ball provides a somewhat different view of Elisabeth (Mrs. Merlin) Ennis in "The 'Three Crosses' of Mission Work." Ball argues that her work as author of the "Three Crosses" play performed at the Angola Jubilee in 1930 demonstrated that missionaries shared with the Portuguese "a negative evolutionary view of African cultures" (357). See also 331, 336, and 344–47. Perhaps one way to reconcile Elisabeth Ennis's more positive portrayal of local Umbundu culture in her earlier piece with her later valuing of Portuguese colonization and associated devaluing of indigenous social practices is to take note of the very different rhetorical situations. In the earlier piece, she was writing to Protestant women back in the U.S. and encouraging their affiliation with Umbundu counterparts based on a shared gender identity. In 1930, at a public gathering with thousands of attendees during a time of increased Portuguese power that threatened the mission enterprise's viability, ABCFM missionaries, as Ball himself suggests, may have felt the need to salute the colonial enterprise in order "to impress the Portuguese colonial administration and thus protect their [the missionaries'] position within Angola" (337). With the Portuguese having asserted a new level of control in their colony, Ball explains, the "Jubilee celebrations of 1930 took place not only within a Christianizing context, but also against the backdrop of an ultranationalist, authoritarian colonial government" (336). Relations with the Portuguese were not entirely cordial at the time of the Jubilee, as missionary and anthropologist Gladwyn Childs, who was present at the celebration, noted in his report of the event. "The Pageant went off beautifully, except for the part which was to depict the Portuguese discoveries. Much work had been put into this section, but it seems that it was not acceptable to certain of the authorities and was not given at all," Childs commented ("The Guests," 339–40).

31. Hunter, "Women's Missions in History," 27; Arnott, "Kamundongo and Vicinity," 144–45.

paign to teach in the new area, with Stimpson's written report of this controversy taking on an even more resistant tone invoking sarcasm. They were allowed to go, but only after the intervention of Reverend Sanders. Arnott would several times spend six weeks alone at outstations closer to Kamundongo, not only teaching boys and girls, but also helping male Umbundu Christian preachers with sermons. This activity placed her work beyond the traditional category of "Woman's Work for Woman," though certainly her main responsibility—teaching young girls in Kamundongo—remained gender-specific.[32]

Figure 23. Annual Meeting, Kamundongo, 1909. Nellie Arnott (who labeled her own photo) is on the right end of the middle row; Sarah Stimpson is seated next to her. William H. Sanders and Sarah B. Sanders are on the back row, center; Elisabeth L. Ennis and Merlin Ennis (with Merlin, Jr.) are on the front row, left. The animal skins are likely those of two leopards that had been destroying livestock near the Kamundongo mission station and, according to Arnott's "Happenings in Africa," were killed a few weeks before the 1909 Annual Meeting. (Photo courtesy of The Bancroft Library, University of California, Berkeley.)

32. Sarah Stimpson to Miss [Kate] Lamson, August 3, 1909, ABCFM Papers, 15.5: Southern Africa, Women's Board, Vol. 2, Rhodesia, West Central Africa, Zulu, 1900–1914, Documents and Letters, A-Z. Reel 215, Pitts Theological Library, Emory University (original in the Houghton Library, Harvard University). On Arnott's work in outstations see, for example, her diary entries during February 1909 (NJADP) and "Letter from Miss Arnott," *Life and Light*, 430. Andrea L Arrington discusses discrepancies between the theory of suitable gender roles for single women missionaries and their actual activities in an article focusing on Martha L. Moors, a nurse who served at a station of the South Africa General Mission in Angola in the 1920s ("Making Sense of Martha," 276–300).

Overall, readers of Arnott's mission magazine articles would certainly have recognized that her role in Angola was not fully in accord with middle-class gender conventions at home. Indeed, that was part of the appeal of reading mission magazines, since they allowed women and children in the U.S. the vicarious experience of traveling to far-off places and doing socially significant work there. However, in its adaptation of travel literature's features, writing like Arnott's for mission magazines faced some gendered challenges. As Kristi Siegel has explained in her book on *Gender, Genre, and Identity in Women's Travel Writing*, all women's travel writing during this period sought a delicate rhetorical balance between generating "material that was reasonably exciting" and needing "to remain a lady." Accordingly, Siegel suggests, women authors "strained the conventions of femininity, but did not break them."[33] Mary Gaunt's secular account of travel to Africa in 1911, *Alone in West Africa*, offers a useful point of comparison. Gaunt's narrative blends features of sentimental writing with examples of her own intrepid behavior, generating a portrait of exciting travel that still allows her to remain a well-bred lady. Arnott carved out a similar self-portrait. At times she emphasized her mission site's uncivilized natural features and the backwardness of its people (their superstitions, for example) so as to point to the needed interventions which donations from home would address. But at other times, even simultaneously in some pieces, she stressed how her students were following a curriculum parallel to children in the U.S., how her social outreach projects (such as teaching good sanitation practices) mirrored women's benevolent enterprises at home, and how she herself remained the clear embodiment of a middle-class Christian woman. Like many other ABCFM women missionaries of her day, in other words, Arnott crafted chronicles of herself and her work that stretched but did not overturn middle-class gender roles.

While writers such as Arnott may have shaped the perceptions of their home audience about ABCFM mission work, it is also useful to examine what mission publications said *about* her. U.S.-based women editors created accounts of Arnott's mission service in headnotes to some of her articles and in sections for "round-up" reports they wrote about multiple women's mission service at diverse overseas locations. They also wrote some full-scale articles specifically about Arnott as an idealized missionary. In this body of writing about Arnott, editors at *Life and Light* and *Mission Studies* presented her as an exemplar of Christian

---

33. Siegel, *Gender, Genre and Identity*, 2–3.

Motherhood, transporting American domesticity to a stereotyped dark, uncivilized Africa. At times, the need for this portrait undercut Arnott's own view, seen in her journals and articles, that her students and their families were capable and productive in their own right.[34]

A narrative about Arnott was also, implicitly, about the shared values being developed among the mothers, Sunday School teachers, and children studying the exemplary life of this far-away missionary by reading about her in mission magazines published by the women's boards of the ABCFM. Accordingly, some of these articles addressed their audiences as "you" and emphasized readers' own participation in the mission enterprise through support provided in the form of donations and magazine subscriptions. For instance, "At Kamundongo," a 1908 piece in *Mission Studies* (published by the WBMI), designates Arnott as "your own missionary in Africa, Miss Nellie Arnott," stressing bonds between her service and her supporters at home. Emphasizing the crucial contribution that missionary women like Arnott were making by carrying American civilization to peoples otherwise lost to Christianity, this sketch noted: "She has been there three years and has learned the strange language and can . . . teach the boys and girls . . . . [Y]ou know that before the missionaries go to them[,] the people of Africa have no books, no letters and no schools."[35]

One dimension of these accounts of Arnott's work written by others at home in the U.S. invokes the familiar "before and after" pattern. For example, Miss May J. Johnston's article, "A Trip to Kamundongo and Ochileso," credits Arnott and her colleagues with transforming the local people and the setting through their Christian influence—even as, through rhetorically savvy contrasts, Johnston raises the specter of persistent elements that can only be overcome with continued backing from ABCFM supporters at home. Johnston declares that the people of Kamundongo "[f]ormerly" lived "in one-room huts, mudded and thatched, with one door and no window," but that they now have "a village of straight, clean streets, and neat, wattled houses with grass roofs and an adjoining garden," thanks to the guidance of the missionary team. However, even in this Christianized village, troubling signs of the pre-mission past persist, in Johnston's account, as unconverted villagers remain caught up in "fetishism, superstition and witchcraft": "men and

34. For a more detailed discussion of this issue, see Robbins and Pullen, *Nellie Arnott's Writings*, 80–88.

35. L. L. [no name given], "At Kamundongo," 251–52.

women are tortured, poisoned, tried by fire and killed in the belief they have caused another's death by sorcery." In contrasting the still-unconverted dimensions of the community with the order evident in the "missionary compounds," Johnston underlines both material features ("walls are of sun-dried bricks ... and the windows number TEN") and social practices reflecting Christianity's power. In schools, she explains, the young children are learning "sewing, weaving, clay work, songs and games, just as they do in America" from their capable teacher, Miss Arnott. At the same time, however, Johnston reports that although Mrs. Sanders, wife of Arnott's colleague Reverend Sanders, tries to teach the adults basic medical care, "The ignorance and need of the people is [sic] appalling."[36]

Arnott herself continued to express ambivalent, even contradictory attitudes toward the local people with whom she worked in Angola. One consistent aspect of her stance is her concern about the life experiences of young girls and women and her firm belief that a Christian education would bring them temporal as well as spiritual salvation. More specifically, over Arnott's years in Angola, she came to believe that forced or early marriage, the high infant death rate, and the colonial powers' enslavement of some young women could all be addressed through the building of an ABCFM-run Girls' Boarding School serving students from all the various highland mission stations. Arnott thus came to support educational goals that were emerging among ABCFM leaders caught up in the Social Gospel.[37] To gather ideas for such a school, ABCFM officials suggested Arnott visit other American Board schools in South Africa on her way home for her regularly scheduled furlough in 1912. She was especially impressed with the organization and work of Inanda Seminary. Once back in the U.S., she devoted much time to lecturing and fund-raising on behalf of such an institution during an extended cross-country tour that eventually brought her to her parents' home in California.[38]

36. May J. Johnston, "A Trip to Kamundongo and Ochileso," 307–10; see also Robbins and Pullen, *Nellie Arnott's Writings*, 85–87.

37. Hutchison, *Errand to the World*, 91. See also Von Rohr, *Shaping of American Congregationalism*, 373–74.

38. Arnott's instructions to visit South African schools and her trip to Inanda Seminary are described in her Circular Letter of February 17, 1912 ("Loose Letters," NJADP) and her diary entries May 8–14, 1912. Her efforts to raise funds for a Girls' Boarding School in Angola are detailed in a number of her letters and articles, for example, her Circular Letter "To the Friends of Mrs. Jane C. Means" in Ideal Scrapbook,

Arnott seemed poised to assume a leadership role in the girls' school when, having returned to her family home during what she was still viewing as a furlough, she became reacquainted with Paul Darling and accepted his marriage proposal. While the reasons behind her acceptance and the resulting change in her career plans have been impossible to determine, it is clear that she continued to be an active supporter of the ABCFM's mission activities by giving talks and writing articles in the early stage of her marriage. Her scrapbooks, meantime, became a longstanding repository not just of her own personal artifacts of mission service, but also of photos, post cards, and other memorabilia from her former colleagues in Angola, who continued to stay in close touch over the years. Meanwhile, Arnott was likely quite proud when the Means Memorial School, which she suggested be named for her Boston-area mentor Jane Means, opened in 1917.[39]

Arnott's writings, though admittedly biased by her missionary perspective, still provide a valuable snapshot of Angola at a critical time period in the history of the highlands and of ABCFM mission stations there. In Arnott's day, the West Central Africa Mission was, in many ways, aligned with ABCFM goals as articulated by nineteenth-century mission theorists, though Arnott's experiences show that gender roles were more flexible in the field than ABCFM leaders might have wished. During Arnott's service, the West Central Africa Mission faced numerous challenges that came with the extension of Portuguese authority into the highlands. In the years after her departure, the situation in the highlands continued to evolve.

In the 1920s, Portuguese rule drew ABCFM missions much more into the colonial orbit. A decree mandated that instruction in mission schools must be in Portuguese, rather than Umbundu. In addition, new agricultural, taxation and labor policies, as well as the completion of the

---

NJADP. See chapter 6 of Robbins and Pullen, *Nellie Arnott's Writings*," for a full discussion.

39. Arnott left no analysis of her choice to marry, except that she decided "I could never leave Paul again" (Diary, March 1, 1913). She agonized over her decision, however, writing on March 7: "These are days of suffering in spite of the inner joy. To withdraw from the Mission nearly kills me." On the naming of Means Memorial School, see Arnott's letter to ABCFM Secretary James L. Barton, December 9, 1912, (ABCFM Papers, 15.1: Western Africa, Vol. 19, Africa Mission, 1910–1919, Letters A-M, Part I, A-E, Reel 168, Pitts Theological Library, Emory University (original in the Houghton Library, Harvard University). Arnott asks if he has any objection to naming the school in honor of Jane Means; her letter "To the Friends of Mrs. Jane C. Means" also indicates her desire that the school be called Means Memorial.

Benguela railroad into the highlands, brought economic changes, as the long-distance carrying trade of the Umbundu region was undermined. Indigenous Christian leaders such as those Arnott and her colleagues envisioned, however, took the lead in this era in adapting many traditional Umbundu practices to Protestant teachings, thus preserving a strong regional identity that continued to characterize the highlands in subsequent decades. Graduates of Means Memorial School for young women and its companion institution, Currie Institute for young men, provided teachers, medical workers and preachers for a network of Umbundu Protestant communities.[40]

As late as the 1930s, at least, materials pasted in her scrapbook and associated notations show that Nellie Arnott (then Mrs. Paul Darling) was still tracking the work of the institution she had helped to establish. Cards from Marion M. Webster, first dean of Means Memorial, and photos, including one of Mrs. Webster with a class of young women proudly displaying their skillfully woven baskets, attest to her ongoing interest in the school's activities. She also continued correspondence with several of her former students who attended Currie Institute, following their careers as some of them, such as S. K. Ngonga, became recognized as notable preachers and teachers. Her scrapbooks indicate that she saw ABCFM goals successfully realized in the growth of the mission's schools and indigenous leaders, despite economic and social changes in the region. Though the brutal Civil Wars in Angola have left the school and other remnants of the mission stations where Arnott worked inoperable today, elements of her personal experience and its connections to the role women played in ABCFM history of her era are, fortunately, still recoverable today in the multi-faceted archive of her writing.[41]

---

40. Linda Heywood comments extensively on these economic, educational and social changes and on adaptive strategies of Umbundu Protestants in *Contested Power in Angola*, 58–59, 89, 104–17. She finds that Protestant missionaries in the highlands continued in the 1920s and later decades to seek means of protecting the rights of Umbundu Christians, even though they "were careful not to confront the government directly" (116–17). Jeremy Ball comments as well on the "sense of community" that ABCFM mission policies encouraged among Umbundu Christians. He emphasizes, however, that despite their accomplishments, ABCFM missionaries in Angola "also reinforced certain perceptions of Africans through civilizing rhetoric that promoted colonial discourse" in their presentations at the 1930 Jubilee celebration of the mission's founding ("'Three Crosses' of Mission Work," 351–52). At the Jubilee, William Henry Sanders was honored for his fifty years of service in Angola.

41. At the 1930 Jubilee, one of the purposes of the celebration was to highlight the

BIBLIOGRAPHY

American Board of Commissioners for Foreign Missions Archives (ABC 1–91). Houghton Library, Harvard University. By permission of the Houghton Library, Harvard University and by Wider Church Ministries of the United Church of Christ. Cited after the first reference as ABCFM Archives.

American Board of Commissioners for Foreign Missions. Papers of the American Board of Commissioners for Foreign Missions. Unit 1–6 [microform]. (Woodbridge CT: Research Publications, c1983–1985). Pitts Theology Library, Emory University. Originals held at Houghton Library; referenced in this edition by permission of the Houghton Library, Harvard University and by Wider Church Ministries of the United Church of Christ. Cited after the first reference as ABCFM Papers.

Arnott, Nellie J. "Kamundongo and Vicinity." *Mission Studies: Woman's Work in Foreign Lands,* May 1910, 144–45.

———. "Letter from Miss Arnott." *Life and Light for Woman,* September 1909, 430–31.

———. "A Letter from Miss Nellie J. Arnott." In "Lesson: Our New Missionary," *Mission Studies: Woman's Work in Foreign Lands,* October 1908, 315–17.

———. "News from Kamundongo." *Mission Studies: Woman's Work in Foreign Lands,* May 1908, 106–07.

Arrington, Andrea L. "Making Sense of Martha: Single Women and Mission Work." *Social Sciences and Missions* 23 (2010): 276–300.

Ball, Jeremy. "The 'Three Crosses' of Mission Work: Fifty Years of the American Board of Commissioners for Foreign Missions (ABCFM) in Angola, 1880–1930." *Journal of Religion in Africa* 40 (2010): 331–57.

Childs, Gladwyn Murray. "The Guests," *Missionary Herald,* September 1930, 339–40.

———. *Umbundu Kinship & Character: Being a Description of the Social Structure and Individual Development of the Ovimbundu of Angola, with Observations Concerning the Bearing on the Enterprise of Christian Missions of Certain Phases of the Life and Culture Described.* London: Oxford University Press, 1949.

Corr, Donald Philip. *"The Field is the World:" Proclaiming, Translating, and Serving by the American Board of Commissioners for Foreign Missions, 1810–1840.* Pasadena: William Carey Library, 2009.

Cushman, Mary Floyd, M. D. *Missionary Doctor: The Story of Twenty Years in Africa.* New York: Harper & Brothers, 1944.

Darling, Mrs. Nellie Arnott. "A Visit to an African Village, Continued." *Mission Studies: Woman's Work in Foreign Lands,* June 1913, 184–86.

---

accomplishments of both elder and younger Umbundu pastors., according to Frank Knight Sanders (brother of William H. Sanders), who represented the ABCFM at the gathering; one of the young pastors so recognized was Ngonga of Sachikela, likely Arnott's former student (F. Sanders, "Impressions of the Angola Jubilee," 331–32). Ngonga's correspondence with her (S. K. Gonga [sic] to Mrs. Darling, January 21, 1914, and S. K. Ngonga to Mrs. Darling, February 13, 1916), as well as letters from other former students, is in "Loose Letters," NJADP. In an article (included in Arnott's papers) about the family, where the name was spelled "Gonga," she added a handwritten note that he "was about 10 years old when I was his teacher at Sachikela in 1910. I taught him his first English. He was a charter member of the church. Was pastor of the church in 1930." See, in "Loose Letters" in NJADP, John A Reuling, "Family Life in Africa," *The Pilgrim Home,* with Arnott's handwritten date of 1947.

Darling, Nellie Jane Arnott Papers, 1905–1943. BANC MSS 92/901 z. Bancroft Library, University of California, Berkeley. Cited after the first reference as NJADP.

Davis, Grace T. *Neighbors in Christ: Fifty-Eight Years of World Service by the Woman's Board of Missions of the Interior.* Chicago: Woman's Board of Missions of the Interior, 1926.

Ennis, [Elisabeth] Mrs. Merlin. "African Witchcraft." *Mission Studies: Woman's Work in Foreign Lands,* October 1910, 317–19.

———. "The Umbundu Baby and Its Mother." *Light and Life for Woman,* September 1914, 390–96.

Harris, Paul William. *Nothing but Christ: Rufus Anderson and the Ideology of Protestant Foreign Missions.* New York: Oxford University Press, 1999.

Henderson, Lawrence. *The Church in Angola: A River of Many Currents.* Cleveland: Pilgrim, 1992.

Heywood, Linda M. *Contested Power in Angola, 1840s to the Present.* Rochester Studies in African History and the Diaspora Vol. 6. Rochester: University of Rochester Press, 2000.

———. "Slavery and Forced Labor in the Changing Political Economy of Central Angola, 1850–1949." In *The End of Slavery in Africa,* edited by Suzanne Miers and Richard Roberts, 415–36. Madison: University of Wisconsin Press, 1988.

Hunter, Jane H. "Women's Missions in Historical Perspective: American Identity and Christian Internationalism." In *Competing Kingdoms: Women, Mission, Nation, and the American Protestant Empire, 1812–1960,* edited by Barbara Reeves-Ellington, Kathryn Kish Sklar and Connie A. Shemo, 19–42. Durham: Duke University Press, 2010.

Hutchison, William R. *Errand to the World: American Protestant Thought and Foreign Missions.* Chicago: University of Chicago Press, 1987.

Johnston, May J. "A Trip to Kamundongo and Ochileso." *Mission Studies: Woman's Work in Foreign Lands,* October 1908, 307–10.

L.L. "At Kamundongo." *Mission Studies: Woman's Work in Foreign Lands,* August 1908, 251–52.

Means, John O. "The Proposed Mission in Central Africa." *Missionary Herald,* November 1879, 443–60.

Nevinson, Henry W. *A Modern Slavery: With an Introduction by Basil Davidson.* New York: Harper, 1906. Reprint, London: Harper & Bros. Background Books, 1963.

Robbins, Sarah and Ann Ellis Pullen. *Nellie Arnott's Writings on Angola, 1905–1913: Missionary Narratives Linking Africa and America.* Anderson, SC: Parlor Press, 2011.

Robert, Dana L. *American Women in Mission: A Social History of Their Thought and Practice.* Macon: Mercer University Press, 1996.

———. *Christian Mission: How Christianity Became a World Religion.* Chichester, West Sussex, UK: Wiley-Blackwell, 2009.

Sanders, Frank Knight. "Impressions of the Angola Jubilee." *Missionary Herald,* September 1930, 331–33.

Sanders, William H. "Reminiscences." American Board of Commissioners for Foreign Missions Archives, 1810–1961. ABC 76:2, Personal Papers. Houghton Library, Harvard University.

Satre, Lowell J. *Chocolate on Trial: Slavery, Politics & the Ethics of Business.* Athens: Ohio University Press, 2005.

Siegel, Kristi, ed. *Gender, Genre, and Identity in Women's Travel Writing.* New York: Peter Lang, 2004.

Soremekun, Fola. "The Bailundu Revolt, 1902." *African Social Research* 16 (1973): 447–73.

———. "Religion and Politics in Angola: The American Board Missions and the Portuguese Government, 1880–1922." *Cahiers d'études africaines* 11, no. 3 (1971): 341–77.

Stover, Bertha D. *Women of West Central Africa.* Chicago: Woman's Board of Missions of the Interior, 19—[undated].

Strong, William E. *The Story of the American Board: An Account of the First Hundred Years of The American Board of Commissioners for Foreign Missions.* Boston: Pilgrim, 1910.

Tucker, John T. *Drums in the Darkness.* New York: George H. Doran, 1927.

Von Rohr, John. *The Shaping of American Congregationalism.* Cleveland: Pilgrim, 1992.

Woodside, Thomas W. "Is the African Worthwhile?" *Missionary Herald*, July 1908, 320–21.

10

The International Institute in Spain: Alice Gordon Gulick and Her Legacy

Stephen K. Ault

T HE INTERNATIONAL INSTITUTE IN Spain once attracted attention
from thousands of American college and university women. Yet, in
the United States today, it is perhaps one of the lesser-known creations
of missionaries from the American Board of Commissioners for Foreign
Missions (ABCFM). Even so, the International Institute, which has survived religious persecution, the perils of two wars, and almost 40 years
of fascist dictatorship, is now the oldest U.S. educational and cultural
institution in Spain. The role it played on two fronts—advancing the
education and condition of Spanish women and bringing education in
Spain into the modern era—makes the International Institute a remarkable testimonial to the dedication of its missionary founders, and to the
idea of the value of education for women that they brought from New
England to Spain in 1872.

The connections between the International Institute and the AB-
CFM were sometimes complex. Nevertheless, those ties to the ABCFM
and to Boston are integral to the early history of the International Institute. Even the handsome Congregational House on Beacon Street, which
was the headquarters of the ABCFM, has a link to the International Institute, as explained further on.

Spain in the nineteenth century was an inhospitable place for
both Protestantism and women's education. Given the vigilance of the
Spanish Inquisition, which remained active until 1834, the Protestant
Reformation had never taken hold in Spain, which was, in fact, one of

the pillars of the Counter Reformation. Protestants had no influence in early nineteenth century Spain, which remained for most of the century the European country most closed to evangelical propaganda. The few Protestants in Spain were almost all poor and from lower social classes, which meant that their chapels and schools required support from abroad. This gave their faith an alien quality that created antagonism on the part of the people and the authorities. The Protestants had few intellectuals or members of the social elite to give them prestige in the face of the overwhelming power, resources, and traditional importance of the Catholic Church in Spanish society.[1]

Yet change was coming. The nineteenth century was a tumultuous time in Spain. Early in the century, the country was engulfed by the Napoleonic peninsular wars. The unpopular King Fernando VII, known from Goya's unflattering portraits, was succeeded by his infant daughter, Isabel II, after a change in the laws of succession permitted a female to take the throne. The adult Isabel's corrupt and chaotic rule led to her overthrow and exile in 1868, and this, in turn, led to the creation of the Spanish Constitution of 1869. The Constitution was singular because it established, for the first time in Spanish history, religious liberty. Its proclamation of freedom of conscience encouraged Protestant missionaries to attempt to evangelize in Spain in order to liberate Spaniards from what they considered backward, medieval Catholicism.

Given this opening, the ABCFM authorized the sending of missionaries to Catholic Spain in 1871. These were among the first missionaries into "papal lands" sent by the Board, which had only just taken over responsibility for the area from the American and Foreign Christian Union.[2] Among those charged with bringing the Protestant Gospel to Spain were William Gulick and his new wife, Alice Gordon Gulick. Gulick was born in Hawai'i. He was one of eight children (seven of whom became missionaries) whose parents who were among the earliest missionaries to the Islands.[3] Alice Gordon Gulick was born in Auburndale,

---

1. De Zulueta, *Cien años de educación*, 56, 69.

2. The American and Foreign Christian Union (AFCU) was established in 1849 as a result of a merger of three missionary societies. By 1860, it had over 200 representatives overseas. As major Protestant denominations set up their own missionary programs, the AFCU had to cut back its activities, and by 1884, the principal focus of the AFCU was the American Church in Paris. See American and Foreign Christian Union, "AFCU History," n.p.

3. Thirty-two members of the Gulick family worked as ABCFM missionaries for a

Massachusetts, and was the daughter of James M. Gordon, a banker and the treasurer of the ABCFM. The primary motive for Alice to go to Spain was the missionary enterprise she was to share with her new husband, whom she married only one week before leaving for Spain. However, her religious faith was accompanied by a strong belief in the power of higher education to create a new type of spiritual and moral woman.

Alice Gulick was a lively and athletic young woman who had studied at Mount Holyoke Seminary. At Mount Holyoke, the first American women's college, she was shaped by the legacy of Mary Lyon, who believed that her students would be effective participants in the great task of renewing the world. After graduating, Alice studied and taught music in Boston. Then she returned to Mount Holyoke to teach philosophy from 1868 to 1870. On October 3, 1870, she married a young tutor from Amherst College, Alvah Bayless Kittredge, who, already gravely ill with tuberculosis, died the day after the wedding. However, Alice's spirit was not crushed by the loss. Even as a young girl, she had shown interest in the missionary enterprise, and a little more than a year after her bereavement, she married the aspiring missionary William Gulick. Following a farewell service at the Shawmut Church on Tremont Street in Boston on December 18, 1871, she set off with William on her first transatlantic voyage, going to Spain as a representative of the ABCFM and the Woman's Board of Missions.[4]

Before settling in northern Spain, the Gulicks toured the whole country, and Alice began to understand the position of women in Spanish society—particularly after she saw a woman hitched to an ox, pulling a plough. She recognized that many women were treated as beasts, trained only for a life of servitude. Even women of higher stations were, in her words, either playthings or housekeepers. Insofar as Spanish girls had any kind of education, they were prepared for life as ornamental ob-

---

total of over 750 years of service. Peter and Fanny Gulick, who went to Hawai'i in 1827, were the first in the family to work for the ABCFM. After 47 years in Hawai'i, Peter and Fanny joined their missionary son Orramel in Kobe, Japan, where they died in 1877 and 1883, respectively. See Putney, "The Legacy of the Gulicks," 29.

4. William's oldest brother, Luther, and his wife Louisa (Lewis) joined William and Alice on the voyage to Spain and settled in Barcelona. William and Luther were the senior missionaries. A younger brother, Thomas, and his wife Alice (Walbridge) arrived in Santander in 1873 to assist in the missionary efforts, but in 1875 moved to Zaragoza, where they worked until ill health forced them to leave Spain in 1883. See Putney, "The Legacy of the Gulicks," 33.

jects, having been taught a bit of French and the catechism. Often, they also learned how to embroider and perhaps to play a tune or two on the piano. Alice was underwhelmed by the elite Spanish girls' achievements: "She may not know the capital cities of Europe or in which direction to travel to reach America, but she must know how to walk gracefully somewhere."[5]

Alice Gulick was even less impressed by education for the masses in Spain. Their schools, to her horror, were dark, gloomy places, where students were crammed together with barely-educated and untrained teachers who were incapable of keeping order, much less creating conditions for learning. At that time, in 1872, almost two-thirds of Spain's eighteen million people were illiterate. Of course, educational opportunity for girls and women was particularly limited, and, according to Alice, generally non-existent. In some provinces, she said, education remained in "medieval obscurity."[6]

Against this background, Alice Gulick conceived of what was to be her life's work: creating a center where young Spanish women could receive teaching of the very best quality—a place where the pedagogical methods that had produced such fine results in the United States would be applied. This center was to be what she called her "Mount Holyoke of Spain."[7] She was not, admittedly, the only one to have had such an idea; other Mount Holyoke alumnae who had become Congregationalist missionaries had established other miniature Mount Holyokes—in Persia (1843), Turkey (1868) and South Africa (1874). But perhaps nowhere else did this drive, fueled by religious faith and a belief in the improving power of higher education for women, have such an impact as it did in Spain.

The first setting for Alice Gulick's efforts was Santander, on the Cantabrian coast. The Gulicks were thwarted in their hope to settle in Bilbao by the violence of the Carlist wars, which made it impossible for them to reach that important city and forced them to choose the much smaller setting of Santander. There, the Gulicks encountered the limits of Spain's newly-proclaimed freedom of religion, which barely rose to the level of toleration. In Santander (and later elsewhere in Spain), they had difficulty finding a landlord who would permit them to rent

5. Gordon, *Alice Gordon Gulick*, 85.

6. Ibid., 73.

7. Ibid., 88.

a property that would be used for Protestant education and worship. Other obstacles that they encountered included: 1) the restrictions on burials in Catholic cemeteries and lack of proper cemeteries for non-Catholics; 2) lack of official recognition for Protestant schools; and 3) persecution of those who tried to distribute Bibles and pamphlets, particularly during fairs and celebrations.[8] Roman Catholic ecclesiastical authorities, local officials, and ordinary citizens all made life extremely complicated for Protestant Christians in general and for the missionaries in particular. Even when the Gulicks unobtrusively set up their chapel in an old Santander leather and cowhide warehouse, the local boys were sometimes encouraged to throw stones through the windows during religious services. In another instance, the bishop of Oviedo sent a special delegate to a town that William Gulick was visiting in order to subvert the missionary's plans. The delegate promised to celebrate weddings and baptisms free for the villagers and even told them from the pulpit that "taking the life of a Protestant would be a good deed."[9]

In spite of all the obstacles, William Gulick became an integral and important part of the small community of Protestant missionaries—to the extent that he was sometimes called "the bishop of Northern Spain." Alice Gulick also became an invaluable part of the mission effort, ministering to the poor and ill, providing music for services, and beginning a small school—not to mention giving birth to three children in her first four years in Spain. Her health suffered from the cold, humid climate of Santander, and in early 1873 she was battered for the first time by the loss of a child. Mrs. Gulick also had to endure a special type of harassment, for in Spanish eyes she was an anomaly: the wife of a priest. Describing a visit to a small village, she once wrote that "Barnum and all his animals could hardly have excited the curiosity and interest that was attached to a Protestant priest with a wife and child!"[10]

A problem that faced the Gulicks throughout their work in Spain was the difficulty in getting enough financial support from the ABCFM. The couple's frequent illnesses and their growing family meant heavy medical expenses, and their salaries did not enable them to cover their

---

8. De Zulueta, *Cien años de educación*, 67.

9. Ibid., 81. Thomas Gulick was nearly shot dead by anti-Protestant Spaniards during the course of his missionary service in Zaragoza. See Putney, "The Legacy of the Gulicks," 33.

10. Gordon, *Alice Gordon Gulick*, 57.

costs. The Board, which was focused on its missions in other parts of the world, wanted to reduce costs in Spain, not increase them. It was therefore often unresponsive to their requests for personal aid and funding for missionary projects.[11]

Undeterred by the Board's stinginess, Alice Gulick started a small boarding school in her home in Santander in 1877, putting herself on the road to establishing the International Institute. Almost from the outset, she had support from other American college women, feminists of the time, and missionaries, who believed in women's education and saw it as a necessity if Spain were to enjoy the benefits of a liberal, tolerant society. In their view, women in Spain needed to be educated, to become independent, and even to earn a livelihood, preferably as teachers, further extending the benefits of education across Spanish society. Young women college graduates came from the United States to assist Alice, who had already begun to talk to them of her hope that the little school in her home was the precursor of a large, well-equipped institute, a Mount Holyoke of Spain.

The funds for the expenses of the boarding school at this stage came from the Woman's Board of Missions, an affiliate of the ABCFM. Its branches in Springfield and, later, Woburn, Massachusetts, paid Alice Gulick's salary: $600 a year. Year after year, the Gulicks had to fight for the pitifully small amounts they were seeking for Alice's school. Eventually the ABCFM came up with some funding, but chastised the Gulicks for spending too much on it. They also balked at the cost of providing the Gulicks with a chapel and a home of their own in Santander. There was one proposal from the Gulicks, however, that the Board did approve in 1880: moving the couple's mission and Alice's school to San Sebastián, an elegant beach-front city where the Gulicks hoped to find less hostility, better weather, more middle-class students, and better communications. After the Gulicks' arrival in San Sebastian in 1881, Alice's school grew and began to be known as the Colegio Norteamericano. In 1883, E. K. Alden and N. G. Clark of the ABCFM came to San Sebastián and were impressed enough that they gave the Gulicks permission to rent the entire building where they were living so that there would be enough space for the boarding school and a basic mission school. The schools grew, with the boarding school training students who went on to teach in the

11. De Zulueta, *Cien años de la educación*, 79.

mission schools. The Gulicks even began a night program to combat adult illiteracy.

The growing fame of Alice Gulick's school (and the location of San Sebastián on the Madrid-Paris route) attracted American visitors, including Jane Addams, founder of Chicago's Hull House.[12] In ten years in Santander, only one American had come to visit the Gulicks. Emboldened by the newfound popularity of her school, Alice grew more insistent on the need for it to have a center of its own, not just space in an apartment building. She lobbied N.G. Clark, the head of the ABCFM, and Mrs. Albert Bowker, the president of the Woman's Board, for more material support for the school. With a building of its own and adequate resources, the school would, according to Alice, attract more paying students. It would also bring over more young American women college graduates to assist in enriching its program.

In November 1884, Alice Gulick complained to N.G. Clark that her school lacked a library, proper furnishings, basic scientific equipment such as microscopes and telescopes, and gymnastic equipment (the last a nod to an important innovation in American education that her nephew Luther Gulick, a pioneer in physical education, was championing at Springfield College in Massachusetts).[13] Only months later Alice wrote Clark again, asking that he send her one or two young women teachers to take charge of the advanced classes: "If we are going to have a Mount Holyoke of Spain, we need teachers from Mount Holyoke, or loyal to the principles of the ABCFM."[14] Unheeded and exhausted, she obtained a leave to come home to the United States in 1887 to regain her energy and to work for the success of her San Sebastián school.

---

12. Gordon, *Alice Gordon Gulick*, 105.

13. De Zulueta, *Cien años de la educación*, 105.

14. Ibid.

Figure 24. Alice Gordon Gulick, n.d. Photo courtesy of the Hawaiian Mission Children's Society Library.

The Prudential Committee of the Board ultimately authorized Alice Gulick to engage in direct fundraising for her school, although N.G. Clark noted that he did not expect that she would obtain many contributions. The Board still wanted Alice to cut costs and was not particularly interested in her goal of a Mount Holyoke of Spain. The ABCFM expected the Gulicks to find a more modest dwelling for themselves and to place an emphasis on preparing teachers for mission schools. Spain lacked importance for the ABCFM, which was focusing its efforts on women's higher education in Turkey and India. Alice had to contend with Clark's view that her school was a purely educational venture, while she saw it as one of the most effective evangelical efforts of the mission. It certainly was successful, with teachers instructing over 500 students in Spain and in one French location. The school continued to grow and experimented with innovations such as a kindergarten and instruction for teachers of what is now called early education.

An exceptional milestone for Alice's school occurred in June 1891 when four of its students presented themselves for government examinations for the *bachillerato* diploma and received outstanding grades. This was a modern first for Spain: young women prepared by women. The conservative sister of one of the professors assessing the young students in this public oral examination demanded to know why he had not found some basis for giving them lower grades or failing them. "How could I?" he told her, "in the presence of so many teachers, scholars and visitors, for they could all hear as well as I, and the girls' responses were absolutely correct." "The devil himself is helping those girls!" was his sister's response.[15] Three of these young women continued their studies at the university level and were able to earn bachelor's degrees—two in Philosophy and Letters and one in Pharmacy—from the University of Madrid. In that same period, 1895–1900, only eleven women received the bachelor's degree in all of Spain, and, as noted, three of them did their university work entirely at the International Institute.

What Alice Gulick had accomplished softened the resistance of the ABCFM to her plans, for her school's successes were easing the way for Protestantism in Spain by breaking down some of the religious prejudices in the country. Her own personality had won many friends for her project in Spain, and the academic success of her students brought her endeavor to the attention of leading Spanish educators, who became allies of the International Institute in the years ahead.

Once the ABCFM had given Alice Gulick permission to raise funds for the College Hall and campus that she hoped to have for her school, she dedicated her life to finding the resources that would make her dream for Spanish women a reality. Although she had previously been appalled by the thought of going from stage to pulpit to platform asking for money for her work, she became a powerful and effective speaker. She managed to connect with women who shared her interest in women's education and who had resources to help advance that cause. These included many women in the Boston area, including Alice Freeman Palmer, the president of Wellesley College. Although suffering terribly from seasickness, Alice Gulick made numerous voyages to the U.S. by steamship in order to raise money for her Spanish school all

15. Gordon, *Alice Gordon Gulick*, 112.

across the nation. She even sought funds in Hawai'i, where she and her husband had gone to see his family and birthplace.

In late 1892, a new entity, the International Institute for Girls in Spain, was incorporated as a nonsectarian charitable corporation by an act of the Massachusetts Legislature. The new entity reflected a desire to collect funds for a permanent home for the school in a way that was separate from the ABCFM and the Woman's Board. It was also a response to Spanish legal reality: religious corporations were prohibited from buying property in Spain. The new International Institute saw itself as cooperating with the ABCFM. Indeed, members of the Board such as Samuel Capen (President of the ABCFM) and Charles Rutan also served as presidents of the International Institute. (It was Rutan, of the Boston architectural firm of Shepley, Rutan & Coolidge, who designed the Congregational House and who may have participated in planning for the International Institute's building in Madrid during his tenure as the Institute's president.)

The 400th anniversary of the Spanish discovery of the New World and the Columbian Exposition in Chicago gave Alice Gulick additional opportunities to raise funds. The International Institute was awarded prizes and medals at the Chicago exposition to honor its work in Spain. Another boost for the school came from Alice Freeman Palmer, the former Wellesley College president who served as president of the International Institute from 1898 to 1901. She suggested that American university women who were aware of the privileges of enjoying the benefits of higher education had a duty to share that privilege with their sisters in Spain by supporting Alice Gulick's cause. Donors to the Institute received special certificates that showed Queen Isabel opening her jewel boxes for Columbus. The imagery suggested that it was time for grateful American women to honor the queen's gift by making possible the building of a center for women's education in Spain.

The Spanish-American War of 1898 disrupted the work of the school, which moved across the French border to Biarritz for the safety of the students and faculty. Stranded in the United States by the war, Alice Gulick and her daughter Grace aided Spanish prisoners of war who were held at Camp Long on Seavy Island, New Hampshire. Alice's exemplary conduct in nursing the wounded and writing to the families of the prisoners impressed both Spanish officers and the American military, including Admiral William Sampson.

A further act of the Massachusetts Legislature authorized the International Institute to acquire property and build anywhere in Spain. The Gulicks' contacts among the country's liberal educators, politicians, and intellectuals urged them to move the Institute to Madrid, the political, intellectual, and educational capital of the country, and they took this advice, buying a small mansion on Fortuny Street, close to the main boulevard, the Paseo de la Castellana. With the addition of two adjacent plots on Miguel Ángel and Rafael Calvo Streets, they created a campus with plenty of room for the spacious College Hall that Alice Gulick had long envisioned.

A meeting at the Old South Church, Boston, on January 25, 1903 brought together powerful forces that turned that vision into a reality. Samuel Capen of the ABCFM, then president of the International Institute, Harvard University president Charles Eliot, and the Rev. Mr. Edward Everett Hale, and others spoke on behalf of raising funds for the building. President Eliot asked the audience to contribute to honor Alice Gulick's work and sacrifices. The meeting led to the formation of the International Institute League, with chapters across the United States. The organization urged college women to support the school and contribute to the advancement of their sisters in Spain.

Alice Gulick did not live to see the opening of the renovated Fortuny building or the construction of College Hall, which, instead, became her memorial. Weakened by her exertions, the loss of her adult son James Gordon in 1900, and the suicide of her sole surviving son Frederick in 1902, she died of tuberculosis in London in September 1903. The opening class day ceremonies at Fortuny became her funeral. Seven years later, the newly-completed College Hall, located at Miguel Ángel 8, was dedicated to her.

The loss of Alice Gulick was a blow to the International Institute. Yet, the school survived and flourished. Led by William Gulick and his successors, the Institute collaborated with progressive forces, including the Institución Libre de Enseñanza, that were trying to regenerate Spanish education. American women, spurred on by Alice's example, went to Madrid to teach for the Institute, and to support the experimental programs of the Junta para Amplicación de Estudios in which the Institute participated, such as the coeducational Instituto-Escuela and the Residencia de Señoritas for university students. Women faculty such as Mary Louise Foster of Smith College, who designed and equipped a chemistry laboratory for women students, brought what Santiago Ramón y Cajal called "the most fertile contribution": "brains of women teachers and scientists capable of leaving a mark on this country."[16] The Institute enhanced its English language offerings, established one of Spain's first lending libraries, and offered the country's first courses in library science. In 1930, the International Institute welcomed students from Smith College in the first organized U.S. study abroad program in Spain.

Forced by the Spanish Civil War to suspend activities in Madrid, the International Institute supported its Spanish friends in exile in France, Mexico and the U.S. The Institute was unable to return to Miguel Ángel 8 until 1950. During the dictatorship of Francisco Franco, the International Institute became a forum for the free expression of ideas, a place to obtain books prohibited elsewhere in Spain, and a site where intellectuals banned from university faculties were able to teach and speak.

Today, the International Institute continues its dedication to advancing women's interests and to promoting women's contributions to society within the context of a program of educational and cultural exchange between Spain and the United States. The Institute houses American university study abroad programs from leading institutions such as Boston University, Stanford University, Syracuse University, University at Albany (SUNY), the University of Southern California, and Washington University. Thousands of students have been introduced to Spanish culture by these programs. Spanish students, for their part, benefit from the Institute's North American Language and Culture Program, which specializes in teaching English to Spaniards. The Institute's 80,000-volume Library helps both English and Spanish-speaking readers to understand one another's cultures. A wide-ranging program of lectures, concerts, and colloquia that emphasize the U.S.-Spain connection continues to enrich Madrid's busy cultural scene.

While responding today to the conditions of a vibrant, democratic Spain, the International Institute honors the legacy of Alice Gordon Gulick and her dedication to the value of education and intellectual growth to a modern nation. A product of the work of the ABCFM and of the tensions between its evangelical objectives and the goals of this dynamic woman, the International Institute has, through its remarkable history, indeed left its mark on Spain.

16. Piñón, "El Instituto Internacional y la educación," n.p.

BIBLIOGRAPHY

American Foreign and Christian Union. "AFCU History." Accessed July 31, 2011. Online: http://www.afcubridge.org/History%202.htm.

Gordon, Elizabeth Putnam. *Alice Gordon Gulick: Her Life and Work in Spain.* New York: Fleming H. Revell, 1917.

Grigas, Carol S. "Mission to Spain: Alice Gordon Gulick and a Transatlantic Project to Educate Spanish Women." PhD diss., Washington State University, 2004.

Piñón Varela, Pilar. "El Instituto Internacional y su contribución a la educación de la mujer en España." Madrid, February 22, 2007. Unpublished talk.

Putney, Clifford. "The Legacy of the Gulicks, 1827–1964." *International Bulletin of Missionary Research* 25 (2001) 28–35.

Zulueta, Carmen de. *Cien años de educación de la mujer española.* 2nd ed. Madrid: Castalia, 1992.

11

Early Nineteenth Century Missionaries to Hawai'i and the Salary Dispute

Paul T. Burlin

THERE ARE FEW SUBJECTS that are more controversial in the much-contested history of Hawai'i since the arrival of the foreigner than the role and impact of the missionaries in the Island Kingdom. This is particularly true of those missionaries sent forth by the Boston-based American Board of Commissioners for Foreign Missions (ABCFM) beginning in 1819.

The historiographical debate, at times more characterized by the heat than by the light it has shed on the missionaries, needs a heavy dose of nuance. For those on the Left and for Hawaiian nationalists generally, there is more-or-less a straight line from the arrival of the First Company of ABCFM agents in 1820 leading to the Great *Mahele* and the acquisition of Hawaiian land by foreigners, including many of the missionaries themselves as well as their descendents. What will be argued here is that while it is undisputable that many of the missionaries acquired land and other forms of wealth in the islands and they worked hard to impose a capitalist political economy on the Hawaiian people, it is not true that there was consensus on this within the missionary community, particularly if one pays close attention to chronology and precise historical context. As a matter of fact, at times it seems as if some of the earlier missionaries were at war with the market revolution and the laissez-faire capitalist values of the main chance that were so much in evidence during the first half of the nineteenth century in the United

States. The salary controversy within the missionary community in Hawai'i in the 1830s is an illuminating case in point.[1]

Prior to discussing the salary issue, however, it is necessary to put the dispute into historical context, a context that was in part defined by the worldview held by many of the missionaries who left the United States under the auspices of the ABCFM during the first half of the nineteenth century. Many of those missionaries were graduates of Andover and other Calvinist-oriented theological seminaries.

What characterized Andover Theological Seminary specifically was a conservative Calvinist perspective, the particular nemesis of which was the theological liberalism and Unitarianism that had come to pervade Harvard College. In fact, Andover was founded specifically in response to the Unitarian capture of the Harvard College Hollis Professorship of Divinity in 1805.

There were a number of Congregational theological groups that collaborated to establish the new seminary. These involved Calvinists of various stripes, including Hopkinsians or New Divinity clerics. While they had their own intramural theological differences, they shared an aversion not only to what had transpired at Harvard, but also to the consequences of that occurrence; namely, the cosmopolitan and urbane theology which extended to the wealthy parishes of mercantile Boston. It was among the elites of Boston and the churches they attended that Unitarianism held sway.[2]

Among the theological groups that founded Andover, the "New Divinity" party was of particular importance in terms of fostering the missionary impulse.[3] The New Divinity theology was associated with Samuel Hopkins, one of Jonathan Edward's most influential students. Hopkins modified his mentor's theology in a way that shifted empha-

1. The historiography on the role and the impact of the missionaries to Hawai'i is lengthy. A few of the works that stand out are Silva, *Aloha Betrayed*, Trask, *From a Native Daughter*, Kame'eleihiwa, *Native Land, Foreign Desires*; Daws, *Shoals of Time*; and Kuykendall, *The Hawaiian Kingdom*. On the market revolution see Sellers, *The Market Revolution*. For a work that well documents Protestant dissent regarding the emerging liberal capitalist order, see Hanley, *Beyond a Christian Commonwealth*.

2. On the founding of Andover and the theological perspectives represented in that effort, see Woods, *History of Andover Theological Seminary*, 17–46. Also see, Howe, *The Unitarian Conscience*, 1–23. For an excellent description of the intellectual and theological trends in Boston Congregational Churches as many evolved toward Unitarianism, see Field, *The Crisis*, especially 47–81.

3. Kling, "The New Divinity." On the role of New Divinity Theology and Andover Theological Seminary, see Harris, *Nothing but Christ*, 59–60.

sis from a preoccupation with one's personal salvation to a perspective wherein "disinterested benevolence" towards others and the world more broadly were most important. The historian Joseph Conforti has captured this distinction quite well. He wrote that:

> Love of God and neighbor and not the saving of one's soul became the core of Hopkinsianism. The true Christian must lose himself in a cause higher than his own salvation—namely, the temporal and eternal well-being of others . . . Hopkins' innovations in the theory of true virtue represented an important shift away from the equivocal legacy of Edwards on the issue of worldly action in the direction of an emphatic endorsement of social reform. Where Edwards saw true virtue as essentially a matter of right affections, Hopkins viewed it as right actions.[4]

This theological perspective played a large role in the Second Great Awakening that began in the 1790s and then ebbed and flowed well into the first half of following century. Historians have long noted the connection between the evangelical piety of the Second Great Awakening and the multitude of reform movements that emerged during the first half of the nineteenth century. Professors and students at Andover and other conservative Congregational seminaries are a case in point.[5]

For example, the Reverend George Shepard, a Congregational minister in Hallowell, Maine and later a faculty member at the Bangor Theological Seminary (an institution very much shaped by New Divinity thought) made the link between conversion and a Christian life of service very explicit. In a letter to a parishioner of his who was "indulging some hope" as to receipt of grace, Shepard wrote that conversion was not enough; to be authentic it had to result in taking action in the name of the faith. Shepard wrote:

> It is important that we *should do* something for Christ in order to brighten and confirm our hope in him. This should be the great object of the Christian, *to promote* the kingdom of the Savior. We should live to serve him. Some make it their prominent object to keep alive their hopes. They think more of their *hope* than they do of the service of Christ. This is selfishness. If we serve Christ faithfully—the hope will take care of itself.[6]

---

4. Conforti, *Samuel Hopkins*, 121. Also see, Burlin, *Imperial Maine*, 7–8.

5. Walters, *American Reformers*, 21–37.

6. George Shepard to Ebenezer Dole, Jr., May 31, 1834 (emphasis in the original)

Enoch Pond, the first Professor of Systematic Theology at Bangor, and a man whose New Divinity credentials were impeccable, argued that missionary activity was the litmus test that certified to the authenticity of an individual believer's conversion experience and faith. He wrote that "The missionary movement of our times—the effort now making for the salvation of the world—is the natural fruit of our revivals of religion; I might even say a *necessary* fruit, without which the genuineness of our revivals might well be suspected, and they could hardly have manifested themselves as the work of God."[7] It is important to note that a number of Pond's students, most notably Daniel Dole, Elias Bond, and Cyrus Hamlin, took up the missionary mantle, the first two in Hawai'i.

There was one other important element that characterized the ABCFM missionaries of the early nineteenth century, and it is important to keep that element in mind. In a very real sense Hopkins' "disinterested benevolence" was rooted in what Edmund Morgan referred to as the "Puritan dilemma."[8] According to Morgan, the Puritan or Calvinist dilemma was a function of their belief that they were to be *in* the world, but not *of* the world. All Calvinists were supposed to discern their divinely ordained "calling," and then pursue that vocation in a diligent manner, all the while, however, they were to do it for God's glory, not for personal gain, whether spiritual or temporal. This was the "worldly asceticism" described and analyzed in such a penetrating fashion by Max Weber.[9]

If the Second Great Awakening, and the reform efforts it helped spawn, were important during the first half of the nineteenth century, another major occurrence that characterized the period was the so-called "market revolution." The possible relationships between these important historical phenomena are as fascinating and important as they are elusive.[10] It is hard to imagine, however, that the sweeping changes that took place in the American political economy during the period, along with the attendant alteration in peoples' values and behavior, bore no relationship to the sustained level of religious revivals and reform initiatives which took place at the same time.

(M 47) DFP/BC.

7. Pond, *The World's Salvation*, 51 (emphasis in the original). Also see Burlin, *Imperial Maine*, 11–16.

8. Morgan, *The Puritan Dilemma*.

9. Weber, *The Protestant Ethic*, especially, 95–183.

10. On the complexity of the issues involved, see Noll, *God and Mammon*, 3–22.

What exactly was occurring in the economic sphere in the United States during the antebellum period, and how might those changes have impacted the ABCFM missionaries who took up residence and work in the Hawaiian Islands and elsewhere? One of the most insightful analyses of possible connections between the market revolution, religion, and reform is provided by Charles Sellers in his book of that title.

It is Seller's contention that the advances in transportation extended the reach of the Atlantic coastal and international markets into the rural interior of the country. The extension of the capitalist marketplace brought with it new values and commercial behavior that were characterized by economic calculation and production for profit. These new developments clashed with what Sellers believes had been predominate in the interior; namely, subsistence agriculture, values oriented to production for use, and economic relationships based on barter, cooperative communities, and very limited and peripheral transactions at local stores.

According to Sellers, the stresses generated by this cultural conflict, coupled in time as they were with economic and social dislocations resulting from a declining availability of land that stemmed from the rising population, all combined to produce the physic energy that generated and sustained the revivals of the Second Great Awakening. As he puts it, with regard to those caught up in the evangelical fervor of the Second Great Awakening, "Hope for God's grace and a better world to come sustained them through this world's tribulations. Only by a headlong flight into domesticity, benevolence, and feeling could they tolerate the market's calculating egoism."[11]

Needless to say, the Puritan dilemma was difficult for any Calvinist to bear at any point in time; however, it was no doubt even more so as the market revolution transformed the political, economic and social landscape of the United States. The revolution was not, after all, just a matter of new economic opportunities opening up; it also ushered in a new set of values and way of looking at the world that placed calculation and individual self-interest at the center of one's existence. It is important to recall that Adam Smith's *Wealth of Nations* which was published in 1776, slowly, but surely helped to foster a laissez-faire liberal capitalist political economy predicated on the cardinal assumption that the pursuit of individual self-interest was the key to a good society and a promising future. It is hard to imagine a more nourishing ground

11. Sellers, *Market Revolution*, 202.

for strident cultural conflict within American society. Furthermore, it would be surprising had missionaries who were born and raised in this environment not been affected by the turbulent cross-currents set loose across the country.

There is no question that the missionaries who ventured forth to Hawai'i and elsewhere were inspired by the revival culture of the Second Great Awakening. There are numerous personal testimonies to that fact. Many testified to the classic conversion experiences associated with evangelical faith and not infrequently saw their calling and work in the context of post-millennial belief. Most of the ABCFM missionaries were from modest circumstances in rural communities that may well have been experiencing the very social, economic, and existential stresses that Sellers argues were occurring during the period in question.

Given this background, it should not be surprising that the issue of salaries became a bone of contention within the missionary community in Hawai'i. It is important to remember that the issue of God and Mammon was as old as the Puritan experiment itself. The famous case of Robert Keayne in mid-seventeenth century Boston is a case in point.[12] While much had changed in New England, and the United States more broadly, by the beginning of the nineteenth century, the tension between the temporal and spiritual remained a constant dilemma for those of even a softened Calvinist perspective.

The salary issue was initially raised relative to the mission to Hawai'i at least as early as 1831; however, it had come up even earlier regarding the ABCFM's outpost in India. In 1830, for example, Jeremiah Evarts, the organization's secretary at the time, wrote from the Boston headquarters to the missionaries in Bombay that the level of compensation was an important and sensitive one for a variety of reasons. If compensation were high it would raise the eyebrows of the public on which the organization depended for donations to its cause.

Going further, Evarts connected the appropriate level of compensation to the character of the missionaries themselves. He wrote: "We doubt not from what we know of your characters, that you will prefer New England simplicity, to anything in India that is not consistent with it. It is the best stile of living for missionaries everywhere." Evarts concluded his letter with a postscript, noting that, "The subject of salaries is a great one. Neither you nor we should be hasty in deciding upon it. It

---

12. Bailyn, *The New England Merchants*, 39–44.

has lain with great weight upon our minds. My own impression is, that there is real danger in allowing a larger sum than would be on the whole best for the cause of Christ."[13]

As noted above, the salary issue was raised the following year with regard to the mission to the Sandwich Islands, as the Hawaiian archipelago was often called in those years. Originally, the missionaries there were supported by a common stock system with a depository located in Honolulu and administered by Levi Chamberlain, the mission's "secular agent." Individual missionary families would apply to Chamberlain for supplies based on their expressed need. The system has often been referred to as a "primitive communist" one.

Rufus Anderson, who would loom large and long in the annals of the ABCFM, wrote to the Hawaiian Mission in 1831 broaching the subject of substituting salaries for the existing common stock depository system. He indicated in his letter that the Prudential Committee, the day-to-day governing body of the Board, had long had the matter under consideration. Their concerns seem to have related primarily to saving money for the organization. He asked the missionaries to take up the subject at their next annual General Meeting and to advise Boston as to their thoughts on the issue in due course.[14]

It is important to note that in the same letter Anderson discussed the selling of books to native Hawaiians. Access to religious material provided by the Sandwich Islands Mission's printing operation was deemed important for the cause. However, Anderson believed that it was not a good idea for the "evangelists" to do the selling. He wished that a good, "disinterested" merchant could be found to take on the task, but he knew of none. Were such an individual to be found this would allow the clergy to rid themselves of "secular" concerns, much as Jesus' apostles had done when they made the choice to follow him. While part of the Secretary's concern was certainly related to the question of the optimal use of the

13. Evarts to Graves et alia, July 31, 1830, ABCFM Records, microfilm reel #12, ABCFMCL. Peter S. Field's analysis of the split in the Standing Order in early nineteenth century Massachusetts between the "orthodox" (the camp of most, if not all of the ABCFM missionaries to Hawai'i) and the "Brahmins," adds yet another possible dimension to the tension between God and Mammon for the missionaries at the time. Unfortunately, that possibility cannot be explored here. See Field, *Standing Order*, 141–79, especially 150–65.

14. Rufus Anderson to the Sandwich Islands Mission, November 16, 1831, GLC/HHS.

missionaries' time, it is also clear that it was connected to concerns about their character and spiritual well-being.

The question of compensation and the corresponding missionary standard of living had several dimensions for the ABCFM. First, there was the simple matter of stretching the financial resources of the organization, a commodity that was seldom in abundant supply. Secondly, as noted before, there was the matter of public relations. The organization relied heavily on donations from churches scattered throughout New England. Were there to be a shift to salaries, those had to be set at a point that was adequate given the circumstances of the missionaries, but not at a level that would raise the eyebrows of cash-strapped New England parishioners.

Finally, there was a theological dimension to the issue. This may well have been the most important aspect for many of those involved, particularly some of the missionaries on "heathen ground" (as they called it) in Hawai'i. The missionaries sent abroad by the ABCFM were mainly Congregationalists or Presbyterians, and as noted previously, they were heirs to Calvin and the Puritan dilemma. To be *in* the world but not *of* the world was their persistent and peculiar burden. Each person was to find and pursue his or her divinely inspired calling (worldly vocation), but that pursuit must always be for the greater glory of God, not for personal aggrandizement, material or otherwise. The issue was all the more compelling and loaded with meaning for missionaries, those who had left family, friends, and the relative security of home shores for the unknown in order to advance the cause of Christianity.

One of the critics of a possible shift away from the common stock system to salaries was Jonathan Green, a member of the Third Company who had been ordained in the rural Vermont town of Brandon, and who arrived in Hawai'i with his wife in 1828. Green made a tour of the Pacific Coast of North America for the ABCFM and then was stationed at various locations in Hawai'i including Lahaina, Hilo, and Wailuku. Eventually Green resigned from the ABCFM because he felt the organization took too circumspect and compliant a position relative to American slavery.[15]

Green weighed in on the salary issue quite strenuously. He argued in an 1832 letter that individual salaries would have a "secularizing" effect on the missionaries, opening the door to personal calculations of profit

15. *Missionary Album*, 104–5.

and loss and individual advantage where they simply did not belong. In concluding his letter, Green indicated that disinterestedness or at least the appearance of it was important to the missionary cause. He wrote:

> In supporting us by fixed salaries, you would take from us the ability of standing up before the world as men who demonstrably show that they seek not their own but the things of Jesus Christ!! You are well aware of the charge of the foreign resident at these Islands. Now I take it upon me to say that with nothing in our character and circumstances are these men so much affected as with the fact that we are self-devoted men and women who have given ourselves to Christ—and the heathen to toil till we die merely for our support from year to year.

He then concluded by saying: "I do therefore humbly and earnestly entreat you to save us from the change in our present mode of living which would so obviously increase our cares as individuals, secularize us as a mission and in its influence deprive us of being regarded as disinterested men—a privilege which I value more than untold gold and silver."[16]

Green was certainly not the only one to voice an opinion about the proposition to substitute salaries for the common stock system. In a joint letter sent from the Lahaina station, William Richards, Lorrin Andrews, and Ephraim Spaulding wrote at length on the subject. They noted that the current system was theoretically open to abuse insofar as some missionaries might be tempted to a more lavish use of the common stock than was necessary, and they thought that this evil would be curbed by individual, fixed salaries. However, they favored the existing system because:

> Though we may now some times fail in economy and self denial, where we should not if we had fixed salaries, yet we sincerely believe this loss to the Board is far less, than the value of time which would be required to manage our salaries ourselves. We do sincerely believe too that much more would be to be feared from a secular spirit, in case of salaries, than now to be feared from a disposition to have the bounties of the Board.[17]

16. Jonathan Green to Rufus Anderson, October 17, 1832, microfilm reel # 797, ABCFM/CL.

17. William Ellis, Lorrin Andrews, and Ephraim Spaulding to Rufus Anderson, November 27, 1832, microfilm reel # 797, ABCFM/CL.

Another missionary, Samuel Whitney, also had severe reservations about a salary system. First, he was not at all convinced that it would save the ABCFM any money. Second, he argued that were salaries to be provided, they would need to be at a sufficient level that the missionaries would not need to supplement their compensation through other means. He wrote, "[I]t appears to me that if you give your missionaries a salary, it must be a *liberal one* as the subject involves a subject of much greater magnitude than *economy*, I mean, the *general good*."[18]

Whitney had traveled to the Marquesas and Society Islands on behalf of the Sandwich Islands Mission and had observed the situation on the latter islands with the British missionaries located there. They received salaries, but they were insufficient for their support and they were consequently forced to engage in trade with the natives and other foreigners. According to Whitney, this diverted some of their time and energy away from their purpose for being on the islands in the first place.

Furthermore, he wrote that the Society Islands missionaries told him that trade "produces a worldly spirit, coldness, in our prayers and preaching. It brings us in contact with one of the worst passions in a native's heart (covetaness) [sic]." If that were not bad enough, when the missionaries struck a particularly profitable bargain for themselves with the natives, other foreigners were quick to inform the islanders of the fact. In addition, since the missionaries also traded with the foreign ships that made call there, they were developing the reputation in the Pacific as merchants, not missionaries. Whitney told Anderson that he had heard from "men of judgment and sound principles" that a "temporizing spirit is apparent in those missionaries."[19]

Not all of the missionaries were adamantly opposed to the substitution of salaries for common stock. Artemas Bishop, a member of the Second Company who arrived in Hawai'i with his wife in 1823, was ambivalent about the whole matter. In a letter to Rufus Anderson in 1832 he said that at the mission's last annual meeting, most of the older missionaries were against the idea and the younger ones tended to favor salaries.

---

18. Samuel Whitney to Rufus Anderson, December 25, 1832, microfilm reel # 797, ABCFM/CL (emphasis in the original).

19. Ibid.

Bishop indicated that he helped to support himself by the sale of books and that his only concern about the current system was that he had no way to garner the resources to provide for the education of his children once they reached the age of twelve. If the ABCFM were to undertake to provide for the education of the children then "Begone care and salaries all together." However, further on in the same letter he indicated that salaries were probably a good idea, and he was content to simply to express his opinion on the matter and then let the Prudential Committee make a decision.

Bishop does not appear to have been concerned that secular affairs would dampen the missionary spirit. Of course, he put his finger on a huge issue, namely the education of the missionaries' children. That problem would be resolved roughly ten years later with the founding of Punahou on Oahu.[20]

Gerrit Judd, the Sandwich Islands Mission's physician who arrived in Hawai'i in 1828, wrote at great length to Boston on the issue of salaries as well. In a long letter to Anderson, he said:

> This subject has begun to be agitated with us the last year or two, although when I arrived nothing could be more popular than the system of common stock was with the mission almost without exception. For two or three years we went on to perfect this system by means of resolutions, (copies of which you have received), and had any one in those days broached sentiments favorable to a salary system he would have been considered almost a traitor to our cause.[21]

However, with the growth of the mission and more and more families to support (according to Judd, 57 adults and 44 children), he believed the common stock system was becoming impractical. Furthermore, and of greater importance, perhaps, is that Judd believed the missionary families were no longer really living by the strict rules of the common stock system. He said that "While we *call nothing our own* we both *speak* and *feel* mine and thine."[22]

In addition, Judd noted that at least some of those currently still in favor of the common stock system had rejected a resolution at the

20. Artemas Bishop to Rufus Anderson, October 3, 1832, microfilm reel # 797, ABCFM/CL.

21. Gerrit Judd to Rufus Anderson, October 15, 1832, microfilm reel # 798, ABCFM/CL.

22. Ibid. (emphasis in the original).

Mission's 1831 General Meeting to the effect that missionaries should only be allowed to trade insofar as it directly served the purposes of native instruction, presumably by selling religious books to them. That resolution was rejected, however, according to Judd because members wanted to be able to trade to render themselves more comfortable. From his perspective then, at least some of the rhetoric about disinterestedness and secular matters expressed by those arguing against a salary system were, to put it bluntly, disingenuous.

Finally, while it is possible to go on with myriad examples of missionary opinion on the salary matter, one more is in order. Peter Gulick corresponded with Boston as well. He seems to have had no ambivalence about the matter. He wrote:

> Since opinions are requested, with regard to the mode of supporting missionaries . . . my judgment is in favor of salaries. From the fact that this method, involves a greater degree of personal interest, I believe it would contribute to the increase of economy, in our various expenditures . . . But as the majority of the brethren think differently, I will forebear.[23]

About the same time that the salary controversy gained traction, other issues involving God and Mammon raised their heads. One was the arrival on the islands of members of Ladd and Company, a group of merchants with close, if not official, connections to the ABCFM. Dubbed derisively as the "pious merchants" by those who feared their mercantile competition and their favored position with the missionary community, the partners of the firm, William Ladd, Peter Brinsmade and William Hooper seem to have been the "disinterested" businessmen for whom Rufus Anderson had wished.[24]

In that regard, it is clear that the Ladd and Company partners had the support of William Reed who was a wealthy Marblehead, Massachusetts merchant and a member of the ABCFM's Prudential Committee. At one point a few years after the Company had set up operations in Honolulu, Reed wrote to the partners, indicating that he hoped "the future will enable you to fulfill your utmost (reasonable) wishes in the acquisition of property." He went on to say that it was his "fondest wish" that Ladd and

23. Peter Gulick to Rufus Anderson, October 22, 1832, microfilm reel # 797, ABCFM/CL.

24. For evidence of this connection, see William Reed to Levi Chamberlain December 20, 1832, Chamberlain letter book, 1822–1844, MSL, HMCSL.

Company would demonstrate to the Hawaiian people that trade could be conducted on the basis of good Christian principles. Reed's bracketing of the word "reasonable" suggests that he was sensitive to the history of merchants exploiting the Hawaiian people. Perhaps, he appreciated the Calvinist dilemma as well.[25]

It is clear from the record that Ladd and Company, particularly Peter Brinsmade, a licensed Congregational minister who had briefly attended Andover Theological Seminary, was initially received quite well by the missionary community. However, as his and the Company's affairs became ever more convoluted, grandiose and ultimately scandalous, many of the Hawai'i-based missionaries condemned both his and the Company's practices.[26]

It was not just Ladd and Company that could provoke missionary ire. Jonathan Green got himself into very deep hot water with the ABCFM when a letter of his was published in the *Boston Recorder*.[27] In that letter he claimed that the expansion of trade as conducted in Hawai'i was "digging the grave of the people" and, by implication, the Sandwich Islands Mission was complicit in this nefarious state of affairs. Green's letter brought the wrath of the mission down upon him and he was more or less censured at the General Meeting that the missionaries held in Honolulu in 1838.[28]

Levi Chamberlain, the secular agent for the mission, personally took Green to task at the time. He told Green that he knew a good deal about trade having had a long business career prior to joining the ABCFM. Trade was not the issue according to Chamberlain, but how that trade was conducted. It needed to be conducted in a Christian manner and, if so conducted, was not antithetical to the faith or to what the mission was trying to accomplish in Hawai'i.[29]

In the same communication, Chamberlain told Green that the latter's letter would have the effect of undermining the resolve and support

25. William Read to Ladd and Company, September 1836, file labeled "September-October 1836," HSP/MHS. Also see Burlin, *Imperial Maine*, 25–26.

26. Burlin, *Imperial Maine*, 21–49.

27. "Letter from the Sandwich Islands, *Boston Recorder*, June 23, 1837.

28. Bingham, Tinker, and Chamberlain to Rufus Green, June 1, 1838, Green Letters, MLC, HMCSL.

29. Levi Chamberlain to Rufus Green, April 20, 1838, Chamberlain Letters, MLC, HMCSL.

of individuals such as William Reed. Chamberlain was well aware of the connection between Reed and Ladd and Company and he hoped that the latter would demonstrate the compatibility between Christianity and trade, properly conducted.

So, what is one to make of these dust-ups among the missionaries to Hawai'i? While the salary matter was a complicated one, and the Boston office may have been primarily motivated by a desire simply to save money, it did strike a much deeper nerve in the missionary community in Hawai'i. The issues of disinterestedness and self-denial were very important for at least some of the missionaries. They went to the heart of what they thought they were about. There is no better statement about the importance of these values than the sermon given by the Reverend Samuel Spring at the ordination of the ABCFM's very first missionaries in 1812.

Spring, a Congregational minister in Newburyport, Massachusetts, was a major player in the founding of both Andover Theological Seminary and the ABCFM. At the ordination in Salem, Massachusetts, the clergyman said:

> [Y]ou must be the subjects of deep humility and much self-denial. One man cannot serve two masters. He cannot serve God and mammon. He cannot seek his own glory and the glory of Christ. You must practice self-denial among the heathen in a conspicuous manner, before you can inculcate it with advantage and success.[30]

The problem was, of course, that this was always much easier said than done.

Ultimately, the strained financial circumstances of the ABCFM, particularly following the Panic of 1837, made it increasingly difficult for the organization to support its large number of missionaries in Hawai'i and elsewhere in the world. As a result of those circumstances and Rufus Anderson's desire to establish self-sustaining native churches, the missionaries in Hawai'i were gradually weaned from direct support. In that process the missionaries took title to some of the mission's property in the islands, most notably the houses in which they lived and the surrounding property.[31]

30. Samuel Spring, "The Charge," a sermon delivered at the ordination of the first ABCFM missionaries, located at the Congregational Library, Boston, Massachusetts.

31. For the impact of financial difficulties in 1837 on missionary opinion regarding

With the Great *Mahele* in the 1840s, many missionaries and other foreigners took title to more land in the islands and in the process the Hawaiian people lost nearly everything. While that was not the intention of the missionaries, that was certainly the result of the capitalist political economy they always sought to impose. Indeed, their critique of the traditional Hawaiian system as exploitative of the commoners only served to open the door to a new and foreign form of exploitation and disenfranchisement.

In the case of the missionaries to Hawai'i, their shifting posture toward the acquisition of land and other forms of wealth in Hawai'i was at least partially a result of the ambiguity toward God and Mammon inherent in their Calvinist faith. During periods of intense religious sentiment such as the Second Great Awakening, it was possible for some of the missionaries to live with the tension created by "worldly asceticism." When the fervor waned, however, the seductions of the marketplace were simply too much for many of them and their descendants to bear. However, at least as late as 1869, Daniel Dole, a member of the Ninth Company which arrived in Hawai'i in 1841, admonished his son, Sanford, to be careful of "prosperity" as it could be dangerous. He reminded his son that he was not "his own," but belonged to God and should first and foremost serve his purposes. The adage came directly from Calvin's *Institutes of the Christian Religion*, a book the senior Dole had in his library. Given the subsequent revolutionary role that Sanford would play in Hawai'i, it is questionable whether the Calvinist dilemma was an issue for him and his generation of missionary descendants at all.[32]

If there is some sort of "lesson" here for early twenty-first century people, it might be to be extremely cautious about intervening in other lands and other cultures. Unintended consequences are almost always a by product of such efforts. In the case of Hawai'i, those consequences were nefarious in the extreme.

ABBREVIATIONS

ABCFM/CL: Records of the American Board of Commissioners for Foreign Missions (microfilm collection) Congregational Library, Boston, Massachusetts.

salaries, see Harris, *Nothing But Christ*, 62–65.

32. Daniel Dole to Sanford Dole, February 11, 1869, Daniel Dole Papers, HMCSL.

DFP/BC: Dole Family Papers (M47) Special Collections, Hawthorne Library, Bowdoin College, Brunswick, Maine.

GLC/HHS: General Letters Collection, Hawaiian Historical Society, Honolulu, Hawai'i.

HMCSL: Hawaiian Mission Childrenís Society Library, Honolulu, Hawai'i.

HSP/MHS: Hooper-Sturgis Papers, Massachusetts Historical Society, Boston, Massachusetts.

BIBLIOGRAPHY

Bailyn, Bernard. *The New England Merchants in the Seventeenth Century*. Cambridge: Harvard University Press, 1979.

Burlin, Paul T. *Imperial Maine and Hawaiëi: Interpretive Essays in the History of Nineteenth-Century American Expansion*. Lanham, MD: Lexington Books, 2006.

Conforti Joseph A. *Samuel Hopkins and the New Divinity Movement: Calvinism, the Congregational Ministry, and Reform in New England Between the Great Awakenings*. Grand Rapids: Christian University Press, 1981.

Daws, Gavan. *The Shoals of Times: A History of the Hawaiian Islands*. Honolulu: University of Hawaii Press, 1968.

Field, Peter S. *The Crisis of the Standing Order: Clerical Intellectuals and Cultural Authority in Massachusetts, 1780–1833*. Amherst: University of Massachusetts Press, 1998.

Hanley, Mark Y. *Beyond A Christian Commonwealth: The Protestant Quarrel with the American Republic, 1830–1860*. Chapel Hill: The University of North Carolina Press, 1994.

Harris, Paul William. *Nothing but Christ: Rufus Anderson and the Ideology of Protestant Foreign Missions*. New York: Oxford University Press, 1999.

Howe, Daniel Walker. *The Unitarian Conscience: Harvard Moral Philosophy, 1805–1861*. Middletown, CT: Wesleyan University Press, 1988.

Kame'eleihiwa, Lilikālā. *Native Land, Foreign Desires*. Honolulu: Bishop Museum Press, 1992.

Kling, David W. "The New Divinity and the Origins of the American Board oCommissioners for Foreign Missions." *Church History* (December 2003): 791–819.

Kuykendall, Ralph S. *The Hawaiian Kingdom*, 3 vols. Honolulu: University of Hawaii Press, 1938–1967.

Missionary Album. *Portraits and Biographical Sketches of the American Protestant Missionaries to the Hawaiian Islands*. Honolulu: Hawaiian Mission Children's Society, 1969.

Morgan, Edmund S. *The Puritan Dilemma: The Story of John Winthrop*. Boston: Little,Brown & Company, 1958.

Noll, Mark A., ed. *God and Mammon: Protestants, Money, and the Market, 1790–1860*. New York: Oxford University Press, 2002.

Pond, Enoch. *The World's Salvation*. Boston: Massachusetts Sabbath School Society, 1845.

Sellers, Charles. *The Market Revolution: Jacksonian America, 1815–1846*. New York: Oxford University Press, 1991.

Silva, Noenoe K. *Aloha Betrayed: Native Hawaiian Resistance to American Colonialism*. Durham: Duke University Press, 2004. Trask, Haunani-Kay. *From a Native Daughter: Colonialism and Sovereignty in Hawaiëi*. Monroe, ME: Common Courage Press, 1993.

Walters, Ronald G. *American Reformers, 1815–1860*. New York: Hill & Wang, 1978.

Weber, Max. *The Protestant Ethic and the Spirit of Capitalism*. New York: Charles Scribner's Sons, 1958.

Woods, Leonard. *History of Andover Theological Seminary*. Boston: James. R. Osgood & Company, 1885.

12

Titus Coan: "Apostle to the Sandwich Islands"

Donald Philip Corr

Although Titus Coan led the Hawaiian Great Awakening, he has received scant attention from scholars and other biographers. Arguably the second most important ABCFM missionary to the Sandwich Islands, behind Hiram Bingham, this Presbyterian in a predominantly Congregational organization provided protean service to the Hawaiian people and to the Christian cause.[1]

The three categories sketched in the previous sentence provide a paradigm for understanding the life of Titus Coan and his abundance of interests and involvement. While a major Christian leader in Hawai'i, he served in the shadow of Hiram Bingham. He was a Presbyterian who worked with mostly Congregationalists. He claimed to have great love for the Hawaiian people, while also exhibiting a common nineteenth century condescension toward indigenous peoples.

This duality is first evident when one compares his birth and upbringing with his eventual involvement with the global mission endeavor. Apart from his being related to the evangelist Asahel Nettleton, there is little indication in his early years and young adulthood of the career path he would eventually take.

Of his birth Coan wrote, "I was born on the first day of February, Sunday morning, 1801, in the town of Killingworth, Conn[ecticut]. My physical constitution was good, my health was perfect, and my childhood happy." While his good constitution, excellent health and positive

---

1. Elkhe, "Enthusiastic Religion."

outlook in life would serve him in good stead in his mission service, no relative or friend identified what he would do for most of his adult life.[2]

In his late teens he became a teacher. Again, teaching would come in very helpful in Hawai'i, yet as far as he knew he would continue to teach in Upstate New York for decades. His future first wife was also a teacher. At the age of 25 he rode his horse one day past another school-house. When he looked through the windows he "saw a face that beamed on me like that of an angel. The image was deeply impressed, and still is ineffaceable." Coan wrote those words fifty-five years after first seeing Fidelia Church.[3]

Both of their lives took a significant turn when they were caught up in the upstate New York part of the rolling Second Great Awakening. Influenced by his cousin, Asahel Nettleton, and the attorney-turned-evangelist Charles G. Finney, Fidelia and Titus experienced a deepening of faith and dedication to serve the Lord throughout the rest of their lives.[4]

Titus and Fidelia would become leaders in the Auburn part of the revival. Uniting with the Presbyterian Church in Auburn, Titus and Fidelia asked for divine guidance for their lives. For Titus, this meant enrolling in Auburn Seminary and beginning correspondence with the ABCFM. The seeming contradiction of a Presbyterian applying to serve with a primarily Congregational organization is not as great as it would appear. At the time of Coan's matriculation at Auburn, the ABCFM was the only American foreign mission organization. In addition, several Reformed denominations, including Presbyterian, were involved with the Board. Missionaries from those denominations served with the Board, and leaders of those denominations, at times, were the featured speakers at the organization's annual meeting.[5]

Coan was placed on a mission fast track education program. While at Auburn Seminary, the man who would become identified with mis-sions in Hawai'i was asked by Board leaders to go to a very different location in the world. He received a letter from Rufus Anderson, the Secretary of the ABCFM. Written on June 19, 1833, at the Mission Rooms, Anderson invited Coan to join William Arms on an "exploring mission" to Patagonia, the southern cone of South America. Almost fifty

2. Titus Coan, *Life*, 2.

3. Ibid., 9.

4. Titus Coan, *Patagonia*.

5. Corr, "The Field is the World."

years later Coan would write about this experience in his first of two published books, *Adventures in Patagonia.*[6]

While the letter exchanges between Anderson and Coan indicate Coan's "no ordinary degree of pleasure" in responding to Anderson's invitation, scholar Margaret S. Ehlke wonders whether Coan was indeed sanguine about the possibility of a Patagonia mission. Was there complex struggle within this part of the dilemma inconsistency? Lydia Coan's *Memorial Volume* provides the summary of Coan's trip.[7]

Coan threw himself into the project and served diligently. After dedicating approximately a year to everything involved in the exploratory trip, he would recommend against the ABCFM establishing a mission to Patagonia at the time.[8]

Coan returned to Connecticut on May 7, 1834 and, in the same year, was called to serve in what were then known as the Sandwich Islands. He and Fidelia were married on November 3, 1834. On November 23 at Park Street Church in Boston, the couple received their instructions and commissioning along with the rest of the Seventh Company of the Sandwich Islands missionaries. "On December 5th they set sail from Boston harbor, bound for Cape Horn and the Sandwich Islands" on the ship *Hellespont.*[9]

After a relatively uneventful journey, Fidelia and Titus Coan arrived in Honolulu on June 6, 1835, at the time of the General Meeting of the Sandwich Islands Mission. Coan wrote glowingly in his autobiography of their arrival and welcome in Honolulu, describing in detail the diverse group of veteran missionaries and their families that ushered them to the Rev. Hiram Bingham's house. [10]

Among the members of the Hawaiian mission and their "flocks of precious children," Titus no doubt met his future second wife, Lydia Bingham, who as a baby in 1835 would have been in her mother's arms. Fidelia, Titus, and the other arrivals received a warm welcome from the Hawaiian people and were guests of honor at a royal banquet. From

---

6. Schneider, "The Senior Secretary"; and Titus Coan, *Patagonia*, 9–12.

7. Titus Coan, *Patagonia*, 13; Ehlke, "Enthusiastic Religion"; and Lydia Bingham Coan, *Memorial Volume*, 9–10.

8. Titus Coan, *Patagonia*, Chapters 1–12; and Ehlke, "Enthusiastic Religion," 70–74.

9. Ehlke, "Enthusiastic Religion," 75–77.

10. Ibid., 94–96.

Honolulu they sailed to Hilo on the Big Island of Hawai'i. At the time Hilo was "one of the most remote posts in the Sandwich Islands."[11]

An interesting contrast to note is the extent of Coan's training and the remoteness of his post. Nevertheless, on July "the 21st we saw the emerald beauty of Hilo, and disembarked with joy and thanksgiving." The Coans would eventually build their own home and call it (along with their surrounding land) their "Emerald Bower."[12]

From that home Coan would go forth to become the leader of the Hawaiian Great Awakening. Before he could lead that movement, however, he needed to be able to converse and, ultimately, preach in the Islanders' vernacular. Along with Fidelia, he experienced the baby steps of language learning. Under the tutelage of their Hawaiian teacher, "a good man named Barnabas," they were patiently drilled "in the language of the people. By reading, trying to talk, teach and write, we crept along, without grammar or dictionary, the mist lifting slowly before us, until at the end of three months from our arrival, I went into the pulpit with Mr. Lyman, and preached my first sermon in the native language."[13]

Lydia Bingham Coan wrote in the *Memorial Volume* how for a time, "his lips were held by an unknown tongue, from direct efforts with the natives . . ." "But when the new language had been to some degree acquired, and three months after landing, he had preached his first Hawaiian sermon, he began the touring, a marked feature" of the rest of his years in Hawai'i.[14]

Along with the difficulty of learning a new language, Coan's ability to travel was significantly impaired. Coan wrote, "For many years after our arrival there were no roads, no bridges, and no horses in Hilo, and all my tours were made on foot." Coan's treks across the Big Island, especially in the early years, are legendary.[15]

Both his language learning and travels had a greater purpose: to proclaim and share the Gospel to Hawaiians, with the goal of seeing them become Christians who would then develop into lifelong disciples. This central purpose defined Coan's mission and provided a unifying point for his apparent dualities.

11. Lydia Coan, *Memorial Volume*, 34–36; and Ehlke, "Enthusiastic Religion," 97.

12. Titus Coan, *Life*, 24.

13. Ibid., 27.

14. Lydia Coan, *Memorial Volume*, 39.

15. Titus Coan, *Life*, 15, 31.

Not long after his arrival and acquisition of the language, Coan began the development of the multi-year phenomenon he is best known for: the Hawaiian Great Awakening. Taking place approximately one century after the English-speaking Great Awakening, the Hawaiian beginning date is not definite, but its conclusion can be given with precision. Coan began preaching and sharing in earnest during the latter part of 1836. In his autobiography he indicates the heart of the Great Awakening took place during the years 1837 and 1838. It concluded with the regrettable events surrounding the overwork of Hawaiians related to the arrival of the United States exploratory mission in 1840.[16]

Ample material exists, both contemporaneous to the events and up to the present, to shed light on the developments of the Great Awakening. Titus Coan preached wherever and whenever he had the opportunity and to whomever listened. Near the end of his life he wrote the Rev. S. E. Bishop saying, "These days and years I never rose to address a native audience without feeling an assurance that a Divine power rested upon me, and that 'Death and Hell' could not withstand the Word of God, but that it was the 'sword of the Spirit, quick and powerful;' that it was the 'fire and hammer,' and the gleaming battleaxe of Jehovah, ordained to conquer Satan and sin; and that it is in *deed* and truth, 'the power of salvation' to all who believe, whether speaker or hearer."[17]

Coan was nevertheless discrete in the discussion of his preaching style. He credited any strong response by the audience to the work of the Holy Spirit. One may, however, read between the lines when he wrote, "The word fell with power, and sometimes as the feeling deepened, the vast audience was moved and swayed like a forest in the wind." Coan vividly described his goal in preaching by observing his resolution "to keep the holy law of the Everlasting God constantly blazing before the midst of all the people, and to hold the claims and sanctions of the gospel in near and warm contact with their frigid hearts."[18]

---

16. Ibid., 42, 66–67.

17. Titus Coan, *Life*, 42–67; Lydia Coan, *Memorial Volume*, 44–61 and passim; Hiram Bingham, *A Residence of Twenty-One years*; Miller (ed.) "To Raise the Lord's Banner"; Anderson, *History of the Sandwich Islands Mission*; Samuel Colcord Bartlett, *Historical Sketch of the Missions of the American Board in the Sandwich Islands, Micronesia, and Marquesas*; Phillips, *Protestant America and the Pagan World*; Davis, *Evangelism in Hawaii*; Ehlke, "Enthusiastic Religion," 107–36; and Corr, "The Field Is the World," passim.

18. Titus Coan, *Life*, 46; Corr, "The Field Is the World," 75–77. Coan's remark about

As was the case in some of the frontier revivals in America, physical demonstrations occurred during the Hawaiian Great Awakening and natural phenomena were given spiritual application. Coan indicated on "some occasions there were physical demonstrations which commended attention." Such demonstrations occurred during very plain and kindly conversations at the Coan home, as well as during sermons preached to large groups. In one instance, Coan wrote that he was preaching on the subject of "Repentance toward God and faith in the Lord Jesus" when an emotional outbreak occurred. It is not known how Coan preached on this subject; however, he related an incident of a man who had been gazing with intense interest at the preacher, who suddenly burst out in a fervent prayer, with streaming tears, saying: "Lord, have mercy, I am dead in sin." The weeping spread to the entire congregation, which was "moved as by a common sympathy."

Coan did not seek to whip up the crowd. Instead, he stood quietly for twenty minutes. When he could be heard, he cautioned and encouraged the multitude. He warned them, "lest they should feel that this kind of demonstration atoned for their sins, and rendered them acceptable before God." He assured "them that all the Lord required was godly sorrow for the past, present faith in Christ, and henceforth faithful, filial, and cheerful obedience. A calm came over the multitude, and we felt that 'the Lord was there.'"[19]

As can be discerned from the above report, the New Measures of Charles Grandison Finney were evident during the Hawaiian Great Awakening. In his *Life*, Coan notes similarities between the Hawaiian Great Awakening and the revivals that took place in Upstate New York and elsewhere. Fidelia Coan saw it as a "work of the Spirit."[20]

While not all leaders approved of everything that happened during the Hawaiian Great Awakening, Hiram Bingham gave a qualified *imprimatur*, noting that the hearers experienced conviction of sin. In a letter dated April 26, 1838, he related, "The Lord has condescended to bless the preaching of the gospel by our missionaries here to an unusual degree." He wrote that preaching should be expected to produce results "when

---

"frigid hearts" was published in the *Missionary Herald* 36 (July 1840) 247.

19. Titus Coan, *Life*, 49–50.

20. Ibid., 49.

it is proclaimed in its naked simplicity." He indicated that he preached many times in many places to large audiences.[21]

When it came to measures and means used during the Great Awakening, the consensus was most missionaries in Hawai'i, including Coan, used methods acceptable to leaders in the Islands and in America. Rufus Anderson noted the "means employed were those commonly used during times of revival in the United States, such as preaching, the prayers of the church, protracted meetings, and conversations with individuals, or small companies." Most of the time of these protracted meetings was taken up with "plain preaching of revealed truth, with prayer in the intervals."[22]

Coan was cautious and conservative in the preparation for and length of time prior to membership. He wrote, "After the lapse of three, six, nine, or twelve months, as the case might be, selections were made from the lists of names." In some cases, Coan required a longer wait than Bingham. Furthermore, he turned down almost half of the people on his list. "From my pocket list of about three thousand, 1,705 were selected to be baptized and received to the communion of the church on the first Sabbath of July, 1838."

He explained the "selection was made, not because a thousand and more . . . were to be rejected, or that a large proportion of them did not appear as well as those received, but because the numbers were too large for our faith, and might stagger the faith of others."[23]

In his letters, Coan reveals the deep sense of responsibility he feels for the souls to whom he preached and with whom he talked. A nuance in this revival mentality is the depth to which Coan holds himself responsible for the eternal destination of the people with whom he spoke and among whom he served.

In a November 24, 1837, letter to a Mr. Lyons, Coan wrote words deleted in Lydia Bingham Coan's *Memorial Volume*. They reappear in Ehlke. In a way similar to the restored Finney text, the deleted and then restored words are found in italics below:

"If I can judge of my own feelings, I never took hold of the work of pulling sinners out of the fire with more faith and more unshaken confidence of success than at this time, and I never saw God's work more

21. Bingham, *Residence*, 520–521; and *Missionary Herald* 34 (1838) 484.

22. Anderson, *Sandwich Islands*, 142, in Corr, "The Field is the World," 78.

23. Titus Coan, *Life*, 54–55, quoted in Corr, "The Field is the World," 82–83.

manifest. *When my dear brother, I say again that we and this mission are red with the blood of souls. Our unbelief has sent thousands down to endless burnings . . . It is so-and what we will now, we shall find it so in the day of Decision.* Only let us preach the gospel in living faith, and under the awful pressure of the world to come, and I defy this people . . . to sleep. Why they might as well sleep under a cataract of fire."[24]

While attending the 1870 Annual Meeting of the American Board, Coan developed a comparison between the nations coming to Christ and sunrise on a volcano.

> I have seen Mauna Kea veiled with the mantle of night, and casting its gigantic shadow of darkness upon us. Again I have seen it when the first rays of the rising sun began to gild its summit. Watching it for a little while, the light poured down its rocky sides, chasing the night before it, until the mighty pile stood out clothed in burnished gold, and shining like a monarch arrayed in robes of glory.
>
> And when I gazed upon that platform in Brooklyn, and cast my eyes upon the great assembly which filled the house, I said in my heart, "When will Polynesia and Micronesia display such a gathering of wisdom, piety, and moral power? A brighter than a natural sun begins to illume the darkness of those lands, chasing away the night of ages; but when will the full-orbed Sun of Righteousness ascend to the zenith and pour a flood of light and glory over all our benighted islands?" And then I reflected that even these lights of the Christian churches were yet to flicker as distant tapers before the coming glories of Zion, as predicted in the sixtieth chapter of Isaiah.[25]

Coan's observation provides a transition from the Revivalist aspect to the Renaissance Man. Titus Coan brought his intellectual curiosity to bear in all areas of life. While his overriding focus was to preach the gospel and to save individuals from the fires of hell, he could and did bring together the study of volcanoes and other scientific matters.

W. D. Alexander provides a summary of Coan's labors in the *Memorial Volume*: "No history of the two volcanoes of Mauna Loa and Kilauea can be written which will not be largely based on Mr. Coan's writings. This fact will be evident to any one who will read Dana's 'Geology' or Brigham's 'Monograph on Hawaiian Volcanoes.' "On several ques-

24. Lydia Coan, *Memorial Volume*, 43; and Ehlke, "Enthusiastic Religion," 112.

25. Titus Coan, *Life*, 218–19.

tions of geology he has furnished valuable data, such as the manner in which lava streams advance many miles over the surface of the earth without being fed by fissures or vents from below; the formation of lava tree moulds, etc. On the one occasion he risked his life in attempting to measure the heat of the liquid lava in the South Lake of Kilauea with a pyrometer furnished by Prof[essor] Dana."[26]

Perhaps holding to the "gap theory" of Genesis, Chapter One, Coan wrote in his autobiography about the Islands giving "evidence of having been raised up from the depths of the ocean by volcanic fires." He also wrote that various "volcanic products" testify to "the terrific rage of Plutonic agencies in unknown ages past." The ongoing importance of Coan's observations of the activity of the Big Island's two volcanoes was recognized by his *Life*, with its multiple chapters referencing volcanoes. The book was provided in digital form in 1997 by Edward Coan and Ken Rubin, web master of the Hawai'i Center of Vulcanology.[27]

Titus Coan was an avid reader of the *American Journal of Science and Arts* (AJSA), and both he and Fidelia had letters published therein. In his first letter dated February 21, 1852, Coan vividly describes an eruption of Mauna Loa: "old lion is again out of his den, his eyes flash fire and his roar is awful." "Another correspondent" (Fidelia Coan) also describes the eruption at Mauna Loa. She had two letters published in the AJSA: one on February 23rd, the other on the 26th.

Her first letter begins with another "eruption is now taking place on Mauna Loa. It presents a scene of sublimity unsurpassed." In the February 26th letter she combined her own observations with what she has heard from her husband. "I add a line to the above to inform you that up to this date the action of the late eruption is undiminished. Truly our island is on fire. A line from Mr. Coan informs me that he passed within five or six miles of a stream of lava, yesterday, which was burning its path through the woods, in the direction of Puna."[28]

After her second letter, Mrs. Coan wrote an update from Alta, California. She expressed concern, indicating the lava "is gradually fill-

26. Lydia Coan, *Memorial Volume*, 219.

27. Titus Coan, *Life*, 160, chapters VI (60–81), XVIII (262–69), XIX (270–79), XX (279–88), XXI (289–312), XXII (313–26), XXIII (327–35). In an October 2009 reply to an e-mail from Corr, Edward Coan indicates that he decided to digitize the autobiography of Titus Coan upon the "request of Ken Rubin."

28. Fidelia Coan, "Scientific Intelligence," 106–7.

ing up all the inequalities of the ground," and it was supposed at that date [March 2?] that it would ultimately reach the sea, and discharge itself into the bay of Hilo. In her February 26th letter, Fidelia had written, "I need not add that we are all deeply interested in knowing when, and where, and how, this fiery flood is to reach the sea. The locality of its source almost precludes the hope that its progress can be as harmless as on a former occasion."[29]

With the volcano located near where the Coans lived in Hilo, their geological interest coincided with existential concern. In his autobiography, Titus Coan indicated his friend and colleague Dr. Wetmore "decided to return to Hilo, apprehensive that the stream might reach the sea before we could return from the crater, and that our families might need his presence."

Coan could not resist staying on the slope of the volcano. Together with his elderly Hawaiian assistant he "pressed on." "At half-past three P.M. I reached the awful crater, and stood alone in the light of its fires." It was a moment of unutterable interest. His scientific interest and spiritual outlook merged as he thought of biblical passages, such as Moses on Mount Sinai and elsewhere. He was soon joined by the assistant who "shouted: '*Kupainaha i keia hana mana a ke Akua mana loa!*'—'Wonderful wonderful is this mighty work of Almighty God.'" Coan concluded this vignette by rhetorically asking "Could I help embracing the old man and praising the Lord?"[30]

In volcanic areas, earthquakes are usually precursors to eruptions. Such was the case in 1868. Coan reported on the earthquake from perspectives both ecclesiastical and geological. In discussing a house of worship and the earthquake he wrote, in "1868 an awful earthquake tore in pieces stone walls and stone houses, and rent the earth in various parts of Hilo, Puna, and Kau. Had we built according to our original plan and agreement with the mason, 'our holy and beautiful house' would have become a heap of rubbish, and our hearts would have sunk within us with sorrow. How true that 'a man's heart deviseth his way, but the Lord directed his steps.'"[31]

Later in the autobiography, Coan focused on how earthquakes preceded volcanic eruptions. He first noted, "From time immemorial

29. Ibid., 107.
30. Titus Coan, *Life*, 281–86.
31. Ibid., 86–87.

earthquakes have been common on Hawaii." He next linked earthquakes and volcanic activity. On 'the 27th of March, 1868, a series of remarkable earthquakes commenced. Kilauea was unusually full and in vehement action."[32]

To round out a consideration of Titus Coan as a scientific Renaissance man, it is intriguing to learn of his friendship with Charles Darwin. While no doubt Coan knew of the controversies raging around Darwin (the two men died the same year) they appear to have had an amicable relationship as indicated through their limited correspondence.

Near the beginning of his *Patagonia* book, Coan wrote "I have . . . taken the liberty to quote from the voyages of . . . Prof[essor] Charles Darwin and others." In his *Life*, he spoke of "Mr. Darwin describing a similar climb which he took in the island of Tahiti."[33]

Until now Coan's somewhat incongruous personality has been examined; the next apparent contradiction looks outward to Coan's relationship with the Hawaiians and the sailors to whom he ministered. Coan had a conflicted view of Hawaiians. On the one hand he revealed a paternalistic perspective on the Hawaiian people; on the other hand was his professed love for and passionate service to them.

In fairness, it needs to be noted that many contemporaries shared Coan's views. Certainly all ABCFM missionaries of his time did so. Neither their views nor Coan's, however, were simplistic. Witness his complex view of and service to the Hawaiian people, both of which are evident in the "Hawaiian character" pages listed in the index of his *Life*.[34]

At times Coan wrote of the Hawaiians as benighted, savage, prone to alcoholism, and with a tendency to lie. On the positive side, he characterized them as very hospitable and loving. Docility as a trait he believed could be either a positive or negative. "They are docile. Few, if any, of the races of men would believe with such simple faith, or, if I may call it, credulity. This trait, though it exposes them to deceitful wiles, also disposes them to listen to correct and useful teachings."[35]

32. Lydia Coan, *Memorial Volume*, 128.

33. Titus Coan, *Patagonia*, 7; Titus Coan, *Life*, 184; and Dana, "Science and the Bible."

34. Titus Coan, *Life*, 338.

35. Ibid., 252–53.

Coan took it upon himself to speak on how young Christian Hawaiian women should comport themselves. Focusing more on gender-related church leadership matters than cultural issues, he took the basic nineteenth century evangelical Protestant position on the role of women in the church.[36]

Coan trained many Hawaiians to be pastors and missionaries. He warned against prematurely allowing Polynesians to lead their churches. He also evaluated the areas of weakness he saw in Hawaiian pastors. The first three points are valid from a biblical perspective while the fourth is a Western imposition of the priority of record keeping and statistics. "Nearly all of our native pastors have been slack in church discipline, indiscriminate in receiving to church communion, and remiss in looking after our wandering people, so that our church statistics are in so confused a state as to be past remedy."[37]

The Hawaiians called Coan "Papa." While the term does have paternalistic overtones, it also evidences the deep respect and love they appear to have had for him. Through caring enough to learn the Hawaiian's language, proclaiming the Gospel to them, treating their medical needs until the arrival of Dr. Wetmore, providing hospitality in his home; and loving some aspects of the island culture, Coan showed his life was all about serving the Hawaiian people.

He did not, however, ignore the needs of non-Hawaiians who would pass through the port of Hilo. Coan carried on a robust ministry to seamen. He ministered to them while he was still learning the Hawaiian language. When he did establish regular preaching times in Hilo, he would—after preaching several times to Hawaiians on a Sunday—at "3 p.m. preach in English to seamen, and English speaking residents and visitors."[38]

Under Coan's inspiration and influence, several "masters and officers gave up Sabbath whaling, and instead held religious meetings with their men on the Lord's day." To further encourage those who "went down to the sea in ships," Coan penned a pamphlet entitled "The Sailor's Sabbath." He wrote, it was "easy to show from all history, from observation, and from innumerable *facts*, that the highest state of civilization,

36. Titus Coan, "The Appropriate Duties of Christian Females, In Public and Social Worship."

37. Morris, "Hawaiian Missionaries Abroad, 1852–1909"; and Titus Coan, *Life*, 250.

38. Ehlke, "Enthusiastic Religion," 143–45.

refinement, enterprise, intelligence and temporal prosperity, can never exist without the [keeping of] the Sabbath."

Coan next rhetorically asked and substantively answered eight questions pertaining to the realities a sailor faced in keeping the Sabbath. He concluded with this hopeful vision of the future: "May the time hasten when the Sabbath sun shall be hailed joyfully by every seaman—when the Bethel Flag shall wave aloft on every ship, and when every ocean and sea shall echo the glad anthem of the sailor, as his song of praise is borne on the breath of Heaven into the ear of Him 'who made the sea and the dry land.'"[39]

According to Ehlke, Coan discharged the duties of a seaman's chaplain. These duties included "nursing sick seamen, burying their remains when they did not recover, caring for their secular affairs and writing their parents . . . [I]t was a post that Coan filled in addition to his ministry with the Hawaiian people of Hilo and Puna."

Coan's labors as a seamen's chaplain show how far he would go to reach out to people of all backgrounds with the good news of the Christian faith. "In this labor for seamen I have been led to correspond with the American Bible, Tract, Peace, Temperance, and Seamen's Friend Societies, and have obtained Bibles and tracts in the English, French, German, Spanish, Portuguese, Swedish, Danish, and Chinese languages; which with many thousands of tracts have been distributed among these vessels. Some of this 'bread cast upon the waters' has been found again according to the promise."

Among the tracts and books Coan distributed to sailors, officers and others was "The Peace Book" from the American Peace Society. The subject of war and peace reveals another complex aspect of the personality of Titus Coan. He abhorred war yet saw a place for it on occasion. He understood the need for the Civil War, while he lamented French military action in the Pacific. [40]

Coan's passion for peace is reflected in the twenty-five letters he wrote to the journal *Advocate of Peace*. The chief object of his first letter was to inform the Society's Corresponding Secretary of a donation of one hundred dollars on its way from the Haili church. "It is but a mite that we are able to cast into your treasury; but be assured, dear Sir, we do it with cheerful hearts, and with many prayers and warm desires, that

39. Titus Coan, "The Sailor's Sabbath: or, a word from a friend to seamen."
40. Titus Coan, letter (April 26, 1859), *Advocate of Peace* (September 1859) 335.

the principles your Society advocates, may spread and prevail until they fill the earth with peace and goodwill."[41]

The cash-strapped American Peace Society used Coan's letter to appeal for funds. Years later, Rev. S. Hopkins Emery twisted Coan's views to fit his categorical pacifist views. He imposed a pacifist cast upon Coan whom he heard "in the city of Providence, and was greatly interested in his statements concerning his work in general, and especially the teachings of the mission from the beginning on the subject of war . . ." Emery was impressed by Coan's ability to persuade the violent and cruel Hawaiians "in favor of peace. The mission appears to have adopted the principle of the early Christians, that it is unchristian to fight."

Emery also felt that Coan has "encouraged his [Haili] church—the largest probably, but by no means the wealthiest in the world—to contribute with exemplary liberality to the Treasury of the American Peace Society." Emery revealed his bias when he noted with disapproval the Sumatra martyrs Lyman and Munson "were found with weapons of offence as well as defence [sic] in their hands."[42]

Coan often wrote to Joel and Hanna Bean, his "widely known and esteemed members of the Society of Friends." In a fascinating August 1865 letter to them, Coan opened with his "thoughts of love to Christian friends so congenial and so dear."[43] Three years later he told the Beans, war "will never be abolished by the timid, the conservative and the wise men of this world, who call peace men and Peace Societies foolish and fanatical; you who say 'you must take the world as you find it . . .'"

Yet Coan did accept the world as he found it when there was no other choice. When in the United States in 1870 the Coans visited the Gettysburg battlefield. While lamenting the death and destruction of the Civil War, Coan opined the battle of Gettysburg and the entire war were necessary. Echoing Lincoln he wrote, "The scars of war are everywhere . . . But our country needed this fiery chastisement, and it will be better in the end if so be that the North and South understand and profit by the lesson."[44]

---

41. A typewritten page in the Coan Papers at the Library of Congress lists 25 letters to the *Advocate of Peace* from Titus Coan between February of 1849 and April of 1882.

42. Non-sourced (1871?) article, a copy of which was provided to Corr by the Library of Congress.

43. Lydia Coan, *Memorial Volume*, 96–96.

44. Titus Coan, *Life*, 215.

Coan addressed the disparity of holding a strong peace position together with support for the Civil War by saying, "Our sentiments may appear paradoxical; but we must still say, that we hate war, and we reaffirm and reiterate the opinion that, if all Christians would view the subject in the light of the Gospel, and would follow the simple and *safe* example of Christ in this matter, war in Christian lands would be *impossible.*"

Coan puts the onus on Christian leaders in the South when he writes, "Had the religious teachings in the South been what they *should* have been, slavery, with its blinding defiling, and maddening power, had long since disappeared from that fair heritage of our fathers, and this awful rebellion would never have been."

Still, Coan was a believer in reconciliation. In his letter to the Beans, he addressed the need to maintain friendship while disagreeing on various matters. So "deep is our respect, so tender and true our love for you, and for all the consistent members of your Society, that you might ever express any sentiment in which we may accidentally and honestly differ without the least fear that our Christian fellowship would be interrupted. 'How good and how pleasant it is for brethren to dwell together,' [Psalm 133] not in *uniformity*, but 'in unity.'"

This leads to Coan's discussion of the assassination of Abraham Lincoln, the Union leader of the bloody internecine conflict: "But suddenly all was changed. The sea, the sky and the fields were darkened—a sigh of sorrow, a wave of woe swept over us. Our sunny islands were draped in mourning. Abraham Lincoln is *dead!* 'A prince and a great man is fallen!' *Treason* has murdered *Mercy.* Thus we wept. But still we looked up to the High Throne of Heaven and saw our Father there."[45]

Coan was militantly against potential and actual French naval actions in the Pacific. He wrote of one battle on a small island: "The French did not conquer it without loss of blood and treasure." He asked several rhetorical questions: "Why should the professed disciples of the 'Prince of Peace' endeavor to propagate the Christian religion by the use of fire and sword? And why do men who call themselves 'priests of the Most High God' call in the aid of weapons, and go and come and live under the cover of cannon? Did the Captain of our salvation teach His disciples such doctrines?"[46]

45. Lydia Coan, *Memorial Volume,* 121.
46. Titus Coan, *Life,* 166.

The use of French military might provides the transition from Coan's unique perspective on war and peace to his relationship with other religions. Coan represents a paradox on this subject as he adamantly opposed Catholics and Latter Day Saints on his own turf, while remaining congenial when on theirs.

Serving more than a century before Vatican II, Coan needs to be understood in the context of his time. He did speak disparagingly about the Roman Catholic priests. While suggesting his was only "a hasty sketch of the introduction of Catholicism into these Islands," Coan nevertheless wrote of Hilo and Puna experiencing "their full share" of the "persistent aggression of the Catholics." "Priests were early stationed in these and the adjoining districts, and they at once took a bold and defiant stand. These emissaries confronted me everywhere."[47]

By contrast, when Coan visited Catholic leaders on their home turf, Coan could be quite congenial both in manners and conversation. When first on their way to the Sandwich Islands, Coan and his shipmates put in at Lima. "With the courteous Bishop of Lima, we went through the Cathedral, he bowing and crossing himself as he passed by the various pictures and statues, telling us of the guardian care of the different saints over the city." Similarly, when Coan visited a Catholic facility during his second sojourn in the Marquesas Islands, he indicated that he and his friends "called on the bishop, who received us politely, and entered into free conversation with us, and with the two English gentlemen, residents, he visited us with great urbanity, and introduced us to the two Sisters."[48]

When it came to the arrival of Latter Day Saint missionaries arriving in 1850, Coan noted not "many years after the introduction of the papal priests came a drove of Mormon emissaries. These spread themselves in squads all over the group [of islands] like the frogs of Egypt." Perhaps he was mindful of the locust swarms the Mormon settlers faced in their early years in the Great Salt Lake Basin. He also indirectly noted the Old Testament military organizational structure found in Mormon planning and implementation.

Coan wrote of the Mormons: "They made an early descent upon Hilo. At first they employed flattering words . . . Finding that they could not prevail by flattery, they assumed a bold front, denounced the American missionaries as false pretenders, deceivers, and blind guides,

47. Ibid., 94.
48. Ibid., 22–200.

without baptism, without ordination, and without credentials from heaven."[49]

Yet when Titus and Fidelia Coan visited Salt Lake City, they apparently had a pleasant visit with several of the Mormon missionaries whom we had seen in Hilo. No evidence of acrimony between Coan and those missionaries can be detected from the existing evidence when they met on the latters' home turf.[50]

Mention of the Coans' time in Salt Lake City provides transition to the Coan's next tension of time and place: while spending most of their adult life in Hawai'i, they returned to the United States for almost a year during parts of 1870 and 1871. Coan had been invited by the American Board to come to the United States as early as 1867, but he pleaded pressing church service in Hawai'i. In a letter to his sister-in-law he wrote, "I see that you and other friends are indulging strong expectations of seeing us again in the land of our birth. We do not yet feel confident on the subject. Cares seem to thicken and labors to multiply as life advances. It now looks as though we could not go before 1869, and before that time who can tell what will be?"[51]

Fidelia's health proved to be a reason for the couple ultimately traveling to the United States in 1870. They thought a change of climate and being able to visit doctors would help Fidelia's condition. Though the visit did not help, they were welcomed as heroes.[52]

In the *Memorial Volume*, Lydia Coan quotes from Dr. Field's introduction to *Adventures in Patagonia:* "Fame of the missionary had gone before him, and wherever he came among the churches he was welcomed with an enthusiasm such as hd not been manifested since the heroic [Adoniram] Judson came back from Burmah years before."[53]

In 1880, a brief article in the *New York Evangelical Journal* noted, "Dr. Coan, the venerable missionary . . . visited his native country, and spent some months seeing old friends and old places, and making many new friends who had come up amid the old surroundings to fill the places of their fathers. Whoever saw him then will have delightful

49. Ibid., 101–3.

50. Ibid., 213.

51. Lydia Coan, *Memorial Volume*, 115.

52. Titus Coan, *Life*, 202.

53. Lydia Coan, *Memorial Volume*, 127.

memories of that beloved patriarch." He told the story of his life "with childlike simplicity."[54]

The Coans traveled to many locations in the United States and had many meetings. "During their absence from Hawaii they visited twenty States and Territories, and Mr. Coan's talks in large and smaller assemblies numbered two hundred and thirty-nine." In his *Life*, Coan expressed his joy at the diversity of denominations present at the various meetings: "They are exhilarating, and one thing which charmed me, if possible more than any other, was the fact that partition walls were gradually giving way between different evangelical denominations."[55]

They arrived in San Francisco on May 5, 1870. After spending two weeks in California, they took a train to Salt Lake City. He described a Sabbath there. Seeing "the prophet and several of the Apostles at a service in "the great tabernacle," he wrote disapprovingly of "a singular observance of the Lord's Supper, the elements being distributed by laughing boys, while a speaker was haranguing the audience without making a single allusion to the death of Christ, to the ordinance which commemorated that event." He "saw the foundation of the great temple."[56]

The Coans "spent a little time in Iowa" and then spent two weeks in Chicago. They continued eastward to Niles, Michigan. His three week stay in Niles was "one continued ovation."[57]

Prior to Niles, the Coans had been in Oberlin, Ohio. There Titus attended "the meeting of the General Congregational Conference of the State." He noted, "I had a most interesting season and saw about two hundred ministers and delegates of the first order of intelligence and piety. I was the guest of Presidents Fairchild and Finney, of Professors Cowles and Morgan. On the Sabbath I spoke four times. The last time, in the evening, was before an assembly of some two thousand five hundred. I have never met a more enlightened, attentive and appreciative audience than in Oberlin. The college is a great success, and Oberlin is a place of marked intelligence and goodness."[58]

Coan's time in Oberlin gives insight on his development from a revival convert to an equal with the world-renowned Charles Finney.

54. *New York Evangelical Journal* (188[0?]) n.p.

55. Lydia Coan, *Memorial Volume*, 128.

56. Ibid., 213–14.

57. Lydia Coan, *Memorial Volume*, 128.

58. Ibid., 128.

Nowhere was this more prevalent than when Finney and Coan co-officiated at a communion service. "Rosell T. Cross remembered a meeting in the Second Church in Oberlin in June [sic?] 1870 when 'the Communion was administered by Mr. Finney and Titus Coan, the great Hawaiian missionary. Probably no two men then living had led more souls to Christ. It was an impressive communion service.'"[59]

The Coans would hopscotch around the northeastern United States for the rest of their trip. In late October they arrived in Brooklyn to attend the annual meeting of the ABCFM. This was the first time "we had the privilege of attending this annual gathering." Coan enjoyed and being a center of attention at the meeting: "Here we met missionaries and men of distinction from the Orient and the Occident, from every continent, and from many an island of the globe. Never shall I forget that great congregation of glowing faces and earnest listeners."[60]

The Coans visited Washington D. C. in March of 1871. Coan characterized it as one of the "happiest weeks" of their trip. In the company of the Howard University president, they attended the school's commencement at a crowded church. While in the nation's capitol, he met with congressmen, senators, and President Ulysses S. Grant. Ehlke notes, "Coan had fought many of his battles with critics during the Great Awakening in the evangelical press in America with such vigor and style that few dared to question his motives." She avers that Coan "was his own best publicist, and this contributed no doubt to the extraordinary welcome which led them to the White House in Washington, D. C."[61]

While in the United States, Titus Coan visited at least four seminaries. He spent some time in the area of his birth and early years. "Our visit to Killingworth, my native town, was full of interest. Tender memories of childhood and youth often drew tears. Sixty-nine years had swept along the flood of time since my eyes first saw the light of day, and forty-four since I had left the home where I was born and nourished." After two long paragraphs of description and comparison, he concludes his reflection on his nostalgic visit with these words: "Thankful for one more view

59. Roselle Theodore Cross, "Memories of Charles G. Finney," n.d., quoted in Dupuis and Rosell, eds., *The Restored Memoirs of Charles G. Finney*, 313.

60. Corr, "The Field is the World," 56–130; and Titus Coan, *Life*, 218.

61. Ehlke, "Enthusiastic Religion," 257.

of my boyhood's home, with chastened reflections I turned from it for the last time."[62]

Along his American trail the missionary would write at least one letter to Lydia Bingham. From Brooklyn he informed her, "Our friends here are legion and they almost kill us with kindness."[63]

Whatever the reasons—press of people, weather, the continued course of the disease, or a combination of those and more—her condition continued to worsen. Lydia Coan wrote in a bridge section of the *Memorial Volume* of the "rapid and alarming decline of Fidelia's health," explaining that "she and Titus returned to the quiet home in the tropics, leaving much unseen and unsaid, but followed by many prayers and remembered in loving appreciation."[64]

Fidelia Church Coan died on September 29, 1872. The one whose angelic face had smitten Titus Coan so many decades before was laid to rest. Writing of the place where his body would be buried a little over ten years later, Coan opines, "The cemetery is in a beautiful place; the towering mountains are upon the west and south. East and north stretches the ocean, and a glorious emerald landscape is on every side. The soft breezes . . . do not wake the sleeping form that awaits the behest of Him who is 'the Resurrection and the Life.' The soul unfettered, unchained, has drawn nearer than they to the throne."[65]

A little over a year later, on October 13, 1872, "Titus Coan would marry the 38-year old Lydia Bingham, the youngest daughter of the Rev[erend] Hiram Bingham." This development indicates another aspect of Titus Coan: that during his life he had two wives and loved each dearly while married to them.[66]

Fidelia Coan became acquainted with Lydia Bingham when she and Titus lived in Hawai'i. After he brought Lydia by "the Emerald Bower" for an unannounced visit, Fidelia wrote him a letter admonishing him: "I very much wish Lydia Bingham could come up with you while the house was clean, the supplies fresh and the peaches not quite gone." Without suggestion of suspicion or scandal, Lydia once "accompanied him on

62. Titus Coan, *Life*, 219–21.

63. Lydia Coan, *Memorial Volume*, 129.

64. Ibid., 132.

65. Titus Coan, *Life*, 221–22.

66. Ehlke, "Enthusiastic Religion," 258.

an excursion to the volcano. Coan continued on to Kalapana from the volcano" and sent a letter with Lydia for Fidelia.[67]

As mentioned above, Titus Coan married Lydia Bingham a little over a year after Fidelia died. Ehlke provides the bridge between the two wives. "A vigorous, loving man, Titus Coan followed the example of Finney in this aspect of his life. Fidelia had taught him the blessedness of the marital state and he did not wish to go on alone."[68]

Not all in Coan's family were pleased with his second marriage. One wonders whether Titus Munson Coan indirectly expressed his displeasure in subtle ways in his capacity as the final proofreader of his father's *Life*. Very little mention is made of Lydia Bingham or of her as Lydia Coan. When we read that "Miss Bingham came to Hilo," it is in the context of her stepping down as the head of the Honolulu school, not because of marrying Titus Coan![69]

No description or mention is provided of the marriage, which combined arguably the two greatest Hawaiian Congregational families. Did Titus Munson Coan resent his father's marriage to someone not much older than he? Unfortunately, this remains a mystery.

Less mysterious is how Coan's daughter, Hattie, felt about his second marriage. Ehlke writes that it "greatly disturbed" her. She refused to attend the wedding supported by 'others who feel that the step is such an one as they would not take,' reported Mr. Castle to his children. Mr. Castle felt sorry for all concerned as he felt it to be a 'perfectly right and proper' step if 'the parties choose.'"[70]

In her summary of the situation, Ehlke transitions to the positives of Lydia's service to Titus Coan. "Coan's daughter, Harriet, found it difficult to accept a younger woman in her mother's place, a view shared by some in the missionary community. The second Mrs. Coan proved to be a loyal companion, assisting her husband in editing his two volumes of reminiscences."[71]

The devotion and love between the two are evident in their writings. To her brother, Coan refers to her as "My L[ydia]." A few months later he movingly describes his feeling for her as he watches her departure

---

67. Ibid., 258.

68. Ibid.

69. Titus Coan, *Life*, before the "Preface" and 243.

70. Ehlke, "Enthusiastic Religion," 259–60.

71. Ibid., 267.

from Hilo harbor for a visit to Honolulu: "You steamed out of the bay splendidly at four P.M. I gazed at the vessel which bore away the dearest earthly treasure of my heart."[72]

Titus Coan's second marriage provides the pivot to yet another aspect: his vital last years, followed by a brief time of decline before his death. Lydia showed her devotion to Coan through her assistance in his writing two books. Because of the public's enthusiastic response to *Adventures in Patagonia*, Coan decided to write his *Life*. Near the end of his autobiography he described how his book would not have been published without his wife's help: "The foregoing pages have been written among interruptions and anxieties, but, they make some partial record of a life preserved by its Giver in many scenes of danger and crowned with many blessings. And among its chief blessings I would recognize God's goodness in granting me precious partners in my lifework [including Fidelia] . . . [Lydia as my] faithful helpmeet is the strength and support of my age. But for her suggestions, and her patient labors in copying the manuscript of this volume, I should not have undertaken, at my time of life, the task of writing it."[73]

Coan wrote the preceding words in 1881. He continued to live an active life as pastor, preacher for over a year. Then he suffered a stroke and experienced many "wearisome . . . days and nights" before his death. Nevertheless his faith remained strong. "Let patience have her perfect work, *her perfect work*. That is my motto. I say it to myself every day and God helps me. We have everything to be thankful for; the Lord is very good to us."[74]

---

72. Lydia Coan, *Memorial Volume*, 145, 151.

73. Lydia Coan, "A Brief Sketch of the Missionary Life of Mrs. Sybil Mosely Bingham"; and Titus Coan, *Life*, 335.

74. Lydia Coan, *Memorial Volume*, 202.

Figure 25. Titus Coan, n.d. Photo courtesy of Edward J. Coan.

Although he was physically an invalid, Coan was granted a "re-markable degree of memory and great clearness of mind" during the "weeks of waiting." Hawaiians came to be with him and show their re-spects. "Aged men, who in their prime had been the companions of the beloved missionary in his tours, came long distances to speak once more with their revered teacher."[75]

75. Ibid., 202–3.

As Coan's death drew near, three physicians attended him: his dear friend Dr. Wetmore, his son Titus Munson Coan, and Dr. Kittredge. The Library of Congress papers include "notes on [the] last illness of Titus Coan."[76]

The aged missionary died on December 1, 1882. Except for his date of death, he prepared the following to go on his marble tombstone:

TITUS COAN.

February 1ˢᵗ, 1801.

December 1ˢᵗ, 1882.

HE LIVED BY FAITH.

HE STILL LIVES

BELIEVEST THOU THIS?

JOHN 11 26.77

A memorial service was held at Coan's Haili Church on March 25, 1883. Hawaiians and haoles alike shared their memories of the man who had served his Lord and touched so many lives. Dr. Wetmore noted that Coan "certainly labored diligently and faithfully in his master's vineyard." The Reverend S. Damon, a missionary to seamen, noted that the "grand business of Mr. Coan's life has been to preach the Gospel among the Hawaiians, and right nobly has he performed his life-work."[78]

A "Native Parishioner" named Paakaula shared that Coan "was strong, without discouragement, in the work of the Lord, with all meekness, content and deep reverence. He treated with kindness the poor, the afflicted, the sick; and to all he was constant in the preaching of the kingdom of God."[79]

As to his legacy, his hometown of Killingworth has a "Titus Coan Road" as well as a marker for his birthplace. In the Pacific, the Titus Coan Endowment plays a significant role in the finances of the Hawai'i Conference of the United Church of Christ.

A complex man with many dualities, Titus Coan stayed focused throughout his life in Hawai'i on "preaching Christ and Him cruci-

76. Coan Papers, Container 17.

77. Lydia Coan, *Memorial Volume*, 248.

78. Written document by Dr. Wetmore provided by the Lyman House Museum archivist, Libby Burke; and Lydia Coan, *Memorial Volume*, 248.

79. Ibid., 227–28.

fied." This led to the deepest level of his legacy, namely the influence he had on lives—Hawaiians, seamen, and others. Proclaiming the Gospel, Coan prepared these people for church membership, and pastored them through the years, showing that he was indeed "The Apostle to the Sandwich Islands."[80]

BIBLIOGRAPHY

Coan, Fidelia Church. "Scientific Intelligence." *American Journal of Science* 14 (September 1852) 106–7.

Coan, Lydia Bingham. "A Brief Sketch of the Missionary Life of Mrs. Sybil Mosely Bingham" (1895).

———. *Titus Coan: A Memorial Volume.* Chicago: Fleming H. Revell, 1884.

Coan, Titus. *Adventures in Patagonia: A Missionary's Exploring Trip.* New York: Dodd, Mead and Company, 1880.

———. "The Appropriate Duties of Christian Females, in Public and Social Worship." Honolulu,1862.

———. *Life in Hawaii: An Autobiographic Sketch of Mission Life and Labors, 1835–1881.* New York: Anson Randolph and Company, 1882.

———. Papers. Library of Congress (MSS76760).

———. "A Sailor's Sabbath: or, a word from a friend to seamen." Honolulu, 1846.

Corr, Donald Philip. "'The Field Is the World': Proclaiming, Translating and Serving by the American Board of Commissioners for Foreign Missions." Pasadena: William Carey Library Dissertation Series, 2009.

Dana, James Dwight. "Science and the Bible: a review of 'the six days of creation' of Prof. Taylor Lewis." Andover, MA: Warren F. Draper, 1856.

DuPuis, Richard A. and Garth M. Rosell. *The Memoirs of Charles G. Finney: The Complete Restored Text.* Grand Rapids, Michigan: Academie Books, 1989.

Ehlke, Margaret S. "Enthusiastic Religion and the Lives of Titus and Fidelia Coan, Missionaries to Hilo." Master's Thesis: University of Hawaii at Manoa, 1986.

Morris, Nancy Jane. *Hawaiian Missionaries Abroad, 1852–1909.* Manoa: University of Hawaii Press, 1987.

Phillips, Clifton Jackson. *Protestant America and the Pagan World: The First Half Century of the American Board of Commissioners for Foreign Missions* (Cambridge, MA: East Asian Research Center, Harvard University Press, 1969.

Schneider, Robert Alan. "The Senior Secretary: Rufus Anderson and the American Board of Commissioners for Foreign Missions, 1810–1860." Ph.D. dissertation, Harvard University, 1980.

80. Preliminary death notice in the *New York Times*; and "Brief Sketch of an Old Missionary," *New York Times* (January 5, 1883).

13

Christianity Builds a Nest in Hawai'i

Regina Pfeiffer

IN ANCIENT HAWAI'I, *PALA'IE*, a game that imitated a bird trying to land in its nest, was popularly played by children and adults. The players would attempt to swing an attached coconut-husk ball to a nest that was made by looping the coconut leaf's rib into an oval. *Pala'ie*, the bird, is looking for its home, trying to nest. It searches and searches, finally to land. The seemingly endless voyage of the first groups of missionaries from the American Board of Commissioners for Foreign Missions (ABCFM) who came to Hawai'i in the early 1820s might have felt similarly to the bird searching for its nest. The missionaries faced a long, arduous journey that included cramped and poorly ventilated quarters with little room for mobility and privacy. The first group of missionaries, led by Hiram Bingham and Asa Thurston, sited land on March 30, 1820, and anchored on April 4 off the shores of the island of Hawai'i, commonly known today as the Big Island. While the earliest missionaries weren't necessarily seeking to relocate permanently, they did arrive with the intention of Christianizing the pagans and turning the heathens away from their evil lives. Thus, they hoped to create a new Christian society filled with faith in the one God, righteousness and the ethics of hard work and decent living. As with the game *pala'ie*, sometimes the bird lands in the nest in totality, while at other times it barely lands. The hope of the missionaries that the Hawaiians would become not only Christian but also temperate and civilized persons met, in some instances, with success. But at other times it met with resistance.

Because of the depth of this topic, perhaps the best way to illustrate the reactions of the Hawaiians to the missionaries and to gauge how well the missionaries succeeded is to examine the lives of four significant Hawaiian women who had great influence in their time. The first two, Queens Keʻōpūʻolani and Kaʻahumanu, had a significant impact in the changes of Hawaiian culture and society in their time. In addition, these two women lived under the ancient system and made the transition from the Hawaiian religion to Christianity. The other two, Princess Bernice Pauahi Bishop and Queen Emma Rooke, left legacies that continue to serve Hawaiians today. While many other representatives of Hawaiian reactions could be selected, these women embraced Christianity in varying ways that serve to explain the multitudinous responses to the foreign missionaries. In addition, these women share some common backgrounds. All four women were related in some manner to King Kamehameha the First, who united the islands under one rule. Second, they were educated by the missionaries either formally or informally. Third, all were closely connected to the monarchy of their time in significant ways either as regent, wife or potential candidate for succession. Fourth, they were instrumental in developing either laws or institutions that impacted greatly on the society of their time. Finally, since women under the Hawaiian cultural system were denied access to many religious rituals and activities, these women represent and reinforce how Christianity effected change in the society.

When the missionaries arrived in Hawaiʻi, also known as the Sandwich Islands, they did not enter an empty nest. Hawaiian culture and religion had existed for centuries and were undergoing drastic changes as a result of Western contact. In other words, Christianity's enduring influence developed not because the missionaries exerted a great conversion among the peoples, but rather through several factors, many of which were instituted by the Hawaiian leadership or monarchy in its early years. A short history will explain how a culture and its religion changed radically in a brief span of time.

The islands of Hawaiʻi, situated as they are in the Northern Pacific region, went unnoticed by many of the early European explorers who traveled the vast oceanic area. Much of the early navigation in the Pacific region had centered in the South and Western areas and their multitude of archipelagos. For the most part, the Northern Pacific region had remained unexplored. Captain James Cook is credited with the first major contact between the European countries and Hawai'i. His arrival on January 18, 1778, in the waters surrounding the occupied Westernmost islands of the archipelago initiated a new period in Hawaiian history. While it would take another 42 years before an organized group of Christian missionaries arrived in the islands, the Hawaiian culture and society would undergo gradual and, finally, radical changes within that same time period.

The community that Cook first encountered and observed was ruled by a complicated *kapu* system with its variety of *kānāwai*, laws. *Kapu* can be translated in various ways, including "sacred" or "forbidden." These two meanings co-exist and express both the socio-political and religious realms. To separate the socio-political aspect of the culture from the religion is impossible for pre-Western contact Hawai'i. The two complemented and supported one another. Religious beliefs shaped the structure of the society, which in turn maintained and supported the spiritual life of the Hawaiians. This needs further explanation.

The Hawaiian social system prior to and immediately following the influx of European and American visitors had several strata or classes. The highest stratum was that of the *ali'i*, the chiefs. Within this level was a further subdivision between the high chiefs and lesser ones. In either case, the *ali'i*, both men and women, were believed to be descended from *na akua*, the gods. As such, their persons, their belongings, their shadows, and the ground upon which they walked were *kapu*. Their spiritual power, their *mana*, existed even in the smallest lock of hair or fingernail. By wearing the personal body parts of *ali'i*, such as hair, or through possessing objects used by them, the *mana* could be transferred or increased. Because of the potential exploitation of spiritual *mana*, special attendants carefully guarded the *ali'i's* personal effects. In addition, *ali'i* enjoyed privileges reserved for them alone. Certain foods, activities and worship were *kapu* or sacred for *ali'i*.

The next stratum, the *kāhuna*, closely worked with the *ali'i* to sustain the religious life of the people. The term, *kāhuna*, is often misused and should be translated to mean "expert" or "the master of." This group maintained the spiritual life of the people through the administration of *heiau*, the temples. While some *heiau* were dedicated for sacrificial purposes or in preparation for war, many others were devoted for other specific activities such as farming, fishing, or medicine. The *kāhuna* were trained in *pule*, prayer, and in the arts for one particular field. For example, *kāhuna laʻau lapaʻau* were trained in prayer that accompanied the gathering, preparing and applying of medicinal plants for people's physical and spiritual well-being. To be *kāhuna* meant many years of rigorous study under the tutelage of an older expert.

The *makaʻāinana*, the largest stratum, sustained the life of the society through planting, fishing, and building. They lived on the lands that the *aliʻi* governed, the *ahupuaʻa*, a land district from the mountain to the sea. While the *aliʻi* governed and benefited from the work of the *makaʻāinana*, they had a reciprocal responsibility to govern fairly and protect the people within the land district over which the *aliʻi* had jurisdiction. Some have compared the system to a feudal one but that is perhaps an oversimplification. The concepts of *ʻohana* (family) and *pono* (justice and care) underscored the system so that reciprocity existed among *aliʻi*, *kāhuna* and *makaʻāinana*.

While the *kapu* system could be considered onerous, particularly for women to whom some of the more restrictive rules were directed, and *makaʻāinana*, whose life was endangered by even the slightest infraction or disrespect to the *aliʻi*, its foundation lay within the religious beliefs of the community. The *kapu* system first and foremost honored the gods and goddesses, maintained the sense of awe engendered by the natural landscape of the islands, and sustained the existent social structure. Success in war, good health, plentiful crops, and all other facets of life depended on the goodwill and appeasement of the myriads of gods and goddesses, including *ʻaumakua*, family or ancestral spirits. For the most part, the Hawaiian religion was poly- and pan- theistic, incorporating animistic tendencies that emphasized the habitation of gods and goddesses in the natural surroundings. One of the most commonly known aspects of Hawaiian religion—still prevalent in custom if not belief—is the myth of *Pele*, the goddess of fire and volcanoes, who supposedly resides in *Halemaʻumaʻu* crater on the island of Hawaiʻi. Her story is part of a religious and cultural system that honored many gods and goddesses, and that remained in effect until the death of the islands' first king in 1819.

Kamehameha the Great, the first *aliʻi* and *mōʻī*, king, to unite the islands under one rule, utilized and enforced the *kapu* system with its various laws, *kānāwai*, to his advantage. Despite Kamehameha's reliance on the ancient ways, discontent with the *kapu* system was occurring. As contact with Westerners increased, the validity and sustainability of the system was questioned. The people of Hawai'i were being ravaged by disease and death despite strict adherence to the land's religious and social life. But those who broke the *kapu*, including visitors from other lands and Hawaiian women who boarded the ships and ate pork that was forbidden to them, seemed to receive no retribution for their transgressions.[1] These factors, among others, began to erode belief in the system itself, particularly in the power of the gods. Even in 1812, Kamehameha heard a prediction that the gods themselves would be overthrown.[2] Not many years later, that predication came true. Kamehameha's favorite wife, Ka'ahumanu, and his most sacred wife, Ke'ōpū'olani, were instrumental in the abolishment of the *kapu* system.

After Kamehameha's death, the royal women collaborated to persuade Kamehameha II, Liholiho, to eat in public with them. Under the ancient system, men and women ate in separate *hale*, houses. By persuading the king to eat with them in public, they were challenging the prevailing customs and belief. After this public event, the *kapu* system with its restrictive laws, *kānāwai*, was broken. Its breaking was challenged by the Kekuaokalani, the nephew of and the one entrusted with Kamehameha I's personal god. But after a brief battle between him and Kamehameha II, the temples and idols were destroyed. The system that had sustained the religious and social structure of the islands was abolished permanently in November 1819.

While the people of the islands were in the midst of socio-religious change, the ABCFM was preparing to send its first group of missionaries to Hawai'i. The interest in the islands for missionary activities stemmed from a meeting with a Hawaiian youth, Henry Opukaha'ia, called Obookiah in New England. He had left the islands soon after the death of his parents and arrived in the United States in 1809 on a ship commanded by Captain Brintnall.[3] At a chance meeting at Yale College, the young man was befriended by Edwin W. Dwight.[4] Dwight agreed to teach him to read and write. Eventually, Opukaha'ia lived with Dwight's relative, Dr. Timothy Dwight, who was the president of Yale. In 1810, Opukaha'ia moved into the home of Samuel J. Mills, whose son, also named Samuel, was among the members of the "Haystack Prayer

1. Daws, *Shoal*, 57.
2. Charlot, "A Note," 375.
3. Kuykendall and Day, *Hawaii*, 43.
4. Lyons, "Obookiah," 42.

Meeting," the group that eventually formed the ABCFM.[5] Opukaha'ia, four other young Hawaiians, and others from various regions of the world, entered the Foreign Mission School at Cornwall, Connecticut. The Hawaiian men were being prepared to accompany the first group of missionaries to the Hawaiian Islands. However, Opukaha'ia, who converted and was baptized, died in 1818, about a year before the first group of missionaries left on October 23, 1819. Three of the young Hawaiians joined the first group of missionaries, out of whom Hiram Bingham and Asa Thurston emerged as the group leaders.[6]

Figure 26. Henry Opukaha'ia. Engraving by Daggett, Hinman & Co.
From E. W. Dwight, *Memoir of Henry Obookiah, a Native of the Sandwich Islands*
(New York: American Tract Society, [1831?]), n.p.
Image courtesy of the Congregational Library, Boston.

Because of their interactions with Opukaha'ia and the other Hawaiian men, the missionaries left the shores of New England expecting to convert the Hawaiian people from their pagan belief in gods and goddesses, and to temper their heathen ways. When the group reached Hawai'i, however, they learned that Kamehameha I had died and that the religious system had been abolished by the Liholiho, the successor to the throne. Although the way for evangelization had been cleared,

5. Ibid., 43.
6. Garrett, *To Live*, 37.

Liholiho and the regent *kuhina nui*, Queen Ka'ahumanu, were not eager to embrace another religious tradition. Ka'ahumanu, as *kuhina nui*, served more as the co-regent, reigning with Kamehameha II and later with his successor and brother, Kamehameha III. She exerted great influence, so much so that Kamehameha II made no decision regarding the missionaries until she was available. The decision was made to allow the missionaries to remain for one year on probation, and to require that they split into two groups: the main one to be in Honolulu, and the other one to be in Kailua-Kona on the island of Hawai'i.

Christianity as a religion was not a new phenomenon in the islands because many of the visiting foreign ships had had chaplains aboard. In addition, some Hawaiians had converted to Christianity earlier, such as the governor of O'ahu, Boki, who had been baptized by French chaplains. Yet no prior systematic efforts or group of missionaries, such as the London Missionary Society (which had been active in other Pacific islands), had attempted to convert the Hawaiian people to Christianity. Thus, the missionaries from the ABCFM, with their Second Awakening thrust and their Calvinistic tendencies, established the first Christian mission in the islands. The year-long probation and residence initially allowed by Queen Ka'ahumanu and the king, Liholiho, became the fruitful beginning of several more ABCFM companies of missionaries and the sustainable establishment of Christianity in Hawai'i.

Conversion and the Christianization of Hawaiian society were the main goals of the missionaries, and the strategy by which to attain these was through a two-fold approach, *palapala*, literacy, and *pule*, prayer. The missionaries began the process of converting the Hawaiian oral language into a written form in order to translate the Bible. In their first order of business, the missionaries developed a written form of the language and established schools, primarily for adults. They also lived temperately, built churches, and held regular worship services. They hoped that, by their example, the Hawaiians would be led not only to read and write but also to embrace the Christian lifestyle. Yet in the first years after the establishment of the mission, few persons of consequence in Hawaiian society became actively associated with the Christian religion and its missionary church.

One exception to this was Queen Ke'ōpū'olani. Born about 1778, Ke'ōpū'olani was the highest ranking wife of Kamehameha I because of her parentage.[7] Her status as high chiefess was due to the fact that she was the child from a marriage between a royal brother and sister, and custom held that the greatest *mana*, spiritual power, was derived from this form of marriage. As the highest ranking wife of Kamehameha, she had been carefully guarded and received many honors under the *kapu* system. For example, during one of her illnesses before the abolishment of the *kapu*, human sacrifice had been offered for her recovery.[8] However, despite the privileges she enjoyed as the highest ranking wife of Kamehameha, she had rejected the system that afforded her and her children special status. She had had several children, only three of whom lived to adulthood. Her son, Liholiho, became Kamehameha II, while his brother, Kauikeaouli became Kamehameha III. Her third child was a daughter, Nāhiʻenaʻena, who accompanied her mother when the court was moved from Kailua-Kona to Honolulu.

When the missionaries first visited Kamehameha II, Keʻōpūolani was present in the court. According to her biographer, William Richards, she not only welcomed the missionaries, but also had no reservations about their establishment.[9] Although she supported their arrival and establishment, Keʻōpūolani did not receive formal religion instruction from the missionaries until 1822. By February 1823, she asked for an instructor to remain with her. Taua, a native teacher from the Society Islands who had accompanied William Ellis of the London Missionary Society to Hawaiʻi, became her personal instructor. Taua taught her about Christianity and prayer. As a sign of her conversion, Keʻōpūolani rejected one of her two current husbands, Kalaimoku, and kept only Hoapili as her legitimate spouse.

By the time of the arrival of the second group of missionaries in April 1823, Keʻōpūolani was seriously ill. She moved from Waikiki to Maui and requested that two of the new company join her there. William Richards and Charles Stewart were selected and traveled with her to establish the mission on Maui. She generously contributed to the establishment of the mission by building a worship house, a school house and two houses for the missionaries, and by treating Richards and Stewart as if they were her sons. Within a little more than month after the completion of the house of worship, Keʻōpūolani's health deteriorated rapidly. During her illness,

7. Sinclair, "Sacred Wife," 4.
8. Richards, *Keopuolani*, 6.
9. Ibid., 8.

she was often encouraged by others to give up Christianity. Yet she continued her instruction, admonished others to embrace the Christian way of life, and prayed regularly, even asking others to leave her presence so that she might pray. As her illness progressed, she instructed her family not to follow the mourning traditions of the Hawaiians. She wanted no one to gouge out their eyes or teeth, and she asked to be buried rather than have her bones stripped of flesh and deposited in hiding. She directed that her young son, Kauikeaouli, and her daughter, Nāhiʻenaʻena, receive instruction in Christianity. Furthermore, Keʻōpūʻolani asked to be baptized before she died, which occurred one hour before her death on September 16, 1823. She was the first Hawaiian person of royal birth to be baptized, and she wholeheartedly embraced Christianity as her new religion.

Unlike Keʻōpūʻolani, Queen Kaʻahumanu was not eager to embrace a new god. Nor did she want to adopt the laws and restrictions incumbent in a new belief. Born as early as 1772 or as late as 1777, Kaʻahumanu was the favored wife of Kamehameha I. As his favorite wife, she enjoyed special privileges denied to his other wives and often accompanied him to meet visitors from other nations. As Kamehameha was dying, he appointed her as *kuhina nui*, the regent and co-ruler with Kamehameha II. Because she was older than the new king and had more experience in diplomatic relations, she was the center of political authority, so much so that the missionaries were required to wait until her return from a fishing trip before being approved to remain in the islands. Even though she allowed them to remain, her only interest consisted in learning how to write, *palapala*. One story goes that, as she was playing cards, which the missionaries deplored, Mr. and Mrs. Bingham visited her to present her with a copy of the new spelling book. After they offered to give her instruction, she consented immediately and put aside her card game to learn *palapala*. Upon leaving, Mrs. Bingham invited her to the Sunday services the next day. While Kaʻahumanu did attend, the hope of her conversion was short-lived, for she devoted her efforts to ruling rather than learning more about Christianity.

Within four years, however, her attitude would change. After the king, Liholiho departed the islands to visit Great Britain, Kaʻahumanu began attending services regularly with her husbands, King Kaumualiʻi and Prince Kealiʻiahonua, both of whom she had married to secure the throne of Kamehameha II. Mr. Bingham suspected that her purpose in attending services was not piety but rather other reasons that might advance her role as *kuhina nui*. Soon, though, with the death of her husband, Kaumuali'i, and the defection of Keali'iahonua, Ka'ahumanu began in earnest to study *palapala* and *pule* while on Kaua'i after a revolt. On her return to O'ahu, she knelt at the altar in the church on the next Sabbath.

From that time onward, Ka'ahumanu embraced Christianity, even more so after the death of Liholiho in 1824. She was baptized in 1825, and, as continuing *kuhina nui* for Kamehameha III, she was instrumental in the passing of *kānāwai* to suppress drunkenness, theft, gambling, dancing and violation of the Sabbath. She also encouraged the banishment of the Roman Catholic priests who had arrived in 1827. She felt that the Hawaiian Kingdom should have only one religion—the Christianity of the ABCFM missionaries. When she died in June 1832, she was extolled as one who had rejected the heathen ways and had championed Christianity and the missionaries.

During the waning years of Ka'ahumanu's rule as *kuhina nui* was born Bernice Pauahi Bishop on December 19, 1831. Her father was Abner Paki and her mother, Konia, was the daughter of the first-born son of Kamehameha the Great, Ka'oleioku. When Pauahi was born, she was adopted, *hanai*, by Kina'u, a daughter of Kamehameha the Great. Within the first year of Pauahi's life, Kina'u became the next *kuhina nui* after the death of Ka'ahumanu in 1832. Kina'u, who had been baptized in the same year as Ka'ahumanu, retained many of the stringent laws against immorality that had been supported by ABCFM missionaries, and she trained her adopted daughter, Pauahi, religiously as well as politically. Pauahi continued to live with Kina'u and her sons until Kina'u gave birth to a daughter. She then returned briefly to live with her birth parents but soon entered a school established principally for the children of the *ali'i*. This was the Hawaiian Chiefs' Children's School (HCCS), later called the Royal School. Pauahi and her *hanai* brothers, Lot, Moses, and Alexander, attended and boarded at the school together.

Established in 1839, the HCCS was instituted to educate select *ali'i* children. Kamehameha III, who had been educated by Bingham from the first missionary group, requested that suitable teachers for the children be selected from among the missionaries. While the early thrust of the missionaries had been the education of adults, they began to teach the Hawaiian children and established schools for that purpose.

Many of these schools were open to all children regardless of family status and background, for the missionaries brought with them the ideal of democratic equality. However, since the *ali'i* children, by virtue of their genealogy, were destined to become the monarchs of the future, Kamehameha III and his advisers wanted them educated by the missionaries apart from other children.

Amos Cooke and his wife Juliette Montague were selected as the teachers of the HCCS, even though neither one had extensive experience in educating children or adults. According to George Kanahele, Amos Cooke had worked as a bookkeeper and clerk in a general store in his native New England.[10] Juliette Montague Cooke, however, had taught in a school for nine months before she left for Hawai'i. Hardworking, industrious, steadfast and sincere, the Cookes accepted the position at the HCCS with some misgivings. Mrs. Cooke, in a letter to her sister-in-law, writes "Mr. C told you probably of the new appointment we have as teachers for the Young Chiefs. We do not feel it to be a very desirable situation but very necessary that some one should occupy it as these children would be going to destruction unless someone should take charge of them."[11]

While educating the young *ali'i* was the purpose for establishing the HCCS, the Cookes also felt that the saving of the souls was of primary importance. In the same letter cited above, Juliette Cooke wrote, "May we have assistance from on High and see these young princes converted, and if they are permitted to rule, may they rule in the fear of God."[12] The school's curriculum included daily prayer, reading theology and weekly attendance at Sunday services in addition to other subjects.

The parents of the children at the HCCS treated the Cookes as they would treat anyone who became a *hanai* parent, and they gave the couple the main responsibility for the care of their offspring. In addition, Kamehameha III and the birth parents supplied the funding for the school and provided for the material needs of the children. The children, in essence, were living with the Cookes in the manner of a young person studying with a *kāhuna* in ancient Hawai'i. Under the tutelage of the Cookes, it was hoped, the children would be prepared for the roles they would have in the future as leaders of the Hawaiian kingdom. From

10. Kanahele, *Pauahi*, 19.

11. Richards, *Amos Starr Cooke*, 180.

12. Ibid., 181.

the Cookes' letters and journals, it seems as if one of the favored young people among the sixteen students in their care was Bernice Pauahi.

Pauahi excelled in her studies, and when she was older, assisted with instructing some of the other students. She frequently helped Mrs. Cooke on special occasions and entertained guests when they arrived. In her final years at the HCCS, one of the visitors, Charles Reed Bishop, showed a marked interest in her. Pauahi, who may have been promised in marriage to Lot, was encouraged by the Cookes to consider Bishop as a suitable partner. In one of his letters, Mr. Cooke wrote, "We would much prefer her to take up with such a man than with either of the Princes now absent with Dr. Judd in Europe. In my opinion, they both are unworthy of her."[13] The Cookes supported her decision to marry Bishop despite the opposition of her parents. She married Bishop at the school with the Cookes as witnesses instead of in the presence of her parents, Paki and Konia.

A few years after her marriage, Pauahi and her parents were reconciled. She then moved into the home called Hale'akala. There she held sewing circles, entertained guests, and held meetings for the Stranger's Friend Society for the relief of destitute persons. Although she had friends from other Christian communities, she maintained close ties with the Cookes and the Kawaiaha'o Church, which had been founded by missionaries from the ABCFM. She was received into its communion in July 1867.[14] Perhaps the deed for which Pauahi is most famous is the legacy she left in her will. Having inherited a sizeable amount of land from her parents, and then her cousin, she stipulated in her will that funds from the lands would be used for the purpose of establishing and maintaining a school that would give preference to children of Hawaiian ancestry. In her will she specified that trustees for the school, as well as teachers, must be Protestant, although she did not restrict the selection to any particular Protestant denomination.[15] However, most of the original trustees were missionaries of or related to the ABCFM community. The schools began in the late nineteenth century, with the Boys' School opening in 1887 and the Girls' School in 1894. Each school had a vocational focus, and the one for girls had a course of study similar to that taken by Pauahi at the Hawaiian Chiefs' Children's School in the 1840s.

13. Ibid., 383.
14. Krout, *Hon. Bernice*, 120.
15. King and Roth, *Broken Trust*, 302.

One of Pauahi's fellow students at the HCCS was Emma Rooke. About four years younger than Pauahi, Emma was also descended from the Kamehameha line but more indirectly. The natural daughter of George Nae'a and Fanny Kekelaokalani, she was born on January 2, 1836. Like Pauahi, Emma was adopted, *hanai*, in her case by her mother's sister, Grace, and her husband, Dr. Thomas Rooke. Emma's mothers were the daughters of John Young and Kuamo'o Ka'oana'eha, the niece of Kamehameha the Great. John Young had served as an adviser to Kamehameha during the king's bid to unite the islands. Thus, Kamehameha had arranged for Young's marriage to his niece in gratitude. Emma had the blood of an Englishman as well as the blood of *ali'i* in her veins. Her adoptive father, Dr. Rooke, had been born in Hertford, England. Young Emma was taught the native languages of both of her parents and grew up in a bilingual home. But her contact with other children was limited, partly because she was the only child of the Rookes (who wanted to protect her), and partly because, as an *ali'i* child, her *kapu* status meant that she could have few playmates. Rather than associating with other children, Emma spent much of her early years in the company of her physician father and other adults. Her life changed radically when she began boarding at the HCCS in January 1842, when she was six. She was among the last of the students to board there.

Emma entered the HCCS humbly, accompanied by her father rather than by a retinue of servants (*kahu*). Her humble entrance must have pleased the Cookes, although they seem not to have given her as much approbation as they gave to Pauahi. A few days after Emma's arrival, Mr. Cooke wrote, "She has not yet learned to obey."[16]

There are relatively few journal entries by the Cookes regarding the behavior of Emma during her years at their school. Their opinion of her, however, can be gleaned from Mr. Cooke's letter to his sister in 1855 about the upcoming marriage of Emma and Alexander, who was King Kamehameha IV and one of the Cookes' former students. In the letter, Cooke wrote, "We hear he is to marry Emma Rooke, of English descent, one of our old scholars. She is very pretty and modest, and a suitable wife for a king. Oh, that they might both become Christians."[17] In another letter about Alexander and Emma's upcoming marriage, Cooke wrote, "The latter frequently calls upon us, tho [sic] the former never

16. Richards, *Amos Starr Cooke*, 231.
17. Ibid., 434.

does. We do not covet their intercourse except as far as shall be for their temporal and eternal good."[18]

Emma had remained as a student at the Hawaiian Chiefs' Children's School until the Cookes left it in 1850. She continued her studies with Sarah Von Pfister, a governess whom her parents had employed. Even though Emma had stayed for many years with the Cookes, she did not embrace the Christian faith as propounded by them. Her father and her governess, both Anglicans, were instrumental in developing her Christian faith in that tradition. When she married Alexander Liholiho, King Kamehameha IV, on June 19, 1856 at Kawaiahaʻo Church, the ceremony was Anglican rather than Calvinist. While some may have wondered how an Anglican service could be performed in the Congregationalist church, no one objected.

Efforts had been attempted in previous years to establish the Anglican Church in Hawaiʻi, but nothing had become of them. Anglicans who desired services in their faith relied on chaplains aboard passing ships. Yet, through the efforts of Emma and Alexander, the Anglican Church would be established. On December 5, 1859, Hawaiʻi's minister of foreign affairs wrote on behalf of the king to the Hawaiian consul in London, seeking to establish the Anglican Church in Hawaiʻi, and offering to donate land for the building of an Anglican cathedral. Two years later, after much discussion and many requests, including one to Queen Victoria, Rev. Thomas Nettleship Staley was consecrated on December 15, 1861, as the first Anglican bishop of Hawaiʻi. He reached the islands in October 1862.

Bishop Staley meant as his first order of business to baptize Prince Albert, the child of Emma and Alexander. But the prince, who died before the bishop's arrival, ended up by necessity being baptized by a Congregationalist pastor, Rev. Ephraim Clark, who performed the Anglican rites. At the service, it was not the prince but rather his hitherto unbaptized mother, Emma, who had the honor of being baptized first. Her husband, Alexander, was also baptized. A month later, both were confirmed in full Anglican liturgical celebration with members of the House of Nobles, the royal court, and the consular corps in attendance. The couple received their first communion the following Sunday, the first Sunday of Advent. Within a month after the arrival of Bishop Staley, Queen Emma patronized the beginning of a college for Hawaiian

18. Ibid., 437.

Girls, now known as St. Andrew's Priory. Her husband contributed his private funds for the erection of the school's building. Emma remained a faithful and active member of what became known as the Hawaiian Reformed Catholic Church, even going so far as traveling to England to solicit funding to support the building of St. Andrew's Cathedral.

Of the four royal women discussed in this paper, Queen Emma is the only one who, while embracing Christianity, rejected that form of it as proffered by the missionaries. The others maintained close alliances with not only the Christian faith but also with the missionaries from the ABCFM. Despite the fact that Emma in this scenario is in the minority, she in fact represents much of the reaction by Hawaiians to the missionaries and the rigid Christian lifestyle they supported. It is estimated that, by the mid-1830s, the Native membership in the Christian church led by the missionaries was below one percent.[19] By 1870, fifty years after the initial missionary company had arrived, only about a fourth of the Hawaiian native population were members of the fifty-eight churches established by the missionaries or the native pastors. Gavan Daws indicates that, while the Hawaiian kingdom could be described as Christian, it was due in part to missionaries from other Christian communities, such as Catholics, Mormons and Anglicans.[20] Furthermore, the laws of the land, which the earliest groups of missionaries had influenced, were changing. Dances, theatrical performances, and alcohol consumption eventually were no longer forbidden. An excellent example of the failure of the missionaries to create a Hawaiian society based on particular Christian principles was the restoration of the hula by King David Kālākaua. He, too, had been among the pupils of the Chiefs' Children's School who subsequently rejected the strict upbringing practiced and engendered by the ethical principles of the missionaries.

Marie Gabriel Bosserant d'Anglade, the French consul during the time of Kālākaua, provides a plausible reason for the failure of the missionaries' hope for a civilized Christian society in imitation of their New England style. He writes, "The missionaries were not satisfied merely with inculcating Biblical principles. What they wanted was to change

19. Osorio, *Dismembering*, 19. Low church membership figures can be misleading, because missionaries from the ABCFM maintained extremely strict standards for membership in their churches. As a result, they admitted into membership only a small fraction of the Native Hawaiians who attended church. See Putney, *Missionaries in Hawai'i*, 48–49.

20. Daws, "Decline," 31.

habits and institutions immediately – to destroy the past. They ignored the fact that here was a race already many centuries old, and they did not see that the transformation they were seeking to bring about could be neither abrupt nor radical."[21] The chief failure of the missionaries was their inability to recognize that the nest into which they were attempting to land their brand of Christianity was formed already into its particular shape. The bird's landing was partially successful, but it missed remaining steady and secure.

With the advent of the Hawaiian sovereignty movement in the latter twentieth and early twenty-first centuries, the use of the word "missionary" among the Native Hawaiians began to provoke mixed reactions and feelings. One feeling people have is a deep mistrust and animosity toward anything remotely connected to the missionaries and their descendants. Part of the reason for animosity against the missionaries is that their descendants, such as Lorrin Thurston, the grandson of Asa Thurston who arrived with the first group, planned and executed the overthrow of the Hawaiian nation and its queen in 1893. Although a formal apology was issued in 1993 by the Hawai'i Conference of the United Church of Christ, the successor of the ABCFM mission, it did little to appease many Native Hawaiians who still view the action as illegal and unchristian. In addition, many of the prominent businesses of the twentieth century, such as Castle and Cooke, and Alexander and Baldwin, had been started by either the missionaries or their descendants. These businesses controlled many of the economic conditions in Hawai'i, bringing in immigrants to work in the sugarcane and pineapple fields and controlling other ventures, such as shipping. Non-Native economic and political control of the islands alienated many Native Hawaiians.

Despite the negative viewpoints in Hawai'i toward the missionaries and their descendants, the islands have more adherents to Christianity than to any other religious tradition. The U.S. Census Bureau's 2011 Statistical Abstract National Data Book indicated that 35.6 percent of Hawai'i' s population is Christian.[22] How many of those Christians are Native Hawaiians is not identified, but a study by Kamehameha Schools, *Ka Huaka'i 2005: Native Hawaiian Educational Assessment*, shows that 42.2 percent of Hawaiian families attend religious services regularly.[23]

21. Bosserante, *Tree*, 34.

22. http://www.census.gov/compendia/statab/cats/population/religion.html.

23. Kana'iaupuni, *Ka huaka'i*, 61.

Hawai'i remains largely a Christian state despite the mixed feelings that Native Hawaiians have in regards to the missionaries. Many of those feelings as previously mentioned are negative. But not all Native Hawaiians abhor the missionaries and their descendents. Some prefer instead to admire the missionaries' courage, tenacity, and devotion to God and their mission. The bird did land in its nest, just not as the missionaries had envisioned.

BIBLIOGRAPHY

Bosseront d'Anglade, M.G. *A Tree in Bud: The Hawaiian Kingdom 1889–1893.* Translated by Alfons L. Korn. Honolulu: University of Hawaii Press, 1987.

Charlot, John. "A Note on the Hawaiian Prophecy of Kapihe." *The Journal of Pacific History.* 39, no. 3, (2004): 375–377.

Dana, Robert. "Evangelist or Homemaker? Mission Strategies of Early Nineteenth-Century Missionary Wives in Burma and Hawaii." *International Bulletin of Missionary Research.* 17 Issue 1 (1993): 4–10.

Daws, Gavan. "The Decline of Puritanism at Honolulu in the Nineteenth Century." *The Hawaiian Journal of History* 1 (1967): 31–42.

———. *Shoal of Time: A History of the Hawaiian Island.* New York: Macmillan Company, 1968.

Fornander, Abraham. *Ancient History of the Hawaiian People to the Times of Kamehameha I Originally published as: Volume II: An Account of the Polynesian Race Its Origins and Migrations.* Honolulu: Mutual Publishing, 1996.

Garrett, John. *To Live Among the Stars: Christian Origins in Oceania.* Fiji: Oceania Printers, 1982.

Grimshaw, Patricia. *Paths of Duty: American Missionary Wives in Nineteenth-Century Hawaii.* Honolulu: University of Hawaii Press, 1989.

Handy, E.S. Craighall, et al. *Ancient Hawaiian Civilization: A Series of Lectures delivered at the Kamehameha Schools, Revised Edition.* Rutland, VT: Charles E. Tuttle Co., 1965.

———, and Mary Kawena Pukui. *The Polynesian Family System in Ka'u, Hawai'i.* Wellington, NZ: The Polynesian Society, 1958.

Kanahele, George. *Pauahi: The Kamehameha Legacy.* Honolulu: Kamehameha Schools Press, 1986.

———. *Emma: Hawaii's Remarkable Queen.* Honolulu: The Queen Emma Foundation, 1990.

Kana'iaupuni, S.K., N. Malone and K. Ishibashi. *Ka huaka'i: 2005 Native Hawaiian Educational Assessment.* Honolulu: Kamehameha Schools, Pauahi Publications, 2005.

King, Samuel P. and Randall W. Roth. *Broken Trust: Greed, Mismanagement and Political Manipulation at America's Largest Charitable Trust.* Honolulu: University of Hawaii Press, 2006.

Krout, Mary. *The Memoirs of Hon. Bernice Pauahi Bishop.* Reprint. Honolulu: The Kamehameha Schools Press, 1958.

Kuykendall, Ralph S. *The Hawaiian Kingdom 1854–1874 Twenty Critical Years*. Honolulu: University of Hawaii Press, 1953.

———, and A. Grove Day. *Hawaii: A History from Polynesian Kingdom to American Statehood*. Englewood Cliffs, NJ: Prentice-Hall, 1948.

Langlas, Charles and Jeffrey Lyon. "Davida Malo's Unpublished Account of Keo[set macron over o]pu[set macron over u]olani." *Hawaiian Journal of History*. 42 (2008): 27–48.

Linnekin, Jocelyn. *Sacred Queens and Women of Consequence: Rank, Gender and Colonialism in the Hawaiian Islands*. Ann Arbor: The University of Michigan Press, 1990.

Lyons, Jeffrey K. "Memoirs of Henry Obookiah: A Rhetorical History." *The Hawaiian Journal of History* 2004 38 (2004): 35–57.

Malo, David. *Hawaiian Antiquities: Moʻolelo Hawaiʻi*. translated by Nathaniel B. Emerson. Honolulu: Bernice P. Bishop Museum Press, 1951.

Mellen, Kathleen. *Hawaiian Heritage: A Brief Illustrated History*. New York: Hastings Publishers, 1963.

Osorio, Jonathan. *Dismembering Lāhui: A History of the Hawaiian Nation to 1887*. Honolulu: University of Hawaii Press, 2002.

Potter, Norris, et al. *The Hawaiian Monarchy*. Honolulu: Bess Press, 1983.

Putney, Clifford. *Missionaries in Hawaiʻi: The Lives of Peter and Fanny Gulick, 1797–1883*. Boston: University of Massachusetts Press, 2010.

Rappolt, Miriam E. *Queen Emma: A Woman of Vision*. Kailua: Press Pacifica, Ltd. 1991.

Rezentes, William C. III. *Ka Lama Kukui Hawaiian Psychology: An Introduction*. Honolulu: Aʻaliʻi Books, 1996.

Richards, Mary Atherton. *Amos Starr Cooke and Juliette Montague Cooke: Their Autobiographies Gleaned From Their Journals and Letters*. Reprint. Honolulu: Daughters of Hawaii, 1987.

———. *The Hawaiian Chiefs' Children's School: 1839–1850*. Rutland, VT: Charles E. Tuttle Company Publishers, 1970.

Richards, William. *Memoir of Keopuolani, Queen of the Sandwich Islands*. Missionary Paper, American Board of Commissioners for Foreign Missions no. 12. Boston: Crocker and Brewster, 1835.

Sinclair, Marjorie. "The Sacred Wife of Kamehameha I: Keopuolani." *Hawaiian Journal of History* 5 (1971): 3–23.

Thompson, Katherine Shirley. *Queen Emma and the Bishop. Revised Edition*. Honolulu: Daughters of Hawaiʻi. 1987.

U.S. Census Bureau. *The 2011 Statistical Abstract: National Data Book*. http://www.census.gov/compendia/statab/cats/population/religion.html.

14

"'We will banish the polluted thing from our houses': Missionaries, Drinking, and Temperance in the Sandwich Islands"

Jennifer Fish Kashay

IN JUNE 1836, THE Reverends William Richards and Ephraim Spaulding wrote a temperance report covering the years 1823 to 1835, which they sent to the American Board of Commissioners for Foreign Missions (ABCFM) in Boston. This report detailed the history of drinking and temperance in the Sandwich Islands (Hawai'i), noting that "Missionaries, here, have had the credit of making all the offensive & rigid laws, & thus robbing the poor sailor of his rights & privileges."[1] The Reverends denied this claim, insisting that the "laws, so *grievous* to be borne, have been made & are sustained solely by the civil authority, to whose province they *alone* belong."[2] To those scholars who are familiar with the American mission in Hawai'i, these protestations seem disingenuous at best. The ABCFM evangelists were and are still well known for meddling in the Sandwich Island kingdom's civil affairs. However, the missionaries' concerns about the consumption of alcoholic beverages were more complicated then one might assume. Throughout the 1820s, many members of the mission, including its leader Hiram Bingham, regularly bought and drank hard liquors, wine, and brandy. It was not until January 22, 1830 that the mission's General Meeting draft-

1. Ephraim Spaulding and William Richards, "A brief history of Temperance for twelve years, at three Sandwich Islands, viz. Maui, Molokai & Lanai," to ? at ABCFM, received June 10, 1836, ML, vol. 4, HMCS.

2. Spaulding and Richards, "A brief history," June 10, 1836. ML, vol. 4, HMCS.

ed resolutions with regard to alcoholic beverages, concluding that they would "wholly abstain from the use of ardent spirits of every kind; and that, excepting as a medicine prescribe by a temperate physician, we will banish the polluted thing from our houses."[3] What then motivated this seemingly abrupt turnabout? Both religious and social forces at home in the northeastern United States and social, political, and religious factors in Hawai'i created the momentum that led to the evangelists' embrace of almost total abstinence.

There are numerous monographs and texts that mention drinking in the Sandwich Islands during the early 19th century, as well as the various efforts to stop it. Most allocate only a few pages to the topic.[4] The only article devoted to the subject is Richard A. Greer's 1994 essay on grog shops and hotels in Honolulu.[5] His work does a good job of describing the drinking culture of the port and the political maneuverings of different factions of chiefs, resident foreigners, and missionaries over the issue of drinking and temperance. However, none of the monographs, or Greer's article, analyzes the circumstances and motivations that led the ABCFM's evangelists in Hawai'i to embrace an almost total abstinence from alcohol. Yet, an analysis of these circumstances and motivations are the only way to undermine the common stereotype and simplistic understanding of these missionaries as dour Puritanical combatants of every type of pleasure and diversion. Thus, this essay is meant to complicate our understanding of the ABCFM missionaries in Hawai'i, especially with regard to the subject of drinking and temperance.

A variety of sources provide an understanding of the temperance movement in the United States and the Sandwich Islands and how the ABCFM missionaries in Hawai'i came to embrace it. Secondary sources like W. J. Rorabaugh's, *The Alcoholic Republic*; Paul Johnson's, *A Shop Keeper's Millennium*; and James A. Rohrer's, "The Origins of the Temperance Movement" give a general understanding and knowledge of the social, religious, economic, and political factors that led specific types of individuals and groups in the US to embrace temperance.[6] Likewise, the ABCFM's journals' *The Panoplist* and its later version *The Missionary*

3. GMM, Jan. 22, 1830, HMCS.

4. See Kuykendall, *The Hawaiian Kingdom*, 28, 84, 126, 130, 161–63. Daws, *Shoal of Time*, 68–69, 75–76.

5. Greer, "Grog Shops and Hotels," 35–67.

6. Rorabaugh, *The Alcoholic Republic*. Johnson, *A Shop Keepers Millennium*. Rohrer, "Origins," 228–35.

Herald provide specific essays and sermons either arguing for temperance or reporting on temperance efforts at home and in its missions abroad. In Hawai'i, primary sources such as mission account books, correspondence between the ABCFM and its evangelists, General Meeting minutes and reports, newspapers and periodicals such as *The Hawaiian Spectator* and *The Sandwich Island Gazette and Journal of Commerce*, and correspondence between the evangelists show the drinking habits of the early missionaries, their eventual repudiation of alcoholic beverages, and efforts by various Hawaiians and foreigners to stop or continue drinking alcohol. Finally, along with the previous newspapers, the journals of foreign sojourners and missionaries, and published accounts, biographies, and autobiographies provide varying views of the drinking habits of those at the islands, as well as temperance.[7]

DRINKING IN THE UNITED STATES AND HAWAI'I

The ABCFM missionaries in Hawai'i came mostly from the northeastern United States, especially New England, as did many of the other foreign sojourners in the islands. As such, as successive companies arrived in the 1820s, the evangelists showed themselves to be a part of—as opposed to set apart from—the American drinking culture that has been so well described by W. J. Rorabaugh and other scholars. Alcohol had been a part of American life since the first settlers' colonized Jamestown and New England. The Virginia colonists, Pilgrims, and Puritans brought beer and wine with them on their voyages to the new world, and all colonists generally drank rum, whiskey, and other alcoholic beverages in "huge quantities."[8] Moreover, Puritans, their Congregational and Presbyterian descendants, and early Republic statesmen such as George Washington, Benjamin Franklin, and Thomas Jefferson did not disapprove of imbibing, but rather the excessive use of drink.[9] Both Increase Mather and his son, Cotton, saw wine and rum as a "good creature of God," but thought that too much of either came from Satan, the destroyer of "good [o]rder."[10]

7. Many university libraries have copies of *The Panoplist* and *The Missionary Herald*. I read them at the HLUMH and online at Google Books. *The Hawaiian Spectator*, vols. 1 and 2 can be found at HMCS. *The Sandwich Island Gazette and Journal of Commerce* can be found at HHS.

8. Williams, *Rum*, 62, 69–70. Carlson, "Uneasy About Alcohol," 34.

9. Williams, *Rum*, 70. Carlson, "Uneasy about Alcohol," 34–35. Rorabaugh, *The Alcoholic Republic*, 5–6.

10. Increase and Cotton Mather quotes are found in Williams, *Rum*, 72–73.

Throughout the colonial period and the early republic, Americans viewed various types of alcoholic beverages as both healthful and as an essential medical remedy for a variety of ailments. Americans used rum to warm the body and as a cure for colds, flu, fevers, and the lassitude of the tropics. They also believed that both rum and whiskey served to aid digestion. [11] Thomas Jefferson saw wine as a healthy alternative to whiskey. When speaking of the possibility of a tax on wine, Jefferson declared, "I think it is a great error to consider a heavy tax on wines as a tax on luxury. On the contrary, it is a tax on the health of our citizens." [12] In contrast, Rorabaugh argues that most Americans considered whiskey part of the national heritage, believing it was "healthful because it was made of a nutritive grain, that it was patriotic to drink it because corn was native," and that it had "wholesome, American qualities . . ." [13] Clearly, the missionaries in Hawai'i continued to believe that alcohol had medicinal qualities since its use for this purpose—rather than for communion—was the major exception to their resolution of total abstinence. [14] As if to confirm this, account books show that the mission's medical department ordered 4 ¼ gallons of rum between May 22, 1826 and Dec. 1, 1827. [15]

The evangelists who came to the islands in the early years of the mission did not have a problem with their own personal consumption of "ardent spirits." The mission used a common stock system for supplies and its secular agent, Levi Chamberlain, kept track of purchases and requests in a series of account books. In the early years, Chamberlain kept detailed records, noting requests by individual members of the mission for various items, including alcohol. A sampling of these account books shows that all 11 of the male evangelists ordered alcoholic spirits at least once, and often regularly. Between May 1826 and July 1827, [16] Hiram

11. Williams, *Rum*, ch. 16., Rorabaugh, *Alcoholic Republic*, 113–19.

12. Thomas Jefferson to William H. Crawford, Nov. 10, 1818, in Hailman, *Thomas Jefferson on Wine*, 354.

13. Rorabaugh, *Alcoholic Republic*, 90–91.

14. GMM, Jan. 22, 1830, HMCS.

15. AB23, SIMC, May 22, 1826, Sept. 9, 1826, Dec. 1, 1827, HMCS.

16. The period 1826–27 was chosen because Account Books 23 and 27 provide detailed information about all purchases made by the evangelists, including their names. Other account books often list the names of stations rather than individuals, and often use terms such as "sundries" rather than detailing specific purchases.

Bingham—the mission's leader who was stationed at Honolulu—ordered on separate occasions the following:

qt rum
1 bottle rum
3 pints rum
1 gal[lon] rum
2 bottles port wine
1 gal[lon] wine
1 doz[en] porter, 1 gal[lon] brandy
1 gal[lon] brandy, 2 ½ gal[lons] wine
½ gal[lon] wine
1 qt rum
4 gal[lons] wine
3 ½ gal[lons] rum
2 gal[lons] brandy
2 bottles port wine
2 ½ gall[ons] wine, 3 qts brandy
2 bottles port wine[17]

One does not have to assume that Bingham drank these gallons of wine, brandy, rum and the like all by himself. Undoubtedly being stationed at Honolulu, the center for commerce and trade in the islands, meant that Bingham entertained visiting sea captains and dignitaries. Nonetheless, this is a large amount of alcohol for a fifteen month period. Moreover, Bingham must have had some grand parties since, at times, he ordered large quantities of alcohol very close together. For example, he bought one doz[en] bottles of porter, and a gallon of brandy on Nov. 20, 1826, and five days later on Nov. 25 1826, he purchased one gallon of brandy and two-and-one-half gallons of wine.[18] Was all of the former alcohol consumed before the purchase of the latter? While it is impossible to know for certain, the timing of these purchases seem to prove the assertion.

Bingham's fellow missionaries also made use of alcoholic beverages. A sampling of accounts from 1826 through 1827 includes Elisha Loomis—the mission's printer—who bought various quantities of wine, rum, and brandy on 6 separate occasions and Dr. Abraham Blatchely,

17. AB23, SIMC, May 15, 1826; June 17, 1826; July 24, 1826; Sept. 26, 1826; Nov. 8, 1826; Nov. 20, 1826; Nov. 25, 1826; Mar. 15, 1827; Apr. 13, 1827; May 2 to Aug. 8, 1827, HMCS. AB27, SIMC, Dec. 6, 1826; July 7, 1827, HMCS.

18. AB23, SIMC, Nov. 20 1826 and Nov. 25, 1826, HMCS.

who received two quarts of rum on July 7, 1826 and four gallons of brandy, one-half gallon of rum, and two gallons of gin on November 6th of that same year.[19] Sometimes, Chamberlain recorded purchases by station rather than by name. For example, during the same period he sent the evangelists on Kaua'i nine quarts of brandy and one gallon of wine, and to Waiakea,[20] a total of thirteen quarts of rum, two gallons of brandy, fifteen bottles of wine, and two bottles of port for "MG" and "MR," presumably Mr. Joseph Goodrich and Mr. Samuel Ruggles.[21]

Whether the missionaries' use of ardent spirits was excessive is a matter of opinion. Rorabaugh shows in 1820 that per capita Americans consumed four point seven gallons of spirits, two gallons of wine, fifteen gallons of cider for a total of three point six gallons of pure alcohol. By 1830, the total of pure alcohol had risen to three point nine gallons.[22] Of course, these statistics include women and children, who mostly did not consume hard liquor and, for children, wine. Presumably, then, men drank much more than these statistics indicate. While we cannot know how much of the alcohol bought by the male evangelists was imbibed by them or their family members, the above numbers indicate that their drinking habits fit well within the drinking patterns found in the United States.

If most of the evangelists in the Sandwich Islands drank alcoholic beverages regularly, most of the other foreign sojourners drank them prodigiously.[23] Since Captain James Cook's so-called discovery of the Sandwich Islands in 1778, Europeans, Americans, and other foreigners had been visiting the islands to resupply their ships in the China trade, and some had taken up residence permanently. According to one visitor "Most of the[se] agents at the Sandwich Islands divide the 24 hours into three parts, Drinking, Gambling and Sleeping."[24] Alcohol helped ease the boredom of island life. Almost all social occasions involved drinking as men imbibed at dinner parties, while they played cards and other

---

19. For Loomis's purchases see AB23, SIMC, May 22, 1826; June 17, 1826; Jan. 1, 1827, Jan. 6, 1827; Jan. 22, 1827; Jan. 22, 1827. For Blatchely see Ibid., July 7, 1826 and Nov. 6, 1826.

20. Waiakea was the mission station at Hilo on the Big Island.

21. AB28, SIMC, 1826–1827, HMCS.

22. Rorabaugh, *Alcoholic Republic*, Table A1.1, 232.

23. Kuykendall, *Hawaiian Kingdom*, 161–62.

24. Dixie Wildes to Josiah Marshall, MLB, March 15, 1824, HHS.

games, or bet on races. Most of all, they drank in the seedy grog shops that lined the harbors of Honolulu and Lāhainā. As two missionaries noted, "The only standard acknowledged here . . . [is] if a man keeps sober enough to walk upon a straight line, or toe the mark in business, he does well."[25]

As in America, alcohol consumption often had serious consequences. It caused mutinous behavior among ship crews, led some sailors to desert their posts, and in too many cases resulted in violence. For example, in March 1824, a number of whale shipmasters formed a temperance society specifically due to the "sweeping and desolating contagion which . . . breeds mutiny among crews. . . ."[26] Or consider the case of the British Captain, Lord Byron. On June 6, 1825, he endeavored to impress the islanders by parading his men in front of them. Instead, during the drill, one of his men, "gloriously Drunk[,]" threw down his musket and refused to "exercise no more for anyone."[27] Desertion also proved a constant problem for the captains who lay over at the islands. No doubt, alcohol gave many a deserter the necessary courage to abandon his duties as when on July 21, 1816, "6 or 7 sailors of the ship *Atala*, left on account of drunkenness [sic] . . ."[28]

Sometimes the consequences of the over consumption of liquor proved even worse. Moreover, combat did not remain the sole provenance of the common seamen. For example, fighting often broke out when intoxicated seamen encountered their rivals from other ships among the harbor dives as on September 5, 1814 when a number of soused sea captains took part in a drunken altercation. Or consider the battle between two inebriated crews of sailors described by John Colcord:

> this time in a midnight revel some men belonging to the Ship Daniel 4th of London were going on board their Ship [and] were hailed by some officers on board the American Brig Convoy[.]

25. Spaulding and Richards, "A Brief History," received June 10, 1836, copied from their journals, September 13, 1824, ML, vol. 4, HMCS.

26. Spectator, "Good Devised," BC, March 31, 1824, HHS.

27. Reynolds, "Journal," June 6, 1825, in King, ed., *Journal*, 94. Lord Byron had come to the islands to return the bodies of Kamehameha II and his queen—who died on a visit to King George—to their homeland. See also, Marin, "Journal," July 21, 1816, in Gast, *Marin*, 220.

28. Marin, "Journal," July 21, 1816, in Gast, *Marin*, 220. See also, Marin, September 11–12, 1814, in Gast, *Marin*, 213. John C. Jones to Henry Clay, July 8 [?], 1826, July 1, 1827, ACL.

The men thought themselves. . . [safe] & gave a saucy answer.
Stephens, Joiner & Perkins were the names of the three Mates
who jumped into the Convoy's boat & gave chase to the men
in the Ship Daniel's boat. A Battle Ensued. One of the men was
beaten & thrown overboard & next morning was found lying
across one of the Ships Cables. Drowned.[29]

Not only did they fight with one another, but drunken sailors also
fought with their Hawaiian hosts. For example, on December 15, 1815,
drinking resulted in a brawl that included more than a thousand Hawaiians
and a smaller number of foreigners. Similarly, on October 31, 1823, a quarrel broke out at Jean Rives' grog shop between intoxicated mariners and
some Sandwich Islanders. The Hawaiians showered the white men with
stones as they fled into the water towards their vessel. After this incident,
the chiefs shut down the notorious dive. Yet, it hardly put a dent in the
liquor traffic among the grog ships that lined Honolulu harbor.[30]

The fighting that accompanied alcohol consumption was common
among western sailors throughout the world. In American, British, and
European ports, authorities endeavored to contain such activities by limiting shore leave and preventing drinking on board ship. However, in the
Sandwich Islands, no structure existed to deal with the excessive drinking and riotous behavior of foreigner visitors, and brawling occurred
on a much larger scale. Until the arrival of Captain Cook, alcohol was
unknown to the Hawaiians. Although they had their own form of intoxi-
cant made from the *ti* root, it did not cause the same aggressive behavior
that spirits did. From the 1790s through the mid-1820s, the Hawaiian
chiefs were at a loss as how to cope with the problem. Increasingly, the
riotous actions of westerners undermined the Hawaiian social order.
For their part, the small expatriate community and visiting seamen
remained undisturbed by the violence and upheaval that periodically
disrupted their lives.[31]

29. Colcord, "Journal," [November 22 or 23, 1826] 9, HSA. See also, Reynolds,
"Journal," November 23, 1826, in King, ed., *Journal,* 165.

30. Marin, "Journal," September 5, 1814, December 10, 1815, in Gast, *Marin,* 213,
218. See also Marin, September 25, 1821, in Gast, *Marin,* 256 and Reynolds, "Journal,"
August, 7, 1826, in King, ed., *Journal,* 146. Various Authors, SIMJ, October 31, 1823,
HMCS.

31. Stark notes that the British navy gave a liquor ration that included grog (rum
mixed with water, lime, or lemon juice) and a half-pint rum ration. She also points
out that the Admiralty halved the half-pint ration in 1824. Stark, *Female Tars,* 173.
Similarly, Byrn contends that just because the British Admiralty acquiesced to the tra-

The white foreign residents were not alone in their drinking. Both Kamehameha II (Liholiho) and Kamehameha III (Kauikeaouli) drank prodigiously. While some high chiefs saw an alliance with the ABCFM missionaries as a pathway to increased power, both Liholiho and Kauikeaouli preferred the foreign residents' alcohol and amusements to the Christians' religious services, schools, and general decorum. Both Kings found it difficult to deal with the massive cultural transformation that had occurred as a result of foreign incursion and the 1819 "over-throw" of the *kapu*, or religious, system that previously had supported the King's (*Mōʻī*'s) power. As a result, they dealt with the stress of the on-going situation by drinking inordinate amounts of alcohol. The ABCFM missionaries and other western visitors to the islands often noted that Liholiho spent most of his time in a state of inebriation, creating confusion wherever he went. For example, on February 7, 1821, missionary wife Maria Sartwell Loomis pointed out, "This *poor King* has left his book for his bottle & for a number of months past has hardly been free from intoxication."[32] Often describing the *Mōʻī* as "crazy with liquor," she concluded, "We are in need of rulers, but do not regret his departure, for all is confusion while he stays."[33] In fact, usually, as many as one hundred chiefs and, perhaps, commoners formed a noisy and disorderly train that followed Liholiho on his drunken escapades around the islands. On one such occasion, the King sailed to Kauaʻi where he reported to the missionary Samuel Whitney that he had been inebriated for twenty-five days in a row. The *Mōʻī* also told Whitney that "he had got drunk and run away."[34]

Likewise, Kauikeaouli had a severe drinking problem. As a child, Kamehameha III took part in the drinking, gambling, and other amuse-

---

ditional drinking rights of seamen, it did not mean they condoned drunkenness. After 1756, regulations emphasized that officers should give sailors watered-down alcohol and that officers should prevent the smuggling of liquor on board ship. Furthermore, the Admiralty prosecuted seamen for intoxication. However, they considered sailors inebriated only when they could no longer perform their duties. Byrn, Jr., *Crime and Punishment in the Royal Navy*, 131. These rations probably did not have the same effect as the unwatered alcohol that sailors drank in the grogshops of Lāhainā and Honolulu.

32. M. Loomis, "Journal," February 7, 1821, HMCS.

33. M. Loomis, March 10, 1821, January 1, 1822, February 22, 1822, HMCS.

34. S. Whitney, "Journal," January 28, 1822, HMCS. Marin notes Kamehameha II as being drunk on a number of days, including February 6, 1820, March 10, 1820, May 20–23, 1821, March 1, 1822, etc. Marin, "Journal," in Gast, *Marin*, 247–48, 250–51, 262. S. Whitney, "Journal," January 28, 31, 1822, HMCS.

ments of the resident foreign population.[35] By the time he reached adulthood in the early 1830s, he was a full blown alcoholic. The Christian chiefs and missionaries tried to rein in his behavior, but the foreign population egged him on. As a way of rebelling, periodically the King went on spectacular drinking binges, and just like his brother surrounded by a retinue of hundreds who followed his lead. These episodes caused chaos, and a great deal of consternation for the ABCFM evangelists and the Christian chiefs who had formed an alliance with them.

Obviously, it did not take long for the ABCFM's missionaries to understand that excessive drinking not only undermined the social order and civil authority in the islands, but also their efforts to convert the Hawaiians to Christianity. For example, on September 10, 1824, one of the missionaries—probably the Rev. William Richards—wrote, "Hoapili Wahine's school is all *drunk* & *broken* up—no hope of reorganizing"[36] The next day he went on to complain, "*There is no restraint by principle, law or* modesty, & all expostulation & entreaty are equally vain. And all this evil is the result of their intercourse with foreigners."[37] Incidences such as this convinced the evangelists that if they were to convert the populace, they must win over the King and high chiefs (*ali'i nui*) first. The commoners followed the example of the chiefs, and if the *ali'i nui* drank excessively and ignored the overtures of the missionaries, so would they.

What occurred, then, was a constant war between the evangelists and most of the other resident foreigners for the hearts, minds, and bellies of the chiefs. For example, on March 24, 1822, resident traders endeavored to lour Kamehameha II away from the missionaries' worship service with promises of food and wine.[38] In that instance, their ploy did not work, but more often than not the foreign community found success.

---

35. Reynolds, "Journal," January 21, 1831, HHS. Levi Chamberlain to Jeremiah Evarts, September 11, 1826, ML, vol. 2, HMCS. Reynolds, "Journal," May 24, 26, 1828, in King, ed., *Journal*, 228. Chamberlain to Evarts, September 11, 1826, ML, vol. 2, HMCS. In 1824, Ka'ahumanu and the other chiefs had given Boki his position as guardian because the chief's trip to London with Liholiho had given him great *mana*. Later, they may have regretted their decision, since Boki became the leader of those who opposed the Christian chiefs and their missionary supporters.

36. Spaulding and Richards, "A brief history," June 10, 1836, ML, vol. 4, HMCS. Spaulding and Richards, "A brief history," June 10, 1836, ML, vol. 4, HMCS.

37. Spaulding and Richards, "A brief history," June 10, 1836, ML, vol. 4, HMCS.

38. Various Authors, SIMJ, Mar. 24, 1822, HMCS.

Even Kāmamalu, Liholiho's favorite wife, recognized that his drinking undermined the missionaries' "good influence": according to the Queen, the commoners imitated his example when he "gets drunk, disregards the Sabbath, neglects instruction, & does wickedly."[39] Excessive alcohol use therefore directly impacted the ability of the evangelists to fulfill their mission. Nonetheless, it would take a combination of social and religious forces at home in the United States, as well a the social, religious, and political realities in the islands to force them to give up their own consumption of alcohol and make their declaration of total abstinence.

THE TEMPERANCE MOVEMENT
IN THE UNITED STATES AND HAWAI'I

Scholars who study the American temperance movement situate its origins in the first three decades of the 19th century, pointing out that it coincided with the Second Great Awakening. According to James A. Rohrer, the early movement centered in the northern and western counties of New England and radiated outwards. Regardless of class, evangelicals expressed great concern that ardent spirits undermined self control, threatened families, and lured young people from the fold of evangelical families. In the decade before 1815, evangelicals' perceptions of liquor changed from an acceptance of moderate use to its condemnation. During this time, Methodists and Quakers began to enforce their own bans on liquor and New Light Presbyterian and Calvinists took on leading roles in transforming their followers' perceptions of ardent spirits.[40] W. J. Rorabaugh asserts that a number of "reformed-minded ministers" launched the anti-liquor campaign in 1810. He associates the beginnings of temperance with evangelical Calvinists and the founding of Andover Theological Seminary. He notes that it was after a Monday night meeting at the seminary that Jeremiah Evarts began writing a series of strongly worded antiliquor articles in *The Panoplist*.[41] In contrast, in areas outside of New England, the temperance movement may have started later. Paul Johnson contends that in upstate New York, the

---

39. Various Authors, SIMJ, October 11, 1823, HMCS.

40. Rohrer, "Origins," 229–30.

41. Rorabaugh, *Alcoholic Republic*, 191.

"temperance question was nonexistent in 1825. Three years later it was a middle-class obsession."[42]

Evangelical churches thus took the lead in the fight against intemperance.[43] The ABCFM's mouthpiece, *The Panoplist*—later called *The Missionary Herald*—provides plenty of evidence for this so-called war, and for changing ideas about the place of alcohol in the ministry and the orthodox church. In particular, the September 1812 issue presented reports and resolutions from the most prominent religious organizations and religious reformers in the Northeast. Beginning in 1811, the General Association of Massachusetts—the ministerial body that founded the ABCFM—called for a committee to study the issue of intemperance. This group cooperated with working groups of the General Assembly of the Presbyterian Church and the General Association of Connecticut, and also communicated with a similar association in New York.[44] In 1812, Ezra Stiles Ely, Secretary of the General Assembly of Presbyterian Churches, reported that his committee resolved that it be

> earnestly recommended to all the ministers and elders in the Presbyterian church to abstain entirely from the use of ardent spirits themselves, and in their families; to refrain from offering them to friends; and to exclude them from all their judicatories and ecclesiastical meetings; excepting always, however, from this recommendation, those cases in which ardent spirits may be necessary as a medicine.[45]

This sounds similar to the statement issued by the members of the Hawaiian mission 18 years later. In the same issue, Samuel Worcester and Jeremiah Evarts wrote a report for the temperance committee in New Hampshire, pointing in particular to the vast amount of money spent on hard liquor "without any possible advantage, and thus exhibit

---

42. Johnson, *A Shop Keeper's Millennium*, 55.

43. Rohrer argues that beginning in 1812, the "Connecticut General Association of Congregational Churches and the General Assembly of the Presbyterian Church initiated a war against intemperance." Rohrer, "Origins," 230.

44. The meetings of these different groups led to the establishment of the Massachusetts Society for the Suppression of Intemperance in 1813. E.C. Tracy, *Memoir*, 75–76. "Report on the Intemperate Use of Spirituous Liquors," *The Panoplist and Missionary Magazine*, vol. 5, no. 4, September 1812, 183–84, HLUHM.

45. Ezra Stiles Ely, "To the Chairman of the Committee appointed by the General Association of Massachusetts for the suppression of intemperance, etc.," *Panoplist*, vol. 5, no. 4, 184.

an example which serves to lead others into a course of evil habits."[46] They asserted further that it was the duty of every minister to examine the subject in the pulpit and to "*abstain even from the appearance of evil*" when it came to drinking.[47]

It is important to note that not only did they work as temperance crusaders, but Samuel Worcester and Jeremiah Evarts held prominent roles in the ABCFM and other religious and reform organizations in New England. Worcester was elected Corresponding Secretary of the ABCFM in 1810. Evarts served as Treasurer from 1811–1820 and Corresponding Secretary from 1821 until his death in 1831.[48] Evarts helped organize the Massachusetts Bible Society, and served as a manager of the American Bible Society, a committee member of the Connecticut Education Society, and as a Vice President of the American Education Society. Furthermore, he wrote frequently against the evils of slavery and supported prison reform.[49] Both Worcester and Evarts were officers of the Massachusetts Missionary Society and worked on its periodical, *The Massachusetts Missionary Magazine*.[50] Evarts served as the editor (1805–20) of the journal, and continued to do so when it merged with *The Panoplist*, and eventually *The Missionary Herald*. These men proved to be ardent temperance crusaders, leaders in the missionary movement, and dedicated social reformers.

Surely the evangelists in Hawai'i were aware of the temperance movement at home, and the views of individuals and religious organizations about the subject. When a student at Andover Theological Seminary in 1816, Hiram Bingham walked to the offices of *The Panoplist* in Boston to obtain a subscription for The Female Charitable Society, clearly demonstrating that he was familiar with the publication.[51] The next year, Samuel Worcester gave a sermon at Salem, Massachusetts titled, "The Drunkard a Destroyer" that later was published in pam-

---

46. Samuel Worcester and Jeremiah Evarts, New York, Jan. 22, 1812, *Panoplist*, vol. 5, no. 4, 185.

47. Worcester and Evarts, *Panoplist*, vol. 5, no. 4, 186.

48. J Tracy, *History*, 30. Maxfield, *The Formation*.

49. Tracy, *Memoir*, 79–91.

50. *Constitution of the Massachusetts Society for the Suppression of Intemperance and Report of the Board of Counsel, May 28, 1813*.

51. Hiram Bingham to parents, Nov. 27, 1816, in Miller, *Selected Writings*, 75.

phlet form.[52] In 1818, while Bingham and his future colleague, Asa Thurston, were at Andover, the Rev. W. Coggswell gave a sermon called "Observations on the evil effects produced by spirituous liquors" in Dedham, Massachusetts that was later issued as a pamphlet by the New England Tract Society.[53] As active members of the evangelical community, Bingham, Thurston, and the other male members of the Hawaiian mission must have read the ABCFM journal's temperance articles and reports that continued to be published regularly and vociferously in the years after 1812.[54] At least some of them had to be aware of Worcester's and Coggswell's sermons and the other temperance literature that circulated throughout the Northeast.[55]

The fact that most of the male evangelists were acquainted with either or both Samuel Worcester and Jeremiah Evarts might lead one to suspect that they were aware of the two men's position on the consumption of ardent spirits. In 1819 before his departure for the Sandwich Islands, Bingham corresponded regularly with Worcester. Whether they spoke about temperance is unknown: Bingham's correspondence does not indicate that they did. But how could the newly ordained minister

52. National Temperance Society and Publication House, *A Hundred Years of Temperance*, 231.

53. National Temperance Society and Publication House, *A Hundred Years of Temperance*, 231. Similarly, the Rev. William Richards graduated from Williams College in 1819 and Andover Theological Seminary in 1822. He too should have been aware of these and other temperance sermons, pamphlets, tracts, and journal articles. Williston, *William Richards*, 7–9.

54. For some examples, see Z.X.Y., "On the Ruinous Effects of Ardent Spirits," *The Panoplist and Missionary Magazine*, vol. 12, no. 5, May 1813, 536–38; Z.X.Y., "On the Gradual and Insidious Progress of Intemperance," Ibid., vol. 9, no. 3, August 1813, 97–103; A.B., "Caution Against Promoting Intemperate Drinking," Ibid., vol. 12, no. 10, Oct. 1816, 460–62; F., "Intemperance. An Allegory.," Ibid., vol. 13, no. 5, May 1817, 207–10. In the early 1820s, there were almost no temperance articles and reports in *The Missionary Herald*, perhaps because Worcester and other temperance crusaders were publishing temperance tracts and sermons under the auspices of the New England Tract Society, the Massachusetts Society for the Suppression of Intemperance, and other temperance organizations. For a list of temperance literature, see Appendix A, *One Hundred Years of Temperance*, 230–38. See also, *Report of the Board of Counsel*, June, 1820 and Sprague, *Address Delivered*. From 1825 onward, *The Missionary Herald* began to publish articles on the ill effects of drinking and the temperance movement more frequently.

55. For a list of temperance literature from the 1760s through the 1830s, see Appendix A, National Temperance Society and Publication House, *One Hundred Years of Temperance*, 230–38, Google Books.

about to embark on a mission not know of Worcester's views concerning the clergy and the consumption of hard liquor?[56] All of the first company of missionaries to the Sandwich Islands met Worcester and Evarts at Park Street Church in Boston where they were given their orders and organized into a mission church before their departure.[57] Furthermore, after their arrival in the Sandwich Islands, the male evangelists corresponded with both Evarts and Worcester frequently.[58] Undoubtedly Hiram Bingham, Levi Chamberlain, Asa Thurston, Elisha Loomis, and the others understood the position of Worcester, Evarts, the Presbyterian church, and various temperance societies of their homeland on the evils of ardent spirits, the unnecessary expense of their purchase of it, and the negative example they gave when they indulged in alcoholic beverages. Yet, the disapprobation of these individuals and groups were not enough to stop the Sandwich Island missionaries from drinking.

If thousands of miles away from the islands back home in New England, the gathering social and religious forces that waged war against intemperance were not enough to persuade the missionaries in Hawai'i to give up drinking, what could have caused them to finally make that decision? The evangelists' rivalry with other resident foreigners for social and political power—and for the allegiance of the *ali'i nui*—served as a large inducement to embrace temperance. As noted earlier, both the missionaries and the foreign merchants vied for the friendship of the King and high chiefs as a means of power and the achievement of their goals. The missionaries' goal was obvious: they wanted to "civilize" and

56. Hiram Bingham to Rev. Samuel Worcester, April 28, 1819, May 11, 1819, July 16, 1819, etc. in Miller, *Selected Writings*, 85–104. Bingham also corresponded with Jeremiah Evarts before his departure to the Sandwich Islands. As with Worcester, there is no evidence that they discussed the temperance movement. Hiram Bingham to Jeremiah Evarts, Aug. 31, 1819, in Miller, *Selected Writings*, 106–10.

57. Thurston, *Life and Times*, 14.

58. It should be noted that the ABCFM missionaries in Hawai'i corresponded regularly with Samuel Worcester until his death in 1821. A sampling of letters written by the male missionaries to Samuel Worcester and Jeremiah Evarts, includes, Hiram Bingham to Samuel Worcester, May 13, 1820, in Miller, *Selected Writings*, 169–75. Joint letter from Bingham, Thurston, Ruggles, Chamberlain, and Loomis to Sam. Worcester, Corresponding Sec. of the ABCFM, July 6, 1821; Joint letter from Bingham, Ruggles, and Whitney to S. Worcester, Oct. 11, 1821; Joint letter from Bingham, Chamberlain, Thurston, Loomis to the Prudential Com. ABCFM, Nov. 25, 1821, ML, vol. 1, typescript copy, HMCS. Bingham, Thurston, Chamberlain, and Loomis to Jeremiah Evarts, Treasurer ABCFM, February 1, 1822, ML, vol. 1, HMCS.

Christianize the islanders. On the other hand, the local foreign residents wanted to do what they pleased without interference from the evangelists or the chiefs. This meant drinking, gambling, making money, and indulging in other forms of amusement.

In many ways, the fight over alcohol symbolized the divergent goals of the two contending groups of foreigners. It certainly became a point of contention between the two rival groups fairly quickly. Sea captains, sailors, and traders consumed large amounts of spirits while in the Sandwich Islands, and the missionaries greatly disapproved of their excesses. Referring to the foreign community's use of ardent spirits, the mission's printer, Elisha Loomis—who had no problem with his own drinking—commented that "it is a grief to see that most white men . . . are in league with this 'enemy of righteousness.'"[59] When a number of western men literally drank themselves to death, the evangelists became enraged because some of the white residents celebrated the lives of these deceased drunkards. For example, after Captain William Heath Davis died from alcoholism, his "companions in wickedness" attended his funeral "with great pomp and [extolled] his character . . . to the skies . . ."[60] In turn, the ABCFM evangelists angered the expatriate community when they lectured the dead man's friends about the evils of intemperance during a Sunday sermon. The white men had attended services mostly out of boredom, but during one particular oration that focused on the circumstances of Davis's death, the offended hearers "turned their backs upon the worship of God & left the house."[61] Similarly, after the Reverend Asa Thurston preached a sermon on "the evils of intemperance" that offended the traders, the U.S. Agent for Commerce, John Coffin Jones, and several other residents set up their own alternative Sunday service.[62] On another occasion, a drunken Frenchman actually interrupted Sunday worship and later bothered the evangelists at the mission house. This incident caused one of the missionaries to exclaim, "More impropriety has been hitherto exhibited at our Church by white men than by the natives; & much more settled, obvious, violent, & deadly opposition to the Gospel has been manifested by a considerable proportion of the

59. Elisha Loomis, "Journal," April 16, 1820, in Gulick, *The Pilgrims of Hawaii*, 81.

60. William Ellis to Tyerman and Bennet, February 18, 1823, LMSC, HMCS.

61. Various Authors, SIMJ, December 1, 1822, HMCS.

62. Ellis to Tyerman and Bennet, February 23, 1823, LMSC, HMCS. See also, Various Authors, SIMJ, December 1, 1822, HMCS.

whites than we have yet perceived in the whole nation of the Sandwich Islands."[63] Obviously, drinking only increased the tension between the merchant and missionary factions.[64]

At this juncture, the Calvinists clearly comprehended the negative influence of the white men on the Hawaiians. They pointed out that "hundreds of untaught natives witness[ed] the actions of unrestrained lust, the wild & wicked vagaries—the shameless & sinful impurities of debauched, profane, *inebriated whites*, who proudly call themselves *christians* [sic] . . ."[65] They believed the foreigners especially endangered Kamehameha II and pleaded that American Christians pray for the King who had been ensnared by white men that "countenance[d] the grossest excesses by those whose birth and education ought to have furnished them with better principles[,] who are lovers of pleasures & of gain more than love of God."[66] Gradually, the drinking, gambling, and amusements of the other whites came to occupy more and more of the missionaries' attention, leading the clergymen to question whether their civilizing mission should include members of their own race. Yet if drinking and its consequences meant that white residents were in need of "civilization" just as much as the Hawaiians, how could evangelists like Loomis criticize their compatriots when they drank liquor as well? How could the missionaries continue to buy alcohol and imbibe without seeming like hypocrites?

Perhaps the missionaries' hypocrisy became more evident because some of the *ali'i nui* whom they had converted showed themselves to be ardent crusaders against all kinds of vice, including intemperance. In particular, Hoapili, the Governor of Maui, fought a vigorous war against drunkeness. Beginning in 1826, Governor Hoapili tabooed the manufacture, sale, and use of alcohol on Maui, Moloka'i, and Lana'i, punishing those who were caught by imposing fines or other penalties on the offenders. According to the ministers William Richards and Ephraim Spaulding, Hoapili went so far as to fine a "man of some distinction" twenty picals of sandalwood, worth $160, for selling a single bottle of

63. Ellis to Tyerman and Bennet, September 7, 1823, LMSC, HMCS.

64. On the death of Captain Lewis from drinking, see M. Loomis, "Journal," November 26, 1822. For the death of Oliver Holmes, see Levi Chamberlain to Jeremiah Evarts, August 27, 1825, ML, vol. 2, HMCS.

65. First set of italics mine. Various Authors, SIMJ, December 17, 1821, HMCS.

66. Various Authors, SIMJ, December 30, 1821.

alcohol.[67] Sailors and seamen responded to the Governor's temperance restrictions with "violence & rage," claiming that their "rights & privileges" had been denied, while other foreigners smuggled liquor or sold spirits in "*secret, transient, walking grogshop[s]*."[68] Nevertheless, the Governor remained firm in his resolve to keep liquor out of the areas that he ruled.

Interestingly, despite Governor Hoapili's ban on the use of alcohol, between August 7, 1826 and January 8, 1828, the mission's secular agent, Levi Chamberlain sent to the mission station at Lāhainā, on separate occasions

> 2 gallons of Madeira wine
> 2 ½ gals of rum
> 1 ½ pints of rum
> 1 ½ pints of rum
> 2 bottles of rum[69]

The Reverend William Richards and his wife Clarissa had been stationed at Lāhainā since 1823. It was Richards who in 1824 had so vigorously denounced the foreigners for their bad influence on the Hawaiians when it came to drinking. In fact, he had concluded that if Satan had "any weapon of his more powerful than all others, it is intoxicating drink."[70] Yet, somehow Richards had the gall to ignore Hoapili's taboo on alcohol. Were these many gallons of rum and wine used solely for medicinal purposes? It seems unlikely. Did Richards's own sense of Christian superiority make him think that he could resist Satan's "weapon" when others, i.e. Hawaiians, merchants, and sailors could not? Why would someone who worked so hard to impose Christian morality on others refuse to live as the kind of example of which his superior at the

67. Spaulding and Richards, "A brief history," received June 10, 1836, ML, vol. 4, HMCS. Likewise, a report in *The Missionary Herald* notes that in December 1828, Hoapili fined a man who sold a bottle of rum $200. Although the article does not specify the race of the man, he was most likely white. "Sentence of a Sandwich Island Governor," *The Missionary Herald*, vol. 25, no. 8, August 1829, 261, Google Books.

68. Spaulding and Richards, "A brief history," received June 10, 1836, ML, vol. 4, HMCS.

69. AB23, Aug. 7, 1826, Nov. 20, 1826, Jan. 20, 1828; AB27, July 7, 1827; AB28, no date, SIMC, HMCS.

70. Excerpt from Richards's journal, September 11, 1824, in Richards and Spaulding, "A brief history," received June 10, 1836, ML, vol. 4, HMCS.

ABCFM, Jeremiah Evarts, had insisted upon?[71] Moreover, there is no evidence that Governor Hoapili fined Richards for breaking the taboo as he had the "man of some distinction." Did the clergyman hide his stash of alcohol from the Governor? If so, maybe at some point Richards thought that all of this secrecy was just too much.

Other high chiefs also endeavored to outlaw liquor. As early as December 1823, Kaumualiʻi, the high chief who governed Kauaʻi, had sent a crier around the island forbidding the distillation and drinking of ardent spirits.[72] In 1828, the missionary Peter Gulick noted the chiefs continued to keep the commoners from drinking alcohol on the island of Kauaʻi.[73] In 1825, on the island of Hawaiʻi, the Reverend Artemas Bishop reported that "Drunkness [sic] is suppressed by law and a heavy fine imposed upon the transgressor. In my whole [preaching] tour I saw but one man intoxicated, whereas two years since it was a most common thing to see whole villages given up to intemperance."[74] While the *aliʻi nui* on other islands found success, at Honolulu on Oahu it proved much more difficult to restrict drinking. Periodically, various Christian chiefs tried to enforce anti-liquor taboos, but their efforts were undermined by Kamehameha III, the resident foreign merchants, and the other high chiefs who belonged to the anti-missionary faction.[75] It was much easier for the high chiefs to control the Hawaiian common people and the relatively few foreigners at the more remote islands than the foreign residents and visiting sailors at the busy port of Honolulu.

71. I would point out that this was not the only instance when the Reverend William Richards's actions contradicted the "civilized" behavior that he and the other missionaries insisted that the Hawaiians embrace. In "Competing Imperialisms and Hawaiian Authority: The Cannoning of Lāhainā in 1827, I point out that it was Richards who insisted that Governor Hoapili release Captain Elisha Clarke, whom Hoapili had taken prisoner because he and his men had violated the taboo on prostitution. See Jennifer Fish Kashay, "Competing Imperialisms and Hawaiian Authority: The Cannoning of Lāhainā in 1827," *Pacific Historical Review*, 77, 3, 2008, 369–90.

72. Artemas Bishop, "Journal," Dec. 29, 1823, (Nov. 1, 1823–Mar. 11, 1824 sent to Jeremiah Evarts), ML, vol. 2, HMCS.

73. Peter Gulick to J. Evarts, Aug. 15, 1828, ML, vol. 2, HMCS.

74. A. Bishop to J. Evarts, 1825, received Dec. 12, 1826, ML, vol. 2, HMCS.

75. Levi Chamberlain to Rufus Anderson, Feb. 13, 1837, ML, vol. 2, HMCS. Hiram Bingham to Jeremiah Evarts, Oct. 15, 1827 (typed transcript gives the date as Dec. 15, 1827), BP, HMCS. Hiram Bingham's Deposition to John Coffin Jones, Jr., August, 18, 1829, ML, vol. 2, HMCS. Translation of a Statement Signed by Kauikeaouli, Oahu, Oct. 7, 1829, ML, vol. 3, HMCS.

In the end, the social, religious, and political expediencies in the Sandwich Island combined with the momentum of the temperance movement in the United States to force the ABCFM evangelists to give up drinking and make a very public declaration for temperance. Apparently, the missionaries could no longer get away with drinking liquor. Tellingly, just five weeks before they made their declaration of abstinence, the Rev. Ephraim Clark complained in a letter to Jeremiah Evarts that he had heard from a sea captain "how our characters are assailed by the leading men among the residents. We are drunkards, adulterers, Sabbath breakers, &c, ... The ears of every visitor are assailed with these things . . . ."[76] While it was unlikely that the missionaries were adulterers and Sabbath breakers, the fact that they drank alcohol meant that the foreign community had the means to assassinate their characters.[77] The evangelists' own actions created this chink in the armor of their defenses against their enemies.

In their resolution for total abstinence, the evangelists now seemed to publically acknowledge what they had recognized for years: alcohol consumption undermined their mission. In point four of their resolution, they declared, "we view with deep regret the widening & deepening streams of liquid poison which are turned upon these islands, and which . . . we fear will yet sweep away some of the strongest barriers to the introduction of vice and misery, which, by the blessing of God, we have here erected . . ."[78] Yet, this point seems specious at best. Since the mid-1820s, ali'i nui like Hoapili and Kaumuali'i had kept most of the Hawaiian commoners from drinking with their taboos against alcohol. And while drinking would continue to be a problem at Honolulu—and in the 1830s when Kamehameha III's drinking was out of control—at the time of the missionaries' resolution, it seemed less likely that "streams of liquid poison" would "sweep" away the progress they had made against vice and misery. Or, to put it another way, while the ABCFM evangelists continued to drink, it was their ali'i nui allies who had erected the barriers against vice and misery.

76. Ephraim W. Clark to Jeremiah Evarts, Dec. 12, 1829, ML, vol. 3, HMCS.

77. There are two notable exceptions when, indeed, members of the mission did commit adultery. However, this occurred later than the period of time under examination here.

78. GMM, Jan. 22, 1830, Folder General Meeting Minutes May 16th 1825–June 28, 1832, HMCS.

More important than their seeming desire to keep their accomplishments from being undermined by the devastating effects of alcohol, the missionaries came to realize that they were no longer part of the mainstream when it came to the consumption of ardent spirits. The evangelist now understood that in the United States, especially among evangelicals, the temperance movement had become a powerful force, and they worried about being left behind, or worse, seeming to hinder God's work. The missionaries own words tell the story. The second point of their declaration of temperance noted that they "rejoice[d] in the success with which a merciful God is crowning the efforts made by christians [sic] and ministers of the Gospel in our own country to check the progress of intemperance . . ."[79] In turn, they pledged their cooperation with Christians and ministers to stop the "*plague*."[80] The missionaries' resolution for total abstinence was not just passed at their General Meeting, but also published in *The Missionary Herald*. It is here that their fears of being left behind are seen most clearly. In an addendum not seen in their original resolution, the ABCFM's evangelists proclaimed

> We feel that we may not—cannot be behind our brethren in the United States, in expressing and exhibiting our abhorrence of this foe to God and man.[81]

Finally, after ten years of drinking at the Sandwich Islands, the missionaries had caught up with the sentiments of their brethren in the United States.

In his study of upstate New York, Paul Johnson points out that "temperance advocates had been drinking all their lives, for until the middle 1820s liquor was an absolutely normal accompaniment to whatever men did in groups."[82] This describes the male missionaries in 1820s Hawai'i as well: they drank alcohol because it was a normative part of American culture. According to Johnson, as society and the economy changed in the first decades of the 19th century, an anxious middle class saw the collapse of old social controls and placed the blame for this squarely on increased consumption of hard liquor. More particularly, the seemingly abrupt shift to a war against intemperance came at a time when the transformation of the work place separated masters from

79. GMM, Jan. 22, 1830, HMCS.

80. Ibid.

81. "General Letter Respecting the Meeting," *The Missionary Herald*, vol. xxvi, no. 10, Oct. 1830, 319.

82. Johnson, *A Shop Keeper's Millennium*, 56.

workers, changing the former into businessmen. As they absented themselves from the workshop, these businessmen called for new standards
of behavior and discipline from workers, which included the purging
of alcohol from the work place.[83] In the Sandwich Islands, there was
also a collapse of social control that led to excessive drinking. This was
the result of foreign invasion and cultural degradation, rather than the
collapse of socio-economic relations between masters and workers. In
Hawai'i, missionaries drank out of custom, foreign residents drank out
of boredom, Hawaiian chiefs and commoners drank because of cultural
malaise, and sailors drank to release the frustrations of long voyages,
under strict control with long periods of boredom.

Missionaries began thinking about temperance for several reasons.
In part, they began to realize that their own consumption of alcohol was
out of step with mainstream evangelicals and temperance crusaders in
the United States. Moreover, they saw drinking as inimical to their efforts of evangelization. Most importantly, the consumption of alcohol
served as a nexus of contention that primarily was about power and
control. When the ABCFM evangelists drank alcohol, they gave their
enemies—the local foreign merchants—the power to criticize them. For
a number of powerful ali'i nui who had aligned themselves with the mission, anti-liquor taboos served to demonstrate their power and control
over other chiefs, commoners, sailors, and foreign residents. Unlike
Johnson, at least for the missionaries and the Christian chiefs, temperance was not about discipline and regularity. Or at least not the social
control of the shop associated with the time clock. For the chiefs, temperance was about asserting their traditional forms of control over all of
those they considered lesser beings. For the missionaries, temperance
was about shoring up their defenses against their enemies in the islands;
exerting social control over Hawaiians and foreigners so as to further
their mission; and exercising self control so as to be in sync with their
colleagues in America.[84] The consumption of wine and hard liquor was
such a normative part of American culture that it took time for the mis-

83. Johnson, *A Shop Keeper's Millennium*, 57.

84. According to Daniel Walker Howe, evangelical social reformers sought both lib-
eration and control as part of the redemptive process. Through conversion, evangelicals
were liberated from the temptations of Satan and thus were free to exercise self-control
and personal autonomy. Consequently they sought "responsible personal autonomy"
for themselves and, in turn, wished to liberate and create self discipline in others. Howe,
What Hath God Wrought, 193.

sionaries in the Sandwich Islands to come around to Samuel Worcester's and Jeremiah Evarts' views on drinking and temperance. The timing of their declaration is significant. As noted before, Johnson states that in upstate New York, the "temperance question was nonexistent in 1825," but by 1828 it was a "middle-class obsession."[85] Likewise, in the 1820s, for the ABCFM evangelists in Hawaiʻi, temperance was just not a part of their thinking. But once they decided to embrace temperance in 1830, the missionaries would pursue it with passion.

BIBLIOGRAPHY

Archival Sources

HHS: Hawaiian Historical Society
        BC: Broadside Collections
        MLB: Marshall Letter Book
        The Sandwich Island Gazette and Journal of Commerce
        Stephen Reynolds, Journal, typed transcript

HLUHM: Hamilton Library, University of Hawaiʻi Manoa
        The Missionary Herald
        The Panoplist

HMCS: Hawaiian Mission Children's Society Library
        BP: Bingham Papers, 1825–1828, photocopies
                from Houghton Library, Harvard
        GMM: General Meeting Minutes, Folder General
                Meeting Minutes May 16th
        1825–June 28, 1832
        LMSC: London Missionary Society Collection
        ML: Missionary Letters, vols. 1–8, type transcript
        SIMC: Sandwich Island Mission Collection
                AB23: Account Book 23
                AB27: Account Book 27
                AB28: Account Book 28
        SIMJ: Sandwich Island Mission Journal
        The Hawaiian Spectator, vols. 1 and 2
        Maria Loomis, Journal
        Samuel Whitney, Journal

85. Johnson, *A Shop Keeper's Millennium*, 55.

HSA: Hawaiʻi State Archives
ACM: America Consul Letters
John Colcord, Journal, typed transcript

Published Primary Sources

Constitution of the Massachusetts Society for the Suppression of Intemperance and Report of the Board of Counsel, May 28, 1813. Boston: Samuel T. Armstrong, 1813. Online: http://webcache.googleusercontent.com/search?q=cache:11oShVYwKZYJ:www .globalministries.org/resources/mission-study/what-is-haystack/haystack_ timeline/part-6-home-missionary-movement.html+Samuel+Worcester+and+Mas sachusetts+Missionary+Magazine&cd=4&hl=en&ct=clnk&gl=us

King, Pauline, ed. Journal of Stephen Reynolds: Volume I: 1823–1829. Salem, Massachusetts: The Peabody Museum of Salem, 1989.

Miller, Char. Selected Writings of Hiram Bingham, 1814–1869, Studies in American Religion, 31. Lewistown, NY: The Edwin Mellen Press, 1988.

Sprague, Charles. Address Delivered Before the Massachusetts Society for the Suppression of Intemperance. Boston: Bowles and Dearborn, 1827. The Missionary Herald, Google Books.

Thurston, Lucy G. Life and Times of Mrs. Lucy G. Thurston. Honolulu: The Friend, 1934.

Unknown. Report of the Board of Counsel to the Massachusetts Society for the Suppression of Intemperance, June, 1820, Boston: Sewell Phelps, 1820.

Secondary Sources
Journal Articles

Carlson, Peter. "Uneasy About Alcohol." American History, 43, 5, (2008), 32–39.

Fish Kashay, Jennifer. "Competing Imperialisms and Hawaiian Authority: The Cannoning of Lāhainā in 1827." Pacific Historical Review, 77, 3, (2008), 369–90.

Greer, Richard A. "Grog Shops and Hotels: Bending the Elbow in Old Honolulu." The Hawaiian Journal of History. 28 (1991) 35–67.

Rohrer, James A. "The Origins of the Temperance Movement: A Reinterpretation." Journal of American Studies. 24, 2, (1990), 228–35.

Books

Byrn, Jr., John D. Crime and Punishment in the Royal Navy: Discipline on the Leeward Islands Stations, 1784–1812. England: Scholar Press, 1989.

Daws, Gavan. Shoal of Time: A History of the Hawaiian Islands. Honolulu: University of Hawaiʻi Press, 1968.

Gast, Ross. Don Francisco de Paula Marin: A Biography. Honolulu: University of Hawaiʻi Press, 1973.

Gulick, Orramel Hinckley. The Pilgrims of Hawaii: Their Own Story of Their Pilgrimage from New England and Life Work in the Sandwich Islands, Now Known as Hawaii. New York: Fleming H. Revell Company, 1918.

Hailman, John. *Thomas Jefferson on Wine*. Jackson, Mississippi: University of Mississippi Press, 2006.

Howe, Daniel Walker. *What Hath God Wrought: The Transformation of America, 1815–1848*. Oxford: Oxford University Press, 2009.

Johnson, Paul. *A Shop Keepers Millennium: Society and Revivals in Rochester, New York, 1815–1837*. New York: Hill and Wang, 1978.

Kuykendall, Ralph S. *The Hawaiian Kingdom, 1778–1854, Vol. 1, Foundation and Transformation*. Honolulu: University of Hawai'i Press, 1965.

Maxfield, Charles A. *The Formation and Early History of the American Board of Commissioners for Foreign Missions*, No pages. Online: http://webcache.google usercontent.com/search?q=cache:UefHzoMcI1kJ:www.maxfieldbooks.com /ABCFM.html+Samuel+Worcester+and+ABCFM&cd=2&hl=en&ct=clnk&gl=us

National Temperance Society and Publication House. *A Hundred Years of Temperance, A Memorial Volume of the Centennial Temperance Conference held in Philadelphia, PA, Sept. 1885*. New York: National Temperance Society and Publication House, 1886. Google Books.

Rorabaugh, W.J. *The Alcoholic Republic: An American Tradition*. New York: Oxford University Press, 1979.

Stark, Suzanne J. *Female Tars: Women Aboard Ship in the Age of Sail*. Annapolis, Maryland: Naval Institute Press, 1996.

Tracy, Ebenezer Carter. *Memoir of the Life of Jeremiah Evarts*. Boston: Crocker and Brewster, 1845.

Tracy, Joseph. *History of the American Board of Commissioners for Foreign Missions*. New York: M.W. Dodd, 1842.

Williams, Ian. *Rum: A Social and Sociable History of the Real Spirit of 1776*. New York: Nation Books, 2005.

Williston, Samuel. *William Richards*. Cambridge, Mass.: Privately Printed, 1938.

15

Domesticity Abroad: Work and Family in the Sandwich Islands Mission, 1820–1840

Char Miller

"Of all the trials incident to missionary life, the responsibility of training up children, and of making provision for their virtue and usefulness . . . is comparatively speaking, the only one worthy of being named."

—LUCY G. THURSTON[1]

HIRAM AND SYBIL BINGHAM, pioneer missionaries to Hawai'i, hoped that the birth of their first son, Levi, would help usher in a new era in the Islands; that his arrival on January 1, 1820 would prove "the harbinger of peace to the mission." In naming him after Levi Parsons, a friend of the family and a missionary who had recently given his life to the Lord's cause in the Middle East, they expected that the peace the child would bring would be that of a Christian missionary. Their wish was that he "be one among the many whom God will raise up to fill in some important sense, heavenly plans."[2]

That heaven itself figured in those plans was not quite what Hiram and Sybil Bingham had envisioned. Less than three weeks after his birth, Levi Bingham died. In death, as in his short life, the child had a public role to play. His burial was the first in the Sandwich Islands Mission's brief history, and, as a result, his parents and their colleagues used the

1. Thurston, *Life and Times*, 101–2.
2. Hiram Bingham to Jeremiah Evarts, 11 January 1823, Hawaiian Mission Children's Society (HMCS).

opportunity to further the Lord's case before the Hawaiian people. "The king and principle chiefs and distinguished women" of the Islands were invited to the funeral, which was designed to display the solemnity and decorous nature of true Christian burials. It was, all in the mission agreed, a sharp (and welcome) contrast to the explosive, often riotous, grief that marked the deaths of Hawaiian royalty. The missionaries hoped that the Islanders would absorb the lesson Levi's death offered and begin to practice Christian customs. If they did so, then Levi Bingham's death would indeed have fulfilled "heavenly plans."[3]

The circumstances surrounding Levi's death revealed the extent to which the Bingham family's grief formed a part of the mission's work. They were not, of course, the only missionaries to learn how profoundly intertwined issues of work and family could be. This interconnection lay at the core of the missionary experience, as American and English missionaries to Oceania came to recognize. There was a reason for the centrality. The English and American mission boards believed that in general Christian families, not individual missionaries, were the most effective means of inculcating Christian values and beliefs abroad. Their views were widely shared. Many believed that the nuclear family was the key social institution of Western civilization and culture, through which the blessings of Christianity would best flow. The sanctification of the family ensured that a missionary's public role and private life were inextricably linked. The mission boards, and the missionaries themselves, were convinced that this interconnection would sustain the missionary in time of need, provide immunization against sexual temptation, and enable potential converts to witness how true Christians lived and worked.[4]

That at least was the theory that emerged from discussions within the American Board of Commissioners for Foreign Missions (ABCFM), the major force behind American mission work in the early nineteenth century. Founded in 1810, the ABCFM launched its evangelical crusade during the War of 1812, sending out its first mission to India in 1813. After creating two more missions, one in Ceylon (present day Sri Lanka) in 1816, and another to Native Americans in 1817, it established the

3. Ibid., Thurston, *The Missionary's Daughter*; Barrere and Sahlins, "Tahitians," 19–35.

4. Miller, *Fathers and Sons*; Humphrey, *The Promised Land*; Andrew, *Rebuilding the Christian Commonwealth*, Dibble, *A History of the Sandwich Islands*; Silverman, "To Marry Again," 64–75; Howe, *Where The Waves Fall*.

Sandwich Islands Mission in 1820. Many other ABCFM missions would follow, but the Sandwich Islands one was particularly notable, because it served as a test case of the strength and effectiveness of the Christian crusade in that region, especially of the contribution of missionary families to that cause. Indeed, everything that the Sandwich Islands Mission did, for good or ill, would set a precedent for future American missions in the Pacific (and elsewhere), and nowhere was this more true than in the arena of work and family relations. By exploring this dynamic interaction, then, one can gain a deeper sense of the texture of the missionaries' lives, their perceptions of their work, and the image of themselves that they hoped to project, all matters of great importance to a fledgling mission.[5]

These issues are important in another respect, for they illuminate questions of considerable scholarly concern: to what degree does work shape the conditions of family life, and to what extent does the reverse hold true? Academics from a variety of disciplines have long focused on the first question, assuming that economic and social forces outside the home have largely determined the course of life within it; in these analyses, the family is usually seen as a dependent variable. But beginning in the 1980s, historians and sociologists, among others, began exploring the ways familial concerns have influenced (if not significantly set) the conditions for work. As historian Tamara Hareven pointed out, the family also can operate as an independent variable (in her words, as an "active agent") and thereby shape the context in which its members work. But, she cautions, being "an active or passive agent does not imply that the family was in full control of its destiny." The crucial historical question is under what conditions has the family been "able to control its environment and under what circumstances did its control diminish?"[6]

The experience of the Sandwich Islands missionaries fully underscores the complexity of Hareven's argument. Their families' life was not simply dependent on work for its character: the Christian missionaries' cultural vision of the private (and nuclear) family, for example, clearly influenced the way the men and women of the Sandwich Islands Mission sought to convert the Hawaiian people. Yet it is just as clear

5. Humphrey, *The Promised Land*; Andrew, *Rebuilding the Christian Commonwealth*; Miller, *Fathers and Sons*.

6. Hareven, *Family Time and Industrial Time*, 4; Kanter, *Work and Family*, 53–58; Papanek, "Men, Women and Work, 852–72.

that the particular (and often contested) social circumstances in which the missionaries labored significantly altered their families' lives. This is important for it suggests that the Hawaiians helped shape the context of mission work. They did so in the public arena by determining when (or if) to convert to Christianity. More subtly, they also helped determine some aspects of private life within the missionaries' compounds. In this sense, they were the audience for whom the American missionaries labored, and thereby helped set the stage for, gave meaning to, and defined the tenor of the cross-cultural dialogue that ensued between these two sets of actors.

Questions concerning this dynamic relationship arose even before the missionaries boarded the brig *Thaddeus* and sailed from Boston in October 1819. Not all supporters of the missionary movement were convinced, as was the ABCFM leadership, that it was appropriate to send married couples to raise the Lord's banner in foreign lands. To meet this challenge, the ABCFM arranged a series of public ceremonies at each step of the mission's formation: at the ordination of its two missionaries, Hiram Bingham and Asa Thurston, in September; at these two men's respective weddings several weeks later; and at a final religious service just before the mission sailed during which sermons were delivered stressing the prominent role missionary family life would play in Christianizing the Hawaiians. To those who reproached the women who chose to go to the Islands, the Rev. Thomas Gallaudet, who officiated at the wedding of Hiram Bingham and Sybil Moseley, declared that all Protestants should feel "grateful ... to those willing to take their lives in their hands ... [and], in some measure, to fulfill our obligation to our Saviour." The women's devotion and piety, he continued, would have an additional benefit. Was not woman, he asked, "sent by Heaven as a helpmate for man; designed to share and soothe his sorrows; to participate in and lighten his cares[?]" If so, then missionary women, because of their strength, would at times "invigorate" their missionary husbands' "languishing efforts in the path of duty." Or they might extricate the mission "from difficulties which his boasted sagacity cannot surmount," all the while, "like the vestal virgin of old, keeping bright the light of domestic piety." The women, in short, would prod their husbands onward, contributing to and standing as a symbol of all that their husbands hoped to accomplish in the Islands.[7]

---

7. Gallaudet, "An Address," 12.

Gallaudet's argument was deeply imbued with the antebellum American concept of domesticity, which imputed particular moral strengths and religious virtues to women, traits that putatively arose out of their nurturing and maternal characters. Yet Gallaudet's emphasis upon domesticity did not mean that he (and, by extension, the ABCFM) supposed that the women's only value lay within the mission home; there was more to it than that. It was these women's special mission, the Rev. Samuel Worcester, secretary of the ABCFM, declared, "To shew to the rude and depraved Islanders an effective example of the purity and dignity and loveliness—the salutary and vivifying influence—, the attractive and celestial excellence, which Christianity can impart to the female character." To fulfill that obligation, the women needed to step outside the mission's walls, entering Hawaiian society (and homes) to "inculcate conjugal fidelity and domestic attachment, parental care and filial obedience" as well as "to educate the rising generation [and] to ameliorate the condition of the female sex." The women in the Sandwich Islands Mission were to play an active and public role in the reformation of Hawaiian society.[8]

Gallaudet and Worcester neatly fit their arguments to their culture's prescription for women's proper sphere of activity. Their hope was to justify the ABCFM's conviction that missionary families must form the core of the Christian crusade. This conviction ultimately would expand the boundaries of the women's "sphere." In the meantime Gallaudet's and Worcester's arguments quieted the critics, stilling what one friend of the Sandwich Islands Mission described as "the barking of little dogs." But neither the mission's supporters nor its critics could have foreseen the disquiet that would emerge from the exportation of domesticity, and from the notion that members of the mission—especially its women— had critical public and private roles to play. This situation occasionally would engender tensions that members of the mission could not easily resolve or reconcile.[9]

But at first all seemed propitious. When the missionaries reached the Islands in the Spring of 1820, they were cheered to learn that the *kapus* (taboos) had been broken, and that the fabric of Hawaiian soci-

8. Degler, *At Odds*; Cott, *The Bonds of Womanhood*; Welter, "The Cult of True Womanhood, 151–74; Worcester, "Instructions to the Sandwich Islands Mission"; Gallaudet, "An Address," 8; Ralston, "'Christian Woman,'" 489–521.

9. Thurston, *The Life and Times*, 7.

ety and religion appeared to be rapidly unraveling. They expected that this situation would increase their prospects for success, and were particularly intrigued by what this might mean for the missionary women. "Jehovah cast down the idols of the heathens of this land," one male missionary wrote, "and actually prepared the way for our female helpers to be well received, and to be treated with much kindness and to be made extremely useful." One benefit was simply the women's presence: it showed the mission's "Pacific design" and ensured that "the blessings of civilization [will] be imparted and the privileges of Christian religion secured to this people much earlier than could be done without them."[10]

Women may have accelerated the process of conversion, but Hawai'i did not represent a speedy victory for the forces of Christ. As with other missionaries in the Pacific, the Americans in Hawai'i found that their inadequate knowledge of its culture hampered, and often undermined, their efforts. They assumed, for example, that the breaking of the kapus shattered the people's allegiance to traditional forms of worship, an assumption that badly underestimated the enduring faith the Hawaiians placed in their gods, and lulled the missionaries into a false sense of the inevitability of the Christian conquest. Inadequate, too, was their understanding of the vital role women played in Hawaiian culture and politics. Reared in a society in which women and men operated in separate spheres, in which domesticity defined—even circumscribed—women's activities, the American missionaries at first ignored the significant positions held by and the respect granted to women of royal blood.[11]

As important as these and other misconceptions were in determining the speed and scope of the mission's success during the initial period of contact, there was another factor that especially shaped the influence that the American women were able to exert in the missionary cause. Upon their arrival in the Islands, the women were confronted with the conflict imbedded in their assigned positions as public and private figures; they quickly discovered that to be fully active in mission work outside the home and to be exemplars of domestic virtue within it, was a very complicated process. This was largely due to the mount-

10. Bingham to Jackson, February 1821, HMCS; Webb, "The Abolition of Taboo Systems in Hawaii," 21–39.

11. Ralston, "The Role of the Kamehameha Family"; Webb, "The Abolition of the Taboo System," 21–39; H. Bingham to Rev. William Jackson, February 1821; Miller, *Fathers and Sons*, Chapter Two; Kashay, "Problems in Paradise," 81–94.

ing chores the women assumed within the mission family, which were particularly onerous at the Honolulu station. In a letter to her sisters back home, Sybil Bingham outlined the tasks she confronted during one arduous period in the summer and early fall of 1822. The mission family in Honolulu, she wrote, comprised four "distinct families, united in one, all having children—all having infants, with eighteen or twenty native children divided among them, two native youths, Thomas and Nonorei, and one young man, Mr. Harwood, from New England." This assembly was crammed into "one frame house, containing five rooms, 12 ft. by 12 ft. above and below . . . with a stone room and eating room on the ground cellar." Not all of these rooms, however, were designed for the inhabitants' exclusive use. One was considered as necessary for "common resort," leaving four "in which to place the beds of eight parents and their little ones, and accommodate the gentlemen, two of the three desiring separate beds." Things only got worse when several other missionaries arrived for a visit, at which point the Binghams (and their child) moved up into the "upper half story" of the house. "The roof was low," Sybil reported, "but a field bedstead could stand," and with two trunks serving as chairs, this small, cramped space was their home for many months. The shortage of space forced all in the mission to show "patience and prudence, to sustain the character of good neighbors."[12]

Personality conflicts were the least of Sybil Bingham's worries, however. "Ways and means must be devised," she wrote, "and labor done that so many might be fed, each day, with food convenient for them." That was no small task, especially as most of the women at the station were already weary. For a while, "Mrs. Loomis superintended the domestic concerns, though hardly able to keep about, from the great exertion she had made." But Mrs. Chamberlain, "having care of the washing and ironing . . . with the daily charge of the visiting gentlemen—her husband, feeble—one or two children ill . . . felt it difficult to take care of the cellar kitchen." Soon thereafter "Mrs. L. gave up and took to her bed. Mrs. C. felt it her duty, rather than mine, to take the place below," but in time Mrs. Chamberlain also had to withdrew when her husband "had a most violent attack of rheumatism and required [his wife's] whole attention." Sybil Bingham, who had been caring for the children and teaching school, now felt she had no alternative—she closed her school for several months and "went below—stood at the helm, and except [for] a few of the first days of my

12. Sybil Bingham, Diary, 81.

labor, had the care of seeing that 50 were fed with something, three times a day." That regimen took its toll: when Sybil Bingham's health failed the women reluctantly asked Mr. Harwood, their guest from New England, to tend to the kitchen until one of the women was healthy enough to relieve him.[13]

The missionary women's response to their burdens was not to ask their husbands for relief; to have done so would have been to draw them away from *their* missionary endeavors. Rather, they wanted Hawaiian laborers to assume some of their domestic chores. Yet even this understandable desire caused some to worry that, by hiring others, they were neglecting their proper duties, thereby diminishing the value of domesticity as an ideal the Hawaiians should absorb. (And when critics of the mission in the U.S. and Hawai'i later charged that the missionary women lived off the labor of others, the women were doubly chagrined). Yet Lucy Thurston found such concerns wrongheaded. She made it a point to advise all of the evangelical women who came to Hawai'i after the first contingent of missionaries "that to live a holy life is one thing, and to sap one's constitution in the ardor of youthful feelings is quite another." The experiences of Lucy Thurston, Sybil Bingham, and the others in their cohort made one thing clear: "Do not be devoted to domestic duties. Trust to natives." If they did not do so, their health would fail and their ability to contribute to the cause would be, perforce, limited.[14]

The women's health tended to fail in any event. As Hiram Bingham advised the ABCFM, "most of the females of the mission suffer materially from debility which is in part attributed to the climate and in part to the hardships and privations they have suffered." Laura Judd agreed: "My constitution suffers from the continual debilitating effects of a tropical climate," she wrote a friend; "I feel the need of bracing winters." Others felt similarly, sought out those winters, and left the missionary field for the United States. For those who stayed, the struggle continued. "My own dear wife has been confined to the couch about 20 days with alarming symptoms of a broken constitution," Hiram Bingham reported in late 1825. "She has been ill about three months and is now lower than Mrs. Stewart or any other member of the mission." Bingham's only hope

---

13. Ibid., 80–81.

14. Thurston, *Life and Times*, 136–37, 130; Raltson, "'Christian Woman, Pious Wife, Faithful Mother, Devoted Mother,'" 489–91.

was that the Lord "will raise [Sybil] up again and enable her to bear her equal part with her husband in winning the nation to Christ."[15]

His was a vain hope, and no one knew that better than his wife. She and the other women recognized that increases in domestic labor and declines in physical health restricted their direct contributions to the mission cause. At best, they were able to shape their mission work around the needs of their families. "My mornings are devoted to the cares of my family," Laura Judd declared, "and I am to be an exemplary wife and mother and housekeeper so that my husband may be known when he sits among the elders of the land." In this way she would at least have an indirect influence on the mission's success. When possible, usually during the afternoons, she was able more directly to shape events, by teaching "native schools" or to set aside some time "to meet with a circle of females . . . to read and explain the scriptures." But even such a limited schedule was hard to maintain, especially when illnesses intervened. Health permitting, Charlotte Baldwin allowed, "I meet with different attributed classes three afternoons a week." But her health was unsteady, so her teaching schedule was inconsistent. Family cares intruded as well. As Lucy Thurston observed, the only time that she could give to the Hawaiians, and it was not much, was the time she could "redeem" from her family. Most found, as did Sybil Bingham, that "time seems divided into little parcels" and "the days and hours, filled with little, busy cares." There was little question of the missionary women playing an "equal part" in the Christian crusade, as Hiram Bingham had hoped. They simply did not have the time for purely missionary work.[16]

No wonder that a tone of frustration occasionally crept into the women's letters and diaries. Exhausted by domestic cares, they could rarely participate in the grand reformation of Hawai'i that had drawn them there in the first place. "I sometimes grieve," Sybil Bingham confided, "that I can no more devote myself to the language and the study of the Bible," activities that characterized male missionary work and which were necessary for effective proselytizing. Her grief, however, was checked by her religious devotion and the larger theological framework

15. Hiram Bingham to Jeremiah Evarts, 18 October 1825, HMCS; Laura Judd to Lydia Finney, 10 December 1832 in O'Hara, et al., *Awakening the Silent Majority*.

16. Laura Judd to Lydia Finney, 10 December 1832, Charlotte Baldwin to Mrs. Sophronia Baldwin, 7 October 1829, HMCS; Thurston, *Life and Times*, 101; Sybil Bingham, Diary, 90–91.

in which she and all missionaries operated. "I believe that God appoints my work; it is enough for me to see that I do it all with an eye to his glory." Sybil Bingham also achieved solace in a more secular manner: "I am allowed to aid [Hiram] whose constant employment is in the way of direct efforts for good." By indicating that only male missionaries could be constantly and directly engaged in the Lord's work, by conceding, as Lucy Thurston put it, that "the missionary best serves his generation who serves the public and his wife best serves her generation who serves her family," the women of the Sandwich Islands Mission conformed nicely to Rev. Thomas Gallaudet's vision of the "heaven-sent helpmate." But they also acknowledged that they could not consistently meet that other expectation of them, that they be active, public figures.[17]

The dilemmas of missionary womanhood were intensified by those of missionary parenthood. The children of the mission brought into focus the inescapable interconnection of work and family. Their births brought great joy to their parents, but created yet another public responsibility. "Our patrons expect, the world expects, the heathen themselves expect, that [the children] will rise up and reflect honor upon an enlightened origin," one missionary mother wrote. As such, the children from birth were taught from infancy to lead emblematic lives. Their parents also used them to score points with Hawaiians. When in 1822, Sybil Bingham and Maria Whitney visited Liholiho and members of the royal family, they brought their children with them to facilitate dialogue. "We would by all means win their favor and confidence if we could," Sybil Bingham indicated, so "sister Maria and I took our sweet babes that they might plead for us." That one of these sweet babes was only a few weeks old, suggests how soon the children took on public personas.[18]

Infants were one thing, but full-fledged children were another. Their lives and needs posed major questions concerning missionary childrearing practices. Was it possible, the missionary parents wondered, to raise dutiful Christian children in a land they considered savage and "polluted"? The stakes were high and the situation complex. If the children stayed with their parents, they ran the risk of being "corrupted" by the surrounding culture, and should that occur (and most felt certain that it would), then the mission's image of Christian decorum and familial piety would be forever tarnished in Hawai'i and in the United States.

17. Sybil Bingham, Diary, 98; Thurston, *Life and Times,* 120.
18. Thurston, *Life and Times,* 114; Sybil Bingham, Diary, 45b.

Equally worrisome was the possible result of sending the children back to the U.S. for education. If the mission parents did so, they risked offending domestic Christians' abiding attachment to the concept of domesticity, which made glorious the mother-child bond. Finally, if the children were sent to the U.S., they (and their families) could not serve as role models in Hawai'i. The mission family struggled with this conundrum for twenty years, a struggle that consumed considerable energy. The struggle also revealed the important role the Hawaiians played in mission life, and it highlighted important differences in parents' perceptions of the purposes and principles of missionary service.[19]

The first significant test case involving the children did not lift the hearts of the Sandwich Islands mission family. Indeed, the situation surrounding the Chamberlain family served as a warning about the dangers associated with children on missionary ground. Daniel and Jerusha Chamberlain had sailed to Hawai'i on the *Thaddeus* in 1820, but unlike the rest of the pioneer company, they brought a large family with them. Their children ranged in age from two to thirteen, and their ages proved a problem. Eager and able to range beyond the mission compound, and thus beyond parental supervision, the Chamberlain children came into regular contact with Hawaiians, whom one missionary called "this rude people, where delicacy is scarcely known or thought of." This "contaminating intercourse" apparently began to leave its mark, and the Chamberlains and the other missionaries labored "long and hard to give [the] children suitable instruction and to watch over them." This solicitude proved ineffective, for the missionaries believed that 1820s Hawai'i lacked "the firmness of Christian discipline" which would reinforce their teachings. No matter what they did (or said), there was little the mission could do to prevent the Chamberlain children and their younger peers from "coming into close contact with the natives." The only solution available was for the Chamberlains to leave the Islands. This decision was strongly supported by a visiting deputation of English missionaries from Tahiti, where similar problems with missionary offspring had been faced and a similar decision reached.[20]

The Chamberlains' decision was not without its problems, however. The Sandwich Islands Mission recognized that it might be some

19. Hiram Bingham, *A Residence*, 331–33.

20. Hiram Bingham et. al. to Jeremiah Evarts, 20 March 1823, HMCS; Tyerman and Bennett to ABCFM, *Missionary Herald*, 104.

time before Hawai'i adopted "the firmness of Christian discipline," which meant that during the interim many, if not all, of the missionary children (and possibly their parents) would have to leave the Islands. Not only would the ABCFM and its domestic supporters disapprove of this policy—for if all left, how would the mission continue?—but the absence of intact, nuclear families among the missionaries might extend the period required to bring about the evangelization they so desired. The Chamberlain family's experience offered little comfort.

The first generation of missionaries nonetheless had to come to terms with the issue of their offspring, though they were not united in the resolutions they reached. Two responses emerged, and these were partly determined by the missionaries' geographic locale and by how individual families viewed their role in the mission. Those in Honolulu, for example, strongly favored sending the children back to the mainland, usually without their parents. Aware that this decision challenged accepted views of childrearing, not to mention the mission's purported commitment to domesticity, the missionaries on O'ahu argued that theirs was not a normal situation and that they should not be judged by standards applied in America. They were, after all, living in Honolulu, a place filled with boisterous foreigners, innumerable grog shops, and other dens of iniquity.

Honolulu was also dangerous, and the parents especially feared for their children's physical safety and psychological security. "Their nursery is as it were on the field of battle," Hiram Bingham wrote the ABCFM in 1828 shortly after sending his daughter Sophia back to the United States. Her departure took place amid violent attacks by sailors on the missionaries, whom the sailors believed were responsible for the curtailment of prostitution. "We fled with [Sophia] from the war on Kauai; we carried her asleep into Mr. Richard's cellar when Lahaina was fired on—but we could not easily hush her cries, when I and my house were mob'd at Honolulu nor will she soon lose the impression that we are here in continual danger from the assaults of wicked men." The locale of Sophia's parents' missionary work clearly shaped her childhood, exposing her to considerable hostility, and it also deprived her of friends, since there were few other missionary children near enough to be her companions (at the time of her departure she had a sister six years younger) and none outside the mission who were acceptable to her parents. The senior Binghams were not about to repeat the Chamberlains' experience.

Sophia, and her case were typical, "had no school, no society suited to her age," deprivations from which she was "likely to suffer more and more" as time passed. At least in the United States, among friends and family, Sophia would be safe and not so "emphatically alone."[21]

The Binghams were not alone in making the difficult decision to send a child home. The exodus began slowly in the late 1820s as those children born earlier in the decade reached that age, somewhere between ages eight and twelve, when their parents feared the consequences of their continued residence among the Islanders. Children from the Ruggles, Whitney, Bishop, and Richards families followed Sophia Bingham to America. The trickle of departures turned into a flood by the middle of the next decade. In 1834 alone, nine children were expected to leave for the mainland. Five years later, on the twentieth anniversary of the mission, the total number of departed children was large. According to Lucy Thurston, "more than forty missionaries' children have been conveyed away by parents, that have retired from this field of labor. Eighteen have been scattered about in the fatherland without parents." These figures reflect the pervasiveness of the problem and suggest that few, if any, of the mission families were untouched by it. Moreover, these numbers suggest that the need for continual reinforcements of the mission from the United States was not simply a result of the missionaries' success in spreading Christ's message, but was also due to the mission's failure to solve the critical issue of childrearing.[22]

Some parents sent their children back to the U. S. to lessen their familial obligations so that they might more effectively fulfill their obligation to the Lord. It was, one wrote, a question of balance. Children helped to sap their parents' strength, vigor that might be best expended on the "thousands of another language [who] are looking to them for attention, care and instruction." The missionary's first duty, then, lay with those they had come to convert. As Samuel Whitney, a father of four, commented, "If I had not sent away my children, 1835 would not find me at the Sandwich Islands." The missionary women's first duty also lay with the Hawaiians, or so Hiram Bingham advocated. "The theory that it is the duty of a missionary mother to guide, watch over and educate her children, whatever else she may do or fail to do," he wrote, required

21. Hiram Bingham to Jeremiah Evarts, 15 October 1828, HMCS; Zweip, "Sending the Children Home," 39–68.

22. Thurston, *Life and Times*, 148; Bingham, *A Residence*, 333.

some revision. Fathers and mothers "are jointly bound to provide for their children, and train them up for Christ and heaven," he declared, "but not necessarily under the same roof." The missionary mother "who is qualified to give her own offspring a thorough education on missionary ground . . . is, or ought to be, qualified to teach a multitude of those whose mothers cannot teach them well at all." It made sense (and possibly more converts) for the missionary mother "to instruct the multitude . . . while the missionary child is committed to the hands of others, either on missionary ground or far over the sea."[23]

This pragmatic assessment had its emotional costs. "To turn our little ones from us," Sybil Bingham wrote, "sometimes literally forcing them from our arms as we embark them upon the wide waters" was painful. Ironically, some of that pain was eased by the support given to the mission policy by the very Hawaiians whose characters seemed to warrant breaking up mission families. For instance, Ka-'ahu-manu, *Kuhina* or executive officer of Hawai'i, agreed with the missionaries that hers were a "depraved people." Her words not only gave her an active voice in determining the mission's course of action but also sanctified it. The missionary women used her assessment in their letters home to justify a decision they knew would not be well received. Such justification, of course, could not fully quell parental "apprehensions for the rocks and shoals that [lay] in their [children's] course." Sending his daughter Sophia to the United States was a "severe struggle," Hiram Bingham acknowledged, "and the path has never...been sufficiently marked to induce us to walk in it without shrinking." Yet walk in it he did, and, once having made the decision, Bingham was "comforted . . . in the reflection that we have do . . . for what the good of the child and the cause of the mission required." In so saying, he spoke for many who believed, even if with heavy hearts, that mission work set the conditions for family life.[24]

He did not speak for everyone. A minority acted on the belief that the needs of the family should shape the work environment. This group probably included some of those who resigned from their positions and left the Islands with their families, unwilling as they may have been to separate from their children. It certainly included Lucy Thurston, who sharply disagreed (and made her disagreement public) with the ap-

23. Hiram Bingham to Jeremiah Evarts, 15 October 1828, HMCS; Samuel Whitney quoted in Thurston, *Life and Times,* 118; Bingham, *A Residence,* 331–33.

24. Sybil Bingham to Mrs. Willard, 30 November 1828, HMCS.

proach those in Honolulu took on this issue. "To send away children at an age so early, while I am sustained in active life, is what every feeling in my heart revolts against," she declared, indicating she was more willing than some to reduce significantly her missionary endeavors for the sake of her children. Her husband, she explained, was "entirely devoted to works of a public nature. My duties are of a more private character," a division of labor with which she was happy. Nor did she feel "like some of our mothers, that children must be sent away or ruined. I harp upon another string, and say, make better provision for them, or [ruination] will be the likely result."[25]

The provisions she made to prevent what she considered the ruination of her children revolved around the physical layout of her mission home. Her general principle, she advised a cousin who was establishing a mission in Turkey, was that "houses and dooryards must be laid out to meet the character of the people and the exigencies of the times." Both demanded that missionaries protect themselves, and, although missionaries are "public characters and their houses, public houses," this did not mean that the entire house need be open to the public. Privacy must be maintained, and the way to do this was to create an architecture that showcased the family and separated it from non-Christians, thereby displaying the family's purity and keeping it pure.[26]

The ideal home for the "pioneer missionary," Lucy Thurston wrote, would "consist of three distinct departments, so closely connected, that one lady could superintend them all. One department would be for children, one for household natives, and one for native company." This structure made the house at once accessible and defensible. It also let "each class know its place," she commented, "and the whole (would) move on without collision." Determined to order the family's life and its interactions with the Hawaiians, the senior Thurstons constructed their home at Kai-lua on the island of Hawai'i according to Lucy Thurstons' principles. Set behind and above the village on an "arid slope," the Thurston homestead of five acres was entirely "enclosed with a stone wall three feet wide and six feet high, with simply the front gate for entrance." From that gate to "each side of the front door" ran two walls parallel to the walkway, effectively sealing off the adjacent yards. Similar partitioning, shaped by the family's needs, occurred within the house. There

25. Thurston, *Life and Times*, 101.
26. Ibid., 101–2.

were public reception rooms from which one could enter the front yard that were designed for Hawaiian visitors. Other rooms (and yards) were off-limits to all but the immediate family, and the Hawaiians evidently understood this. They "know precisely where to enter, the yard and the house," Lucy Thurston wrote, "and they have learned where to stop." Should Hawaiian visitors wander off course, there were stymied by the one door that led to the Thurston's rooms, and to the family's separate backyard. Guarding that portal was none other than Lucy Thurston, who took her gate-keeping duty seriously. "If I am entertaining company in the sitting room [I can remain] . . . devoted to the natives [but] still [be] porter to the only door that leads into the children's special enclosure, and have the satisfied feeling of their being safe, beyond the reach of native influence." Yet Islander influence was more pervasive than Lucy Thurston recognized. The very erection of such elaborate architectural defenses an indicates how influential the Hawaiians had been in molding the contours of mission-family life.[27]

Few in the mission were as systematic as the Thurstons had been in developing such an exclusive architecture. Fanny Gulick had a fence constructed around her family home at Wai-mea, a physical marker of her "strict injunction that [she] laid upon all intercourse with the natives" with her children. As she advised her stateside family: children "cannot remain among the heathen without danger of ruin, unless some spot is provided where they may be secluded most of the time from debasing sights and sounds." Those in Honolulu felt similarly. They also erected a fence around the mission compound to fend off the "moral dearth" around them. But they found that it had relatively little impact due to the central location of the mission in a port town significantly larger than Kai-lua and Wai-mea. Yet they knew as well that they could not maintain total separation because the instructions that the Sandwich Islands Mission had received from the Prudential Committee of the ABCFM before leaving the United States stipulated that they must inculcate Christianity and civilization. To achieve this goal, they had to engage with the island peoples, not isolate themselves from them. Whatever their homes' defensive posture, then, these buildings must also serve as welcoming symbols of the larger, religious and cultural changes to come. "Aim at nothing short of covering those islands with fruitful fields, and pleasant dwellings, and schools and churches," The ABCFM's charge

27. Ibid., 76, 84–85.

declared, and "of raising up the whole people to an educated state of Christian civilization."[28]

The very houses in which the missionaries lived, and the churches in which they led prayers, were to reflect the mission's presence and act as agents of change. Lucy Thurston spoke to this aspiration when, after a new church was erected in Kai-lua, she noted approvingly that it gave "quite an American look to our village," an appearance she hoped would inspire greater piety and decorum. Similarly inspired were those missionaries who left Hawai'i in 1833 to establish a new (and ill-fated) mission in the Marquesas Islands; there, they constructed a compound designed to radiate moral order and influence outward among the Marquesan people. Although this particular missionary compound failed in its task (the Marquesas mission collapsed after less than a year in the field), Lucy Thurston took comfort from the survival of her station, where she dealt what with what she described as "the double responsibilities" missionaries faced—"of molding heathen, and of forming the characters of our children." Both, she felt, could be accomplished simultaneously on missionary ground.[29]

For all it success, the Thurston compound had its drawbacks. "Think of children, cut off from the benefits of the sanctuary, of schools, of associates," she wrote, "of children thus exiled I am the mother." This isolation would continue, she knew, until her progeny reached maturity. When "an employment, trade or profession for future life was chosen," she acknowledged, "the Sandwich Islands is no longer the place for them." Her acknowledgment that the missionary child's life cycle determined the make-up of the mission family meant that it was only a matter of time before Lucy Thurston's family was broken up. In 1839, she and her children sailed from Hawai'i, leaving Asa Thurston behind. On this voyage, she was joined by Hiram and Sybil Bingham and their remaining children. Although Lucy Thurston eventually would return to Hawai'i, the senior Binghams never did, and their departure marked the close of the pioneer era of the mission.[30]

28. Putney, *Missionaries in Hawai'i*, 51; "Instructions from the Prudential Committee of the ABCFM,"x–xi; Damon, Letters, 261; Schultz, "Empire of the Young."

29. Herbert, *Marquesan Encounters*, 24-30; Bingham, Jr., *Voyage*; Miller, "Text in Context,"47–63.

30. Bingham Jr., *Voyage*, 98, 101.

This era's conclusion was marked in other ways, too. In 1841, Punahou, a boarding school for missionary children, was established, keeping many missionary children in the Islands, though separated from the Islanders. The school's founding and growing success suggested that "the firmness of Christian discipline," the lack of which had earlier prompted so many families and children to leave Hawai'i, had become pervasive enough that missionary men and women could stay and contribute more fully to a broad range of missionary endeavors. This Americanization came too late for the families of the pioneer generation of the mission. As Lucy Thurston understood, her peers' decision to send children home was reached in response to "the wants of our world, [and is] probably destined only to flourish while the science of missions is in its infancy." One indication that the Sandwich Islands Mission had matured was that the particular trials of the pioneer missionary, those deeply rooted in the complex interaction between work and family, no longer formed the core of the missionary experience. They were but part of the mission's past.[31]

BIBLIOGRAPHY

Andrew, John. *Rebuilding the Christian Commonwealth: New England Congregationalists and Foreign Missions.* Lexington: University Press of Kentucky, 1976.

Baldwin, Charlotte to Mrs. Sophronia Baldwin, 7 October 1829. HMCS.

Barrere, Dorothy and Marshall Sahlins. "Tahitians in the early history of Hawaiian Christianity: The Journal of Toketa." *Hawaiian Journal of History,* 13 (1979).

Bingham, Hiram. *A Residence of Twenty One Years in the Sandwich Islands.* Hartford: Hezekial Huntington, 1849.

Bingham, Hiram to Rev. William Jackson, February 1821. HMCS.

Bingham, Hiram to Jeremiah Evarts, 11 January 1823. HMCS.

Bingham, Hiram et. al. to Jeremiah Evarts, 20 March 1823. HMCS.

Bingham, Hiram to Jeremiah Evarts, 18 October 1825, HMCS.

Bingham, Hiram to Jeremiah Evarts, 15 October 1828. HMCS.

Bingham, Hiram Jr.. *Voyage to Abaiang,* Vol. II, HMCS.

Bingham, Sybil. Diary. Bingham Family Papers, Yale University Library.

Bingham, Sybil to Mrs. Willard, 30 November 1828. HMCS.

Cott, Nancy. *The Bonds of Womanhood: "Woman's Sphere" in New England, 1780-1835.* New Haven: Yale University Press, 1977.

Degler, Carl. *At Odds: Women and the Family from the Revolution to the Present.* New York: Oxford University Press, 1980.

Dibble, Sheldon. *A History of the Sandwich Islands.* Honolulu: T. H. Thrum, 1909.

Gallaudet, Thomas. "An Address Delivered at a Meeting for Prayer." Hartford: Lincoln and Stone, 1819.

31. Ibid., 139; Varigney, *Fourteen Years in the Sandwich Islands,* 151–53, 189–92; Thurston, *Life and Times,* 117.

Hareven, Tamara. *Family Time and Industrial Time*. New York: Cambridge University Press, 1982.

Herbert, T. Walter. *Marquesan Encounters: Melville and the Meaning of Civilization*. Cambridge: Harvard University Press, 1980.

Howe, K. R. *Where The Waves Fall*. Honolulu: University of Hawaii Press, 1984.

Humphrey, Heman. *The Promised Land*. Boston: Samuel T. Armstrong, 1819.

Instructions from the Prudential Committee of the ABCFM to members of the Mission to the Sandwich Islands. Boston: Samuel Armstrong, 1819.

Judd, Laura to Lydia Finney, 10 December 1832. HMCS.

Kanter, Rossbeth Moss. *Work and Family in the United States: A Critical Review and Agenda for Research and Policy*. New York: Russell Sage Foundation, 1979.

Kashay, Jennifer Fish. "Problems in Paradise: The Peril of Missionary Parenting in Early Nineteenth-Century Hawaii." *Journal of Presbyterian History* 77 (Summer 1999) 81–94.

Miller, Char. *Fathers and Sons: The Bingham Family and the American Mission*. Philadelphia: Temple University Press, 1982.

Miller, Char. "Text in Context: The Journal of an Early 19th Century American Missionary." *Yale University Library Gazette*, 65 (October 1991) 47–63.

O'Hara, Mary et al. *Awakening the Silent Majority: The Changing Role of Women in My Church, Past Present and Future*. New York: Auburn Theological Seminary and Union Theological Seminary, 1975.

Papanek, Hanna. "Men, Women and Work: Reflections on the Two-Person Career." *American Journal of Sociology*, 78 (1973) 852–872.

Putney, Clifford. *Missionaries in Hawai'i: The Lives of Peter and Fanny Gulick, 1797–1883*. Amherst: University of Massachusetts Press, 2010.

Ralston, Caroline. "'Christian Woman, Pious Wife, Faithful Mother, Devoted Missionary': Conflicts in Roles of American Missionary Women in Nineteenth-Century Hawaii." *Feminist Studies* 9 (Fall 1983), 489–521.

Schultz, Joy. "Empire of the Young: Missionary Children in Hawai'i and the Birth of U. S. Colonialism in the Pacific, 1820–1898." PhD diss., University of Nebraska-Lincoln, 2011.

Silverman, Jane L. "To Marry Again," *Hawaiian Journal of History*, 17 (1983).

Thurston, Lucy G. *Life and Times of Mrs. Lucy G. Thurston, Wife of Rev. Asa Thurston, Pioneer Missionary to the Sandwich Islands, Gathered from Letters and Journals Extending over a Period of More Than Fifty Years*. Ann Arbor: S. C. Andrews, 1934.

Thurston, Lucy G. *The Missionary's Daughter: A Memoir of Lucy Goodale Thurston of the Sandwich Islands*. New York: The American Tract Society, 1842.

Tyerman, Daniel and George Bennett to ABCFM. *Missionary Herald*, 19 (April 1823).

Varigney, Charles de. *Fourteen Years in the Sandwich Islands, 1855-1868*. Honolulu: University Press of Hawaii, 1981.

Webb, M. C. "The Abolition of Taboo Systems in Hawaii." *Journal of Polynesian Society* 74 (March 1965) 21–39.

Welter, Barbara. "The Cult of True Womanhood: 1820-1860." *American Quarterly* 18 (Summer 1966) 151–174.

Worcester, Samuel. "Instructions to the Sandwich Islands Mission," in Heman Humphrey, *The Promised Land*. xii-xiv.

Zweip, Mary. "Sending the Children Home: A Dilemma for Early Missionaries." *Hawaiian Journal of History* 24 (1990) 39–68.

For Heaven's Sake

Char Miller

THE AMERICAN CHRISTIAN MISSIONARY project never has been simple, neither for the culture that has promoted it nor for the individuals who have undertaken the difficult task of leaving hearth and home in hopes of converting other peoples and places. This ambition—religious and cultural; personal and political—is also an outgrowth of particular places in time.

This is what these essays, written in commemoration of the 200th anniversary of the American Board of Commissioners for Foreign Missions (ABCFM), reveal. Formally established amid the War of 1812, a conflict that helped to forge a newfound sense of national identity, the ABCFM was a reflection of Americans' perception of their growing significance in the world. Some fused their patriotic passion with a religious zeal to do good beyond our shores. Without such affective impulses, without their intensity and heartfelt quality, it would have been quite difficult to men and women to muster up enough courage to join what grew to be a stream of missionary companies heading out into terra incognita. It was this kind of commitment, averred Hiram Bingham, one of the leaders of the Sandwich Islands Mission (1819), that led his "little band of pilgrims" to chose to leave behind "the loved dwellings of Zion in our dear native land" so that they might labor among "pagans and strangers" in Hawai'i, there to raise the "Lord's Banner."[1]

American missionaries first unfurled Christianity's flag in such disparate landscapes as India, Ceylon, and Turkey, China and the Pacific; later in the nineteenth and twentieth centuries they took the flag further

---

1. Miller, *Selected Writings of Hiram Bingham*, 175, 185.

still, planting it all over the world. But wherever they took it, they came to understand, however imperfectly, that the welter of forces that had forged their piety could also complicate their work.

Consider those who initially launched the missionary crusade. In 1810, undergraduates at Williams College, swept up in the Second Great Awakening, wanted to save those who had not yet heard the Good Word. To do so, they convinced their elders to organize and fund what came to be known as the ABCFM. Their age was a critical part of this narrative: college-aged youth was the defining demographic of those who under the ABCFM's aegis signed on to minister to the native peoples of North America, or board ships for points east and west. They were energetic, unencumbered, hopeful. And their unworldliness and parochial perspectives sat well with the ABCFM leadership, which viewed those qualities as decided assets for those who wished to be devout agents of change. After all, if Hiram Bingham, Robert Wilson Hume, Nellie Arnott, or Ruth Parmalee had known what they were up against they might not have set forth with such confidence and conviction.

Figure 27. Departure of the *Caravan* from Salem, Massachusetts.
The ship left on February 19, 1812, carrying Adoniram and Ann Judson
and Samuel and Harriet Newell to India. Titled "The Departure," the engraving
was created by Alfred Jones (artist) and W. S. Lawrence (engraver).
From John Dowling, ed., *The Judson Offering* (New York: Lewis Colby & Co., 1850),
front. Image courtesy of the Congregational Library, Boston.

Much of the missionaries' seeming naïveté was not naïveté at all, but rather an expression of their being rooted in the manners and mores of their time and country. The women of the Sandwich Islands Mission, for example, were no exceptions to their era's embrace of American Exceptionalism. Even as they eagerly taught school to those who were unlettered, they built fences around their compounds to fend off their students, whom they routinely decried as degraded heathens. Of a piece was Titus Coan's paternalistic approach to his Hawaiian charges. "He had a great love for the Hawaiian people," Philip Corr observes, "while also exhibiting a common nineteenth century condescension toward indigenous peoples."[2]

These Americans were not insulated from other manifestations of their culture, however removed their posts may have been from their native soil. So missionaries in Hawai'i came to understand when shifting attitudes at home towards alcohol compelled them to rethink their personal consumption of spirits. The controversial questions that revolved around their salaries—how much should they receive and in what form would it to be doled out—was part of a larger debate in the United States as laissez-faire capitalism began to rearrange the new nation's class structure and economic relationships.

Just as influential was the emergence of the nineteenth-century women's rights movement. The first generations of women who entered missionary service almost exclusively did so as spouses. Although their commitment was no less than their husbands', and their workload every bit as intense, their standing with the ABCFM was determined by their marital status. Like their sisters and mothers who remained stateside, these women were bound by cultural norms of domesticity, in which women's work lay within the home.

The proper role of women proved to be an elastic concept. For as transitional figures such as Nellie Arnott demonstrated, women could act in a feminine fashion outside the home. Yet through her missionary journalism about her work in Angola, she also revealed to her large American readership that it was possible for unmarried women to function effectively in a foreign and occasionally dangerous environment. In Turkey, Dr. Ruth Parmalee made the same case, pouring her creative energy into bringing health care to the poor and dispossessed; at great risk, she kept open her clinic there during World War I, and left an astonishing eyewitness account of the Armenian Genocide. And while

2. Tocqueville, *Democracy in America*, Part 2, 36; Ross, *Origins of American Social Science*, 22–30.

Alice Gordon Gulick may have married into one of the great American missionary families, her true inspiration was in her beloved alma mater. With the goal of establishing what she touted as a "Mt. Holyoke of Spain," in which, as Stephen Ault writes, "young women would be prepared by young women," she created the International Institute, a pioneering educational venture that transformed Spanish women's opportunities.

Equally transformative, if unexpectedly so, were the people with whom the missionaries came into contact. In this fluid cross-cultural exchange, the Americans occasionally were schooled by those whom they had expected to reform. Consider temperance, a matter of furious debate in the United States. There, abstemious Protestants used the issue to hammer those who imbibed, thereby reinforcing ethnic stereotypes and racial hierarchies. Overseas, however, the issue was much more knotty. U. S. missionaries in Turkey scaled back their alcoholic consumption in synch with prevailing notions within the ABCFM, but they recognized that in so doing they were only playing catch-up with already existing edicts in their Muslim-dominated host country. Similarly, the missionaries in Hawai'i were embarrassed that many of the *ali'i* (chiefs) were well ahead of them in promulgating and enforcing prohibition among their people.

In more subtle ways, formative Christian principles were also tested and at times found wanting. Confirmation of this lies in the intellectual evolution across three generations of the Hume family. Robert Wilson Hume, a member of the second generation of ABCFM missionaries, tended to the spiritual needs of his converts, but unlike his predecessors he was also engaged in elevating their social condition. His son, Robert Hume, became embroiled in what is known as the Andover Controversy, an internal battle among Protestants that deeply divided missionaries and their domestic supporters. After witnessing the profound faith of Muslims and Hindus, Hume joined with those who advocated for a doctrine of "future probation," acknowledging that it was possible "that the heathen who had never heard of Christ might not be condemned to everlasting perdition." This ecumenical stance nearly ended his career, but this same position greatly benefitted the career of his son, Robert Ernest Hume. A liberal theologian, he wrote *The World's Living Religions* (1924), in which he "pointed to spiritual progress on a universal level," that was, in the words of Alice C. Hunsberger, "born of a universal human aspiration to higher faith that had been proceeding through all time and would continue to evolve in the future."

Although this third Hume's openness to the world did not shake his ultimate faith in Christianity's primacy, his family's experience suggests why close analyses of historical contexts and multi-generational influences are so essential. Without these analytical approaches we would miss significant alterations in tone and action, substance and meaning.[3] Without them, we would be unable to decipher the import of that wandering Christian, David Abeel, whose itinerant ministry took him through China and Southeast Asia; we would have no way of comprehending why nineteenth century American missionaries in Turkey turned a blind eye to their resident countrymen's complicity in the opium trade; we would be incapable of appreciating the boundary-crossing implications of educational programs in Asia Minor, where American missionaries first taught Greek and Armenian students, and after World War I Turkish Muslim children; or the even more the striking achievements of the American-trained Japanese evangelists Annaka Kyôkai. And we would fail to see the need to study the impact that indigenous peoples—The Other—had on the successes and failures of the missionary enterprise; this is particularly evident in Hawai'i, as Regina Pfeiffer makes clear, but is essential anywhere that ABCFM-sponsored missions were planted.

What is required for a better understanding of these intensely human dynamics is as necessary for the built environment in which the ABCFM missionaries often operated. Architecture is revelatory. Its framing determines our movements through it. Its massing and volume help structure our behavior. Its siting and detail conveys something of our cultural aspirations. That is why early Pacific missionaries erected pre-fabricated New England-style clapboard buildings in the tropics. Those in Turkey, East Asia, and Spain also sought to convey symbolic messages through the materials they employed to build their schools, homes, and churches. But in the case of some of these facilities, the imported ideals merged with local materials, from landscape planting to design elements, creating architectural hybrids.

In their hybridity lies a larger message about the importance of the ABCFM's two-century-long global engagement. What had been initially conceived as a unilateral American commitment to the expansion of

3. Putney, *Missionaries in Hawai'i*; Miller, *Fathers and Sons*.

Christianity abroad ultimately became a reciprocal process; what had begun as a monologue became a dialogue. From this complex convergence emerged a more mature, nuanced, and international perspective. Saving the world had become a collaborative endeavor.

BIBLIOGRAPHY

Miller, Char. *Fathers and Sons: The Binghams and the American Mission*. Philadelphia, PA: Temple University Press, 1982.

Miller, Char. *Selected Writings of Hiram Bingham, 1814–1869: Missionary to the Hawaiian Islands*. Lewiston, NY: The Edwin Mellen Press, 1988.

Tocqueville, Alexis de. *Democracy in America*. New York: Langley, 1840.

Putney, Clifford. *Missionaries in Hawai'i: The Lives of Peter and Fanny Gulick, 1797–1883*. Amherst, MA: University of Massachusetts Press, 2010.

Ross, Dorothy. *Origins of American Social Science*. New York: Cambridge University Press, 1991.

Subject/Name Index

Barton, James L., xxvii, 75n1, 85–86, 87, 93n57, 96
Barton, Titus Theodore, 5n12
Basel Mission Society, 155
Baysal, Cem, 71n73
Bean, Hanna, 257
Bean, Joel, 257
Bebek Boys Seminary, 53
Bellevue Hospital School of Nursing, 90n53
Berkeley Street Church (Boston), 19
Berry, John Cuting, 171
Bingham, Hiram, 244, 246, 249–50, 269, 274, 277–78, 287, 290–91, 299–300, 301, 312–13, 315, 318, 319–21, 323–25, 328, 331, 332
Bingham, Levi, 312–13
Bingham, Lydia, 246, 263–64. *See also* Coan, Lydia Bingham
Bingham, Sophia, 323–24, 325
Bingham, Sybil, 277, 312–13, 318–21, 323–24, 325, 328
Bingham family, xvii
Birge, John Kingsley, 56–57
Birge, Ruby P., 65
Bishop, Artemas, 236–37, 305
Bishop, Bernice Pauahi, 270
Bishop, Charles Reed, 280
Bishop, S.E., 248
Bishop family, 324
Bissell, L., 112
Blake, Everett (Jack), 65
Blake, Lynda Goodsell, 65
Blatchely, Abraham, 291–92
Blatter, Dorothy, 65
Bliss family, xvii
Blythe, John W., 130n92
Boki, 275
Bombay University, 132
Bond, Elias, 230
Boone, Sally DeSaussure, 160
Boone, William Jones, 160, 161
Bosphorus University, 54
Bosserant d'Anglade, Marie Gabriel, 283–84
Boston University, 225
Bowen, George, 112

Bowen, Marcellus, 56, 58
Bowker, Mary, xxiii, 52, 220
Boys' School (Hawai'i), 280
Boys' School (Izmir), 56
Brainerd, David, 145
Brethren, the, 1, 2
Brewer, Josiah, 37
Bridgman, Elijah Coleman, 36–37, 143, 146, 147, 157, 158, 160, 161, 173
Brinsmade, Peter, 238, 239
Brintnall (captain), 273
British Anglicanism, 169
British East India Company, 30, 44, 102
British and Foreign Bible Society, 103
British Levant Company, 30
Brown, Mrs. Samuel, 158
Brown, Samuel Robbins, 157, 158, 178
Brückner, Gottloeb, 149n18
Burgess, Abbie Lyon. *See* Hume, Abbie Lyon Burgess
Burgess, Abigail (Moore), 115n37
Burgess, Ebenezer, 104, 112, 115n37
Burgess, Mrs. Ebenezer, 104
Burn, Robert, 153
Buyukalkan, Tulin, 65
Byron, Lord (George Gordon), 293

Calvin, John, 241
Capen, Samuel, 223, 224
Carey, William, 4n8, 142n2
Caris, Mary D., 202n27
Carnegie Endowment for International Peace, 132
Castle and Cooke, 284
Central Turkey College, 55
Chamberlain, Daniel, 322–23
Chamberlain, Jerusha, 322–23
Chamberlain, Levi, 233, 239–40, 290–92, 301, 304
Chamberlain (Mrs.), 318
Chandler, Alice, 115n38
Chandler, Charlotte, 115
Chapin, Calvin, 6
Chicago Theological Seminary, 122n61
Chigira, Shōan, 179, 181
Childs, Gladwyn Murray, 197, 204n30
Christie, Thomas, 59, 66